Formal Approaches to Computing and
Information Technology

Springer

London
Berlin
Heidelberg
New York
Barcelona
Hong Kong
Milan
Paris
Santa Clara
Singapore
Tokyo

E. Sekerinski and K. Sere (Eds)

Program Development by Refinement

Case Studies Using the B Method

With 89 figures

 Springer

Emil Sekerinski
Department of Computing and software, McMaster University,
1280 Main Street West, Hamilton, Ontario, L8S 4K1, Canada

Kaisa Sere
Department of Computer Science, Åbo Akademi University, Lemminkaisenk. 14A,
FIN-20520 Turku, Finland

Series Editor
S.A. Schuman, BSc, DEA, CEng
Department of Mathematical and Computing Sciences
University of Surrey, Guildford, Surrey GU2 5XH, UK

ISBN 1-85233-053-8 Springer-Verlag London Berlin Heidelberg

British Library Cataloguing in Publication Data
Program development by refinement. - (Formal approaches to
    computing and information technology)
    1. B (Computer program language)
    I. Sererinski, Emil   II. Sere, Kaisa
    005.1'33
ISBN 1852330538

Library of Congress Cataloging-in-Publication Data
Program Development by Refinement (case studies using the B method)
    / E. Sekerinski and K. Sere.
        p.   cm. — (Formal approaches to computing and information
technology)
    Includes bibliographical references.
    ISBN 1-85233-053-8 (pbk. : alk. paper)
    1. B (Computer program language)   I. Sekerinski, E. (Emil), 1963-
II. Sere, K. (Kaisa), 1954-   III. Series.
    QA76.73.B155 P76   1998   98-25801
    005.13'3 — dc21   CIP

© Springer-Verlag London Limited 1999
Printed in Great Britain

Typesetting: Camera ready by editors
Printed and bound at the Athenæum Press Ltd., Gateshead, Tyne & Wear
34/3830-543210 Printed on acid-free paper

Preface

The Idea of Program Refinement

Programs are complex. They are typically so complex, that they go beyond the full comprehension even of the programmer or team who designed them, with all the consequences this has. How can we cope with such complexity in a satisfactory way?

An approach, advocated for a long time, is to separate a concise specification of a program — the "what" — from a possibly involved implementation — the "how". Once a specification is obtained from the set of requirements on the program, there can still be a large gap to an efficient implementation. The development from specification to implementation can then proceed by a succession of layers, such that each layer is a *refinement* of the previous one. Design decisions can be introduced in refinement steps one at a time. By this, the refinement steps can be kept small and manageable.

Still, the set of all requirements can be far too large to be taken completely into account in the initial specification. Even if they could, they might obscure issues more than clarify them. For example:

- An information system for stored goods needs to produce an error message on illegal input. Yet, the exact wording — and even the language — of those messages is irrelevant for an understanding of the essence of the system.
- A banking application interacts with customers with a graphical interface. Yet the specification of the graphical layout is secondary compared to the specification of the possible transactions.
- For a mailing system the possible physical distribution of the users is an essential requirement. Yet it can be ignored for an initial specification of the logic of message delivery.

Such requirements do not need to be reflected in the initial specification. Rather, they can better be taken into account in subsequent refinement steps. Hence, our picture of program development is that the initial specification is only a partial one, though, by slight abuse, we still refer to it as the specification. Subsequent refinement steps take further requirements into account or represent design decisions (Fig. 0.1).

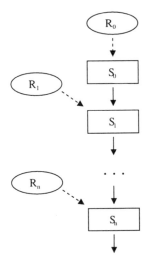

Fig. 0.1. Program Development by Refinement: $R_0, \ldots, R_n$ are the requirements, S_0 is the specification, S_n is the implementation, and the other S_i are intermediate refinements; Solid arrows stand for the refinement relation

The B Method

The B Method is an approach for the industrial development of highly trusted software. It is the outcome of two decades of academic research on program specification and refinement:

- It offers a rich collection of set-theoretic data types for an abstract specification of the state of systems.
- It allows the use of standard first-order predicate logic for the specification of operations on the state.
- It uses a relational semantics for statements and supports consistency and correctness proofs of operations by weakest precondition calculation.
- It supports grouping of operations and encapsulation of state variables in modules, called *machines*.
- It supports *algorithmic refinement* of operations and *data refinement* of state variables in machines.
- It allows the construction of new machines out of existing ones.

Currently there are two commercial tools supporting the B Method, B-Toolkit from B Core, UK and Atelier B from Steria, France. Both tools address issues of documentation, project management, and prototyping which are necessary for large-scale use, beside issues of verification and code generation. The tools achieve a remarkable degree of automation in checking refinements by proof, as well as in project management. Even though the tools are still being further developed, the B Method with its current tool support can be considered the most advanced general purpose environment for producing highly trustworthy software.

Contents of the Book

This book is a collection of case studies in program refinement with the B Method. Each chapter shows a typical program development from problem analysis to implementation with a non-trivial example, using one of the tools. The developments include a discussion and justification of the chosen approach as well as experiences with the tools used. The developments are intended to be representative of a whole class of related problems.

The book is divided in two parts. Part I considers the development of information systems and data structures. These examples demonstrate the typical use of the B Method, in particular the development by a sequence of refinement steps, the consideration of further requirements in refinement steps, and the use of object-oriented models with the B Method. For the benefit of readers who are not familiar with the B Method, the first chapter gives an introduction to it. The other chapters of the first part can be read in any order.

Chapter 1: Introduction to the B Method. This chapter introduces the basic concepts of the B Method, substitutions, statements, machines, invariants, nondeterminism, algorithmic and data refinement, layered development, and refinement and implementation machines. The use of these is illustrated by a series of examples. Also, the impact of the finiteness of numbers and of the memory is discussed and the use of the B-Toolkit library is illustrated.

Chapter 2: Container Station. The container station is an information system with a rather complex structure of the state and an elaborate set of requirements. This chapter exemplifies the use of various set-theoretic data types and operations for describing and manipulating a complex state. Moreover, it shows how the initial specification can be kept abstract and how requirements like fairness of a scheduling strategy and error reporting can be incorporated in refinement steps. This chapter also exemplifies the use of library machines provided with the B-Toolkit for the implementation.

Chapter 3: Minimum Spanning Tree. This chapter is about an algorithm on graphs with a simple abstract specification but an intricate implementation. It shows how introducing further B machines during refinement leads to better modularisation for reuse and helps to keep the proof obligations simpler. The last point is known as *design for provability*. The B machines introduced in the development for maintaining equivalence classes with union-find, priority queues, and heaps, are of interest on their own.

Chapter 4: The B Bank. This chapter develops a simple but complete application for banking over the Internet. An object-oriented model is used as an aid during analysis, which is translated to a B machine which specifies the key functionality. For the implementation, new base machines for persistent object storage and for string handling are introduced. These are of general usefulness. In this chapter, a robust interface with error reporting is built on top of the basic functionality. Thus, this illustrates a combined top-down and bottom-up development. Finally, for working over the Internet and for providing a graphical user interface, general-purpose B machines for interfacing with HTML and CGI are developed.

Part II illustrates refinement for the development of distributed systems and process control systems. These systems are examples of *reactive systems*. A reactive system is a system which maintains an on-going interaction with its environment. Although reactive systems are outside the original scope of the B Method, the connection can be established by the theory of action systems, as presented in the first chapter of Part II. The remaining chapters illustrate this and can be read in any order.

Chapter 5: Parallel Programming with the B Method. By appealing to the theory of action systems, this chapter shows how reactive systems and the parallel composition of reactive systems can be expressed with the B Method. It also shows how the refinement of reactive systems leads to proof obligations which can be mapped to those of B machine refinement.

Chapter 6: Production Cell. This chapter illustrates an approach for developing a control program for a discrete control system by the example of a production cell consisting of several interacting machines. For such a system, it is shown how *safety conditions* can be guaranteed. Refinement is used for decomposing a system specification into a controller and a plant. This chapter presents action systems with a large number of actions but simple data structures and basic action system refinement.

Chapter 7: Distributed Load Balancing. Load balancing in a network of processes can be conveniently specified by disregarding the distribution, assuming that each process has direct access to the load of neighbouring processes. In an implementation however, nodes must either communicate their load explicitly or keep estimates of each other's loads. This chapter illustrates the development of such an implementation by a series of refinement steps using *superposition refinement*, a special form of action system refinement.

Chapter 8: Distributed Electronic Mail System. The previous chapters on action systems have taken the view that only the global state of action systems is observable. By contrast, this chapter takes the alternative view that only external events of action systems are observable. The refinement of event-based action systems is illustrated by the development of a mailing system with communication over a network of nodes with links between them. By disregarding the distribution, the specification can be kept concise. In this development, extensions of the B notation are proposed for supporting such developments.

Smaller B machines are presented with separate explanations, larger B machines are presented with explanations interleaved. For B machines which are longer than just a few pages this *literate style* relates directly pieces of formal text with the corresponding explanation and thus improves readability. This interleaving is supported by both tools which were used.

The appendix summarises the Abstract Machine Notation of the B Method concisely for easy reference when reading the case studies.

The readers are referred to the B-Book by J.-R. Abrial [2] for a definitive and comprehensive reference, with an extensive discussion of the theoretical foundations.

Readership

Firstly, the book is suitable as study material for advanced undergraduate and graduate courses on program refinement. This is supported by fully explained program developments, by suggestions for further extensions of the examples, and by making the examples available on the World Wide Web. The book is also suitable as additional material for self-study.

Secondly, the book aims to show potential users of the B Method what classes of programs can be handled, what the typical size of specifications and refinements are, and what the effort for the examples is. Patterns of solutions are presented, which can then be applied in similar situations in practice.

World Wide Web Page

The code of some examples and additional supporting material, e.g. the B Bank application which can be run from any Web browser, can be accessed through the book's Web page at:

```
http://www.springer.co.uk/comp/support/
```

Acknowledgements

The editors wish to thank to Ib Søerensen of B-Core and Corinne Givois and Denis Sabatier of Steria for their support and all the persons involved in this project for their contributions, comments, and patience. We also wish to thank the Series Editor, Steve Schuman of University of Surrey, UK, as well as Rosie Kemp from Springer-Verlag for their guidance and help during the different phases of producing this volume and the reviewers for their constructive comments.

Contents

Part II. Reactive Systems

5. **Parallel Programming with the B Method** 183
Michael Butler, Marina Waldén

List of Contributors

Michael Butler
Department of Electronics and Computer Science
University of Southampton
Highfield
Southampton SO17 1BJ
United Kingdom
mjb@ecs.soton.ac.uk

Martin Büchi
Turku Centre for Computer Science
Åbo Akademi
Lemminkäisenkatu 14A
20520 Turku
Finland
Martin.Buechi@abo.fi

Ranan Fraer
Future CAD Technologies
Intel Haifa
Israel
rananf@iil.intel.com

Ken Robinson
School of Computer Science and Engineering
The University of New South Wales
Sydney NSW 2052
Australia
K.Robinson@unsw.edu.au

Emil Sekerinski
Department of Computing and Software
McMaster University
1280 Main Street West
Hamilton, Ontario, L8S 4K1
Canada
emil@mcmaster.ca

Elena Troubitsyna
Turku Centre for Computer Science
Åbo Akademi
Lemminkäisenkatu 14A
20520 Turku
Finland
Elena.Troubitsyna@abo.fi

Marina Waldén
Turku Centre for Computer Science
Åbo Akademi
Lemminkäisenkatu 14A
20520 Turku
Finland
Marina.Walden@abo.fi

Foreword
Some Perspective on Refinement

David Lorge Parnas

1 Three Decades of Software by Refinement

Nobody would claim that the subject of this book, designing programs by refinement, is a new idea. As soon as observers began to realise that software development was difficult, and what a mess we were making of it, they began to look for a better way. All of the "better ways", share two ideas:

- Writing code means making design decisions. Don't make many decisions at once; instead, write code in a step-by step process that results in making decisions in a carefully chosen sequence.
- Verify or validate each decision as it is made. If incorrect decisions are made, and subsequent decisions are based on them, those subsequent decisions will have to be reviewed, and may have to be revised. Verification/validation as you go is likely to sáve effort in the long run.

  Program development by refinement adds a third point:

- Begin with a precise statement of what will be done adding details about the implementation with each step. This distinguishes refinement from some other proposals. [1]

When people began to think about refinement, mathematical proof of software correctness was in its infancy. Verification/validation had to be done by other methods. Two early papers that discussed languages in which models could be gradually refined into working code, while the performance and correctness of each new set of decisions was verified by simulation, were [66] and [87]. Current work on refinement assumes mathematical verification of the decisions.

Dijkstra's early work on "structured programming" was certainly one of the most widely discussed approaches to refinement, e.g. [24], but Wirth's work was also very influential [84]. Another version by Mills [54], lives on today as part of the collection of methods known as "Cleanroom". There have been many Ph.D. theses (e.g. [4]) and books (e.g. [52]). The work mentioned just "scratches the surface" of a vast body of literature. The reader of this book should be asking two questions:

---

[1] Some incremental development methods propose an alternative, a "bottom up" approach that requires building a subset and adding functions after the subset is working.

- Why isn't refinement more widely used in industry?
- Why do we need yet another book on the subject?

2 Refinement Remains a Buzzword

When the authors of [66] and [87] read the abstracts of the other paper, each thought that the other had the same idea. However, their ideas could be described by the same abstract, when they met, they discovered that their approaches were quite different. This is true of many approaches to design by refinement. The general description of refinement given above leaves three important questions unanswered:

- In what order should the decisions be made?
- How should decisions be documented?
- How should decisions be verified or validated?

In the sections below, I discuss possible answers to each of these questions.

2.1 Decision Ordering in a Refinement Process

There is room for considerable discussion about the best order for making decisions in a software design process. Unfortunately, people have always been rather vague about it. Below we present a number of incompatible ideas about the order in which decisions should be made.

Top Down Design. The phrase "top down design" has long been popular but its meaning has never been clear. It is assumed that there is a hierarchical structure and the higher levels in the hierarchy should be designed first, with the lower levels being a refinement. Unfortunately, as was discussed many years ago, even the phrase hierarchical structure is a "buzzword" in the software design field [61]. Usually when someone uses the term "top down" they mean one of the forms of refinement mentioned below.

Stepwise Refinement. Although the phrase "stepwise refinement" appears to have been coined by Wirth [84], his approach was close to what Dijkstra had been promulgating, first in technical reports and then in [24]. Programs were refined by writing the major control structures first, using suggestive names for the programs in those structures, and then refining those programs later.

Outside In. Many early systems were developed at great expense, and at the end of the development process it would be discovered that the services provided were the wrong ones or that the user interface was difficult to use. In reaction to many disasters, some authors begin to propose that we should design the outside of a system (the user interface) first and postpone implementation decisions to later stages.

Module Structure First. With the publication of [60], many designers were reminded (a) that programs had to be divided into independent work assignments if development was going to progress at reasonable speed and (b) that there were good ways and bad ways to divide a program into modules. Thus, some people began to argue that the design should begin with decisions about the module structure with later stages refining module specifications into code. One paper that made such proposals explicitly was [65].

Refinement from Program Functions to Code. In a long series of papers (e.g. [53]) Mills and others showed how mathematical functions could be used to describe what a program did and recommended that design of a program always begin with its program function (a mathematical function mapping from its control state to its final state), which would then be refined, in a sequence of small steps, in which program functions for components were written, until one had an implementation. The same philosophy, but other notation, can be found in [68].

Data Refinement. Many authors questioned the stress on control structures found in the papers mentioned above and suggested that refinement could be applied to data as well. They proposed that software design begin with the specification of a series of abstract data types (e.g. [32, 51, 39]).

Most Difficult First. E. W. Dijkstra once suggested that when designing a system the first decisions to be made should be the most difficult ones, those where you are not sure you can find a solution. In this way, you won't waste effort if satisfactory solutions can not be found [23].

Most Solid First. A very different rule was suggested in [62] where it was argued that the first decisions should be those that were least likely to be revised as this would make it easier to build families of programs (product lines) with shared characteristics and design decisions.

2.2 Documentation of Decisions in a Refinement Process

Experienced developers know that design decisions have not been made until they are written down in a precise and binding way. Among those who have advocated refinement in the general sense there are many different ideas about how those decisions can be documented.

Documentation by Writing Code One of the earliest, and most intuitively appealing, approaches to documenting decisions in the refinement process has been to simply write code. Each decision allows some code to be written and further decisions lead to expansion of the code.

2.3 Documentation by Writing Mathematical Models

In some approaches, notably many examples using the Z notation, documentation of design decisions is in the form of a model, an abstract mechanism that behaves as the system being designed is intended to behave [78]. These models are often called "specifications" but they rarely state requirements; instead they are mechanisms that exhibit desirable properties that satisfy unstated requirements. With models, it is often difficult to distinguish the essential from the incidental.

Documentation by Writing Formal Specifications. In the refinement approaches advocated by Dijkstra [25] and Mills [54] and others (e.g. [67, 63]) mathematics is used to write true specifications. In [67] it is suggested that these specifications should be thought of as design documentation and represented in a readable tabular format [42]. Of course, informal documents can serve in this role but there are well-known disadvantages of such imprecise notation.

2.4 Verification Methods in a Refinement Process

In most of the recent work on refinement it is assumed that verification means formal mathematical proof. There are many design decisions that cannot be verified or validated in that way. Performance characteristics are one example. In earlier work ([66, 87]) simulation was proposed as a verification method. Informal inspection has also proven effective in some cases. When formal proof is considered there are two possible approaches: proof of correctness and proof of refinement. With a correctness proof approach, the refined program is proven correct. In more sophisticated approaches a proof at each step proves only that the newly refined program is actually a refinement of the previous program thus taking advantage of earlier work. There are obvious advantages to proving each refinement correct rather than proving the complete program correct. As is demonstrated by the examples in this book, once we have an abstract statement of what is to be done, proving the correctness of each refinement is generally easier than proving correctness of the program.

3 Refinement in Practice

Although the general idea of designing by refinement was proposed more than 30 years ago, none of the industrial systems that I have examined was produced by such a process. In fact, discussions in the "software engineering" community are headed in very different directions. Fred Brooks adage, "Plan to throw one away, you will anyway" [14] has been taken to heart as more and more practitioners advocating building a "quick and dirty" prototype and then starting over. Incremental approaches such as that advocated by Barry Boehm [12] are considered more realistic than the refinement approaches mentioned here.

Refinement does not seem to have worked in practice. Among the reasons are:

- Impatience: Designers cannot wait to get down to "real" code. They think the decisions made in the early stages of a refinement process are obvious and a waste of time. Unless the "specification language" has "animation" features they find the work uninteresting.

- When people get to the later design stages, they ignore the earlier decisions.
- Verification and validation (by any method) seem to take too much time in a deadline-driven project.
- Many program developers believe that their real skill is the mastery of one of today's complex programming languages and are convinced that the (much simpler) formal languages advocated by the refinement community are too complex and not worth learning.
- Designers find it very hard to express their real design decisions in a refinement process.

4 Some Opinions

Having observed and participated in discussions of refinement for more than 30 years, I am not without some personal opinions on the questions raised above.

4.1 Order of Design Decisions

Although the approaches to choosing a design process outlined in Sec. 2.1 seem contradictory, I find all the arguments valid but oversimplified. Many constraints prevent designers from following any of the simple procedures outlined and they will not be able to produce systems by a pure refinement process. However, they can and should produce a system design and documentation that looks as if a refinement process had been applied [64].

4.2 Documenting Decisions

Refinement processes that only produce code might help in program development, but will not help in the longer, and more expensive, "Maintenance" period. Refinement processes like that suggested by Wirth [84] produce a sequence of programs with increasing length and the structure becomes more and more difficult to see. When changes are required, they are not restricted to a single section of the code.

On the other hand, relying completely on specifications leads to unnecessary concerns about the "composability" of specifications. The easiest way to describe the composition of separately specified components into something larger is to write code that invokes the components that were specified.

It is a mistake to believe that a single notation, either code or specifications, should be used throughout the project. This is not the case in other areas of engineering where a philosophy of design through documentation has long been standard practice [36].

5 The Role of this Book

The attractive feature of this book is its focus on case studies. Those who wish to do further research on refinement need to give serious consideration to the issues raised above, particularly the reason that refinement is not used in more practical projects. If refinement is going to be practical for the majority of software systems produced, the problems posed in this book should be simple. This book poses a challenge. Everyone interested in either applying or studying software development through stepwise refinement should read this book and try to use the case studies either as tutorial examples or as a basis for further study. The extensive but often very vague work on programming methods must be combined with the careful mathematical study of refinement to yield a practical approach.

6 Acknowledgement

Comments by E. Sekerinski on an earlier draft were very helpful.

David Lorge Parnas, P.Eng.
NSERC/Bell Industrial Research Chair in Software Engineering
Director of the Software Engineering Programme
Department of Computing and Software
Faculty of Engineering
McMaster University, Hamilton, Ontario, Canada - L8S 4K1

Part I

Information Systems

1. Introduction to the B Method

Ken A. Robinson

1.1 Machines

In the B Method [2], subsequently referred to as **B**, the specification, design – here called *refinement* – and implementation phases of software development are represented by sets of *Abstract Machines*. A machine is an encapsulation of a state and a set of operations; the state being determined by a set of variables. The notation for describing *Abstract Machines* is known as *Abstract Machine Notation* or *AMN*.

1.1.1 Machine Semantics and Generalised Substitutions

The constructs that determine and change the state of a machine are called *substitutions*; these correspond to what would be called *statements* in a programming language. The semantics of substitutions are defined by *Generalised Substitutions*. The concept of a substitution arises as follows:

- in general, any construct that changes a machine can only do so by changing the state, since the state is the only part of a machine that persists and is changeable;
- the principal construct for changing the state of the machine is the simple substitution $x := E$, which changes the value of the variable x to the value of the expression E. This construction is recognizable as the assignment statement found in all procedural programming languages. Ultimately all substitutions affect the state through simple substitutions.

To define the meaning of a state changing construct we describe the relationship between the *before* and *after* states. This relation is defined by using predicates to define sets of states. Suppose we have a substitution S that is intended to cause a machine to terminate in a state that satisfies the predicate R, then we specify the set of states from which this can happen by the formalism

$$[S]\, R$$

The function $[S]$ is a predicate transformer that maps a predicate on the state after S to the *weakest* predicate that describes the set of possible *before* states. While the notation is different, this concept is analogous to Dijkstra's weakest precondition concept [22].

For the simple substitution $x := E$ we have

Description	Substitution	Semantics
Simple	$xx := E$	$[xx := E]R \Leftrightarrow R[E/xx]$
Skip	$skip$	$[skip]R \Leftrightarrow R$
Choice from set	$xx :\in S$	$[xx :\in S]R \Leftrightarrow [@xx'.$ $xx' \in S \Longrightarrow xx := xx']R$
Choice by predicate	$xx : P$	$[xx : P]R \Leftrightarrow [@xx'.$ $[xx := xx']P \Longrightarrow xx := xx']R$
Multiple	$xx, yy := E, F$	$[xx, yy := E, F]R \Leftrightarrow R[E, F/xx, yy]$
Sequential	$G ; H$	$[G ; H]R \Leftrightarrow [G][H]R$
Preconditioned	$P\|G$	$[P\|G]R \Leftrightarrow P \wedge [G]R$
Guarded	$P \Longrightarrow G$	$[P \Longrightarrow G]R \Leftrightarrow P \Rightarrow [G]R$
Alternate	$G[]H$	$[G[]H]R \Leftrightarrow [G]R \wedge [H]R$
Unbounded choice	$@zz.(G)$	$[@zz.(G)]R \Leftrightarrow \forall zz . ([G]R)$

where xx, yy are variables; E, F are expressions; S is a set; P, R are predicates; and G, H are substitutions.

Table 1.1. Basic Substitutions

$$[x := E]R \quad \stackrel{\triangle}{=} \quad R[E/x]$$

where $R[E/x]$ denotes the substitution in R of the expression E for all free instances of x. Hence the terminology *substitution*.

Table 1.1 shows the basic substitutions. The table is divided into two parts: the first part shows the basic substitutions for assigning a value to one or more variables; and the second part shows the basic compositions of substitutions.

For the specification of large substitutions, a *parallel* composition is available: $S_1 \| S_2$ is the parallel composition of S_1 and S_2. The basic form of parallel composition is the composition of simple substitutions:

$$xx := E \| yy := F \mathrel{\hat{=}} xx, yy := E, F$$

Parallel compositions of more complex substitutions can be expressed as compositions of the generalised substitutions shown in Table 1.1.

Extended Notation. The preceding substitutions are the basic substitutions, but an extended notation is generally used when defining machines. This extended notation has a more *programmatic* appearance, looking similar to the constructs found in programming languages, but these extended constructs are defined in terms of the basic substitutions. There is quite a large variety of the extended forms, and some of them are given in Table 1.2 on the facing page.

The notation displayed in Tables 1.1 and 1.2 on the next page is the publication form. Generally, when writing the source of machines an ASCII notation is used. Table 1.3 on the facing page shows the ASCII equivalences for substitutions where they are substantially different from the publication form.

The presentation of machines here will use the publication form.

Extended form	Definition
BEGIN G END	G
IF P THEN G ELSE H END	$(P \Longrightarrow G) [](\neg P \Longrightarrow H)$
IF P THEN G END	IF P THEN G ELSE *skip* END
CHOICE G OR H END	$G [] H$
SELECT P THEN G WHEN …	
WHEN Q THEN H END	$P \Longrightarrow G [] … [] Q \Longrightarrow H$
VAR z IN G END	$@z.(G)$
ANY z WHERE P THEN G END	$@z.(P \Longrightarrow G)$
LET x BE $x = E$ IN G END	$@x.(x = E \Longrightarrow G)$, where $x \setminus E$
WHILE P DO G	
VARIANT V INVARIANT I END	*see 1.1.1*

where z denotes a list of variables; x denote single variable; and n denotes a list of integer expressions.

Table 1.2. Extended Notation

Publication form	ASCII form
$x :\in S$	x :: S
$P \Longrightarrow G$	P ==> G
$G [] H$	G [] H

Table 1.3. ASCII Equivalent Notation

The While-Loop Substitution. The while-loop construct shown in Table 1.2 has four components:

P: a controlling predicate on the machine state;
S: a substitution;
V: an arithmetic *variant* expression, which is a function of the machine state;
I: an *invariant* predicate on the machine state.

The while-loop is not given a simple substitution semantics. This is because the substitution semantics would involve a least fixed point computation. Instead, an approximation is used. Given the following loop:

WHILE P DO S VARIANT V INVARIANT I END

the following obligations must be proved for some predicate R:

$$I \wedge P \Rightarrow [S] I$$
$$I \Rightarrow V \in \mathbb{N}$$
$$I \wedge P \Rightarrow [n := V][S](V < n)$$
$$\neg P \wedge I \Rightarrow R$$

where n is a *new* variable, that is a variable that is not one of the state variables. If these obligations are discharged then

$$I \Rightarrow [\text{WHILE } P \text{ DO } S \text{ VARIANT } V \text{ INVARIANT } I \text{ END}] R$$

1.1.2 Set Theory and Types

The basis for the mathematical models used in B is set theory. The mathematical toolkit models relations – and subsequently functions and sequences – as sets of pairs. The following definitions of relations and partial functions, illustrate the set-theoretic modelling and the notation.

Construct	Publication	ASCII	Definition
Relation	$S \leftrightarrow T$	S <-> T	$S \leftrightarrow T = \mathbb{P}(S \times T)$
Partial function	$S \nrightarrow T$	S +-> T	$S \nrightarrow T = \{r \mid r \in S \leftrightarrow T \wedge r^{-1}; r \subseteq id(T)\}$

A complete table is given in Sec. 1.7 on page 33 at the end of this chapter.

1.1.3 Types in B

Variables in **B** are strongly typed. This is despite the superficial appearance of it being typeless. Explicit types are not given at the point of declaration of variables – unlike most strongly typed programming languages. Instead, there is a requirement that invariants, preconditions and quantifiers must contain a *constraining* predicate for each variable or operation parameter. A constraining predicate for the variable x has the form: $x \in S$, $x \subseteq S$, $x \subset S$, or $x = E$, where $x \setminus S$, $x \setminus E$.

The meta-predicate $z \setminus E$ ("z not free in E") means that none of the variables in z occur *free* in E. This meta-predicate is defined recursively on the structure of E, but we won't do that here. The base cases are: $z \setminus (\forall z . P)$, $z \setminus (\exists z . P)$, $z \setminus \{z \mid P\}$, $z \setminus (\lambda z . (P \mid E))$, and $\neg (z \setminus z)$.

For the quantifiers:

$$\forall z . (P \Rightarrow Q)$$
$$\exists z . (P \wedge Q)$$
$$\{z \mid P\}$$
$$\bigcup z . (P \mid E)$$
$$\bigcap z . (P \mid E)$$
$$\Sigma z . (P \mid E)$$
$$\Pi z . (P \mid E)$$

and the lambda expression:

$$\lambda z . (P \mid E)$$

the predicate P must constrain the variables in z. Additionally, the predicate P in the substitution $x : P$ must constrain x.

1.2 Specification

In B, specifications are presented as (top-level) machines. The machines present a mathematical model of the required behaviour. There are some constraints imposed on these machines:

MACHINE   *SquareRoot*

OPERATIONS

    sqrt ⟵ *SquareRoot*(*xx*)   ≙
       PRE $xx \in \mathbb{N}$
       THEN
          ANY   *yy*
          WHERE $yy \in \mathbb{N} \wedge square\,(\,yy\,) \leq xx \wedge xx < square\,(\,yy + 1\,)$
          THEN   *sqrt* := *yy*
          END
       END

DEFINITIONS

    square (*x*) ≙ $x \times x$

END

Fig. 1.1. A Square Root Machine

- the *WHILE* substitution may not be used;
- sequential composition may not be used; only parallel composition is available.

To illustrate, we will present two machines.

1.2.1 The Square Root Machine

The *SquareRoot* machine, Fig. 1.1, is a stateless machine (no variables) with a single operation that computes the natural square root of a natural number. Things to notice about this machine are:

- The name of the machine is *SquareRoot*.
- The machine has a definition section defining a simple macro *square*.
- There is a single operation named *SquareRoot*. This operation has a single parameter, *xx* of type $\mathbb{N}$ (natural number), and returns a single result, *sqrt* also of type $\mathbb{N}$.
- The result of the operation is defined by the non-deterministic choice of the variable *yy* to satisfy a predicate, which says that *yy* is the largest natural number whose square does not exceed *xx*.

Note carefully. For technical reasons machine variable names must contain at least two characters. Variable names containing only one character, as for example in the definition of *square*, are *jokers* and represent an arbitrary expression.

1.2.2 The Unique Identifier Machine

As an example of a different machine, Fig. 1.2 on the following page shows the specification of a machine that can be used to allocate a unique identifier from a set. Things to notice about this machine are:

MACHINE   *UniqueID* (*maxids*)

CONSTRAINTS $maxids \in \mathbb{N}_1$

SETS   *IDS*

PROPERTIES   card (*IDS*) $=$ *maxids*

VARIABLES   *usedIDS*

INVARIANT $usedIDS \subseteq IDS$

INITIALISATION $usedIDS := \{\}$

OPERATIONS
     newid ⟵ *allocID* $\hat{=}$
       PRE $usedIDS \neq IDS$
       THEN
         ANY   *nid*
         WHERE $nid \in IDS - usedIDS$
         THEN
           $newid := nid \; \| \; usedIDS := usedIDS \cup \{ \, nid \, \}$
         END
       END ;
     nids ⟵ *FreeIDS* $\hat{=}$
       BEGIN
         $nids := $ card ($IDS - usedIDS$)
       END

END

Fig. 1.2. A Unique Identifier Machine

- The machine has a parameter, which is a non-zero natural number representing the maximum number of identifiers that may be allocated. The constraints on this parameter are specified in the machine's *CONSTRAINTS* section.
- The machine has an abstract set *IDS* specified in the *SETS* section. Somewhere between specification and implementation this set will have to be instantiated to some set of natural numbers. The constraints on this set are specified in the *PROPERTIES* section.
- The machine has a state determined by a single variable *usedIDS*, defined to be a subset of *IDS* in the *INVARIANT* section. This variable models the identifiers already allocated, and hence is initialised to the empty set.
- The machine has two operations: *allocID* which returns an unused identifier, provided that not all identifiers have been allocated; and *FreeIDS* that returns the number of identifiers remaining to be allocated. This operation is required for a caller of *allocID* to ensure that the precondition is satisfied.
- The specification of *allocID* uses non-deterministic choice from the set of unused identifiers.

1.3 Refinement

Refinement is the term given to the process of taking a specification through a sequence of design steps towards implementation. Very simply, P is refined by Q if Q is a satisfactory replacement for P in any situation in which P is defined. Notice that this does not mean that Q is equivalent to P; it may be that the behaviour of P is non-deterministic, and Q discards some of the non-determinism.

In general, a distinction is frequently made between *procedural* or *algorithmic* refinement, in which only the algorithmic component of an operation is refined. This is like changing the algorithm. The other form of refinement is *data* refinement, in which the state of the machine is also changed, that is, we choose a new set of variables to model the behaviour, and of course we have to change the algorithm as well.

The formal definition of refinement in **B** does not distinguish between procedural and data refinement, but to illustrate these two aspects of refinement we will give examples that illustrate the distinction.

1.3.1 Procedural Refinement

To illustrate procedural refinement we will refine the operation in the *SquareRoot* machine. Any refinement of the *SquareRoot* operation is clearly procedural refinement as this machine has no state. The specification of the *SquareRoot* operation is declarative in that it simply asserts the property that the result should satisfy, and does not give any hint as to how the result can be computed. The first step of refinement suggests an algorithm for computing the result. There are many such algorithms of which we will suggest only one here, and we will also give some idea of where the algorithm comes from.

In the specification machine we choose the value of the variable yy to satisfy the predicate

$$square(yy) \leq xx \wedge xx < square(yy + 1)$$

This choice cannot be made simply, as the value chosen has to satisfy two conjuncts. Thus we need an implementation strategy. We can observe that is relatively easy to choose a value that satisfies either conjunct, so a possible strategy is to use two variables. We represent the two arguments to *square* in the above predicate by two different variables, as in

$$square(yy) \leq xx \wedge xx < square(zz)$$

then we can suggest an algorithm in which we choose arbitrary initial values for yy and zz that satisfy the above predicate and then modify yy and zz maintaining the above predicate and moving the values of yy and zz closer together until $yy + 1 = zz$. At that point yy will satisfy the specification.

The refinement is shown in Fig. 1.3 on the next page.

REFINEMENT   *SquareRootR*

REFINES   *SquareRoot*

OPERATIONS

   $sqrt \longleftarrow SquareRoot(\ xx\ )$ $\widehat{=}$
   ANY $yy\ ,\ zz$
   WHERE $yy \in \mathbb{N} \wedge zz \in \mathbb{N} \wedge$
      $sqinv\ (\ xx\ ,\ yy\ ,\ zz\ ) \wedge$
      $zz = yy + 1$
   THEN
      $sqrt := yy$
   END

DEFINITIONS

   $square\ (\ x\ )\ \widehat{=}\ x \times x\ ;$
   $sqinv\ (\ x\ ,\ y\ ,\ z\ )\ \widehat{=}\ y < z \wedge square\ (\ y\ ) \leq x \wedge x < square\ (\ z\ )$

END

Fig. 1.3. Square Root Refinement

1.3.2 Data Refinement

In contrast to the refinement of *SquareRoot*, we will present a refinement of *UniqueID* in which we change the representation of the state. The refinement of the state of a machine is determined by the operations that need to be supported, as distinct from the operations that might be supported. In many cases the operations do not need the full capability of the abstract state and a concrete state can be chosen that discards some of the abstractions. In the case of the *UniqueID* machine we make the following observations:

- The abstract set *IDS* could be replaced by the set of natural numbers 1..*maxids*. We then know that identifiers are actually natural numbers.
- We don't need to allocate identifiers non-deterministically, we could allocate them sequentially starting from 1.
- Since there is no operation by which identifiers can be returned, we can simulate the set of used identifiers very simply: we simply need a natural number variable that records the last allocated identifier. Then if that variable is *lastID* the *usedIDS* set is implicitly 1..*lastID*.

The refinement is shown in Fig. 1.4 on the facing page and the following features should be noted:

- The abstract set *IDS* is instantiated to the set 1..*lastID* in the PROPERTIES clause.
- The machine has a single variable *lastID* whose type is $\mathbb{N}$, given in the INVARIANT section.

REFINEMENT   *UniqueIDR*

REFINES   *UniqueID*

PROPERTIES   *IDS = 1 .. maxids*

VARIABLES   *lastID*

INVARIANT   *lastID* $\in \mathbb{N} \wedge$ *usedIDS = 1 .. lastID*

INITIALISATION   *lastID* := *0*

OPERATIONS
    newid $\longleftarrow$ *allocID* $\hat{=}$
      BEGIN
        newid := *lastID + 1* $\parallel$ *lastID* := *lastID + 1*
      END ;
    nids $\longleftarrow$ *FreeIDS* $\hat{=}$
      BEGIN
        nids := *maxids − lastID*
      END

END

Fig. 1.4. Unique Identifier Refinement

- The INVARIANT not only specifies an invariant on the state of the refining machine, but it also expresses the refinement relation between the state of this machine and the state of the refined machine. The refinement relation shows how the *refining* machine models the *refined* machine. In this case, the set *usedIDS* is simulated by the set 1 .. *lastID*.
- The INITIALISATION establishes the invariant.
- The operations are now expressed as simple deterministic computations.

1.3.3 Refinement and Non-Determinism

While both specification machines use non-determinism in the definition of their operations, the uses are quite different:

1. The result of the *SquareRoot* operation is defined using non-deterministic choice, but in that case there is only one possible value. In this case we are using non-determinism to achieve an abstract expression of the requirements, in order to avoid irrelevant details that would be introduced if a constructive definition were given.
2. The non-deterministic choice used in the specification of the operation *allocID* does result in a large number of different behaviours, all of which are acceptable.

In the case of 1) above, refinement consists of devising an algorithm that will compute the required result. Any algorithm – ignoring possible performance requirements – will do. In this case the verification of refinement is concerned with showing that the result is consistent with the specification.

In the case of 2) above, the situation is different. Not only do we need to design an algorithm, but we need to deal with the non-determinism.

We will deal briefly with the formal definition of refinement and how it deals with non-determinism. We will take a very simple example in which we have non-determinism of the second kind, but in which only procedural refinement is involved.

Consider a coin flipping operation. We have a set

$$COIN = \{HEAD, TAIL\}$$

and an operation that flips the coin

$$y \longleftarrow flip \mathrel{\widehat{=}} y : \in COIN$$

Notice that the result of the *flip* operation is specified as non-deterministic choice from a set.

Now suppose that we refine the *flip* operation using exactly the same definition. Is a coin flip refined by any other coin flip?

Let us do a very simple investigation of the formalisation of refinement. We will deal only with refinement between substitutions and we will restrict the discussion to substitutions that are total, ie. precondition *TRUE*.

Suppose we have two substitutions G and H and we want H to be a refinement of G. Suppose that each of G and H returns a result y. In order to distinguish the two results we will rename the result of H to y' and hence also change H to H' in which all instances of y are replaced by y'. We assume that y' is a new variable. Our first guess, from the replacement argument above, might be to say that the condition for refinement is the condition under which both G and H' achieve $y = y'$, that is

$$[H']([G](y = y'))$$

Let's just try that with $G = y := 2 * x$ and $H = y := x + x$.

$$[y' := x + x][y := 2 * x](y = y')$$
$$= [y' := x + x](2 * x = y')$$
$$= 2 * x = x + x = TRUE$$

Now try it on the non-deterministic choice in our *flip* operation. Let us first compute the substitution of *flip* for any predicate R.

$$[y : \in COIN]R$$
$$= [@y'.(y' \in COIN \Longrightarrow y := y')]R)$$
$$= \forall y'.([y' \in COIN \Longrightarrow y := y']R)$$
$$= \forall y'.(y' \in COIN \Rightarrow [y := y']R)$$
$$= [y := HEAD]R \wedge [y := TAIL]R$$

So the condition for *flip* to refine *flip* is

$$[flip']([flip](y = y'))$$
$$= [y' :\in COIN]([y :\in COIN](y = y'))$$
$$= [y' :\in COIN](HEAD = y' \wedge TAIL = y')$$
$$= HEAD = HEAD \wedge TAIL = HEAD \wedge$$
$$\quad HEAD = TAIL \wedge TAIL = TAIL$$
$$= FALSE$$

The problem we have here is due to the non-determinism. Our condition for refinement is insisting that the two machines produce the same results. This is too strong for our notion of refinement. While we may be able to distinguish between two different coin flips, we normally would accept one coin flip as an acceptable replacement for any other coin flip. If we were to compare the results of each we would only want to insist that the result produced by the refinement could have been produced by the refined machine. The result for refinement is weakened to the following

$$[H'](\neg[G]\neg(y = y'))$$

Notice that $[S]R$ specifies the set of states in which S is guaranteed to produce a state satisfying R. Therefore $[S]\neg R$ specifies the set of states in which S is guaranteed to produce a state satisfying $\neg R$. Hence, $\neg[S]\neg R$ specifies the set of states in which it is not possible for S to produce a state satisfying $\neg R$, ie. the set of states for which it is possible, but not guaranteed, for S to produce a state satisfying R. That is the precondition we are interested in for non-deterministic operations.

If you evaluate the new condition for the *flip* machines you will find that the condition reduces to *TRUE*.

In conclusion, the notion of refinement that **B** supports is that for any state for which an operation of the refined machine is defined, then the same operation in the refining machine must do something that is consistent with the refined machine. In any state for which an operation in the refined machine is not defined, the same operation in the refining machine can do anything. Behaviour includes results and also changes of states interpreted according to the invariant in the refining machine.

If an operation of the refined machine could produce more than one result, ie. it is non-deterministic, then the corresponding operation in the refining machine must produce a result that the refined machine could possibly produce. In other words, the result must not be one that the refined machine can never produce.

There are a number of refinement obligations defined within **B**. We will give just one case that will allow us to discuss the refinement of *UniqueID*. Consider a machine M with operations that are parameterless, but which return a result, as characterised below:

MACHINE M
VARIABLES V
INVARIANT I
OPERATIONS
$R \longleftarrow Op \,\widehat{=}$
PRE P
THEN S
END
END

and that this is refined by:

REFINEMENT M_R
REFINES M
VARIABLES V_R
INVARIANT I_R
OPERATIONS
$R \longleftarrow Op \,\widehat{=}$
PRE P_R
THEN S_R
END
END

then the refinement obligation for the refined operation is

$$I \wedge I_R \wedge P \Rightarrow P_R \wedge [S_R'](\neg[S](\neg(I_R \wedge R' = R))) \tag{1.1}$$

where $S_R' = [R := R']S_R'$.
Condition (1.1) splits into two requirements:

$$I \wedge I_R \wedge P \Rightarrow P_R \tag{1.2}$$
$$I \wedge I_R \wedge P \Rightarrow [S_R'](\neg[S](\neg(I_R \wedge R' = R))) \tag{1.3}$$

If S is a deterministic substitution, then condition (1.3) can be simplified to

$$I \wedge I_R \wedge P \Rightarrow [S_R']([S](I_R \wedge R' = R)) \tag{1.4}$$

Informally:

- condition (1.2) requires that the precondition of the operation is not strengthened;
- condition (1.3) requires the new substitution S_R to maintain the simulation of M_R under the refinement relation embedded in I_R. As well, there is a requirement that this condition holds only where the two result values are the same.

Since both machines contain the variable R, it is necessary to rename one of them, and we rename the result variable in the refining machine to R'. Notice that we are using a substitution on a substitution, $[R := R']S_R'$ to change the name of a variable – or more generally a number of variables – in a substitution.

A toolkit will, of course, generate all proof obligations automatically. We will apply the above refinement condition to the *allocID* operation.

IMPLEMENTATION   *UniqueIDRI*

REFINES   *UniqueIDR*

IMPORTS   *ID_Nvar (maxids)*

INVARIANT   *lastID = ID_Nvar*

OPERATIONS

  newid ⟵ *allocID*   ≙
     BEGIN
         ID_INC_NVAR **;**
             newid ⟵ *ID_VAL_NVAR*
     END ;
  nids ⟵ *FreeIDS*   ≙
     VAR   *ll*
     IN
         ll ⟵ *ID_VAL_NVAR* **;**
         nids := *maxids − ll*
     END

END

Fig. 1.5. Implementation of the Unique Identifier Machine

1.4 Implementation

Implementation in **B** is a special refinement step. There can be as many refinement steps as you wish, and then at any stage you can decide to implement. This step can be done only once for each development, and the implementation machine has some very strong constraints:

- The implementation machine has no state of its own.
- To implement the operations, the implementation machine must import other (specification) machines.
- Any parameters of imported machines must be instantiated in the IMPORTS statement.
- The operations of the machine may not directly modify, or reference any of the variables of the imported machines. All interrogation or modification of the state must be achieved by using operations of the imported machines.
- Implementation machines cannot use abstract substitutions like non-deterministic choice and parallel composition.

The purpose of these constraints is

1. to ensure that the implementation is dependent only on the specification of other machines and not on their implementation.
2. to ensure that the implementation is concrete.

An example of a simple implementation is shown in Fig. 1.5. The following feature of the implementation should be noted:

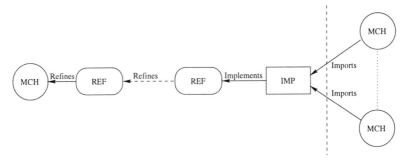

Fig. 1.6. Layered Development

- The imported machine *ID_Nvar* is a renamed instance of a natural number variable machine. The prefix "*ID_*" identifies this instance of the machine. The machine encapsulates a single natural number variable, *ID_Nvar* and a set of natural number operations.
- The parameter of the *Nvar* machine sets the upper bound for values of the variable.
- *ID_INC_NVAR* increments the value of *ID_Nvar*.
- *ID_VAL_NVAR* reads the value of *ID_Nvar*.
- Operations may have local temporary variables.

> **Note:** the machine *Rename_Nvar* is a machine available in the standard library of the B-Toolkit. If the reader has access to a toolkit, then that or a similar machine should be available. The standard library of those toolkits will contain a range of machines that are useful for the implementation of various mathematical and programming constructs.

1.4.1 Layered Development

Machines that are imported into an implementation may be already implemented, as is the case of the *Nvar* machine imported into the *UniqueIDRI* machine, or they may be newly invented machines specified for the purpose of enabling this implementation. In the latter case the new machine will have to be refined and implemented. This process continues, layer by layer, until all the lowest level implementations depend on machines that have been implemented. This leads to a development pattern that has become known as *layered development*. Layered development is illustrated in Fig. 1.6.

The implementation of the *SquareRoot* machine illustrates this layering. The implementation shown in Fig. 1.7 on page 18 illustrates an approach to implementing *WHILE* substitutions. The constraint from the refinement machine

$$sqinv(xx, yy, zz) \land zz = yy + 1$$

is broken into two conjuncts:

1. $sqinv(xx, yy, zz)$ is satisfied by the initialisation of the local variables yy and zz. It is also the main part of the loop INVARIANT.
2. The while-loop is used to satisfy the other conjunct $zz = yy + 1$, by modifying the values of yy and zz under the constraint of the loop INVARIANT.
3. The modification of the variables yy and zz is assigned to an operation of a new machine shown in Fig. 1.8 on the following page.

This strategy allows us to explore different approaches to "moving yy and zz closer together", if we were interested.

Having introduced the *SquareRootUtils* machine, we first refine it to the basic algorithm we wish to use, in Fig. 1.9 on page 19. The final implementation in Fig. 1.10 on page 19 has only one small change: the refinement of the expression $ww * ww \leq xx$ to $ww \leq xx/ww$. The former expression is the one that most directly expresses our requirement, and we could have refined directly to an implementation containing that expression, but if we did then the implementation would be flawed. Since this expression contains a multiplication it is possible for it to overflow, and so we replace the expression by another that meets our needs and, which will not overflow. In using the refined expression we need to be sure that $ww \neq 0$. This is assured by the precondition of the *ChooseNewApprox* operation in the *SquareRootUtils* machine. How?

Note: we should take care with all arithmetic operations and there is a pair of machines, *Scalar_TYPE* and *Scalar_TYPE_Ops*, that specifies the common natural number operations. We should have used these machines in the implementation of our square root machines, but this would have involved introducing the *SCALAR* type early in the development.

1.4.2 Proof Obligations

There are proof obligations associated with each machine in a development. These address the following concerns:

- *Context:* proof that sets satisfying specified constraints and properties exist.
- *Maintenance of invariant:* proof that the invariant is established by the initialisation and maintained by the operations.
- *Satisfaction of refinement relation:* proof that refinement and implementation machines satisfy the refinement constraints.
- *Preconditions:* proof that preconditions for any invoked machine operations are satisfied.

The discharge of proof obligations is a vital part of the B Method. The proofs document the case for your development. If proof obligations are not discharged then, except for the added rigour in specifying machines, there is little significant difference between developing in AMN and in some other programming language. If a toolkit is used then the proof obligations will be generated automatically, and there will be substantial assistance given to the proof of those obligations. That assistance will include automatic proof and various forms of interactive proof, during which you will be required to specify new proof rules.

IMPLEMENTATION   *SquareRootR1*

REFINES   *SquareRootR*

IMPORTS   *SquareRootUtils*

OPERATIONS

   sqrt ⟵ *SquareRoot*(*xx*)   ≘
        VAR   *yy* , *zz*
        IN   *yy* := *0* ;
            zz := (*xx* + *1*) / *2* + *1* ;
            WHILE   *yy* + *1* ≠ *zz*
            DO   *yy* , *zz* ⟵ *ChooseNewApprox* (*xx* , *yy* , *zz*)
            INVARIANT   *yy* ∈ ℕ ∧ *zz* ∈ ℕ ∧ *sqinv* (*xx* , *yy* , *zz*)
            VARIANT   *zz* − *yy*
            END ;
            sqrt := *yy*
        END

DEFINITIONS

   square (*x*)   ≘   *x* × *x* ;
   sqinv (*x* , *y* , *z*)   ≘   *y* < *z* ∧ *square* (*y*) ≤ *x* ∧ *x* < *square* (*z*)

END

Fig. 1.7. Implementation of the SquareRoot Machine

MACHINE   *SquareRootUtils*

OPERATIONS

   yy , *zz* ⟵ *ChooseNewApprox*(*xx* , *yy0* , *zz0*)   ≘
        PRE   *xx* ∈ ℕ ∧ *yy0* ∈ ℕ ∧ *zz0* ∈ ℕ ∧
            sqinv (*xx* , *yy0* , *zz0*) ∧ *yy0* + *1* < *zz0*   **THEN**
            ANY   *ww*
            WHERE   *ww* ∈ ℕ ∧ *yy0* < *ww* ∧ *ww* < *zz0*   **THEN**
                SELECT
                    sqinv (*xx* , *ww* , *zz0*)   **THEN**   *yy* , *zz* := *ww* , *zz0*
                WHEN
                    sqinv (*xx* , *yy0* , *ww*)   **THEN**   *yy* , *zz* := *yy0* , *ww*
                END
            END
        END

DEFINITIONS

   square (*x*)   ≘   *x* × *x* ;
   sqinv (*x* , *y* , *z*)   ≘   *y* < *z* ∧ *square* (*y*) ≤ *x* ∧ *x* < *square* (*z*)

END

Fig. 1.8. Square Root Utility Machine

REFINEMENT   *SquareRootUtilsR*

REFINES   *SquareRootUtils*

OPERATIONS

yy , zz ⟵ *ChooseNewApprox*(xx , $yy0$, $zz0$)   ≘
    VAR ww **IN**
      $ww := (yy0 + zz0) / 2$ **;**
      IF $ww \times ww \leq xx$
      THEN $yy := ww$ **;** $zz := zz0$
      ELSE $yy := yy0$ **;** $zz := ww$
      END
    END

END

Fig. 1.9. Square Root Utility Refinement

IMPLEMENTATION   *SquareRootUtilsRI*

REFINES   *SquareRootUtilsR*

OPERATIONS

yy , zz ⟵ *ChooseNewApprox*(xx , $yy0$, $zz0$)   ≘
    VAR ww **IN**
      $ww := (yy0 + zz0) / 2$ **;**
      IF $ww \leq xx / ww$
      THEN $yy := ww$ **;** $zz := zz0$
      ELSE $yy := yy0$ **;** $zz := ww$
      END
    END

END

Fig. 1.10. Square Root Utility Implementation

Using the B-Toolkit, the square-root development generated 17 proof obligations, of which 4 required interactive proof.

Figure 1.11 on the next page presents all the proof obligations for the *UniqueIDR* machine shown in Fig. 1.4 on page 11. In each proof obligation the following abbreviations are used for parts of the hypotheses:

cst(mch):   constraints: the predicates of the *CONSTRAINTS* clause of machine *mch*;

ctx(mch):   context: predicates of the *PROPERTIES* clause of machine *mch* and subordinate machines;

inv(mch):   invariant: predicates *INVARIANT* clause of machine *mch* together with abstract/concrete equalities of any algorithmically-refined variables;

asn(mch):   *ASSERTIONS* of machine *mch*;

Initialisation . 1

$\quad cst\,(\,UniqueIDR_1\,) \wedge ctx\,(\,UniqueIDR_1\,)$

$\Rightarrow$

$\quad 0 \in \mathbb{N}$

Initialisation . 2

$\quad cst\,(\,UniqueIDR_1\,) \wedge ctx\,(\,UniqueIDR_1\,)$

$\Rightarrow$

$\quad \{\} = 1\,..\,0$

---

allocID . 1

$\quad cst\,(\,UniqueIDR_1\,) \wedge ctx\,(\,UniqueIDR_1\,) \wedge$
$\quad inv\,(\,UniqueIDR_1\,) \wedge asn\,(\,UniqueIDR_1\,) \wedge$
$\quad pre\,(\,allocID\,)$

$\Rightarrow$

$\quad lastID_1 + 1 \in IDS - usedIDS$

---

allocID . 2

$\quad cst\,(\,UniqueIDR_1\,) \wedge ctx\,(\,UniqueIDR_1\,) \wedge$
$\quad inv\,(\,UniqueIDR_1\,) \wedge asn\,(\,UniqueIDR_1\,) \wedge$
$\quad pre\,(\,allocID\,)$

$\Rightarrow$

$\quad lastID_1 + 1 \in \mathbb{N}$

---

allocID . 3

$\quad cst\,(\,UniqueIDR_1\,) \wedge ctx\,(\,UniqueIDR_1\,) \wedge$
$\quad inv\,(\,UniqueIDR_1\,) \wedge asn\,(\,UniqueIDR_1\,) \wedge$
$\quad pre\,(\,allocID\,)$

$\Rightarrow$

$\quad usedIDS \cup \{\,lastID_1 + 1\,\} = 1\,..\,lastID_1 + 1$

FreeIDS . 1

$\quad cst\,(\,UniqueIDR_1\,) \wedge ctx\,(\,UniqueIDR_1\,) \wedge$
$\quad inv\,(\,UniqueIDR_1\,) \wedge asn\,(\,UniqueIDR_1\,) \wedge$
$\quad pre\,(\,FreeIDS\,)$

$\Rightarrow$

$\quad maxids - lastID_1 = \mathsf{card}\,(\,IDS - usedIDS\,)$

Context . 1

$\quad cst\,(\,UniqueIDR_1\,)$

$\Rightarrow$

$\quad \mathsf{card}\,(\,1\,..\,maxids\,) = maxids$

Context . 2

$\quad cst\,(\,UniqueIDR_1\,)$

$\Rightarrow$

$\quad \mathsf{card}\,(\,1\,..\,maxids\,) \in \mathbb{N}_1$

Fig. 1.11. Proof Obligations for the *UniqueIDR* Machine

allocID . 1

1	cst (*UniqueIDR* $_1$)	HYP
2	ctx (*UniqueIDR* $_1$)	HYP
3	inv (*UniqueIDR* $_1$)	HYP
4	asn (*UniqueIDR* $_1$)	HYP
5	$maxids \in \mathbb{N}_1$	1,HypExp.7
6	$IDS = 1 .. maxids$	2,Props.1
7	$usedIDS = 1 .. lastID_1$	3,HypExp.6
8	$lastID_1 \in \mathbb{N}$	3,HypExp.5
9	inv (*UniqueID*)	3,HypExp.3
10	$maxids \in \mathbb{N}$	5,Law.1
11	$usedIDS \subseteq IDS$	9,HypExp.1
12	pre (*allocID*)	HYP
13	$\neg (usedIDS = IDS)$	12,HypExp.2
14	$1 \le lastID_1 + 1$	Law.2
15	$usedIDS \subset IDS$	11,13,UsersTheory.1
16	$lastID_1 < maxids$	7,6,15,UsersTheory.2
17	$lastID_1 + 1 \le maxids$	8,10,16,Law.3
18	$lastID_1 + 1 \in 1 .. maxids$	14,17,Law.4
19	$lastID_1 + 1 \in IDS$	18,6
20	$1 \in \mathbb{N}$	Law.5
21	$0 < 1$	ARI
22	$1 \in \mathbb{N}_1$	20,21,Law.6
23	$lastID_1 < lastID_1 + 1$	22,8,Law.7
24	$\neg (lastID_1 + 1 \in 1 .. lastID_1)$	Law.8
25	$\neg (lastID_1 + 1 \in usedIDS)$	24,7
26	$lastID_1 + 1 \in IDS - usedIDS$	19,25,Law.9
27	*QED*	DED

Fig. 1.12. Proof of *allocID.1* for the *UniqueIDR* Machine

UsersTheory . 1

$$S \subseteq T \wedge \neg (S = T)$$
$$\Rightarrow$$
$$S \subset T$$

UsersTheory . 2

$$S = 1 .. m \wedge T = 1 .. n \wedge S \subset T$$
$$\Rightarrow$$
$$m < n$$

Fig. 1.13. User Theories for Proof of *allocID.1*

pre(opn):   precondition of operation *opn* in this machine.

For the machine *UniqueIDR*, all of the above are empty except the *ctx*, *inv* and *pre* components.

It should also be noted that a subscripted name, as in $lastID_1$, is a reference to the value associated with that name *before* the operation.

As an exercise, the reader should compute condition (1.3 on page 14) for the operation *AllocID* and compare with the proof obligations labelled *allocID.1*, *allocID.2* and *allocID.3*. Substitution distributes through conjunction and in most cases this allows a proof obligation to be separated into a number of simpler obligations. It should be noted that

- *allocID.1* is generated from the $R = R'$ conjunct in condition (1.3 on page 14). The result of the operation in *UniqueID* is *nid*, and *nid* in that machine is specified by non-deterministic choice $nid :\in IDS - usedIDS$. In the *UniqueIDR* machine the result is $lastID_1 + 1$. Thus this condition is a reflection through to the refinement from the non-deterministic choice in the abstract machine *UniqueID*.
- *allocID.2* is generated from the $lastID \in \mathbb{N}$ conjunct of the invariant of the abstract machine *UniqueIDR*.
- *allocID.3* is generated from the $usedIDS = 1..lastID$ conjunct of *UniqueIDR*.

A proof of *allocID.1* is shown in Fig. 1.12. This proof was produced interactively under the B-Toolkit. The two user theories, shown in Fig. 1.13 on the page before, were required.

1.5 An Extended Example

A more extensive example will now be given that demonstrates a longer development sequence and more of the facilities of **B**. The example presented below is adapted from an example in J.P. Hoare [40].

1.5.1 A Simple Data Queue Machine

The *DataQueue* machine models the problem of retaining the chronological order of registration of some customer data or information, given that customers' information may be added to or deleted from the existing collection of data. We model this by having a set of tokens (*TOKEN*) that represents the set of data objects. The data attributes of each object are modelled by a partial function from *TOKEN* to *DATA*. The sequencing is modelled by an injective sequence of tokens. The *DataQueue* machine is parameterised by three items: *DATA:* a non-empty set representing the data in the queue; *anydata:* an element of that set; *maxqueue:* a non-zero constant representing the maximum number of elements in the queue. The parameters remain uninstantiated until the machine is imported into some other machine.

MACHINE   *DataQueue (DATA , anydata , maxqueue)*

CONSTRAINTS   *anydata* ∈ *DATA* ∧ *maxqueue* > 0

SEES   *Bool_TYPE*

SETS   *TOKEN*

PROPERTIES   card (*TOKEN*) = *maxqueue*

VARIABLES   *TokenSeq* , *TokenMap*

The state consists of two variables: *TokenSeq*, representing the (consecutive) sequence of tokens or identifiers, and *TokenMap*, which represents the relation between members of the *TokenSeq* and data items associated with it. The precise meaning of these two variables is given in the machine's *INVARIANT*. The first conjunct constrains *TokenSeq* to be an injective sequence to ensure that any token occurs at most once in the sequence. The second and third conjuncts constrain *TokenMap* to be a total function from all tokens in the sequence *TokenSeq* to *DATA*. As noted earlier, this allows each token to be uniquely identified with a data item, but each data item may have more than one token associated with it.

INVARIANT

TokenSeq ∈ iseq (*TOKEN*) ∧
TokenMap ∈ *TOKEN* ↦ *DATA* ∧
dom (*TokenMap*) = *USED*

INITIALISATION

TokenSeq , *TokenMap* := [ ] , {}

The operations of the machine follow. Some of these operations may succeed or fail, so any specification and implementation might take this into account. For example, adding an item may fail because there can be no more tokens allocated. This is a direct result of the B-Method insisting on specifying finite sets. An attempt to delete an item that is not currently in the queue is regarded as benign and so we will not regard deletion as an operation that can fail. Returning the oldest item can fail if there are no items to return.

OPERATIONS

success , *token* ⟵ *AddItem*(*item*)   ≙
    PRE   *item* ∈ *DATA*   **THEN**
        CHOICE
            ANY   *new_token*   **WHERE**   *new_token* ∈ *TOKEN* − *USED*
            THEN
                TokenSeq := *TokenSeq* ⟵ *new_token*   ‖
                TokenMap (*new_token*) := *item*   ‖
                success , *token* := *TRUE* , *new_token*
            END
        OR
            success := *FALSE*   ‖   *token* :∈ *TOKEN*
        END
    END ;

DeleteItem(*token*)   ≙
    PRE   *token* ∈ *TOKEN*   **THEN**
      IF   *token* ∈ *USED*   **THEN**

$$\textbf{ANY} \quad before , after$$
$$\textbf{WHERE} \quad before \in \text{seq}_1 \; (\; TOKEN \;) \wedge after \in \text{seq}_1 \; (\; TOKEN \;) \wedge$$
$$TokenSeq = before \frown [\; token \;] \frown after$$
$$\textbf{THEN}$$
$$TokenSeq := before \frown after \; \|$$
$$TokenMap := \{ \; token \; \} \lhd TokenMap$$
$$\textbf{END}$$
$$\textbf{END}$$
$$\textbf{END} ;$$
$$success , token \longleftarrow OldestItem \quad \widehat{=}$$
$$\textbf{IF} \quad USED \neq \{\} \quad \textbf{THEN}$$
$$success , token := TRUE , \text{first} \; (\; TokenSeq \;)$$
$$\textbf{ELSE}$$
$$success := FALSE \; \| \; token :\in TOKEN$$
$$\textbf{END} ;$$
$$item \longleftarrow ItemData(\; token \;) \quad \widehat{=}$$
$$\textbf{PRE} \quad token \in USED \quad \textbf{THEN}$$
$$item := TokenMap \; (\; token \;)$$
$$\textbf{END}$$
$$\textbf{DEFINITIONS}$$
$$USED \; \widehat{=} \; \text{ran} \; (\; TokenSeq \;)$$
$$\textbf{END}$$

1.5.2 Refinement of the Data Queue

We will refine the *DataQueue* machine to an implementation. As noted above, to do this we will have to import one or more machines which provide operations that can be used to simulate the operations of the refined machine. The *DataQueue* machine could be refined to an implementation using standard machines in the library of a toolkit, but we will take the development via a different, and somewhat fanciful, route. Instead of refining the sequence using a sequence machine we will refine using a "doubly-linked list" machine (*DList*) as shown in the following refinement.

IMPLEMENTATION *DataQueue_Imp*

REFINES *DataQueue*

SEES *Bool_TYPE*

IMPORTS *DList* (*DATA* , *anydata* , *maxqueue* + *1*)

PROPERTIES *ITEM* = *TOKEN*

INVARIANT

dom (*TokenMap*) = dom (*Contents*) − { *Anchor* } ∧
$\forall ii . (ii \in$ dom (*TokenSeq*) ⇒
   TokenSeq (*ii*) = $Next^{ii}$ (*Anchor*)) ∧
$\forall token . (token \in$ ran (*TokenSeq*) ⇒
   TokenMap (*token*) = *Contents* (*token*))

OPERATIONS

success , token ⟵ *AddItem(item)*   ≘
    BEGIN
       success , token ⟵ *List_Append (item)*
    END ;
DeleteItem(token)   ≘
    BEGIN
       List_Delete (token)
    END ;
success , token ⟵ *OldestItem*   ≘
    VAR   *isempty*
    IN   *isempty* ⟵ *List_Isempty* **;**
       success ⟵ *NEG_BOOL (isempty)* **;**
       token ⟵ *List_Head*
    END ;
item ⟵ *ItemData(token)*   ≘
    BEGIN
       item ⟵ *List_Info (token)*
    END
END

1.5.3 The Doubly-Linked List Machine

The imported *DList* machine specifies a doubly-linked list of items taken from a set *ITEM*. The start of the list is denoted by a variable *Anchor*, and items in the list have forward and backward "pointers", *Next* and *Previous*. The content of each item in the list is established by a function that maps items to values in the parametric set *INFO*. The refinement is based on the following relations extracted from the *DataQueue* implementation:

There are three important points to note:

- In the *IMPORT* clause, the parameters of the *DList* machine are instantiated.
- In the *PROPERTIES* clause, the deferred set *ITEM* of the *DList* machine is equated to the deferred set *TOKEN* of the *DataQueue* machine.
- In the *INVARIANT* clause the state of the *DataQueue* machine is related to the state of the *DList* machine.

The *DList* machine provides the abstract operations of appending, and deleting an item from a doubly-linked list, as well as operations to allow checking to see if the list is empty and returning the first item in the list. The machine is parameterised by *INFO*, a set of items that represents the information content of each list item. These list entries are associated with three separate "pointer" functions: one for the information content, one for the forward link to the next item in the list, and one for the link to the previous item in the list. This may be done in a lower level machine which is imported in the implementation of *DList*. Our specification deals only with the operations allowed on the items in the list (as well as giving invariants and assertions about the list and associated entries). The modelling of the doubly-linked list structure is discussed in the following specification.

MACHINE   *DList (INFO , anyinfo , maxitems)*

CONSTRAINTS   *anyinfo* $\in$ *INFO* $\wedge$ *maxitems* > 0

SEES   *Bool_TYPE*

SETS   *ITEM*

PROPERTIES   card (*ITEM*) = *maxitems*

The *DList* machine models a doubly-linked list. The list is formed from a set of ITEMS. Each item in the set has the following attributes:

Contents: the information associated with the item;
Next: the successor item in the list;
Previous: the predecessor item in the list.

The dummy item **Anchor** has a *Next* value that points to the first item in the list, and a *Previous* value that points to the last item in the list. The first item in the list has a *Previous* link to **Anchor** and the last item in the list has a *Next* link to **Anchor**. If the list is empty then both the *Next* and *Previous* links from **Anchor** point to itself.

The invariant expresses the following properties:

- every item in the list has a *Next* and a *Previous* link, and each link points to a unique item, hence *Next* and *Previous* are bijective functions.
- if you follow a *Next* link and then immediately follow a *Previous* link, you get back to where you started; similarly for *Previous* and *Next* in the other order. Hence, both (*Next* ;*Previous*) and (*Previous* ;*Next*) are the identity relation on the set of *USED* items.
- starting from the **Anchor** you can reach every item in the list by following only *Next* (or *Previous*) links.

VARIABLES

Anchor ,
Contents ,
Next ,
Previous

INVARIANT

Anchor $\in$ *USED* $\wedge$
Contents $\in$ *ITEM* $\twoheadrightarrow$ *INFO* $\wedge$
Next $\in$ *USED* $\rightarrowtail\!\!\!\!\rightarrow$ *USED* $\wedge$
Previous $\in$ *USED* $\rightarrowtail\!\!\!\!\rightarrow$ *USED* $\wedge$
(*Next* **;** *Previous*) = id (*USED*) $\wedge$
Next* [{ *Anchor* }] = *USED*

We can also express the doubly linked list properties by assertions.

ASSERTIONS

$\forall$ *item* . (*item* $\in$ *USED* $\Rightarrow$
    Previous (*Next* (*item*)) = *item*) $\wedge$
$\forall$ *item* . (*item* $\in$ *USED* $\Rightarrow$
    Next (*Previous* (*item*)) = *item*) $\wedge$
$\forall$ *item* . (*item* $\in$ *USED* $\Rightarrow$

$\exists\ ii\ .\ (\ ii \in 0\ ..\ \mathsf{card}\ (\ USED\ ) \land Next^{ii}\ (\ Anchor\ ) = item\ )\ )$

INITIALISATION

    ANY $item\ ,info$ **WHERE** $item \in ITEM \land info \in INFO$
    THEN
        $Anchor := item\ \|$
        $Contents := \{\ item \mapsto info\ \}\ \|$
        $Next := \{\ item \mapsto item\ \}\ \|$
        $Previous := \{\ item \mapsto item\ \}$
    END

OPERATIONS

$success\ ,\ newitem \longleftarrow List\_Append(\ info\ )\quad \hat{=}$
    PRE $info \in INFO$
    THEN
        IF $FREE \neq \{\}$
        THEN
            ANY $item$ **WHERE** $item \in FREE$
            THEN
                $Contents\ (\ item\ ) := info\ \|$
                $Next := Next \lhd\!\!\!- \{\ Previous\ (\ Anchor\ ) \mapsto item\ ,$
                    $item \mapsto Anchor\ \}\ \|$
                $Previous := Previous \lhd\!\!\!- \{\ Anchor \mapsto item\ ,$
                    $item \mapsto Previous\ (\ Anchor\ )\ \}\ \|$
                $newitem := item\ \|$
                $success := TRUE$
            END
        ELSE
            $success := FALSE\ \|\ newitem :\in ITEM$
        END
    END ;

$List\_Delete(\ item\ )\quad \hat{=}$
    PRE $item \in ITEM \land item \in USED - \{\ Anchor\ \}$
    THEN
        $Contents := \{\ item\ \} \lhd\!\!\!\!\!\!- Contents\ \|$
        $Next := \{\ item\ \} \lhd\!\!\!\!\!\!- Next \lhd\!\!\!- \{\ Previous\ (\ item\ ) \mapsto Next\ (\ item\ )\ \}\ \|$
        $Previous := \{\ item\ \} \lhd\!\!\!\!\!\!- Previous \lhd\!\!\!- \{\ Next\ (\ item\ ) \mapsto Previous\ (\ item\ )\ \}$
    END ;

$isempty \longleftarrow List\_Isempty\quad \hat{=}$
    BEGIN
        $isempty := \mathsf{bool}\ (\ Next\ (\ Anchor\ ) = Anchor\ )$
    END ;

$item \longleftarrow List\_Head\quad \hat{=}$
    PRE $Next\ (\ Anchor\ ) \neq Anchor$ **THEN**
        $item := Next\ (\ Anchor\ )$
    END ;

$info \longleftarrow List\_Info(\ item\ )\quad \hat{=}$
    PRE $item \in ITEM$ **THEN**
        $info := Contents\ (\ item\ )$
    END

DEFINITIONS

    $USED\quad \hat{=}\quad \mathsf{dom}\ (\ Contents\ )$ **;**

$FREE \; \widehat{=} \; ITEM - USED$
END

1.5.4 Implementing the DList Machine

When we implemented the *DataQueue* machine by importing the *DList* machine we entered the layered development chain: we are required to implement the *DList* machine. As previously, we will choose to take the refinement a further step, which we will not complete here.

We will specify a *Node* machine in Sec. 1.5.5 on the facing page, which is a more general and less constrained machine than the *DList* machine. The refinement relation between the *DList* machine and the *Node* machine is shown in invariant below.

IMPLEMENTATION   *DList_Imp*

REFINES   *DList*

SEES   *Bool_TYPE*

IMPORTS

    Node (INFO , maxitems) ,
    Anchor_Vvar (NODE)

Notice that this machine also imports the *rename_Vvar* machine from the standard library. The *rename_Vvar* machine provides a single variable of any type. In this case the instantiation *Anchor_Vvar* provides a variable that implements the variable **Anchor** of the *DList* machine.

PROPERTIES $ITEM = NODE$

INVARIANT

    $Anchor = Anchor\_Vvar \;\wedge$
    $\textbf{dom} (\textit{Contents}) = Allocated \;\wedge$
    $\forall \, node \, . \, (\, node \in Allocated \Rightarrow NodeContents \, (\, node \,) = Contents \, (\, node \,) \,) \;\wedge$
    $\forall \, node \, . \, (\, node \in Allocated \Rightarrow NextNode \, (\, node \,) = Next \, (\, node \,) \,) \;\wedge$
    $\forall \, node \, . \, (\, node \in Allocated \Rightarrow PreviousNode \, (\, node \,) = Previous \, (\, node \,) \,)$

INITIALISATION

    VAR   *node*
    IN
        $node \longleftarrow SingleNode \, (\, anyinfo \,) \; ;$
        $Anchor\_STO\_VAR \, (\, node \,)$
    END

The refinement of the operations of *DList* follow.

OPERATIONS

    $success \, , newitem \longleftarrow List\_Append(\, info \,) \quad \widehat{=}$
        VAR   *anchor , newnode , lastnode , ok*
        IN

```
            anchor ⟵ Anchor_VAL_VAR ;
            lastnode ⟵ GetPrevious ( anchor ) ;
            ok , newnode ⟵ NewNode ( info , lastnode , anchor ) ;
            IF    ok = TRUE
            THEN
                SetNext ( lastnode , newnode ) ;
                SetPrevious ( anchor , newnode )
            END ;
            success := ok ;
            newitem := newnode
        END ;
    List_Delete( item )    ≙
        VAR    prev , next
        IN
            prev ⟵ GetPrevious ( item ) ;
            next ⟵ GetNext ( item ) ;
            SetNext ( prev , next ) ;
            SetPrevious ( next , prev ) ;
            FreeNode ( item )
        END ;
    isempty ⟵ List_Isempty    ≙
        VAR    anchor , frst
        IN
            anchor ⟵ Anchor_VAL_VAR ;
            frst ⟵ GetPrevious ( anchor ) ;
            isempty ⟵ EqlNode ( frst , anchor )
        END ;
    item ⟵ List_Head    ≙
        VAR    anchor
        IN
            anchor ⟵ Anchor_VAL_VAR ;
            item ⟵ GetNext ( anchor )
        END ;
    info ⟵ List_Info( item )    ≙
        BEGIN
            info ⟵ GetInfo ( item )
        END
END
```

1.5.5 The Node Machine

The *Node* machine specifies a low level construct that is more primitive than the
DList structure. The *Node* machine specifies a set of objects *NODE*, where each
object has three attributes:

NodeContents: a value of type *INFO*;
PreviousNode: a reference to another node;
NextNode: a reference to another node.

The attributes *PreviousNode* and *NextNode* have been given names that will assist in
understanding how the node machine is used in the implementation of the doubly-

linked structure, but the attributes should have less specific names like *Left* and *Right*. A node is a quite general construct and the nodes are not constrained to be connected in a linear sequence or in any other topology. The invariant of the *Node* machine should be compared carefully with the invariant of the *DList* machine. The nodes are constrained only so that *PreviousNode* and *NextNode* must reference other allocated items. The data model for *NODE* objects is specified through the variables and the invariant of the *Node* machine.

MACHINE   *Node (INFO , maxnode)*

CONSTRAINTS   *maxnode > 0*

SEES   *Bool_TYPE*

SETS   *NODE*

PROPERTIES   card (*NODE*) = *maxnode*

VARIABLES

    Allocated ,
    NodeContents ,
    PreviousNode ,
    NextNode

INVARIANT

    Allocated $\subseteq$ *NODE* $\wedge$
    NodeContents $\in$ *Allocated* $\rightarrow$ *INFO* $\wedge$
    PreviousNode $\in$ *Allocated* $\rightarrow$ *Allocated* $\wedge$
    NextNode $\in$ *Allocated* $\rightarrow$ *Allocated*

INITIALISATION

    Allocated , NodeContents , PreviousNode , NextNode := $\{\} , \{\} , \{\} , \{\}$

Implementation in **B** enforces *full hiding* of imported machines, meaning that the refinement is not allowed to reference directly any of the variables of the *IMPORTED* machines. Hence, in many cases, machines must have operations for inspecting and modifying their own variables. For the *Node* machine we have provided a reasonably complete complement of such operations:

- *SingleNode*: for creating a singleton node
- *NewNode*: for creating an extra node
- *FreeNode*: for freeing a node
- *GetInfo*: for retrieving the value of the *Info* attribute
- *GetPrevious*: for getting *PreviousNode* attribute
- *GetNext*: for getting *NextNode* attribute
- *SetPrevious*: for setting the *PreviousNode* attribute
- *SetNext*: for setting the *NextNode* attribute
- *EqlNode*: for checking node equality

OPERATIONS

    newnode $\longleftarrow$ *SingleNode(info)* $\widehat{=}$
        PRE   *info* $\in$ *INFO* $\wedge$ *FREE* $\neq \{\}$
        THEN

    ANY *node* **WHERE** *node* ∈ *FREE*
    THEN
     Allocated := *Allocated* ∪ { *node* } ‖
     NodeContents (*node*) := *info* ‖
     PreviousNode (*node*) := *node* ‖
     NextNode (*node*) := *node* ‖
     newnode := *node*
    END
   END ;

success , *newnode* ⟵ *NewNode*(*info* , *previous* , *next*) ≙
  PRE *info* ∈ *INFO* ∧ *previous* ∈ *Allocated* ∧ *next* ∈ *Allocated*
  THEN
   IF *FREE* ≠ {}
   THEN
    ANY *node* **WHERE** *node* ∈ *FREE*
    THEN
     Allocated := *Allocated* ∪ { *node* } ‖
     NodeContents (*node*) := *info* ‖
     PreviousNode (*node*) := *previous* ‖
     NextNode (*node*) := *next* ‖
     success , *newnode* := *TRUE* , *node*
    END
   ELSE
    success := *FALSE* ‖
    newnode :∈ *NODE*
   END
  END ;

FreeNode(*node*) ≙
  PRE *node* ∈ *Allocated* ∧
   node ∉ ran ({ *node* } ◁ *PreviousNode*) ∧
   node ∉ ran ({ *node* } ◁ *NextNode*)
  THEN
   Allocated := *Allocated* − { *node* } ‖
   NodeContents := { *node* } ⩤ *NodeContents* ‖
   PreviousNode := { *node* } ⩤ *PreviousNode* ‖
   NextNode := { *node* } ⩤ *NextNode*
  END ;

info ⟵ *GetInfo*(*node*) ≙
  PRE *node* ∈ *Allocated*
  THEN
   info := *NodeContents* (*node*)
  END ;

previous ⟵ *GetPrevious*(*node*) ≙
  PRE *node* ∈ *Allocated*
  THEN
   previous := *PreviousNode* (*node*)
  END ;

next ⟵ *GetNext*(*node*) ≙
  PRE *node* ∈ *Allocated*
  THEN
   next := *NextNode* (*node*)
  END ;

SetPrevious(node , previous) $\hat{=}$
    PRE   *node* $\in$ *Allocated* $\wedge$ *previous* $\in$ *Allocated*
    THEN
       PreviousNode (node) := *previous*
    END ;
SetNext(node , next) $\hat{=}$
    PRE   *node* $\in$ *Allocated* $\wedge$ *next* $\in$ *Allocated*
    THEN
       NextNode (node) := *next*
    END ;
eql $\longleftarrow$ *EqlNode(node1 , node2)* $\hat{=}$
    PRE   *node1* $\in$ *NODE* $\wedge$ *node2* $\in$ *NODE*
    THEN
       eql := **bool** *(node1 = node2)*
    END

DEFINITIONS
   FREE $\hat{=}$ *NODE − Allocated*

END

1.6 Exercises

Exercise 1.1. Take the *SquareRoot* development and discharge all proof obligations.

Exercise 1.2. Investigate alternative refinements for *SquareRootUtilsR*. That is, keep the specification *SquareRootUtils* and refine in different directions to that taken here.

Exercise 1.3. To complete the layered development of *DataQueue*, we need to refine the *Node* machine to an implementation. This is left as an exercise for the reader.

1.7 Logic and Set Theory Notation

In the following tables P and Q denote predicates; x and y denote single variables; z denotes a list of variables; S and T denote set expressions; U denotes a set of sets; E and F denote an expression; m and n denote lists of integer expressions; f and g denote functions; r denotes a relation; s and t denote sequence expressions; G is a substitution.

Table 1.4: Predicate Notation

Construct	Publication	ASCII
Conjunction	$P \wedge Q$	P & Q
Disjunction	$P \vee Q$	P or Q
Implication	$P \Rightarrow Q$	P => Q
Equivalence	$P \Longleftrightarrow Q$	P <=> Q
	$\widehat{=} P \Rightarrow Q \wedge Q \Rightarrow P$	
Negation	$\neg P$	not P
Universal quantification	$\forall z . (P \Rightarrow Q)$	!z . (P => Q)
Existential quantification	$\exists z . (P \wedge Q)$	#z . (P & Q)
Substitution	$[G] P$	[G] P
Equality	$E = F$	E = F
Inequality	$E \neq F$	E /= F

Table 1.5: Set Notation

Construct	Publication	ASCII
Singleton set	$\{E\}$	{E}
Set enumeration	$\{E, F\}$	{E, F}
Empty set	$\{\}$	{ }
Set comprehension	$\{z \mid P\}$	{ z | P }
Union	$S \cup T$	S \/ T
Intersection	$S \cap T$	S /\ T
Difference	$S - T$	S-T
	$\widehat{=} \{x \mid x \in S \wedge x \notin T\}$	
Ordered pair	$E \mapsto F$	E |-> F
	$E \mapsto F = E, F$	
Cartesian product	$S \times T$	S * T
	$\widehat{=} \{x, y . x \in S \wedge y \in T\}$	
Powerset	$\mathbb{P}(S)$	POW(S)
	$\widehat{=} \{s . s \subseteq S\}$	
Non-empty subsets	$\mathbb{P}_1(S)$	POW1(S)
	$\widehat{=} \mathbb{P}(S) - \{\}$	
Finite subsets	$\mathbb{F}(S)$	FIN(S)
Finite non-empty subsets	$\mathbb{F}_1(S)$	FIN1(S)
Cardinality	$\text{card}(S)$	card(S)
Generalised union	$\text{UNION}(U)$	union(U)
	$\widehat{=} \{x \mid x \in S \wedge (\exists s . s \in U \wedge x \in s)\}$	

Table 1.5: Set Notation (continued)

Construct	Publication	ASCII
Generalised intersection	$inter(U)$	$inter(U)$
	$\widehat{=}\{x \mid x \in S \wedge (\forall s . s \in U \Rightarrow x \in s)\}$	
Generalised union	$\bigcup z . (P \mid E)$	UNION (z).(P | E)
	$\forall z . (P \Rightarrow E \subseteq T) \Rightarrow$	
	$\bigcup z . (P \mid E) = \{x \mid x \in T \wedge \forall z . (P \Rightarrow x \in E)\}$	
Generalised intersection	$\bigcap z . (P \mid E)$	INTER (z).(P | E)
	$\forall z . (P \Rightarrow E \subseteq T) \Rightarrow$	
	$\bigcap z . (P \mid E) = \{x \mid x \in T \wedge \exists z . (P \wedge x \in E)\}$	
Set membership	$E \in S$	E : S
Set non-membership	$E \notin S$	E /: S
Subset	$S \subseteq T$	S <: T
Not a subset	$S \not\subseteq T$	S /<: T
Proper subset	$S \subset T$	S <<: T
Not a proper subset	$s \not\subset t$	S /<<: T

Table 1.6: Natural Number Notation

Construct	Publication	ASCII
The set of natural numbers	$\mathbb{N}$	NAT
The set of positive natural numbers	$\mathbb{N}_1$	NAT1
	$\widehat{=} \mathbb{N} - \{0\}$	
Minimum	$min(S)$	min(S)
Maximum	$max(S)$	max(S)
Sum	$m + n$	m + n
Difference	$m - n$	m - n
Product	$m \times n$	m * n
Quotient	m/n	m / n
Remainder	$m \bmod n$	m mod n
Interval	$m..n$	m .. n
	$\widehat{=} \{ i \mid m \leq i \leq n \}$	
Set summation	$\Sigma z . (P \mid E)$	SIGMA(z).(P | E)
Set product	$\Pi z . (P \mid E)$	PI(z).(P | E)
	Condition: $\{z \mid P\} \neq \{\}$	
Greater	$m > n$	m > n
Less	$m < n$	m < n
Greater or equal	$m \geq n$	m >= n
Less or equal	$m \leq n$	m <= n

Table 1.7: Relation Notation

Construct	Publication	ASCII
Relations	$S \leftrightarrow T$	S <-> T

Table 1.7: Relation Notation (continued)

Construct	Publication	ASCII
	$\widehat{=}\ \mathbb{P}(S \times T)$	
Domain	$\mathrm{dom}(r)$	$\mathrm{dom}(r)$
	$\forall r . r \in S \leftrightarrow T \Rightarrow$ $\mathrm{dom}(r) = \{x \mid (\exists y . x \mapsto y \in r)\}$	
Range	$\mathrm{ran}(r)$	$\mathrm{ran}(r)$
	$\forall r . r \in S \leftrightarrow T \Rightarrow$ $\mathrm{ran}(r) = \{y \mid (\exists x . x \mapsto y \in r)\}$	
Forward composition	$p;q$	$p\ ;\ q$
	$\forall p,q . p \in S \leftrightarrow T \wedge q \in T \leftrightarrow U \Rightarrow$ $p;q = \{x,y \mid (\exists z . x \mapsto z \in p \wedge z \mapsto y \in q)\}$	
Backward composition	$p \circ q$	$p\ \mathrm{circ}\ q$
	$\widehat{=}\ q;p$	
Identity	$\mathrm{id}(S)$	$\mathrm{id}(S)$
	$\widehat{=}\ \{x,y \mid x \in S \wedge y \in S \wedge x = y\}$	
Domain restriction	$S \triangleleft r$	$S\ <\mid\ r$
	$\widehat{=}\ \{x,y \mid x \mapsto y \in r \wedge x \in S\}$	
Domain subtraction	$S \triangleleft\!\!\!- r$	$S\ <<\mid\ r$
	$\widehat{=}\ \{x,y \mid x \mapsto y \in r \wedge x \notin S\}$	
Range restriction	$r \triangleright T$	$r\ \mid>\ T$
	$\widehat{=}\ \{x,y \mid x \mapsto y \in r \wedge y \in T\}$	
Range subtraction	$r \triangleright\!\!\!- T$	$r\ \mid>>\ T$
	$\widehat{=}\ \{x,y \mid x \mapsto y \in r \wedge y \notin T\}$	
Inverse	r^{-1}	$r\text{\textasciitilde}$
	$\widehat{=}\ \{y \mid \exists x . x \in S \wedge x \mapsto y \in r\}$	
Relational image	$r[S]$	$r[S]$
	$\widehat{=}\ \{y \mid \exists x . x \in S \wedge x \mapsto y \in r\}$	
Right overriding	$r_1 \triangleleft\!\!+ r_2$	$r1\ <+\ r2$
	$\widehat{=}\ r_2 \cup (\mathrm{dom}(r_2) \triangleleft\!\!\!- r_1)$	
Left overriding	$r_1 +\!\!\triangleright r_2$	$r1\ +>\ r2$
	$\widehat{=}\ r_1 \cup (\mathrm{dom}(r_1) \triangleleft\!\!\!- r_2)$	
Direct product	$p \otimes q$	$p\ ><\ q$
	$\widehat{=}\ \{x,(y,z) \mid x \mapsto y \in p \wedge x \mapsto z \in q\}$	
Parallel product	$p \parallel q$	$p\ \mid\mid\ q$
	$\widehat{=}\ \{(x,y),(m,n) \mid x \mapsto m \in p \wedge y \mapsto n \in q\}$	
Iteration	r^n	$\mathrm{iterate}(r,n)$
	$r \in S \leftrightarrow S \Rightarrow$ $r^0 = \mathrm{id}(S) \wedge r^{n+1} = r;r^n$	
Closure	r^*	$\mathrm{closure}(r)$
	$\widehat{=}\ \bigcup n . (n \in \mathbb{N} \mid r^n)$	
Projection	$\mathrm{prj1}(S,T)$	$\mathrm{prj1}(S,T)$
	$\widehat{=}\ \{(x,y),z \mid x,y \in S \times T \wedge z = x\}$	
Projection	$\mathrm{prj2}(S,T)$	$\mathrm{prj2}(S,T)$
	$\widehat{=}\ \{(x,y),z \mid x,y \in S \times T \wedge z = y\}$	

Table 1.8: Function Notation

Construct	Publication	ASCII
Partial functions	$S \nrightarrow T$	S +-> T
	$\hat{=} \{r \mid r \in S \leftrightarrow T \wedge r^{-1}; r \subseteq \mathsf{id}(T)\}$	
Total functions	$S \rightarrow T$	S --> T
	$\hat{=} \{f \mid f \in S \nrightarrow T \wedge \mathsf{dom}(f) = S\}$	
Partial injections	$S \rightarrowtail\mkern-14mu\nrightarrow T$	S >+> T
	$\hat{=} \{f \mid f \in S \nrightarrow T \wedge f^{-1} \in T \nrightarrow S\}$	
Total injections	$S \rightarrowtail T$	S >-> T
	$\hat{=} S \rightarrowtail\mkern-14mu\nrightarrow T \cap S \rightarrow T$	
Partial surjections	$S \nrightarrow\mkern-14mu\twoheadrightarrow T$	S +->> T
	$\hat{=} \{f \mid f \in S \nrightarrow T \wedge \mathsf{ran}(f) = T\}$	
Total surjections	$S \twoheadrightarrow T$	S -->> T
	$\hat{=} S \nrightarrow\mkern-14mu\twoheadrightarrow T \cap S \rightarrow T$	
Bijections	$S \rightarrowtail\mkern-14mu\twoheadrightarrow T$	S >->> T
	$\hat{=} S \rightarrowtail T \cap S \twoheadrightarrow T$	
Lambda abstraction	$\lambda z . (P \mid E)$	%z.(P|E)
	$\hat{=} \{z, y \mid z \in \{z \mid P\} \wedge y = E\}$	
	where $y \backslash P \wedge y \backslash E$	
Function application	$f(E)$	f(E)
	$E \mapsto f(E) \in f$	

Table 1.9: Sequence Notation

Construct	Publication	ASCII
Empty sequence	$[\,]$	<>
	$\hat{=} \{\}$	
Finite sequences	$\mathsf{seq}(S)$	seq S
	$\hat{=} \{f \mid f \in \mathbb{N}_1 \nrightarrow S \wedge$	
	$\exists n . n \in \mathbb{N} \wedge \mathsf{dom}(f) = 1..n\}$	
Finite non-empty sequences	$\mathsf{seq}_1(S)$	seq1(S)
	$\hat{=} \mathsf{seq}(S) - \{[\,]\}$	
Injective sequences	$\mathsf{iseq}(S)$	iseq(S)
	$\hat{=} \mathsf{seq}(S) \cap (\mathbb{N}_1 \rightarrowtail\mkern-14mu\nrightarrow S)$	
Permutations	$\mathsf{perm}(S)$	perm(S)
	$\hat{=} \mathsf{iseq}(S) \cap (\mathbb{N}_1 \twoheadrightarrow S)$	
Sequence concatenation	$s \frown t$	s^t
Prepend element	$E \rightarrow s$	E -> s
	$\hat{=} [E] \frown s$	
Append element	$s \leftarrow E$	s <- E
	$\hat{=} s \frown [E]$	
Singleton sequence	$[E]$	[E]
	$\hat{=} \{1 \mapsto E\}$	
Sequence construction	$[E, F]$	[E,F]
	$\hat{=} [E] \leftarrow F$	

Table 1.9: Sequence Notation (continued)

Construct	Publication	ASCII
Size	$\mathsf{size}(s)$	`size(s)`
	$\widehat{=} \mathsf{card}(s)$	
Reverse	$\mathsf{rev}(s)$	`rev(s)`
	$\forall i . i \in \mathsf{dom}(s) \Rightarrow$ $\mathsf{rev}(s)(i) = s(\mathsf{size}(s) + 1 - i)$	
Take	$s \uparrow n$	`s /|\ n`
	$\widehat{=} 1 .. n \lhd s$	
Drop	$s \downarrow n$	`s |/ n`
	$\widehat{=} \lambda m . (m \in \mathbb{N} \| m + n)) ; (1 .. n \lhd s$	
First element	$\mathsf{first}(s)$	`first(s)`
Last element	$\mathsf{last}(s)$	`last(s)`
Tail	$\mathsf{tail}(s)$	`tail(s)`
	$\mathsf{first}(s) \rightarrow \mathsf{tail}(s) = s$	
Front	$\mathsf{front}(s)$	`front(s)`
	$\mathsf{front}(s) \leftarrow \mathsf{last}(s) = s$	
Generalised concatenation	$\mathsf{conc}(ss)$	`conc(ss)`
	$\mathsf{conc}([\,]) = [\,]$ $conc(s \leftarrow E) = \mathsf{conc}(s) \frown E$	
Strings	"..."	`"..."`
	Sequences of characters.	

2. Container Station

Elena Troubitsyna

2.1 Introduction

In this chapter we present a development of an information system for container station bookkeeping. Such an information system has to assist the operators in performing routine operations of registration and loading of trucks arriving at the container station. The introduction of the automated bookkeeping system has to improve the efficiency of the operator's work and speed up the reloading procedures.

The information system to be designed is an example of a critical system, in the sense that incorrect or unpredictable behaviour of the system leads to significant money and time losses. Because of that the correctness of the developed software should be thoroughly verified.

We present a process of the software development from an informal task description to a specification close to program code. An elegant way to specify the problem is to start from an abstract specification. A high level of abstraction allows even complicated entities to be expressed succinctly. Performing a number of refinement steps we obtain a final implementation which is translatable to program code. At each stage we carefully explain our design decisions and motivation behind the steps.

The developed system is an example of a complicated information system. To design a logically consistent and well-structured system we use the idea of stepwise introduction of complexity. Namely, we consider each particular refinement step as a way to encompass some requirements of task description left unspecified on a more abstract level. With such an approach each refinement step becomes a goal oriented activity to incorporate some particular design decisions rather than a routine exercise in a logical calculus.

The assistance of B-Toolkit allows a software developer to perform the whole cycle of software development, verification and documentation within a single environment. This is a convenient way to organise a uniform basis for running practical projects. In our case the reader solving exercises can be considered a participant of the project developing some independent modules which will be assembled to constitute the software of the entire extended system.

The rest of the chapter contains the stepwise development of the information system for container station bookkeeping. At first we present the informal task description. Then we explain our understanding of the task and show the corresponding abstract specification. As the next step, we perform the refinement of the initial specification. The development of the implementation is the result of the bottom-up and the top-down design. The experience gained is summarised in the conclusion. Possible extensions to the considered task are suggested as exercises.

2.2 Task Description

The container station is a railway station for reloading freight transported in containers. The containers are brought on trains during the night and early morning. During the morning, empty trucks arrive to fetch the containers. At noon, the empty wagons are rearranged for further transport. In the afternoon, loaded trucks arrive and the containers are reloaded on the trains. The scheme of the container station is presented in Fig.2.1. We consider the morning operations only.

When a truck arrives at the entry, the truck driver registers at the gate. The gatekeeper notes the identification of the container and assigns the truck to an appropriate position in the loading zone. If no such position is free, the truck is assigned a place in the waiting zone. When an appropriate position for loading becomes free, the gatekeeper informs the truck driver to move there. In the loading lane the truck will be loaded by means of a crane. When this is completed, the driver leaves the container station without further notice.

The positions in the loading zone and on the railway tracks are measured in multiples of 10 meters called sectors. It is assumed that a truck occupies one sector in the loading zone. The trucks are only allowed to drive forwards, for safety reasons.

The gatekeeper bases his decisions on the list of the trains with their loaded containers and their respective positions. The positions of the wagons depend on the order of arrival of the trains. The gatekeeper gets this list in the morning before the gate opens.

Using the positions of the containers and the arriving trucks, the gatekeeper compiles a list of reloads to be carried out. Each hour the crane operator gets an updated list of reloads. The crane operator selects reloads from the lists, carries them out, and marks them as done. In order to minimise movement of the crane, the crane operator starts with reloads at sector one and moves to the upper end. Then the crane moves quickly back to the lower end.

In a typical container station, 400 reloads are carried out each morning. The manual operation mode is sometimes very inefficient, especially at peak times, causing long waits or poor use of the crane. Our task is to design an automated bookkeeping system which minimises the average waiting time of the trucks and achieves some degree of fairness among them, so that the truck drivers will not get annoyed. For that purpose, both the gate and the crane will be equipped with a simple computer terminal.

We concentrate on modelling the algorithmic part of the problem and keep the user interface as simple as possible. The design should be reusable for similar container stations.

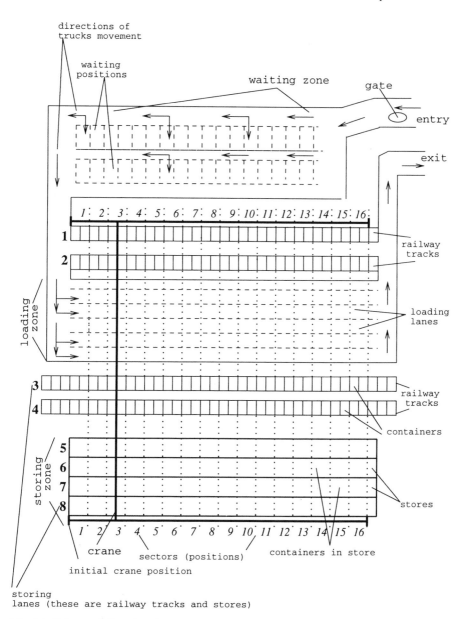

Fig. 2.1. Scheme of Container Station

2.3 Design of Specification

When developing the specification we strive to solve two problems. The first is to develop a data structure and a set of operations which are not redundant (with regards to the number of operations, variables and so on) and which are sufficient to preserve the integrity of the task. The second goal, which is to establish an optimal discipline of truck service in order to minimise the average waiting time of the trucks, is incorporated naturally in the first one.

We start the development by defining the necessary operations and the data structure. While doing the system analysis we bear in mind that there are two operators working at the container station, namely the gatekeeper and the crane operator. Each of them is a user of the information system and we need to organise their work in the most efficient way. Hence, the information system must provide the operators with a set of operations which is sufficient to obtain all data required to conduct their duties.

Considering a simple scenario, i.e. the arrival and the service of a single truck, we identify a set of required operations. Having arrived at the gate the truck becomes a subject of an analysis for the gatekeeper. From the list of the trains the operator extracts the number of the container to be loaded on the truck. Also it is necessary to find a proper position in the loading zone where the loading takes place. The operator can ask the information system about an available position for the truck or to check whether the truck is eligible for a certain position in the loading zone. As soon as this sequence of operations is performed the truck moves to the waiting zone. When the required loading position becomes vacant the truck leaves the waiting zone and proceeds to that position. In the loading zone the truck waits until the crane operator chooses to load it.

Meanwhile the crane moves from the first position to the end of the loading zone. At each sector the crane operator checks the necessity to perform reloads (if any). Naturally, there can be a different number of trucks parked in a certain sector in distinct loading lanes. This number varies form sector to sector and lies in the bounds from zero to the number of loading lanes. The crane operator inputs the current crane position and obtains the number of reloads to be done there. If there are any trucks to be loaded the crane operator chooses one of them. For performing the reloads the operator must learn about the number of the loading lane where the truck is parked and the number of the storing lane where the container to be loaded is kept. Sending the corresponding requests to the system the crane operator obtains this information. As soon as the truck is loaded it leaves the container station. If no more trucks have to be loaded in the current sector the crane operator drives the crane to the next sector.

An analysis of the task description shows that we can identify two main parts of the problem. The first is the management of events that change the state of the container station. For example, arrival of new trucks, departure of trucks, change of the crane position etc. The second part consists of manipulations which provide information to the operators but do not change the current state of the container station. This is information regarding the possibilities of setting trucks in the loading zone, the necessity to perform the reloads etc. We denote the first group of operations as *modifiers* and the second group of operations as *selectors*. Fig. 2.2 presents a list of operations which will be developed to specify the information system for the container station bookkeeping.

Now let us note that our specification should be reusable for similar container stations. Parameterisation makes the specification universal. By defining new values for the parameters we can easily adapt our software to container stations with similar structures. Thus, our specification should have parameters. Let us analyse the scheme of the container station to determine the entities that can be changed without breaking the structure of the container station. It is clear that the number of railway tracks, the width of the storing zone, the number of loading lanes, the number of sectors, and the capacity of the waiting zone differ from station to station. Hence, we can define these entities as the parameters of our specification.

To introduce the necessary variables let us indicate the key entities of the task description. The first basic entity is *trucks*. They can be situated in *the waiting zone* or in *the loading zone*. Let us denote these two sets as *TruckInWaitingZone* and *TruckInLoadingZone*. Moreover, the trucks in the loading zone allocated in the current crane position form a set of the trucks to be loaded next. This is the set *reloading_trucks*. The second entity is the *containers* stored in the container station. We denote them as the set *ContainersInStores*. All containers are separated into two categories: containers which have been assigned to trucks and containers which have not yet been assigned. These assignments establish a relationship between the entities *trucks* and *containers*. The relation between *trucks* and *containers* is denoted as *RequestedContainer*. The third key entity in the task description is *crane*. This entity is characterised by its position. Thus the next variable is *CranePosition*. The last entity of the investigated task is *position in the loading zone*. This entity has direct and indirect relations with all others. Let us mention the most obvious relations. *Any truck* can be situated in the loading zone only in a certain sector (*position*). The set of all positions available for a certain truck is contained in the variable *possible_positions*. On the other hand, not every truck can be put in a certain position. The variable *possible_trucks* is the set of all trucks which can be allocated to the considered position. Now we have defined the basic structure of the specification: the list of parameters, the variables and the operations of the specification. A detailed explanation of the design is given in the text of the specification. However, before presenting the whole specification we have to make a decision concerning the optimisation of the service procedure.

A bottleneck of the container station is the loading zone. Indeed an average service time t of the truck (a period of time from when the truck passes the entrance gate till it leaves the container station) consists of two parts. The first part, t_{wz}, is the waiting time until the proper position in the loading zone becomes vacant. The second part, t_{lz}, is the time which the truck has to wait, once it has moved into the loading zone. (Here we assume that the movement from the waiting zone to the loading zone and the loading process take a negligible amount of time.) It is clear that t_{wz} of any truck consists of the sum of t_{lz} of its predecessors in a certain position

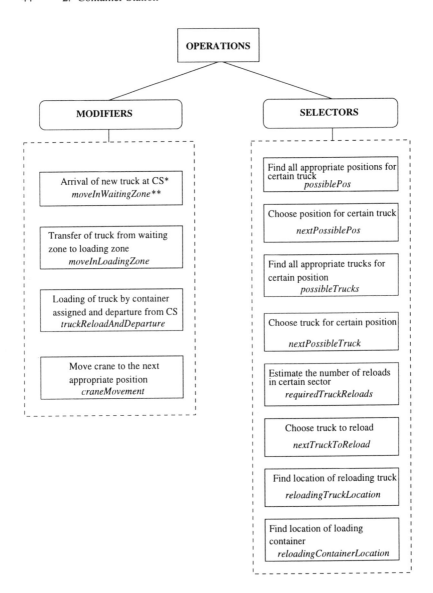

Fig. 2.2. Structure of Specification

in the loading zone. Because of that we argue that the crucial point of minimisation of the average service time t is to optimise the loading procedure, i.e. to minimise t_{lz}.

Our solution is based on the assumption that the movement of the crane from sector to sector is much more time consuming than doing the reloads while staying at the same sector. Because of that we introduce a certain parking discipline for the trucks in the loading zone and a corresponding loading discipline for the crane reloads. Namely, any truck must be parked in the loading zone in such a way that it occupies the same sector as the container to be loaded. (Consider the container station as a xy-plane. Let the positions form x-axis and the lanes y-axis. Then the discipline described means that the truck parked in the loading zone and the container must have the same x-coordinates). The loading discipline forces the crane operator to reload all the trucks in the current position before moving to the next sector. The introduced disciplines speed up the loading procedure, because they exclude the slow crane movement between sectors while loading a truck. Moreover, we come to the conjecture that the utilisation of the crane is significantly improved in comparison to the manual operation.

Now let us make a short comment on specifying a problem within the B-Method. All stages of program derivation - specification, refinement and implementation - can be presented in the B-Method as *Abstract Machines*. To specify the problem we develop the Abstract Machine *CONTAINERSTATION*. The Abstract Machine contains clauses giving global constraints, constants, abstract sets with their properties, a list of variables and operations on them. The presence of these clauses does not put any constraints on the structure of the specification which we have already developed.

MACHINE   *CONTAINERSTATION*
    (*nofRailwayTracks* , *nofStores* , *nofLoadingLanes* , *nofPositions* , *nofWaitingPositions*)

---

nofRailwayTracks: number of railway tracks where wagons with containers are parked.

nofStores: number of line in the area where containers unloaded from wagons are kept. We refer to the parameters *nofRailwayTracks* and *nofStores* indirectly. As it can be seen from the *DEFINITION* clause we denote a sum of these two parameters as *nofStoringLanes*. Besides, for the shortage we extend the notion of storing zone by speaking about the containers kept on the wagons and the containers kept on the stores without making difference between them.

nofLoadingLanes: number of loading lanes for trucks reloads

nofWaitingPositions: capacity of the waiting zone. The waiting zone is the area where trucks are waiting for a permission to move at the loading zone.

There is an assumption that the loading zone, the storing zone and the zone of wagons parking have the same number of positions. The length of a single position is equal to the length of one sector as can be seen in the task description. The positions with the same numbers are opposite each other. The number of those positions is kept in the parameter *nofPositions.*

CONSTRAINTS

> *nofPositions* $\in \mathbb{N}_1$ $\wedge$
> *nofWaitingPositions* $\in \mathbb{N}_1$ $\wedge$
> *nofRailwayTracks* $\in \mathbb{N}_1$ $\wedge$
> *nofStores* $\in \mathbb{N}_1$ $\wedge$
> *nofLoadingLanes* $\in \mathbb{N}_1$

SEES

> *Bool_TYPE*

VARIABLES

> *TrucksInWaitingZone* , *TrucksInLoadingZone* , *ContainersInStores* ,
> *CranePosition* , *RequestedContainer* , *possible_positions* , *possible_trucks* ,
> *reloading_trucks*

TrucksInWaitingZone represents trucks which are parked in the waiting zone.

TrucksInLoadingZone defines a correspondence between coordinates and trucks in the loading zone. Each truck in the loading zone can be uniquely defined by the number of the position and number of the lane in the loading zone.

ContainersInStores contains the correspondence between coordinates and containers in the container station. This variable is similar to *TrucksInLoadingZone*.

CranePositions is the set of all possible positions of the crane. Here is some kind of an artificial digitising of the crane's movement. This is because the crane cannot carry out reloading operations during its movement.

RequestedContainer establishes the correspondence between the trucks and the containers assigned to them.

possible_positions contains information about positions in the loading zone vacant for a certain truck.

possible_trucks represents the trucks which can be parked in a certain position in the loading zone.

reloading_trucks defines the set of the trucks in the loading zone parked in the current crane position.

INVARIANT

> *TrucksInWaitingZone* $\subseteq$ *TRUCKS* $\wedge$
> card (*TrucksInWaitingZone*) $\leq$ *nofWaitingPositions* $\wedge$
> *TrucksInLoadingZone* $\in$ (*1 .. nofPositions*) $\times$ (*1 .. nofLoadingLanes*) $\rightarrowtail\!\!\!\rightarrow$
>   *TRUCKS* $\wedge$
> *TrucksInWaitingZone* $\cap$ ran (*TrucksInLoadingZone*) $= \{\}$ $\wedge$
> *ContainersInStores* $\in$ (*1 .. nofPositions*) $\times$ (*1 .. nofStoringLanes*) $\rightarrowtail\!\!\!\rightarrow$
>   *CONTAINERS* $\wedge$
> *CranePosition* $\in$ *1 .. nofPositions* $\wedge$

$RequestedContainer \in$
   $TrucksInWaitingZone \cup$ ran $(TrucksInLoadingZone) \rightarrowtail$
      ran $(ContainersInStores) \wedge$
$possible\_positions \subseteq (1 .. nofPositions) \times (1 .. nofLoadingLanes) \wedge$
$possible\_trucks \subseteq TRUCKS \wedge$
$reloading\_trucks \subseteq$ ran $(TrucksInLoadingZone)$

The invariant gives the real meaning of the introduced variables in terms of the sets and reflects certain restrictions on the described task.

TrucksInWaitingZone is defined as a subset of all trucks.

The capacity of the waiting zone is restricted, meaning that the number of the trucks in the waiting zone should not exceed it. To show this we put a condition restricting the cardinality of the set *TrucksInWaitingZone* in the invariant.

The invariant defines *TrucksInLoadingZone* as a partial injection. The domain of this injection consists of the coordinates of the trucks in the loading zone. The range contains trucks in the loading zone. Using an injective function guarantees that any position in the loading zone can be occupied by only one truck.

We assume that any truck in the container station can be only in the waiting zone or in the loading zone. In addition, no truck can be in both zones simultaneously. The next predicate in the invariant expresses this assumption. It defines the intersection of the sets of the trucks in the waiting zone and trucks in the loading zone as an empty set.

Any container in the container station has a certain place, either in the storing zone or on the railway tracks. The variable *ContainersInStores* maps the coordinates of each stored container (i.e. the number of the position and the number of the storing lane) to this container. As in the previous case using an injection provides a placement of only one container in one position.

The position of the crane at any time is defined as a natural number in the range from 1 to *nofPositions*, which is the number of the last position.

The variable *RequestedContainer* is defined as a partial injection. The domain of *RequestedContainer* consists of the trucks parked in the waiting and loading zones which have already been assigned to containers. Correspondingly these containers form the range of *RequestedContainer*. In this case the injection shows that only one container can be assigned to a single truck.

In principle, the operator can choose one of several positions for parking a truck in the loading zone. All such possible positions for a certain truck are represented in the set *possible_positions*. This set is a subset of all positions in the loading zone.

Similarly, any position in the loading zone can be occupied by one of several possible trucks. The variable *possible_trucks* is the set of candidates for a certain position in the loading zone.

The variable *reloading_trucks* contains information about the trucks parked in the loading zone which have to be loaded with the assigned containers before the crane can move to the next position.

INITIALISATION

$TrucksInWaitingZone := \{\}$ ||
$TrucksInLoadingZone := \{\}$ ||
$CranePosition := 1$ ||
$RequestedContainer := \{\}$ ||
$possible\_positions := \{\}$ ||
$possible\_trucks := \{\}$ ||
$reloading\_trucks := \{\}$ ||
$ContainersInStores :\in (1 .. nofPositions) \times (1 .. nofStoringLanes) \rightarrowtail \mathbb{N}_1$

The initialisation establishes the state of the container station before the gate is opened and sets the crane in its initial position.

OPERATIONS

$moveInWaitingZone (truck, reqcontainer) \quad \hat{=}$
    PRE
        $truck \in TRUCKS \wedge$
        $truck \notin TrucksInWaitingZone \wedge$
        $truck \notin \text{ran} (TrucksInLoadingZone) \wedge$
        $\text{card} (TrucksInWaitingZone) < nofWaitingPositions \wedge$
        $reqcontainer \in \text{ran} (ContainersInStores) \wedge$
        $reqcontainer \notin \text{ran} (RequestedContainer) \wedge$
        $truck \notin \text{dom} (RequestedContainer)$
    THEN
        $TrucksInWaitingZone := TrucksInWaitingZone \cup \{truck\}$ ||
        $RequestedContainer := RequestedContainer \cup \{truck \mapsto reqcontainer\}$
    END ;

The operation *moveInWaitingZone* models the arrival of a new truck at the container station. In specifying this operation we assume that any arriving truck should be set in the waiting zone (probably, only notionally), regardless of whether an appropriate position in the loading zone might be vacant. This assumption allows us to treat all trucks in the container station as two groups: the first is trucks in the waiting zone and the second is trucks in the loading zone. We assume that there are no trucks anywhere outside these two zones. The following scenario is performed. The truck *truck* arrives at the gate of the container station. On the basis of the ID of the arriving truck the gatekeeper gives an ID of container *reqcontainer* to the truck driver. Afterwards, the truck parks in the waiting zone. In terms of sets this means adding a new element to the set *TrucksInWaitingZone* and a new mapplet to the set *RequestedContainer*.

The precondition of this operation establishes that this is indeed a new truck. This means that this truck has not already been situated either in the waiting zone or in the loading zone. Parking of the truck in the waiting zone is possible if the cardinality of the set *TrucksInWaitingZone*, with the new element added, does not exceed the number of positions in the waiting zone. The last three conjuncts of the invariant establish that the container *reqcontainer* assigned to *truck* is in the storing zone and has not yet been assigned to any truck and that the truck is not assigned to any container as well.

$moveInLoadingZone (truck, pos, ln) \quad \hat{=}$
    PRE

$truck \in TrucksInWaitingZone \land$
$pos \in 1 .. nofPositions \land$
$ln \in 1 .. nofLoadingLanes \land$
$pos \mapsto ln \notin \mathbf{dom} \, (TrucksInLoadingZone)$
THEN
$TrucksInLoadingZone :=$
$\quad TrucksInLoadingZone \cup \{ pos \mapsto ln \mapsto truck \} \, \|$
$TrucksInWaitingZone := TrucksInWaitingZone - \{ truck \}$
END ;

The operation *moveInLoadingZone* corresponds to the transfer of a truck from the waiting zone to the loading zone. The operation has three parameters. The first is the truck which is going to be assigned to the loading zone. The second and the third ones define the loading sector and lane which will be occupied by this truck.

The precondition checks that the truck *truck* can be allocated in the loading zone and the coordinates of the targeting position do not extend beyond the ranges of the loading zone. Next we check the vacancy of the position chosen.

The gatekeeper obtains the coordinates of the position to be occupied after an execution of the operation *nextPossiblePos*. The result parameter *position* returned by the operation *nextPossiblePos* is a pair of the form *(sector, lane)*. To simplify the specification of the operation *moveInLoadingZone* and its further refinement we treat that pair as two distinct input parameters.

The selection of the available loading positions is done on the basis of the parking discipline introduced before. Hence, the input of the coordinates suggested by the system guarantees that the truck *truck* will be parked in a proper position (i.e. the number of the position occupied by a truck in the loading zone will be the same as the number of the position occupied by a container in the storing zone).

$truckReloadAndDeparture \, (truck) \quad \hat{=}$
PRE
$\quad truck \in TRUCKS \land$
$\quad truck \in \mathbf{ran} \, (TrucksInLoadingZone) \land$
$\quad truck \notin reloading\_trucks \land$
$\quad \exists \, pos . \, (pos \in 1 .. nofPositions \land$
$\quad pos \in \mathbf{dom} \, (\{ TrucksInLoadingZone^{-1} \, (truck) \}) \land$
$\quad pos = CranePosition)$
THEN
$\quad TrucksInLoadingZone := TrucksInLoadingZone \mathrel{\rhd} \{ truck \} \, \|$
$\quad ContainersInStores :=$
$\quad\quad ContainersInStores \mathrel{\rhd} \{ RequestedContainer \, (truck) \} \, \|$
$\quad RequestedContainer := \{ truck \} \mathrel{\lhd} RequestedContainer$
END ;

The execution of the operation *truckReloadAndDeparture* corresponds to the reloading of the truck *truck* and its the departure from the container station. To model the reload we remove the container loaded from the set of containers on store. The departure of the truck which is loaded with the given container corresponds to the extracting of the relevant elements from the sets *TrucksInLoadingZone* and *ContainersInStores*. Deleting elements from the sets *TrucksInLoadingZone* and *ContainersInStores* is done by means of *relational anti-range restriction*. Removing an element from *RequestedContainer* is performed as *relational anti-domain restriction.*

The precondition for the operation *truckReloadAndDeparture* ensures that the truck has already been situated in the loading zone. According to the loading discipline introduced the truck can be reloaded only when it occupies the same sector as the crane does. Identifying the truck parking section (denoted as *pos*) we compare it with the current crane position. Only if they coincide will the crane reload the truck and the truck leave the container station.

---

number_candidates ⟵ *possiblePos* (*truck*) $\widehat{=}$
   PRE
      truck ∈ *TRUCKS* ∧
      truck ∈ *TrucksInWaitingZone*
   THEN
     LET *pp* **BE**
       pp =
         dom ({ *ContainersInStores* $^{-1}$ (*RequestedContainer* (*truck*)) }) ◁
         (*1* .. *nofPositions*) × (*1* .. *nofLoadingLanes*) −
           dom (*TrucksInLoadingZone*)
     IN
       possible_positions := *pp* ‖
       number_candidates := card (*pp*)
     END
   END ;

The operation *possiblePos* has the input parameter *truck* and the result parameter *number_candidates*. The goal of this procedure is to give information about the number of the vacant positions which can be occupied by a certain truck. As can be seen from the specification the result parameter is the cardinality of the set *possible_positions*. In this operation we use the same idea of locating a truck in any loading lane in line with an assigned container. Let us consider a way of doing this.

The expression *RequestedContainer(truck)* results in a container being assigned to *truck*. Using the relational inverse *ContainersInStores* with the assigned container as the parameter and taking the domain of this expression we get a sector which is occupied by the considered container. Then we map the resulting sector to the set of all possible positions in the loading zone. We use the operator *relational domain restriction*. This results in the set *resulted_sector* × (1 .. *nofLoadingLanes*). We receive the targeting set after removing all occupied positions.

---

position ⟵ *nextPossiblePos* $\widehat{=}$
   PRE
     possible_positions ≠ {}
   THEN
     ANY *pos* **WHERE**
      pos ∈ *possible_positions*
     THEN
      position := *pos* ‖
      possible_positions := *possible_positions* − { *pos* }
     END
   END ;

The operation *nextPossiblePos* is a logical continuation of the operation *possiblePos*. When the number of positions available for a certain truck has a non-zero value, the operator can choose one of these positions to park a truck there. The operation *nextPossiblePos* has *position* as the result parameter. A position from the set *possible_positions* is chosen non-deterministically by the operation *nextPossiblePos*. Afterwards, this position becomes occupied so we remove it from the set of all possible positions\

---

number_candidates ⟵ *possibleTrucks* (*lane* , *pos*) $\widehat{=}$
    PRE
        lane ∈ *1* .. *nofLoadingLanes* ∧
        pos ∈ *1* .. *nofPositions* ∧
        pos ↦ *lane* ∉ dom (*TrucksInLoadingZone*)
    THEN
        LET   *pt*   **BE**
           pt = { *truck* | *truck* ∈ *TRUCKS* ∧
           truck ∈ *TrucksInWaitingZone* ∧
           ∃ *ln* . (*ln* ∈ *1* .. *nofStoringLanes* ∧
           ContainersInStores (*pos* , *ln*) = *RequestedContainer* (*truck*)) }
        IN
           possible_trucks := *pt* ‖
           number_candidates := card (*pt*)
        END
    END ;

In the previous two operations the operator tried to park a certain truck in the loading zone. Now the operator's task is to find an appropriate truck to occupy a certain position in the loading zone. We use the same technique to solve this problem as was used in the previous two operations. First, the operation *possibleTrucks* informs the operator about trucks suitable for the considered position. The parameters of the operation *possibleTrucks* define the place in the loading zone which is going to be occupied. The precondition ensures us that this place is in the range of the loading zone and is vacant. The result parameter of this procedure is a number of trucks which have been assigned to containers stored in the different storing lanes but in the same sectors *pos*. This number is obtained as the cardinality of the set of all trucks satisfying the mentioned condition.

---

truck ⟵ *nextPossibleTruck* $\widehat{=}$
    PRE
        card (*possible_trucks*) > *0*
    THEN
        ANY   *tr*   **WHERE**
           tr ∈ *possible_trucks*
        THEN
           truck := *tr* ‖
           possible_trucks := *possible_trucks* − { *tr* }
        END
    END ;

If the obtained number of the trucks which fit a certain position is not equal to zero, then the operator can choose any of these trucks arbitrarily. The operation *nextPossibleTruck* chooses non-deterministically a truck from the set of all possible trucks. The chosen truck is removed from the set *possible_trucks*.

$number\_reloads \longleftarrow requiredTruckReloads \ (\ position \ ) \quad \widehat{=}$
    PRE
        $position \in 1 \ .. \ nofPositions \ \wedge$
        $position = CranePosition$
    THEN
        LET tr **BE**
            $tr = \{ \ truck \ \mid \ truck \in \mathsf{ran} \ (\ TrucksInLoadingZone \ ) \wedge$
                $truck \in \mathsf{dom} \ (\ RequestedContainer \ ) \wedge$
                $\exists \ ln \ . \ (\ ln \in 1 \ .. \ nofLoadingLanes \ \wedge$
                $TrucksInLoadingZone \ (\ position \ , \ ln \ ) = truck \ ) \}$
        IN
            $reloading\_trucks := tr \ \parallel$
            $number\_reloads := \mathsf{card} \ (\ tr \ )$
        END
    END ;

The operation *requiredTruckReloads* provides the crane driver with information about the necessity of performing any reloads in the current position *position*. The precondition ensures that the position analysed is indeed the current crane position. The body of the operation forms the set *reloading_trucks* of the trucks parked in the current crane position. The result of *requiredTruckReloads* is the number of trucks which has to be loaded while the crane is in the sector *position*.

$next\_truck \longleftarrow nextTruckToReload \quad \widehat{=}$
    PRE
        $reloading\_trucks \neq \{\}$
    THEN
        ANY tr **WHERE**
            $tr \in reloading\_trucks$
        THEN
            $next\_truck := tr \ \parallel$
            $reloading\_trucks := reloading\_trucks - \{ \ tr \ \}$
        END
    END ;

The operation *nextTruckToReload* is similar to the operation *nextPossibleTruck*. If there are any trucks in the current crane position one of them is chosen to be loaded next.

$trucklane \longleftarrow reloadingTruckLocation \ (\ truck \ ) \quad \widehat{=}$
    PRE
        $truck \in TRUCKS \ \wedge$
        $truck \in \mathsf{ran} \ (\ TrucksInLoadingZone \ )$
    THEN
        LET ln **BE**
            $ln = \{ \ lane \ \mid \ lane \in 1 \ .. \ nofLoadingLanes \ \wedge$
                $\exists \ pos \ . \ (\ pos \in 1 \ .. \ nofPositions \ \wedge$
                $TrucksInLoadingZone \ (\ pos \ , \ lane \ ) = truck \ ) \}$
        IN

trucklane :∈ *ln*
 END
END ;

To load a truck the crane driver has to learn
- the lane of the reloading truck
- the lane where a container assigned to that truck is kept.
The operations *reloadingTruckLocation* and *reloadingContainerLocation* provide the
crane driver with that information. Introducing the parameter *truck* in the first operation
he obtains the lane in the loading zone where the truck to be loaded is parked. The execution of the second operation, *reloadingContainerLocation*, gives the crane driver the
location (the storing lane) of the container which is assigned to be loaded on *truck*. In
both operations only the lanes of the truck and the container are of interest. This is due to
the reloading discipline we introduced (i.e. the sector of the reloading truck, the sector of
the loading container and the sector of the crane are all the same).

---

containerlane ⟵ *reloadingContainerLocation* (*truck*) ≙
 PRE
  truck ∈ *TRUCKS* ∧
  truck ∈ ran (*TrucksInLoadingZone*)
 THEN
  LET *conln* **BE**
   conln = dom ([{ *ContainersInStores* $^{-1}$ (
    RequestedContainer (*truck*)) }])
  IN
   containerlane :∈ *conln*
  END
 END ;
craneMovement ≙
 PRE
  reloading_trucks = {}
 THEN
  IF *CranePosition* ≠ *nofPositions*
  THEN
   CranePosition := *CranePosition* + *1*
  ELSE
   CranePosition := *1*
  END
 END

As soon as all trucks parked in the current crane position are reloaded the crane proceeds
its movement to the next sector. If the end of the loading zone is not reached (i.e. the number of the sector is less then *nofPositions*) the crane moves to the next sector. Otherwise
the crane moves at the beginning of the loading zone in the fast mode.

DEFINITIONS

nofStoringLanes ≙ *nofRailwayTracks* + *nofStores* ;
TRUCKS ≙ $\mathbb{N}_1$;
CONTAINERS ≙ $\mathbb{N}_1$

---

nofStoringLanes is the sum of two numbers: the number of railway tracks and the number of storing lanes. As previously mentioned, this simplification allows containers to be treated uniformly on the trains and in the stores.

TRUCKS: a set of positive natural numbers. It represents an abstract set of all trucks which can appear in the container station at any time.

CONTAINERS: this set of positive natural numbers is the set of containers which can be put in the store in the container station.

END

2.4 Introducing Fairness in a Refinement Step

Solving our task we follow the *stepwise manner* of program derivation. In the previous section we showed the first step of this process, i.e. the design of an *abstract specification* of the considered task. Each step in this derivation should bring us closer to the final *implementation*. Instead of doing a big jump from the abstract specification to the implementation we make an intermediate step. In this step our goal is to fulfil the requirements of the task description which could not be met in the abstract specification.

Let us note the following straightforward fact which points to the direction of the *refinement*. It is well known that a set as used to model the pool of trucks is an unordered structure. Such a structure is appropriate at the abstract level. The problem arises when we recall that the designed system should achieve some degree of fairness among the trucks, so that the truck drivers will not get annoyed. The requirement of fairness means that if two trucks request the same position in the loading zone, then the truck which arrived in the waiting zone earlier must also be parked in this position earlier. Thus the requirement of fairness implies the presence of some order between the trucks. This point gives us a real direction of the refinement for our case: the introduction of ordered structures. The next task is to select the most suitable ordered structure. Everyday experience leads us to the idea of a queue arrangement for the arriving trucks. We choose a sequence as the most natural representation of a queue.

To meet the requirement of fairness we perform *a data refinement*. Hence, we are going to refine the Abstract Machine specification by changing the data structure. Obviously, manipulations with the data structure demand the corresponding changes in the operations basically, to adapt the operations to the new data structure.

Now we have to consider the question to what extent we should be fair? To make this point clearer, let us imagine the following situation. Suppose we have absolute fairness, i.e. we implement the discipline *first in first out* without any exceptions. Moreover, we assume that several trucks arrive at the container station at almost the same time. By chance they might all be parked in the same position in the loading zone. Then in spite of the fact that other positions are empty at this moment, the trucks arriving later should wait in the common queue. This simple example demonstrates that we lose flexibility for the sake of absolute fairness. Thus we do not satisfy the requirement of minimising the average waiting time. It is clear that we should find a compromise solution. We think that giving highest priority to the operator is the most reasonable solution in this conflicting problem. In this case, the situation described above does not lead to a fast growing queue. The operator gives permission to move into the loading zone to trucks behind the trucks assigned to the same position. Here we can speak about queues for certain positions rather than about a common queue of trucks.

We implement these ideas by replacing the set of arriving trucks *TrucksInWaitingZone* by the sequence *TrucksInWaitingZone_seq*. Furthermore, so that the operator's decision when choosing which truck to assign to a certain position is a fair one, we refine the set *possible_truck* to the sequence *possible_trucks_seq*. We refine the specification by means of introducing the new data structure and the requirement of fairness.

REFINEMENT   *CONTAINERSTATIONR*

REFINES   *CONTAINERSTATION*

SEES

  Bool_TYPE

VARIABLES

  TrucksInWaitingZone_seq , *TrucksInLoadingZone* , *ContainersInStores* ,
  CranePosition , *RequestedContainer* , *possible_positions* , *possible_trucks_seq* ,
  reloading_trucks

In the refinement the changed variables receive ending *seq* to distinguish them from their counterparts in the specification.

INVARIANT

  $TrucksInWaitingZone\_seq \in$ iseq ($TRUCKS$) $\wedge$
  $possible\_trucks\_seq \in$ iseq ($TRUCKS$) $\wedge$
  $TrucksInWaitingZone =$ ran ($TrucksInWaitingZone\_seq$) $\wedge$
  $possible\_trucks =$ ran ($possible\_trucks\_seq$)

The invariant indicates the changes in the data structure. The variables which remain unchanged in the refinement are not redefined in the invariant. We introduce the injective sequence *TrucksInWaitingZone_seq* instead of the set *TrucksInWaitingZone*. Indicating that the set *TrucksInWaitingZone* is a range of the sequence *TrucksInWaitingZone_seq* we clarify the correspondence between the variable in the specification and one in the refinement. Introduction of the sequence *possible_trucks_seq* is done in the same way.

INITIALISATION

  $TrucksInLoadingZone := \{\}$ ||
  $RequestedContainer := \{\}$ ||
  $possible\_positions := \{\}$ ||
  $reloading\_trucks := \{\}$ ||
  $CranePosition := 1$ ||
  $TrucksInWaitingZone\_seq := [\ ]$ ||

$possible\_trucks\_seq := [\ ]$ ||
$ContainersInStores :\in (\ 1 .. nofPositions\ ) \times (\ 1 .. nofStoringLanes\ ) \rightarrowtail \mathbb{N}_1$

The initialisation here establishes the same state of the container station as in the specification. The only difference is that we initialise the corresponding variables as empty sequences.

OPERATIONS

$moveInWaitingZone (\ truck\ , reqcontainer\ )$ $\widehat{=}$
    PRE
        $truck \in TRUCKS \wedge$
        $truck \notin \mathrm{ran}\ (\ TrucksInWaitingZone\_seq\ ) \wedge$
        $truck \notin \mathrm{ran}\ (\ TrucksInLoadingZone\ ) \wedge$
        $\mathrm{card}\ (\ \mathrm{ran}\ (\ TrucksInWaitingZone\_seq\ )\ ) < nofWaitingPositions \wedge$
        $reqcontainer \in \mathrm{ran}\ (\ ContainersInStores\ ) \wedge$
        $reqcontainer \notin \mathrm{ran}\ (\ RequestedContainer\ ) \wedge$
        $truck \notin \mathrm{dom}\ (\ RequestedContainer\ )$
    THEN
        $TrucksInWaitingZone\_seq := TrucksInWaitingZone\_seq \leftarrow truck$ ||
        $RequestedContainer := RequestedContainer \cup \{\ truck \mapsto reqcontainer\ \}$
    END ;

In the operation *moveInWaitingZone* we take into account the new data structure. A new arriving truck is prepended to the queue of trucks in the waiting zone. Even if we do not work with the common queue of trucks in the waiting zone directly, we use the order of the arriving truck when considering the truck's line to a certain position.

$moveInLoadingZone (\ truck\ , pos\ , ln\ )$ $\widehat{=}$
    PRE
        $truck \in \mathrm{ran}\ (\ TrucksInWaitingZone\_seq\ ) \wedge$
        $pos \in 1 .. nofPositions \wedge$
        $ln \in 1 .. nofLoadingLanes \wedge$
        $pos \mapsto ln \notin \mathrm{dom}\ (\ TrucksInLoadingZone\ )$
    THEN
        ANY   *oc*   **WHERE**
           $oc \in \mathbb{N}_1 \wedge$
           $oc = TrucksInWaitingZone\_seq^{-1}\ (\ truck\ )$
        THEN
           ANY   *wtrseq*   **WHERE**
               $wtrseq \in \mathrm{iseq}\ (\ TRUCKS\ ) \wedge$
               $\forall ii .\ (\ ii \in 1 .. oc - 1 \Rightarrow$
                 $wtrseq\ (\ ii\ ) = TrucksInWaitingZone\_seq\ (\ ii\ )\ ) \wedge$
               $\forall ii .\ (\ ii \in oc + 1 .. \mathrm{size}\ (\ TrucksInWaitingZone\_seq\ ) \Rightarrow$
                 $wtrseq\ (\ ii - 1\ ) = TrucksInWaitingZone\_seq\ (\ ii\ )\ ) \wedge$
               $\mathrm{size}\ (\ wtrseq\ ) = \mathrm{size}\ (\ TrucksInWaitingZone\_seq\ ) - 1$
           THEN
               $TrucksInLoadingZone :=$
               $TrucksInLoadingZone \cup \{\ pos \mapsto ln \mapsto truck\ \}$ ||
               $TrucksInWaitingZone\_seq := wtrseq$
           END
        END
    END ;

To park *truck* in the loading zone it is necessary to remove this truck from the line of trucks in the waiting zone. The constructions **ANY WHERE** in the operation *moveIn-LoadingZone* are used to introduce the local variables *wtrseq* and *oc*. The variable *oc* contains the number of the *truck* in the queue of waiting trucks. The variable *wtrseq* represents the queue of trucks in the waiting zone with *truck* deleted. The expression with quantifier must show that the order of the other trucks remains unchanged after deletion of a certain truck from the queue.

---

truckReloadAndDeparture (*truck*) $\hat{=}$
    PRE
        truck ∈ *TRUCKS* ∧
        truck ∈ ran (*TrucksInLoadingZone*) ∧
        truck ∉ *reloading_trucks* ∧
        ∃ *pos* . (*pos* ∈ *1* .. *nofPositions* ∧
        pos ∈ dom ({ *TrucksInLoadingZone* $^{-1}$ (*truck*) }) ∧
        pos = *CranePosition*)
    THEN
        TrucksInLoadingZone := *TrucksInLoadingZone* ▷ { *truck* }   ‖
        ContainersInStores :=
            ContainersInStores ▷ { *RequestedContainer* (*truck*) }   ‖
        RequestedContainer := { *truck* } ◁ *RequestedContainer*
    END ；
number_candidates ⟵ *possiblePos* (*truck*) $\hat{=}$
    PRE
        truck ∈ *TRUCKS* ∧
        truck ∈ ran (*TrucksInWaitingZone_seq*)
    THEN
        LET   *pp*   **BE**
            pp =
                dom ({ *ContainersInStores* $^{-1}$ (*RequestedContainer* (*truck*)) }) ◁
                (*1* .. *nofPositions*) × (*1* .. *nofLoadingLanes*) −
                    dom (*TrucksInLoadingZone*)
        IN
            possible_positions := *pp*   ‖
            number_candidates := card (*pp*)
        END
    END ；
position ⟵ *nextPossiblePos* $\hat{=}$
    PRE
        possible_positions ≠ {}
    THEN
        ANY   *pos*   **WHERE**
            pos ∈ *possible_positions*
        THEN
            position := *pos*   ‖
            possible_positions := *possible_positions* − { *pos* }
        END
    END ；
number_candidates ⟵ *possibleTrucks* (*lane* , *pos*) $\hat{=}$
    PRE
        lane ∈ *1* .. *nofLoadingLanes* ∧
        pos ∈ *1* .. *nofPositions* ∧

$pos \mapsto lane \notin$ dom ($TrucksInLoadingZone$)
THEN
    LET pt **BE**
      $pt = \{ truck \mid truck \in TRUCKS \land$
        $truck \in$ ran ($TrucksInWaitingZone\_seq$) $\land$
        $\exists\, ln\,.\, (ln \in 1\,..\, nofStoringLanes \land$
        $ContainersInStores\, (\, pos\,,\, ln\,) = RequestedContainer\, (\, truck\,)\,)\, \}$
    IN

      ANY $wtrseq$ **WHERE**
        $wtrseq \in$ iseq (pt) $\land$
        ran ($wtrseq$) $= pt \land$
        size ($wtrseq$) $=$ card (pt) $\land$
        $\forall\, ii\,.\, (ii \in 1\,..\,$ size ($wtrseq$) $- 1 \Rightarrow$
        $TrucksInWaitingZone\_seq^{-1}\, (\, wtrseq\, (\, ii\,)\,) <$
          $TrucksInWaitingZone\_seq^{-1}\, (\, wtrseq\, (\, ii + 1\,)\,)\,)$
      THEN
        $possible\_trucks\_seq := wtrseq \parallel$
        $number\_candidates :=$ size ($wtrseq$)
      END
    END
  END ;

The number of trucks waiting for permission to move to the considered position is the output result of the operation *possibleTrucks*. Based on the queue of waiting trucks *TrucksInWaitingZone_seq* this operation forms the queue of trucks for the considered position. Such a queue is formed in the local variable *wtrseq* and then stored in the variable *possible_trucks_seq*. The expression with the existential quantifier shows that we form the sequence of the trucks which have been assigned to containers parked in the sector *pos*. The next predicate indicates that the sequence *wtrseq* is formed such that a truck which arrived earlier at the container station is located in the queue before trucks that arrived later.

$truck \longleftarrow nextPossibleTruck$ $\widehat{=}$
  PRE
    card (ran ($possible\_trucks\_seq$)) > 0
  THEN
    $truck :=$ first ($possible\_trucks\_seq$) $\parallel$
    $possible\_trucks\_seq :=$ tail ($possible\_trucks\_seq$)
  END ;

The operation *nextPossibleTruck* performs the fair choice of the next truck to be parked in the loading zone. The design of the operation *nextPossibleTruck* forces the operator to choose the first truck in the queue for a certain position in the loading zone. This operation implements the idea of fairness in the specification of the task.

$number\_reloads \longleftarrow requiredTruckReloads\, (\, position\,)$ $\widehat{=}$
  PRE
    $position \in 1\,..\, nofPositions \land$
    $position = CranePosition$
  THEN
    LET tr **BE**
      $tr = \{ truck \mid truck \in$ ran ($TrucksInLoadingZone$)

$\wedge$ *truck* $\in$ dom (*RequestedContainer*) $\wedge$
$\exists$ *ln* . (*ln* $\in$ *1* .. *nofLoadingLanes* $\wedge$
TrucksInLoadingZone (*position* , *ln*) = *truck*) }
      IN
        reloading_trucks := *tr* $\parallel$
        number_reloads := card (*tr*)
      END
    END ;

next_truck $\longleftarrow$ *nextTruckToReload* $\widehat{=}$
    PRE
      reloading_trucks $\neq$ {}
    THEN
      ANY   *tr*   **WHERE**
        tr $\in$ *reloading_trucks*
      THEN
        next_truck := *tr* $\parallel$
        reloading_trucks := *reloading_trucks* $-$ { *tr* }
      END
    END ;

trucklane $\longleftarrow$ *reloadingTruckLocation* (*truck*) $\widehat{=}$
    PRE
      truck $\in$ *TRUCKS* $\wedge$
      truck $\in$ ran (*TrucksInLoadingZone*)
    THEN
      LET   *ln* **BE**
        ln = { *lane* | *lane* $\in$ *1* .. *nofLoadingLanes* $\wedge$
          $\exists$ *pos* . (*pos* $\in$ *1* .. *nofPositions* $\wedge$
          TrucksInLoadingZone (*pos* , *lane*) = *truck*) }
      IN
        trucklane :$\in$ *ln*
      END
    END ;

containerlane $\longleftarrow$ *reloadingContainerLocation* (*truck*) $\widehat{=}$
    PRE
      truck $\in$ *TRUCKS* $\wedge$
      truck $\in$ ran (*TrucksInLoadingZone*)
    THEN
      LET   *conln* **BE**
        conln = dom ([{ *ContainersInStores* $^{-1}$ (
          RequestedContainer (*truck*)) }])
      IN
        containerlane :$\in$ *conln*
      END
    END ;

craneMovement $\widehat{=}$
    PRE
      reloading_trucks = {}
    THEN
      IF   *CranePosition* $\neq$ *nofPositions*
      THEN
        CranePosition := *CranePosition* + *1*
      ELSE

$$CranePosition := 1$$
END
END
DEFINITIONS

$nofStoringLanes \;\hat{=}\; nofRailwayTracks + nofStores$;
$TRUCKS \;\hat{=}\; \mathbb{N}_1$;
$CONTAINERS \;\hat{=}\; \mathbb{N}_1$

END

2.5 Implementation: Development of Robust Software

In this section, we present a final refinement step resulting in an implementation. Before giving the actual implementation with more specific comments we analyse the constraints put on implementing an Abstract Machine (mentioned in Chapter 1).

First, let us recall that Abstract Machine Implementation has no state of its own. It imports other machines and refers to the variables of the imported machines via the operations of these machines. In our case a main part of the imported machines is renamed instances of standard machines in the library of B-Toolkit. The parameters of the imported machines are instantiated in the IMPORTS statement. In most cases the representation of the data structure entities and the instantiation of the parameters of the imported machines is straightforward. There are two exceptions which we discuss deeper, namely the injections *TrucksInLoadingZone* and *ContainersInStores*.

A Function machine for the Natural Number Function (*Nfnc*) encapsulates a partial function over numbers. The machine has two parameters: *maxint* and *maxfld*. They restrict the range and the domain of the encapsulated partial injection. The type of the encapsulated variable is the most appropriate one to represent the injection *TrucksInLoadingZone*. Because of this we select that machine to be imported and instantiated in the implementation as the machine *TInLoadingZone_Nfnc*. Since the number of trucks ranges over natural numbers we instantiate the first parameter by *maxint*.

However, the domain of *TrucksInLoadingZone* is the Cartesian product of two sets rather than a set of fields as is the domain of the encapsulated variable *TInLoadingZone_Nfnc*. The domain of *TrucksInLoadingZone* defined as (1 .. *nofPositions*) $\times$ (1 .. *nofLoadingLanes*) uniquely determines the maximal number of items in the domain. Hence, we instantiate the parameter *maxfld* of the imported machine by the value (*nofPositions* $\times$ *nofLoadingLanes*).

To establish the correspondence between elements of the domains *TInLoadingZone_Nfnc* and *TrucksInLoadingZone* we notice the following regularity: each element of *dom(TrucksInLoadingZone)* with subscript (($ii + 1$, $jj + 1$)) corresponds to the element of *dom(TInLoadingZone_Nfnc)* with subscript ($ii + nofPositions \times jj + 1$). With that relation we achieve the desired result so we include it as a part of the refinement relation.

The injection *ContainersInStores* is represented by the encapsulated variable of the imported machine *ContInStores_Nfnc*. The same calculations as above are performed for that instance as well.

In principle, the operations of machines in the library of the B-Toolkit are sufficient to implement the designed system. However, applying a slightly more sophisticated approach, namely layered development as suggested in the previous chapter, we obtain a more elegant solution. The necessity of layered design is justified by the following observation. In several operations we need to verify whether a precondition is satisfied or not. This is done by looking for the presence of a certain element in the range of the function. There is no such operation in the Function machine for the Natural Number function. A possible solution to this problem is the direct introduction of the corresponding loops (**WHILE** substitution) in the final implementation. It means that we would have several loops performing the same function and changing slightly according to the context. To avoid repetitions of standard loops, we extend the standard Function machine for the Natural Number function by the operation *IIR* (which stands for *Item In Range*) which will check whether a certain item is in the range of the function. Here we present our solution instantiated as *TInLoadZone1_Nfnc*.

MACHINE   *TInLoadZone1_Nfnc* (*maxint* , *maxfld*)

CONSTRAINTS

    maxint $\leq$ *2147483646* $\wedge$
    maxfld $\leq$ *2147483646*

SEES

    Bool_TYPE

EXTENDS   *TInLoadingZone_Nfnc* (*maxint* , *maxfld*)

OPERATIONS

    res , *ii* $\longleftarrow$ *TInLoadingZone1_IIR_NFNC* (*item*) $\widehat{=}$
      PRE
        item $\in$ *1* .. *maxint*
      THEN
        LET   *tv*   **BE**
          tv = bool (*item* $\in$ ran (*TInLoadingZone_Nfnc*))
        IN
          IF   *tv* = *TRUE*
          THEN
            res := *TRUE* $\parallel$
            ii := *TInLoadingZone_Nfnc* $^{-1}$ (*item*)
          ELSE
            res := *FALSE* $\parallel$
            ii :$\in$ *1* .. *maxfld*
          END
        END
      END

END

The operation *TInLoadingZone1_IIR_NFNC* returns a Boolean value indicating the occurrence of an item in the range of a function and the corresponding position of the item in a domain.

As the next step we implement the designed machine. The implementation is presented as the machine *TInLoadZone11_Nfnc* where the operation *IIR* is refined by a **WHILE** substitution. According to the layered design method we import the extended machines (the same extension is done for the machine *ContInStores_Nfnc*) in the final implementation.

IMPLEMENTATION   *TInLoadZone11_Nfnc*

REFINES

   TInLoadZone1_Nfnc

SEES

   Bool_TYPE

EXTENDS   *TInLoadingZone_Nfnc* (*maxint* , *maxfld*)

OPERATIONS

   res , *ii* ⟵ *TInLoadingZone1_IIR_NFNC* (*item*) $\widehat{=}$

        VAR   *ind* , *domch*
        IN
           ind := *1* ;
           res := *FALSE* ;
           ii := *0* ;
           WHILE   *ind* $\leq$ *maxfld* $\wedge$ *res* = *FALSE*
           DO
               domch ⟵ *TInLoadingZone_DEF_NFNC* (*ind*) ;
               IF   *domch* = *TRUE*
               THEN
                  res ⟵ *TInLoadingZone_EQL_NFNC* (*ind* , *item*)
               END ;
               ii := *ind* ;
               ind := *ind* + *1*
           INVARIANT
               (*res* = *FALSE* $\Rightarrow$ *item* $\notin$ *TInLoadingZone_Nfnc* [*1* .. *ind* − *1*]) $\wedge$
               (*res* = *TRUE* $\Rightarrow$ *item* $\in$ ran (*TInLoadingZone_Nfnc*)) $\wedge$
               ind $\in$ *1* .. *maxfld* + *1*
           VARIANT
               maxfld − *ind* + *1*
           END
        END

END

The last general comment on the implementation concerns error handling. When developing an implementation we assume that any error should invoke a corresponding error message rather than initiate unpredictable system behaviour. Such an approach guarantees the design of robust and user-friendly software. Hence, in any situation the operator should have a meaningful message depicting the current state of the system.

When presenting the abstract specification we tried to describe every particular design decision. However, some explanations were omitted with the hope that the corresponding error messages would provide the reader with information sufficient to reconstruct all the details.

IMPLEMENTATION   *CONTAINERSTATIONRI*

REFINES   *CONTAINERSTATIONR*

SEES

Bool_TYPE , *basic_io* , *String_TYPE* , *Scalar_TYPE*

IMPORTS

TInWaitingZone_Nseq (*maxint* , *nofWaitingPositions*) ,
TInLoadZone1_Nfnc (*maxint* , *nofPositions* × *nofLoadingLanes*) ,
ContInStores1_Nfnc (*maxint* , *nofPositions* × *nofStoringLanes*) ,
CranePosition_set (*1 .. nofPositions* , *1*) ,
RequeCont1_Nfnc (*maxint* , *nofPositions* × *nofStoringLanes*) ,
PosPositions_set ($\mathbb{N}_1$, *nofPositions* × *nofLoadingLanes*) ,
PosTrucks_Nseq (*maxint* , *nofWaitingPositions*) ,
ReloadTrucks_set ($\mathbb{N}_1$, *nofPositions* × *nofLoadingLanes*) ,
WaitingQueue_Nseq (*nofWaitingPositions* , *nofWaitingPositions*)

In the implementation we introduce the auxiliary variable *WaitingQueue_Nseq*.

INVARIANT

$TInWaitingZone\_Nseq = TrucksInWaitingZone\_seq \land$
$\forall (ii , jj) . (ii \in 0 .. nofPositions - 1 \land jj \in 0 .. nofLoadingLanes - 1 \Rightarrow$
    $TrucksInLoadingZone (ii + 1 , jj + 1) =$
        $TInLoadingZone\_Nfnc (ii + nofPositions \times jj + 1)) \land$
    $\forall (aa , bb) . (aa \in 0 .. nofPositions - 1 \land bb \in 0 .. nofStoringLanes - 1 \Rightarrow$
    $ContainersInStores (aa + 1 , bb + 1) =$
        $ContInStores\_Nfnc (aa + nofPositions \times bb + 1)) \land$
    $CranePosition\_sset = \{ CranePosition \} \land$
    $RequeContainer\_Nfnc = RequestedContainer \land$
    $\forall (cc , dd) . (cc \in 0 .. nofPositions - 1 \land dd \in 0 .. nofLoadingLanes - 1 \land$
    $cc + 1 \mapsto dd + 1 \in possible\_positions \Rightarrow$
        $cc + nofPositions \times dd + 1 \in PosPositions\_sset) \land$
    $PosTrucks\_Nseq = possible\_trucks\_seq \land$
    $ReloadTrucks\_sset = reloading\_trucks$

OPERATIONS

moveInWaitingZone (*truck* , *reqcontainer*) $\widehat{=}$
    VAR
        len , *pos* , *parked* , *poss* , *contcheck* , *reqcontcheck* , *tras* , *parklz*
    IN
        len ⟵ *TInWaitingZone_LEN_NSEQ* **;**
        parked , *pos* ⟵
        TInWaitingZone_SCH_LO_EQL_NSEQ (*1* , *len* , *truck*) **;**
        parklz , *poss* ⟵ *TInLoadingZone1_IIR_NFNC* (*truck*) **;**
        contcheck , *poss* ⟵
        ContInStores1_IIR_NFNC (*reqcontainer*) **;**
        reqcontcheck , *poss* ⟵

$$RequeContainer1\_IIR\_NFNC\ (\ reqcontainer\ )\ \texttt{;}$$
$$tras \longleftarrow RequeContainer\_DEF\_NFNC\ (\ truck\ )\ \texttt{;}$$

At first, we check whether the precondition of the operation is satisfied. Since there are many conditions to be checked we use **IF ELSIF END** substitution for that. We could have used the nested **IF THEN ELSE END** constructs but decided not to do it since it deteriorates the presentation.

The nested **IF THEN ELSE** statements are used to establish whether a precondition holds but in the operations where the preconditions are more compact.

IF $\quad truck < 1 \lor truck > maxint$
THEN
$\quad PUT\_STR\ (\ ``\texttt{The truck }"\ )\ \texttt{;}$
$\quad PUT\_STR\ (\ ``\texttt{is badly defined }"\ )\ \texttt{;}$
$\quad NWL\ (\ 1\ )$
ELSIF $\quad len \geq nofWaitingPositions$
THEN
$\quad PUT\_STR\ (\ ``\texttt{The waiting zone is full}"\ )\ \texttt{;}$
$\quad NWL\ (\ 1\ )$
ELSIF $\quad len \neq 0 \land parked = TRUE$
THEN

If the capacity of the waiting zone is not exceeded and the waiting zone is not empty, then we check for the presence of a truck *truck* in the queue of waiting trucks. The value of the variable *parked* equals *FALSE* if there is no *truck* in the waiting zone. It means that after establishing that the capacity of the waiting zone is not exceeded, we will verify the following condition: $truck \notin TrucksInWaitingZone$.

$\quad PUT\_STR\ (\ ``\texttt{The truck }"\ )\ \texttt{;}$
$\quad PUT\_NAT\ (\ truck\ )\ \texttt{;}$
$\quad PUT\_STR\ (\ ``\texttt{is in the waiting zone }"\ )\ \texttt{;}$
$\quad NWL\ (\ 1\ )$
ELSIF $\quad parklz = TRUE$
THEN

If the program fails to find *truck* in the waiting zone, it proceeds by searching for this truck in the loading zone. The following statement must be verified: $truck \notin$ ran (*TrucksInLoadingZone*).

$\quad PUT\_STR\ (\ ``\texttt{The truck }"\ )\ \texttt{;}$
$\quad PUT\_NAT\ (\ truck\ )\ \texttt{;}$
$\quad PUT\_STR\ (\ ``\texttt{is in the loading zone }"\ )\ \texttt{;}$
$\quad NWL\ (\ 1\ )$

If the considered truck is not parked either in the waiting zone or in the loading zone, we continue verification of the precondition. Next, we check whether the input parameter *reqcontainer* has a proper value.

ELSIF   *reqcontainer* $< 1 \lor$ *reqcontainer* $> maxint$
THEN
    PUT_STR (" The requested container ") **;**
    PUT_STR (" is badly defined ") **;**
    NWL (*1*)
ELSIF   *contcheck* $= FALSE$
THEN

The local variable *contcheck* indicates whether *reqcontainer* is stored at the container station or not.

    PUT_STR (" Container ") **;**
    PUT_NAT (*reqcontainer*) **;**
    PUT_STR (" is not ") **;**
    PUT_STR (" in the storing zone ") **;**
    NWL (*1*)
ELSIF   *reqcontcheck* $= TRUE$
THEN

The next statement to be verified is *reqcontainer* $\notin$ ran (*RequestedContainer*), i.e. we have to check whether the desired container has already been assigned to any truck or not.

    PUT_STR (" Container ") **;**
    PUT_NAT (*reqcontainer*) **;**
    PUT_STR (" is already ") **;**
    PUT_STR (" assigned to truck ") **;**
    NWL (*1*)
ELSIF   *tras* $= TRUE$
THEN

Finally, we have to establish that the predicate *truck* $\notin$ dom (*RequestedContainer*) holds.

    PUT_STR (" Truck ") **;**
    PUT_NAT (*truck*) **;**
    PUT_STR (" is already assigned to container ") **;**
    NWL (*1*)
ELSE

At this point we have checked that all conditions of the precondition are satisfied. Thus we now assign the container to the arrived truck and park this truck in the waiting zone.

    RequeContainer_STO_NFNC (*truck* , *reqcontainer*) **;**
    TInWaitingZone_PSH_NSEQ (*truck*)
    END
  END ;
moveInLoadingZone (*truck* , *pos* , *ln*) $\widehat{=}$
  VAR
    len , *parkedInWZ* , *pwz* , *plz* , *vacant* , *tras*
  IN

$$len \longleftarrow TInWaitingZone\_LEN\_NSEQ ;$$
$$parkedInWZ , pwz \longleftarrow$$
$$TInWaitingZone\_SCH\_LO\_EQL\_NSEQ (1 , len , truck) ;$$

The position *(pos,ln)* in the domain of *TrucksInLoadingZone* corresponds to the position *plz* in the domain of *TInLoadingZone_Nfnc*.

$$plz := pos + nofPositions \times (ln - 1) ;$$
$$vacant \longleftarrow$$
$$TInLoadingZone\_DEF\_NFNC (plz) ;$$
$$tras \longleftarrow RequeContainer\_DEF\_NFNC (truck) ;$$
IF $truck < 1 \lor truck > maxint$
THEN
    PUT_STR (" The truck is badly defined ") ;
    $NWL (1)$

If the input parameter *truck* has a correct value, we check whether this truck is parked in the waiting zone or not. According to the developed specification a truck can move to the loading zone only after being parked in the waiting zone. If the truck in question is parked in the waiting zone, the variable *parkedInWZ* has the value *TRUE* and we continue checking the precondition.

ELSIF $len = 0 \lor parkedInWZ = FALSE$
THEN
    PUT_STR (" Truck   ") ; PUT_NAT (*truck*) ;
    PUT_STR (" is not in the waiting zone   ") ;
    $NWL (1)$
ELSIF $pos < 1 \lor pos > nofPositions$
THEN
    PUT_STR (" The requested position   ") ;
    PUT_STR (" is badly defined ") ;
    $NWL (1)$
ELSIF $ln < 1 \lor ln > nofLoadingLanes$
THEN
    PUT_STR (" The requested lane   ") ;
    PUT_STR (" is badly defined ") ;
    $NWL (1)$

Having established that the input parameters *pos* and *ln* are well defined we check whether this position is vacant.

ELSIF $vacant = TRUE$
THEN
    PUT_STR (" Requested place: ") ;
    PUT_STR (" position   ") ;
    PUT_NAT (*pos*) ;
    PUT_STR (" lane   ") ; PUT_NAT (*ln*) ;
    PUT_STR (" is already occupied ") ;
    $NWL (1)$

ELSIF   *tras = FALSE*
THEN
    PUT_STR (" No container ") **;**
    PUT_STR (" is assigned to truck ") **;**
    PUT_NAT (*truck*) **;**
    NWL (*1*)
ELSE

If the desired position is not occupied by any truck the truck *truck* leaves the queue in the waiting zone and parks in the loading zone.

    TInLoadingZone_STO_NFNC (*plz* , *truck*) **;**
    TInWaitingZone_LFT_NSEQ (*pwz* + *1* , *len* , *1*)
END
END ;
truckReloadAndDeparture (*truck*) $\hat{=}$
    VAR
        parkedInLZ , *poss* , *nchosen* , *acpos* , *crpos* , *cont* , *contpos* , *tras*
    IN
        parkedInLZ , *poss* $\longleftarrow$ *TInLoadingZone1_IIR_NFNC* (*truck*) **;**
        nchosen $\longleftarrow$ *ReloadTrucks_MBR_SET* (*truck*) **;**

When calculating the value of *acpos* we use the predicate of the invariant establishing the relation between the elements of the domain of *TrucksInLoadingZone* and *TInLoading-Zone_Nfnc*. The relation is bijective. Hence, we can uniquely calculate the values of both the sector and the lane for any particular value of the field of *TInLoadingZone_Nfnc*.

---

    acpos := (*poss* − *1*) **mod** *nofPositions* + *1* **;**
    crpos $\longleftarrow$ *CranePosition_VAL_SET* (*1*) **;**
    tras $\longleftarrow$ *RequeContainer_DEF_NFNC* (*truck*) **;**
    IF   *truck* < *1* $\vee$ *truck* > *maxint*
    THEN
        PUT_STR (" The truck is badly defined ") **;**
        NWL (*1*)
    ELSIF   *parkedInLZ = FALSE*
    THEN

If the input parameter *truck* has a proper value we check whether the truck *truck* is allocated in the loading zone and is chosen to be loaded next.

    PUT_STR (" Truck ") **;** *PUT_NAT* (*truck*) **;**
    PUT_STR (" is not in the loading zone ") **;**
    NWL (*1*)
    ELSIF   *nchosen = TRUE*
    THEN
        PUT_STR (" Truck ") **;** *PUT_NAT* (*truck*) **;**
        PUT_STR (" is not chosen ") **;**
        PUT_STR (" for reload ") **;**
        NWL (*1*)

Next we have to establish that the truck *truck* occupies the same sector as the crane does. For that we compare the number of the truck sector, *acpos* and the current position of the crane, *crpos*.

      ELSIF $acpos \neq crpos$
      THEN
        PUT_STR (" Truck   ") ; *PUT_NAT* (*truck*) ;
        PUT_STR (" is not under the crane ") ;
        NWL (*1*)
      ELSIF   *tras* = *FALSE*
      THEN
        PUT_STR (" No container ") ;
        PUT_STR (" is assigned to truck") ;
        PUT_NAT (*truck*) ;
        NWL (*1*)
      ELSE

Because the truck *truck* is properly located it is loaded by the container assigned (the container *cont*). So the truck *truck* leaves the container station, the container *cont* is taken from the storing zone and the record about the assignment of the container *cont* to a truck *truck* is erased.

        TInLoadingZone_RMV_NFNC (*poss*) ;
        cont ⟵ *RequeContainer_VAL_NFNC* (*truck*) ;
        contpos ⟵ *ContInStores_VAL_NFNC* (*cont*) ;
        ContInStores_RMV_NFNC (*contpos*) ;
        RequeContainer_RMV_NFNC (*truck*)
      END
    END ;
  number_candidates ⟵ *possiblePos* (*truck*) $\widehat{=}$
    VAR
      len , *cont* , *hh* , *pos* , *poss* , *acpos* , *nl* , *trpos* , *domch* , *parked* , *tras*
    IN
      IF $truck \geq 1 \wedge truck \leq maxint$
      THEN
        len ⟵ *TInWaitingZone_LEN_NSEQ* ;
        IF $len > 0$
        THEN
          parked , *pos* ⟵
          TInWaitingZone_SCH_LO_EQL_NSEQ (*1* , *len* , *truck*)
        ELSE
          parked := *FALSE*
        END ;
        IF   *parked* = *TRUE*
        THEN

The previous part of the operation verified the establishing of the precondition. Next we identify the position of the container *cont* assigned to the truck *truck*. We obtain the position of the assigned container in the domain of *ContInStores_Nfnc* and then extract the number of the sector from it.

$tras \longleftarrow RequeContainer\_DEF\_NFNC\ (\ truck\ )\ ;$
IF $tras = TRUE$
THEN
$\quad cont \longleftarrow RequeContainer\_VAL\_NFNC\ (\ truck\ )\ ;$
$\quad hh\ ,\ poss \longleftarrow ContInStores1\_IIR\_NFNC\ (\ cont\ )\ ;$

The container *cont* is kept in the sector *acpos*. According to the introduced loading discipline the truck *truck* must be parked in the sector *acpos* as well.

$$acpos := (\ poss - 1\ )\ \mathsf{mod}\ nofPositions + 1\ ;$$

The sequence of the statements below is the initialisation of the loop.

$nl := 1\ ;$
$number\_candidates := 0\ ;$
$PosPositions\_CLR\_SET\ ;$

The following loop forms the set of all vacant and appropriate positions for *truck* in the loading zone. Only positions in the sector *acpos* are taken into consideration. On each iteration of the loop we check whether position *acpos* in the line *nl* is vacant or not. If the considered position is vacant we insert it in the set *PosPositions_sset* and increment the counter of available positions *number_candidates*. The loop variable is the number of the currently considered line.

WHILE $nl \leq nofLoadingLanes$
DO
$\quad trpos := acpos + nofPositions \times (\ nl - 1\ )\ ;$
$\quad domch \longleftarrow TInLoadingZone\_DEF\_NFNC\ (\ trpos\ )\ ;$
$\quad$**IF** $domch = FALSE$
$\quad$**THEN**
$\quad\quad PosPositions\_ENT\_SET\ (\ trpos\ )\ ;$
$\quad\quad number\_candidates := number\_candidates + 1$
$\quad$**END** $;$
$\quad nl := nl + 1$
INVARIANT
$PosPositions\_sset =$
$\{\ xx\ \mid\ xx = acpos + nofPositions \times (\ nl - 1\ )\ \wedge$
$\quad (\ xx - 1\ )\ /\ nofPositions\ \mathsf{mod}\ nofPositions + 1 \in$
$\quad\quad 1\ ..\ nl - 1\ \wedge$
$\quad xx \notin \mathsf{dom}\ (\ TInLoadingZone\_Nfnc\ )\ \}\ \wedge$
$number\_candidates = \mathsf{card}\ (\ PosPositions\_sset\ )\ \wedge$
$nl \in 1\ ..\ nofLoadingLanes + 1\ \wedge$
$\mathsf{size}\ (\ TInWaitingZone\_Nseq\ ) \neq 0\ \wedge$
$truck \in 1\ ..\ maxint\ \wedge$
$parked = TRUE\ \wedge$
$pos = TInWaitingZone\_Nseq^{-1}\ (\ truck\ )\ \wedge$
$cont = RequeContainer\_Nfnc\ (\ truck\ )\ \wedge$
$(\ hh = TRUE \Rightarrow cont \in \mathsf{ran}\ (\ ContInStores\_Nfnc\ )\ )\ \wedge$
$(\ hh = FALSE \Rightarrow cont \notin \mathsf{ran}\ (\ ContInStores\_Nfnc\ )\ )\ \wedge$
$poss = ContInStores\_Nfnc^{-1}\ (\ cont\ )\ \wedge$

$acpos = (poss - 1) \bmod nofPositions + 1 \wedge$
$len = \mathsf{size}\ (\ TInWaitingZone\_Nseq\ ) \wedge$
$tras = TRUE$
VARIANT
$\quad nofLoadingLanes - nl + 1$
END
ELSE
 PUT_STR ("No container ");
 PUT_STR ("is assigned to truck");
 PUT_NAT ($truck$);
 NWL (1)
END
ELSE
 PUT_STR ("Truck "); PUT_NAT ($truck$);
 PUT_STR ("is not in the waiting zone");
 NWL (1)
END
ELSE
 PUT_STR ("The truck ");
 PUT_STR ("is badly defined ");
 NWL (1)
END
END ;
$position \longleftarrow nextPossiblePos \quad \widehat{=}$
VAR
 $vacancy , pos$
IN
 $vacancy \longleftarrow PosPositions\_EMP\_SET$;
 IF $vacancy = FALSE$
 THEN

If some positions are available in the loading zone, the operator can choose any of them. The operator expects to get the coordinates of the chosen position in the form *(sector, lane)*. However, these coordinates are represented by an item of the form *sector + lane × nof Positions* in the set *PosPositions_sset*. To provide the operator with meaningful information we convert this item so that the operator gets the final result as a pair consisting of the number of the position and the number of the line. The chosen position is considered to be occupied and is therefore removed from the set of vacant positions.

 $pos \longleftarrow PosPositions\_ANY\_SET$;
 $position :=$
 $(pos - 1) \bmod nofPositions + 1 \mapsto (pos - 1) / nofPositions + 1$;
 $PosPositions\_RMV\_SET$ (pos)
ELSE
 PUT_STR ("There are no vacant ");
 PUT_STR ("positions for the truck ");
 NWL (1)
END
END ;
$number\_candidates \longleftarrow possibleTrucks$ ($lane , pos$) $\widehat{=}$
VAR
 $occupied , ln , trpos , domch , cont , len , parked , assigned ,$

```
        wpos , truck , ind , ptruck , tpos , lwq , tplz
   IN
        tplz := pos + nofPositions × ( lane − 1 ) ;
        occupied ⟵ TInLoadingZone_DEF_NFNC ( tplz ) ;
        IF    lane < 1 ∨ lane > nofLoadingLanes
        THEN
            PUT_STR ( " The lane " ) ;
            PUT_STR ( " is badly defined " ) ;
            NWL ( 1 )
        ELSIF    pos < 1 ∨ pos > nofPositions
        THEN
            PUT_STR ( " The position " ) ;
            PUT_STR ( " is badly defined " ) ;
            NWL ( 1 )
        ELSIF    occupied = TRUE
        THEN
            PUT_STR ( " Position " ) ; PUT_NAT ( pos ) ;
            PUT_STR ( " Lane " ) ; PUT_NAT ( lane ) ;
            PUT_STR ( " is already occupied " ) ;
            NWL ( 1 )
        ELSE
```

If the input parameters are well-defined and they correspond to a vacant position in the loading zone, we can execute the body of the operation. We form the queue of the trucks fitting the position *pos* in the lane *lane* in the loading zone in two steps.

At first, we form an auxiliary queue of the waiting trucks *WaitingQueue_Nseq*. Every element of *ran(WaitingQueue_Nseq)* is such an element of the domain of *TInWaiting-Zone_Nseq* that the corresponding truck fits the desired position, i.e. the ordinal numbers of truck arival are contained in *ran(WaitingQueue_Nseq)*.

```
        ln := 1 ;
        WaitingQueue_CLR_NSEQ ;
        len ⟵ TInWaitingZone_LEN_NSEQ ;
```

The following loop with initialisation forms the sequence *WaitingQueue_Nseq* as described above.

```
            WHILE    ln ≤ nofStoringLanes
            DO
                trpos := pos + nofPositions × ( ln − 1 ) ;
                domch ⟵ ContInStores_DEF_NFNC ( trpos ) ;
                IF    domch = TRUE
                THEN
                    cont ⟵ ContInStores_VAL_NFNC ( trpos ) ;
                    assigned , truck ⟵
                    RequeContainer1_IIR_NFNC ( cont ) ;
                    IF    assigned = TRUE
                    THEN
                        parked , wpos ⟵
                        TInWaitingZone_SCH_LO_EQL_NSEQ ( 1 , len , truck ) ;
                        IF    parked = TRUE
```

THEN

$WaitingQueue\_PSH\_NSEQ\,(\,wpos\,)$

END

END

END ;

$ln := ln + 1$

INVARIANT

$ln \in 1 \,..\, nofRailwayTracks + nofStores + 1 \land$

$\mathsf{ran}\,(\,WaitingQueue\_Nseq\,) =$

$\{\,wp \mid wp \in \mathsf{dom}\,(\,TInWaitingZone\_Nseq\,) \land$

$\quad \exists\,ii\,.\,(\,ii \in 1 \,..\, ln - 1 \land$

$\quad RequeContainer\_Nfnc\,(\,TInWaitingZone\_Nseq\,(\,wp\,)\,) =$

$\quad\quad ContInStores\_Nfnc\,(\,pos +$

$\quad\quad\quad nofPositions \times (\,ii - 1\,)\,)\,)\,\} \land$

$lane \in 1 \,..\, nofLoadingLanes \land$

$pos \in 1 \,..\, nofPositions \land$

$(\,occupied = FALSE \Rightarrow$

$\quad tplz \notin \mathsf{dom}\,(\,TInLoadingZone\_Nfnc\,)\,) \land$

$len = \mathsf{size}\,(\,TInWaitingZone\_Nseq\,) \land$

$tplz = pos + nofPositions \times (\,lane - 1\,)$

VARIANT

$nofRailwayTracks + nofStores - ln + 1$

END ;

$PosTrucks\_CLR\_NSEQ\,;$

$number\_candidates := 0\,;$

$ind := 1\,;$

$lwq \longleftarrow WaitingQueue\_LEN\_NSEQ\,;$

$WaitingQueue\_SRT\_DSC\_NSEQ\,(\,1\,,\,lwq\,)\,;$

To perform a fair choice of the truck which fits a certain position and has arrived before the other trucks fitting that position, we sort the sequence *WaitingQueue_Nseq*. Now on top of the stack *WaitingQueue_Nseq* is the ordinal number of the truck which arrived earliest. Hence if we pop the top of the stack *WaitingQueue_Nseq* and push it into *PosTrucks_Nseq*, then we form the sequence of trucks fitting a certain position in the loading zone in such a way that the first element of this sequence is the truck with the earliest arrival time.

WHILE $ind \le lwq$

DO

$tpos \longleftarrow WaitingQueue\_LST\_NSEQ\,;$

$WaitingQueue\_POP\_NSEQ\,;$

$ptruck \longleftarrow TInWaitingZone\_VAL\_NSEQ\,(\,tpos\,)\,;$

$PosTrucks\_PSH\_NSEQ\,(\,ptruck\,)\,;$

$number\_candidates := number\_candidates + 1\,;$

$ind := ind + 1$

INVARIANT

$ind \in 1 \,..\, lwq + 1 \land$

$\mathsf{ran}\,(\,PosTrucks\_Nseq\,) =$

$\{\,tr \mid tr \in \mathsf{ran}\,(\,TInWaitingZone\_Nseq\,) \land$

$\quad \exists\,ii\,.\,(\,ii \in 1 \,..\, ind - 1 \land$

$\quad RequeContainer\_Nfnc\,(\,tr\,) =$

$\quad ContInStores\_Nfnc\,(\,pos + nofPositions \times (\,ii - 1\,)\,)\,)\,\} \land$

$\forall\,jj\,.\,(\,jj \in 1 \,..\, ind - 1 \Rightarrow$

$$TInWaitingZone\_Nseq^{-1} \ (\ PosTrucks\_Nseq\ (\ jj\ )\ ) <$$
$$TInWaitingZone\_Nseq^{-1} \ (\ PosTrucks\_Nseq\ (\ jj+1\ )\ )\ )$$
$\wedge$
$number\_candidates = \textsf{size}\ (\ PosTrucks\_Nseq\ )\ \wedge$
$ln \in 1\ ..\ nofRailwayTracks + nofStores + 1\ \wedge$
$\textsf{size}\ (\ WaitingQueue\_Nseq\ ) + \textsf{size}\ (\ PosTrucks\_Nseq\ ) =$
$lwq\ \wedge$
$lane \in 1\ ..\ nofLoadingLanes\ \wedge$
$pos \in 1\ ..\ nofPositions\ \wedge$
$(\ occupied = FALSE \Rightarrow$
$tplz \notin \textsf{dom}\ (\ TInLoadingZone\_Nfnc\ )\ )\ \wedge$
$len = \textsf{size}\ (\ TInWaitingZone\_Nseq\ )\ \wedge$
$lwq = \textsf{size}\ (\ WaitingQueue\_Nseq\ )\ \wedge$
$tplz = pos + nofPositions \times (\ lane - 1\ )$
VARIANT
$lwq - ind + 1$
END
END
END ;
$truck \longleftarrow nextPossibleTruck \quad \hat{=}$
VAR
len
IN
$len \longleftarrow TInWaitingZone\_LEN\_NSEQ\ ;$
IF $len > 0$
THEN

The truck which was waiting longer than the other trucks is chosen to be parked in the loading zone.

$truck \longleftarrow TInWaitingZone\_FST\_NSEQ\ ;$
$TInWaitingZone\_TAL\_NSEQ$
ELSE
$PUT\_STR\ (\text{``There are no trucks''})\textbf{;}$
$PUT\_STR\ (\text{``for this position ''})\textbf{;}$
$NWL\ (\ 1\ )$
END
END ;
$number\_reloads \longleftarrow requiredTruckReloads\ (\ position\ ) \quad \hat{=}$
VAR
$crpos\ ,\ trpos\ ,\ posch\ ,\ truck\ ,\ assigned\ ,\ nl$
IN
IF $position \geq 1 \wedge position \leq nofPositions$
THEN
$crpos \longleftarrow CranePosition\_VAL\_SET\ (\ 1\ )\ \textbf{;}$
IF $position = crpos$
THEN

Currently we have established that the input parameter *position* has a proper type and coincides with the current crane position *crpos*. The following initialisation and the loop have to form the set of trucks parked in the sector *position* in the loading zone. The loop variable *nl* shows the number of the lane which we consider. If there is any truck *truck* in the place *(position, nl)* then that truck is put in the set of trucks to be reloaded next. Any occurrence of such truck increments the result parameter *number_reloads*. Initially *nl* is set in unit, the formed set is empty and the number of occurrences is zero.

$nl := 1$ **;**
$number\_reloads := 0$ **;**
ReloadTrucks_CLR_SET **;**
WHILE $nl \leq nofLoadingLanes$
DO
    $trpos := position + nofPositions \times (nl - 1)$ **;**
    $posch \longleftarrow TInLoadingZone\_DEF\_NFNC (trpos)$ **;**
    IF $posch = TRUE$
    THEN
        $truck \longleftarrow TInLoadingZone\_VAL\_NFNC (trpos)$ **;**
        $assigned \longleftarrow$
        $RequeContainer\_DEF\_NFNC (truck)$ **;**
        IF $assigned = TRUE$
        THEN
            ReloadTrucks_ENT_SET $(truck)$ **;**
            $number\_reloads := number\_reloads + 1$
        END
    END ;
    $nl := nl + 1$
INVARIANT
    $nl \in 1 .. nofLoadingLanes + 1 \land$
    $position \in 1 .. nofPositions \land$
    $crpos = CranePosition \land$
    $position = crpos \land$
    $ReloadTrucks\_sset =$
    $\{ tr \mid tr \in \mathsf{ran} (TInLoadingZone\_Nfnc) \land$
        $tr \in \mathsf{dom} (RequeContainer\_Nfnc) \land$
        $\exists xx . (xx = position \times nl \land$
        $xx \bmod nofPositions \in 1 .. nl - 1 \land$
        $TInLoadingZone\_Nfnc (xx) = truck) \} \land$
    $number\_reloads = \mathsf{card} (ReloadTrucks\_sset)$
VARIANT
    $nofRailwayTracks + nofStores - nl + 1$
END
ELSE
    PUT_STR (" The position ") **;**
    PUT_NAT (*position*) **;**
    PUT_STR (" is not the ") **;**
    PUT_STR (" current crane position") **;**
    NWL (*1*)
END
ELSE
    PUT_STR (" Position ") **;**
    PUT_STR (" is badly defined ") **;**
    NWL (*1*)
END
END ;

next_truck ⟵ *nextTruckToReload* $\hat{=}$
   VAR
     relds
   IN
     relds ⟵ *ReloadTrucks_EMP_SET* **;**
     IF   *relds* = *FALSE*
     THEN
        next_truck ⟵ *ReloadTrucks_ANY_SET* **;**
        ReloadTrucks_RMV_SET (*next_truck*)
     ELSE
        PUT_STR (" There is no unloaded trucks ") **;**
        PUT_STR (" in the current position ") **;**
        NWL (*1*)
     END
   END ;
trucklane ⟵ *reloadingTruckLocation* (*truck*) $\hat{=}$
   VAR
     posch , *pos*
   IN
     posch , *pos* ⟵ *TInLoadingZone1_IIR_NFNC* (*truck*) **;**
     IF   *posch* = *TRUE*
     THEN

The coordinates of the truck *(position, lane)* are represented by *pos* in the domain of *TInLoadingZone_Nfnc*.

---

        trucklane := (*pos* − *1*) / *nofPositions* + *1*
     ELSE
        PUT_STR (" Truck ") **;** *PUT_NAT* (*truck*) **;**
        PUT_STR (" is not in loading zone ") **;**
        NWL (*1*)
     END
   END ;
containerlane ⟵ *reloadingContainerLocation* (*truck*) $\hat{=}$
   VAR
     parkedInLZ , *poss* , *cont* , *contpos*
   IN
     IF   *truck* ≥ *1* ∧ *truck* ≤ *maxint*
     THEN
        parkedInLZ , *poss* ⟵ *TInLoadingZone1_IIR_NFNC* (*truck*) **;**
        IF   *parkedInLZ* = *TRUE*
        THEN

If the input parameter *truck* has a proper value and *truck* is allocated in the loading zone, we check whether any container is assigned to this truck.

---

        cont ⟵ *RequeContainer_VAL_NFNC* (*truck*) **;**
        contpos ⟵ *ContInStores_VAL_NFNC* (*cont*) **;**

The coordinates of a container in the storing zone are represented in the same manner as the coordinates of a truck parked in the loading zone. To obtain the number of the lane *containerlane* where the container *cont* assigned to the truck *truck* is kept we use the integer division (as in the previous operation).

```
                    containerlane := ( contpos − 1 ) / nofPositions + 1
            ELSE
                PUT_STR ( " Truck    " ) ; PUT_NAT ( truck ) ;
                PUT_STR ( " is  not  in  the  loading  zone " ) ;
                NWL ( 1 )
            END
        ELSE
            PUT_STR ( " The  type  of  truck  " ) ;
            PUT_STR ( " is  badly  defined " ) ;
            NWL ( 1 )
        END
    END ;
craneMovement   ≙
    VAR
        relds , crpos , newpos
    IN
        relds ⟵ ReloadTrucks_EMP_SET ;
        IF    relds = TRUE
        THEN
            crpos ⟵ CranePosition_VAL_SET ( 1 ) ;
            IF    crpos ≠ nofPositions
            THEN
                newpos := crpos + 1 ;
                CranePosition_RMV_SET ( crpos ) ;
                CranePosition_ENT_SET ( newpos )
            ELSE
                newpos := 1 ;
                CranePosition_RMV_SET ( crpos ) ;
                CranePosition_ENT_SET ( newpos )
            END
        ELSE
            PUT_STR ( " There  is  some  unloaded  trucks " ) ;
            PUT_STR ( " in  the  current  position " ) ;
            PUT_STR ( " Complete  reloading " ) ;
            PUT_STR ( " in  the  current  position " ) ;
            NWL ( 1 )
        END
    END
END

DEFINITIONS
    TRUCKS  ≙  ℕ₁ ;
    CONTAINERS  ≙  ℕ₁ ;
    maxint  ≙  2147483646 ;
    nofStoringLanes  ≙  nofRailwayTracks + nofStores

END
```

2.6 Conclusions

We have shown that we can perform a whole cycle of software development starting from the informal task description to specification close to implementation within the B-Method. The chosen task, the development of an information system for a container station bookkeeping is not trivial and is solved without known recipes. We started from an informal task description and showed that identifying the key entities of that description a designer can easily develop a data structure. When developing the specification we introduced certain service disciplines and argued that these are vital restrictions in order to minimise the service time of trucks and optimise the crane utilisation.

We captured the requirements of the task description in a stepwise manner. We argued that an attempt to meet all requirements already by the specification step increases the complexity of the task drastically and leads to weaker design decisions. Indeed, in the abstract specification we defined the general structure of the system and resolved questions concerning the crane utilisation and the parking discipline. However, the question of the introduction of fairness was postponed and resolved at a refinement step. We discussed an optimal solution compromising a relative fairness with an optimal crane utilisation.

The implementation machine has some very strong constraints (an absence of state of its own, importing of other machines and so on). When developing the implementation we analysed the influence of these constraints on the development process in our particular case. First, we explained the most non-trivial instantiations of the imported machines in full detail. Next, we demonstrated how to apply the layered design method. We argued that the use of that method allowed us to obtain a more elegant and succinct implementation.

At each stage of the development we pointed out the scope of phenomena that had to be considered in making a certain design decision. We appealed to the standard results in queuing theory when optimising the service discipline. Some insights from human-computer interaction theory were used to define the structure of communication of operators with the information system. We used a well-known method of analysing the possible scenarios to define the entire set of operations. Referring to the layered method we showed that it is indeed an applicable and solid method for software development. For the readers who are inspired by the case treated in this chapter we suggest some further extensions of the task.

In the presented case the emphasis was on the design process rather than on the proof of a logical consistency. However, when developing the system this question was not omitted completely. For the developed specification we obtained 31 proof obligations and only a few of them were not proved automatically. The number of proof obligations for the refinement step increased slightly (34 proof obligations had to be discarded) but the proportion of the automatically proved ones decreased significantly (24 proof obligations were proved automatically). The proof of the correctness of the implementation demanded great efforts. About 400 proof obligations were generated and only half of them were proved automatically. Inspite of the large number of undiscarded proof obligations many of them are rather simple and trivial.

2.7 Exercises

Exercise 2.1 (Fairness of Reloads). When specifying *requiredTruckReloads* we assumed that the reloading procedure takes a negligible amount of time. Hence, the order of the reloads does not influence fairness of truck service.

Specify the operation in such a way that the crane operator will choose the truck to be loaded in a fair manner, so that the truck with the earliest arrival time is loaded before the others. (Hint: it will require an introduction of a variable representing the order of the truck arrivals.)

Exercise 2.2 (Add a Second Crane). The task is extended in such a way that the second crane is added. The goal is to achieve better performance (to minimise the further waiting time of the trucks). Suggest different loading disciplines. Which is the best? Specify the extended task.

Exercise 2.3 (Afternoon Operations). In this chapter the afternoon operations are not considered. Try to extend the given specification to incorporate these operations as well. (Note that the variable *ContainersOnStore* is initialised non-deterministically and should obtain some value as a result of the execution of the afternoon operations).

Exercise 2.4 (Different Types of Containers). Specify the following task extension: there are two different kinds of containers at the container station: large containers and small ones. Every truck can take away either two small containers or one large container. Make corresponding changes in the loading discipline.

Exercise 2.5 (Optimisation as Refinement). The presented abstract specification contains a precise specification of the loading discipline. Develop a more abstract specification at first and then, at a refinement step, introduce an optimisation of the loading procedure.

3. Minimum Spanning Tree

Ranan Fraer [1]

3.1 Introduction

The case studies usually found in the B literature present many of the characteristics common to safety-critical software systems. The successful use of B on such systems, as exemplified by several realistic large-size projects [21, 40], has greatly contributed to increasing the interest of industrial practitioners in formal development techniques.

However, safety-critical case studies drawn from industrial practice have little appeal for computer science researchers and students, as few of them have enough time to invest in understanding the specific issues of a particular safety-critical area. For these reasons we feel that a chapter dedicated to a case study on an algorithmic development would provide additional value for readers with a computer science background.

While avoiding the trap of choosing one of the "over-verified" toy programs (like the factorial, greatest common divisor or quicksort), we focus here on a widely-studied problem arising in graph theory: the finding of a minimum spanning tree in a connected weighted graph. The best-known algorithms for solving this problem, due to Kruskal [45], respectively Prim [71], are covered in most algorithms textbooks.

We have chosen to develop Kruskal's algorithm for its use of non-trivial data structures such as priority queues, implemented as heaps [83], and tree representations of disjoint sets [81]. This should be contrasted with the simple data structures (scalars and arrays) usually employed in safety-critical applications. The complexity there lies rather in the large number of variables and the size of the applications themselves.

The intrinsic difficulty of the algorithms employed (Kruskal's algorithm, Tarjan's Union-Find algorithm and the various heap algorithms) are another source of complexity in our case study. This is rarely an issue in safety-critical applications where one can hardly find some simple loops. Nevertheless, in spite of their "algorithm-free" nature, such applications might exhibit non-trivial control structures in the form of involved state automata.

The structure of this chapter follows the structure of the layered B development: each section introduces the specification of a new layer that is used to build the implementation of the layer above. In Sect. 3.2 we define the minimum spanning

---

[1] Work performed at INRIA Sophia-Antipolis, France.

tree problem, and propose an abstract specification of it in B. Sect. 3.3 presents an informal description of Kruskal's algorithm and its correctness proof. As the implementation of the algorithm becomes too complex to be manageable, we decompose it into two subsystems: one allows to manipulate disjoint sets and the other provides the facilities of a priority queue. The two subsystems are then independently refined to implementable code: Sect. 3.4 traces the stepwise refinement from disjoint sets operations to Tarjan's Union-Find algorithm, while Sect. 3.5 describes the implementation of priority queues as heaps. We conclude in Sect. 3.6 with a discussion on the lessons to learn from this chapter.

3.2 The Minimum Spanning Tree Problem

Consider an undirected connected graph $G = (Nodes, Edges)$ and a weight function associating a positive integer cost to each edge. Given $E \subset Edges$, the subgraph $T = (Nodes, E)$ is a *spanning tree* of G if and only if T is a tree. The total cost associated with such a tree is obtained by summing the weights of all edges belonging to the tree. The minimum spanning tree problem requires a spanning tree minimising the cost function to be found.

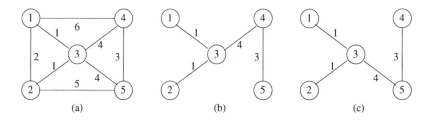

Fig. 3.1. A Sample Graph and its Two Minimum Spanning Trees

The solution of the problem need not necessarily be unique. Consider the graph in Fig. 3.1(a), where

$$Nodes = \{1,2,3,4,5\}$$
$$Edges = \{(1,2),(1,3),(1,4),(2,3),(2,5),(3,4),(3,5),(4,5)\}$$

This graph admits two minimum spanning trees of cost 9, as shown in Fig. 3.1(b) and Fig. 3.1(c).

3.2.1 An Abstract View of a Graph

As the components of the graph will have to be accessed by several modules it is worth encapsulating them into an abstract machine that should be shared by the other modules. We prefer the sharing mechanism provided by the **SEES** clause since it is a full-hiding one, supporting independent refinement of the seen and seeing machines. In our case, this means that the seeing components do not have to depend on a particular representation of the graph, like an adjacency matrix or adjacency lists. Instead of committing from this early stage to such a representation, we shall postpone the choice of the most convenient data structure to the implementation level.

At the specification level we simply model the graph as a finite non-empty set *Nodes*, a relation on this set *Edges* ∈ *Nodes* ↔ *Nodes* and a weight function *weight* ∈ *Edges* → *NAT*. All three components should be declared as abstract constants[2] since they belong to the static part of the specification and they are supposed to be refined in a subsequent implementation. The graph being undirected, we will require that $Edges \cap Edges^{-1} = \{\}$, such that *Edges* contains only one copy of each undirected edge. On the other hand, paths in the graph are better expressed in terms of the "directed" set of edges $All\_Edges = Edges \cup Edges^{-1}$ and the transitive closure of relations. For instance, the connectedness assumption can be simply stated as $All\_Edges^* = Nodes \times Nodes$.

In order to hide completely from the underlying implementation of the graph, some abstract inquiry operations have to be provided. The interface of the machine will thus contain a few primitives to iterate through the edges: the operation *all_unread* declares all edges as unread, *no_more_edges* tests if there are still unread edges and *read_edge* returns the next unread edge together with its weight. All three operations make use of an auxiliary variable *Read* representing the set of already read edges.

The resulting abstract machine, *Weighted_Graph* is presented below. Actually, a complete interface of the graph specification should also include an indexing function mapping *Nodes* to the interval $1 .. n$, where n is the number of nodes of the graph. However, for the sake of simplicity we will identify *Nodes* with $1..n$. This is not necessarily a restriction, as for a non-trivial set of nodes, users of the specification could provide their own indexing function.

MACHINE   *Weighted_Graph*

CONSTANTS   *n , Edges , weight*

DEFINITIONS

$Nodes \; \hat{=} \; 1 .. n$ **;**
$All\_Edges \; \hat{=} \; Edges \cup Edges^{-1}$ **;**
$cost \; \hat{=} \; \lambda E . (E \in \mathbb{P} (Edges) \; | \; \sum edge . (edge \in E \; | \; weight (edge)))$

PROPERTIES

$n \in NAT1 \wedge Edges \in Nodes \leftrightarrow Nodes \wedge weight \in Edges \rightarrow NAT \wedge$
$Edges \cap Edges^{-1} = \{\} \wedge All\_Edges^* = Nodes \times Nodes \wedge$
$\mathsf{card} (Edges) \in NAT \wedge cost (Edges) \in NAT$

---

[2] The **ABSTRACT_CONSTANTS** clause has been recently introduced in the AMN [2]. Although the B-Toolkit does not support this clause yet, it provides an equivalent mechanism of refining constants.

VARIABLES   *Read*

INVARIANT   *Read* $\in \mathbb{P}$ (*Edges*)

INITIALISATION   *Read* := {}

OPERATIONS

 all_unread $\widehat{=}$ *Read* := {} **;**

 b ⟵ *no_more_edges* $\widehat{=}$ *b* := bool (*Read* = *Edges*) **;**

 u , *v* , *w* ⟵ *read_edge* $\widehat{=}$

  PRE   *Read* $\neq$ *Edges*   **THEN**

   ANY   *i* , *j*   **WHERE**

    i $\in$ *Nodes* $\wedge$ *j* $\in$ *Nodes* $\wedge$ (*i* , *j*) $\in$ *Edges* − *Read*

   THEN

    u , *v* , *w* , *Read* := *i* , *j* , *weight* (*i* , *j*) , *Read* $\cup$ { (*i* , *j*) }

   END

  END

END

We will not provide an implementation of this machine here. One could easily imagine how an implementation based on adjacency lists or on an adjacency matrix would look, and how it could be instantiated with the data of a particular graph, like the one presented in Fig. 3.1(a). Alternatively, *Weighted_Graph* might be considered as a basic abstract machine, whose implementation would not be carried out in B, but in a suitable programming language.

Note also that the various integer quantities are constrained to belong to *NAT* or *NAT1*, denoting the intervals $0 .. MAXINT$, respectively $1 .. MAXINT$, where *MAXINT* stands for the largest integer representable on a given architecture. The B-Method ensures that the machine arithmetic is taken into account rather than the infinite set of integers $\mathbb{N}$ in order to ensure that integer values are effectively implementable. This proves to be extremely useful since subtle overflow errors can be easily overlooked in large developments.

3.2.2 Specification of the Minimum Spanning Tree Problem

As a pre-requisite to the specification we have to formalise the notion of the spanning tree. Between the many equivalent definitions of trees, the most suitable for our problem is the one that requires the absence of cycles, and the presence of $n-1$ edges, n being the number of nodes in the graph:

$$Spanning\_Tree \,\widehat{=}\, \{E \mid E \in Forest \wedge \mathsf{card}\,(E) = n-1\}$$

where *Forest* is the set of subsets of edges that induce no cycles. A cycle *C* can be characterised by the property $C^{+} \cap \mathsf{id}(Nodes) \neq \{\}$. Here *C* is considered as a "directed" set of edges, that is a subset of *All_Edges*. Furthermore, in order to avoid fake cycles as $\{(v,u),(v,u)\}$ we will require *C* to contain at most one copy of each undirected edge, that is $C \cap C^{-1} = \{\}$. With these definitions, the minimum spanning tree problem can be formally specified in B by the means of the abstract machine *Min_Spanning_Tree*. Note that we reuse below the definitions of *Nodes*,

All_Edges and *cost* introduced in the machine *Weighted_Graph*. A complete development would require these definitions to be repeated in the current machine.

MACHINE   *Min_Spanning_Tree*

SEES   *Weighted_Graph*

VARIABLES   *Min_Tree*

DEFINITIONS

$\quad$ *Cycle* $\;\widehat{=}\;$ { C | $C \in \mathbb{P}$ (*All_Edges*) $\wedge\; C^{+} \cap$ id (*Nodes*) $\neq$ {}

$\qquad\qquad\qquad \wedge\; C \cap C^{-1} =$ {} } ;

$\quad$ *Forest* $\;\widehat{=}\;$ { E | $E \in \mathbb{P}$ (*Edges*) $\wedge\;$ *Cycle* $\cap\; \mathbb{P}$ ($E \cup E^{-1}$) = {} } ;

$\quad$ *Spanning_Tree* $\;\widehat{=}\;$ { E | $E \in$ *Forest* $\wedge\;$ card (E) = $n - 1$ }

INVARIANT   *Min_Tree* $\in \mathbb{P}$ (*Edges*)

INITIALISATION   *Min_Tree* := {}

OPERATIONS

$\quad$ *min_cost* $\longleftarrow$ *min_spanning_tree* $\widehat{=}$

$\qquad$ **ANY** T **WHERE**

$\qquad\quad$ $T \in$ *Spanning_Tree* $\wedge\;$ *cost* (T) = min (*cost* [*Spanning_Tree*])

$\qquad$ **THEN**

$\qquad\quad$ *Min_Tree* := T $\|$ *min_cost* := *cost* (T)

$\qquad$ **END**

END

The unique operation *min_spanning_tree* is just a simple transliteration of the informal description of our problem: "find a spanning tree minimising the cost function". It is precise enough in describing the "what" of the problem, without giving any hint on the "how" of a possible implementation.

The style of this specification is a generous one: the connectedness assumption guarantees that the graph admits at least a spanning tree. In turn, this ensures the feasibility of *min_spanning_tree*. We will see later that the termination proof of the implementation subtly relies on this property. A defensive specification would omit the connectedness assumption, and require the test to be done inside the *min_spanning_tree* operation:

$\quad$ *connected*, *min_cost* $\longleftarrow$ *min_spanning_tree* $\widehat{=}$

$\qquad$ **ANY**   *ok*, *tree*   **WHERE**

$\qquad\quad$ *ok* $\in$ *BOOL* $\wedge\; T \in \mathbb{P}$ (*Edges*) $\wedge$

$\qquad\quad$ (ok = *TRUE* $\Rightarrow T \in$ *Spanning_Tree* $\wedge\;$ *cost*(T) = min (*cost* [*Spanning_Tree*])) $\wedge$

$\qquad\quad$ (ok = *FALSE* $\Rightarrow$ *All_Edges* $^{*} \neq$ *Nodes* $\times$ *Nodes*)

$\qquad$ **THEN**

$\qquad\quad$ *Min_Tree* := T $\|$ *min_cost* := *cost* (T)

$\qquad$ **END**

As argued in the B-Book [2], generous specifications are more within the constructive spirit of the B-method than defensive ones. However, this is one case where a defensive specification might have been advantageous since connectedness is not that simple to test on the "user's side". Additionally it turns out that Kruskal's algorithm allows this test to be done "for free" internally, while constructing the spanning tree.

When specifying just an algorithm with no meaningful notion of state, a variable-less abstract machine should be preferred. Unfortunately, it is impossible to have both *min_cost* and *Min_Tree* as results returned by *min_spanning_tree*, because *Min_Tree* is a set of edges and not a scalar value. This is due to the definition of refinement requiring refined operations to preserve the signature of their abstract counterparts. As at the implementation level operations can only accept and return scalar values, this constraint is propagated up to the abstract machines.

3.3 Kruskal's Algorithm

3.3.1 A Greedy Strategy

The best-known algorithms for solving the minimum spanning tree problem, due to Kruskal [45] and Prim [71], are based on a greedy strategy. The tree is being built edge by edge, the next edge to be included being chosen by some optimisation criteria. The simplest such criteria would be to choose an edge that results in a minimum increase in the sum of the costs of the edges included so far.

The two algorithms differ in the interpretation of this criteria. Prim's algorithm requires that the set E of edges so far selected forms a tree. Thus, the next edge (u,v) to be included in E, is a minimum cost edge not in E, such that $E \cup \{(u,v)\}$ is also a tree.

On the contrary, Kruskal's algorithm requires only that the set of edges E selected so far form a forest, that it is possible to *complete* into a spanning tree. The edges are considered in nondecreasing order of weight. Thus, the next edge (u,v) to be included in E, is a minimum cost edge not in E, such that no cycle is created by adding (u,v) to E. It is Kruskal's algorithm that we have chosen, due to its manipulation of non trivial data structures such as heaps and tree representation of disjoint sets.

At this point, we are in the position to write down some pseudo-code for the loop described above. This stage in the algorithmic design is closely mirrored in the B development by an early implementation of the abstract machine *Min_Spanning_Tree*:

```
min_cost ⟵ min_spanning_tree    ≘
    VAR    u , v    IN
        Unprocessed := Edges ; E := {} ;
        WHILE    card ( E ) < n − 1    DO
            u , v : ( ( u , v ) ∈ Unprocessed
                ∧ weight ( u , v ) = min ( weight [ Unprocessed ] )) ;
            Unprocessed := Unprocessed − { (u ,v) } ;
            IF    E ∪ { (u , v) } ∈ Forest    THEN
                E := E ∪ { (u ,v )}
            END
        INVARIANT    . . .
        VARIANT    . . .
```

END ;
     min_cost := cost(E)
END

As an example, consider again the graph from Fig. 3.1(a), and suppose that its edges are processed in nondecreasing weight order. In the case of edges of equal weight suppose that $(1,3)$ is processed before $(2,3)$, and $(3,5)$ is processed before $(3,4)$. Then, the sequence of diagrams in Fig. 3.2 illustrates the building of the tree one edge at a time. Note that, in spite of weighing less than $(4,5)$, the edge $(1,2)$ has been rejected at step (c) because of the cycle formed with the already selected edges $(1,3)$ and $(2,3)$.

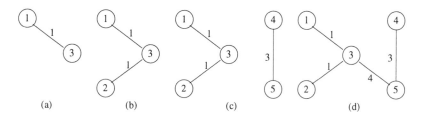

(a)   (b)   (c)   (d)

Fig. 3.2. Successive Stages in Kruskal's Algorithm

3.3.2 Correctness Proof

As we still have to provide an invariant and a variant for the above loop, let us give some insight into the correctness proof of the algorithm. The essential invariant property is that the set of edges E selected so far can be completed into a spanning tree of minimum cost:

$$I_1 \; \hat{=} \; \exists T.(T \in Spanning\_Tree \land E \subset T$$
$$\land \; cost(T) = \min(cost[Spanning\_Tree]))$$

The invariant I_i is verified at the entry of the loop when we have that $E = \{\}$ as $Spanning\_Tree \neq \{\}$ (due to the fact that the graph is connected), so we can choose a spanning tree of minimum cost that will necessarily include E.

Now suppose I_1 to be true before an iteration of the loop and let us prove that it is still true after executing that iteration. The case when the new edge (u,v) introduces a cycle in E is trivial, as E stays unchanged so it can still be completed into a spanning tree of minimum cost. The difficult case is when (u,v) is included in E. If T is a spanning tree of minimum cost containing E, we can again distinguish two cases.

First, if $(u,v) \in T$ then I_1 is again trivially satisfied. Let us consider the second case, when $(u,v) \notin T$. The inclusion of (u,v) in T creates a unique cycle $C \subset T$. But then,

$$I_2 \cong E \in Forest$$

is a second invariant stating that E contains no cycles, so there is at least one edge $(u',v') \in C \setminus E$. It is easy to see that $T' = T \setminus \{(u',v')\} \cup \{(u,v)\}$ is still a spanning tree. It would then be sufficient to prove that $weight(u',v') \geq weight(u,v)$ since this would imply that $cost(T') \leq cost(T)$, so T' itself would be of minimum cost.

As (u,v) is the edge of minimum weight in $Unprocessed$ it would be enough to prove that $(u',v') \in Unprocessed$, or equivalently that $(u',v') \notin Processed$, where $Processed$ is defined as $Edges \setminus Unprocessed$. A simple third invariant states that only processed edges have been selected so far:

$$I_3 \cong E \subset Processed$$

From above we already know that $(u',v') \notin E$. Therefore it remains for us to prove that $(u',v') \notin Processed \setminus E$.

The proof can be completed by considering another invariant property, stating that E is a maximal forest in $\mathbb{P}(Processed)$:

$$I_4 \cong \forall e.(e \in Processed \setminus E \Rightarrow E \cup \{e\} \notin Forest)$$

As $E \cup \{(u',v')\} \subset T$ and T is a spanning tree, we infer that $E \cup \{(u',v')\}$ is necessarily a forest, so from I_4 we obtain that $(u',v') \notin Processed \setminus E$.

Putting all the pieces together we obtain the complete loop invariant:

INVARIANT

$E \in Forest \wedge Unprocessed \in \mathbb{P}(Edges) \wedge E \subseteq Processed \wedge$
$\exists T . (T \in Spanning\_Tree \wedge E \subseteq T \wedge cost(T) = \min(cost[Spanning\_Tree])) \wedge$
$\forall e . (e \in Processed - E \Rightarrow E \cup \{e\} \notin Forest)$

What about the termination proof? A good candidate for the variant of the loop seems to be the number of unprocessed edges $card(Unprocessed)$. It is easy to show that this quantity is strictly decreased at each iteration and that it always stays positive.

A more subtle issue in the termination proof is the partial nature of the min function. More exactly, we are required to prove that $Unprocessed \neq \{\}$ whenever the invariant and the test of the loop, $card(E) < n - 1$, are true. The proof makes use of the invariants I_1 and I_4: suppose that $Unprocessed = \{\}$, then $Processed = Edges$ and from I_4 we infer that E is a maximal forest with respect to inclusion. But according to I_1, E can be completed into a spanning tree, so E itself has to be a spanning tree, which contradicts the fact that E has less than $n - 1$ edges.

It should be noted that indirectly this proof relies on the assumption that the graph is connected. Indeed, this assumption was used to establish that I_1 is satisfied at the entry of the loop. If the graph was not connected, it would have been possible to exhaust $Unproceesed$ before including $n - 1$ edges in E. In this case, a defensive specification should have been used.

3.3.3 Decomposing the Development

This algorithmic refinement of our specification would not be accepted as an implementation in B, because it still uses mathematical notions like sets and relations and abstract operations on them. Further refining of these elements at this stage towards executable code would lead to a much too complicated implementation and make its verification highly expensive.

The *layered development* paradigm proposed by the B method allows the solution of this problem, by breaking a possibly very difficult verification step into a number of smaller and simpler steps. Various structuring mechanisms are provided to decompose a large system description into several subsystems that can be independently refined to implementable code. In our case we can split our development into modules by encapsulating the set variables *Unprocessed* and *E* and the corresponding operations in some abstract machines, and have these machines imported in the implementation.

Further analysis reveals that the variables *E* and *Unprocessed* can be isolated in two different abstract machines. The first one, *Min_Weight_Edge*, will encapsulate the variable *Unprocessed* together with two operations: one for initialising *Unprocessed* to the whole set of edges, and a second for retrieving the minimum weight edge:

MACHINE   *Min_Weight_Edge*

SEES   *Weighted_Graph*

VARIABLES   *Unprocessed*

INVARIANT $Unprocessed \in \mathbb{P}\,(\,Edges\,)$

INITIALISATION $Unprocessed := Edges$

OPERATIONS
   $all\_unprocessed \quad \widehat{=} \quad Unprocessed := Edges$ **;**
   $u\,,v\,,w \longleftarrow min\_weight\_edge \quad \widehat{=}$
      ANY $i\,,j$ **WHERE**
         $i \in Nodes \wedge j \in Nodes \wedge (i\,,j) \in Unprocessed \wedge$
         $weight\,(\,i\,,j\,) = \min\,(\,weight\,[\,Unprocessed\,]\,)$
      THEN
         $Unprocessed\,,u\,,v\,,w := Unprocessed - \{\,(i\,,j)\,\}\,,i\,,j\,,weight\,(i\,,j)$
      END
END

The second abstract machine, *Weighted_Forest*, will encapsulate the variable *E* together with an operation initialising *E* to the empty set, and a "test-and-set" operation that adds an edge *u*,*v* to *E* if no cycle is introduced by this edge. On the other hand, as there is no valid reason to encapsulate the remaining scalar variables, *u*,*v* and *w* we can keep them as local variables at the implementation level. The resulting machine will also have to provide two inquiry operations to retrieve the cardinal and the cost of the set *E*:

MACHINE   *Weighted_Forest*

SEES   *Weighted_Graph*

VARIABLES   *E*

INVARIANT $E \in Forest$

INITIALISATION $E := \{\}$

OPERATIONS

 none_selected $\widehat{=}$ $E := \{\}$ **;**

 add_edge_if_no_cycle(*u* , *v* , *w*) $\widehat{=}$

  PRE

   $u \in Nodes \wedge v \in Nodes \wedge w \in \mathbb{N} \wedge$

   $(u , v) \in Edges - E \wedge w = weight (u , v)$

  THEN

   IF $E \cup \{ (u , v) \} \in Forest$ **THEN**

    $E := E \cup \{ (u , v) \}$

   END

  END **;**

 cnt $\longleftarrow$ *nr_edges* $\widehat{=}$ *cnt* := card (*E*) **;**

 total $\longleftarrow$ *cost_edges* $\widehat{=}$ *total* := *cost*(*E*)

END

The main reason for using a "test-and-set" operation instead of two simpler operations, a "test" one and a "set" one, is that in their implementation, both "set" and "test" would have to call the same "lookup" operation of an imported machine. Merging "set" and "test" into a single operation allows a redundant call of "lookup" to be avoided, which itself is a time-costly operation. Also, note that the "test-and-set" operation is specified in a defensive style by using an **IF** substitution, while a "test" operation would have been specified in a generous style using a **PRE** substitution. This is one of the rare cases where implementation details like efficiency concerns influence the style of the abstract specification.

Now we are able to write a proper implementation of the *Min_Spanning_Tree* machine based on the services provided for us by the two abstract machines *Min_Weight_Edge* and *Weighted_Forest*.

IMPLEMENTATION   *Min_Spanning_Tree_1*

REFINES   *Min_Spanning_Tree*

SEES   *Weighted_Graph*

IMPORTS   *Min_Weight_Edge* , *Weighted_Forest*

DEFINITIONS   *Processed* $\widehat{=}$ *Edges* − *Unprocessed*

INVARIANT   *Min_Tree* = *E*

OPERATIONS

 min_cost $\longleftarrow$ *min_spanning_tree* $\widehat{=}$

  VAR   *u* , *v* , *w* , *c*   **IN**

   all_unprocessed **;** *none_selected* **;** *c* := *0* **;**

   WHILE   *c* < *n* − *1*   **DO**

u , v , w ⟵ min_weight_edge ;
$add\_edge\_if\_no\_cycle$ (u , v , w) ;
c ⟵ nr_edges
INVARIANT
$E \subseteq Processed \land c = \mathsf{card}\ (\ E\ ) \land$
$\exists\ \overline{T}\ .\ (\ T \in Spanning\_Tree \land E \subseteq T$
$\land\ cost\ (\ T\ ) = \mathsf{min}\ (\ cost\ [\ Spanning\_Tree\ ]\ )) \land$
$\forall\ e\ .\ (\ e \in Processed - E \Rightarrow E \cup \{\ e\ \} \notin Forest\ )$
VARIANT $\mathsf{card}\ (\ Unprocessed\ )$
END ;
min_cost ⟵ $cost\_edges$
END

END

One might wonder why the operations *all_unprocessed* and *none_selected*, whose rôle is to initialise the variables *Unproceesed* and *E*, are called here and not in the initialisation of the machine. This is due to the fact that one cannot rely on the initialisation to be executed just before calling *min_spanning_tree*. Indeed, as an operation of an abstract machine, nothing forbids *min_spanning_tree* from being called several times in a row in states satisfying the machine invariant $Min\_Tree \in \mathbb{P}(Edges)$. A rather embarrassing consequence is that subsequent machines in the design would have to provide operations redundant with the initialisations of the respective machines, as it was already the case for *all_unprocessed* and *none_selected*.

The correctness proof of this implementation has already been presented in the previous section. Now, that we have split the initial code into several pieces, we have to make sure that the preconditions of the called operations are satisfied as well. We can regard this as part of the termination proof, and actually we have already established the precondition $Unprocessed \neq \{\}$ of *min_weight_edge* as a termination argument. A second non trivial precondition $(u,v) \in Edges - E$ protects the operation *add_edge_if_no_cycle* and it can be proved from the invariant $E \subseteq Processed$ and the fact that $(u,v) \in Unprocessed$.

Note that some of the invariants of the initial loop, like $E \in Forest$, have now been moved to the invariants of the imported machines where they are simpler to prove. This is part of a general strategy in B, called *design for provability*: establish complex invariants by putting together simple invariants of several modules of the development. The successful application of this strategy is conditioned by a careful design of the architecture of the application, trying to group in the same module variables tightly linked by an invariant, and to separate unrelated variables to different modules, as was the case for *E* and *Unprocessed*.

The structure of the development so far is pictured in Fig. 3.3, where tiling indicates refinement and solid and dashed lines are used to distinguish between **IMPORTS** and **SEES** links. The development will be completed in the next two sections by independently refining the abstract machines *Weighted_Forest* and *Min_Weight_Edge* to the implementable code.

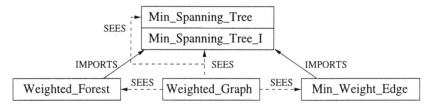

Fig. 3.3. Structure of the Upper Layer of the Development

3.4 The UNION-FIND Algorithm

In this section we propose an implementation of the machine *Weighted_Forest* based on Tarjan's Union-Find algorithm [81]. The various decisions involved in the algorithm will be introduced progressively through a series of stepwise refinements, ensuring in this way a smooth transition from the abstract specification to an executable implementation.

3.4.1 Equivalence Relations

In order to implement the operation *add_edge_if_no_cycle* efficiently, the nodes of the graph should be grouped together in such a way that one may easily determine if the vertices i and j are already connected by the set of edges E selected so far. If they are not, then (i, j) is added to E.

One possible grouping is to place all vertices in the same connected component of E into a set (that would also be a tree, due to the absence of cycles). Then, two vertices are connected if and only if they are in the same set. Mathematically, this can be formalised by defining a partition, or alternatively, an equivalence relation on the set of nodes. While a partition allows the union of two connected components to be expressed easily, an equivalence relation R will be preferred due to the simplicity of the refinement invariant relating it to the set of edges E: $R = (E \cup E^{-1})^*$.

We can then encapsulate R into another abstract machine, *Equivalence*, together with two operations: one setting R to the identity relation, and another "test-and-set" operation that connects two elements if they are not already connected by the relation R. It is still too early to decompose this operation into a "test" operation and a "set" one, for the same efficiency reasons exposed in the previous section.

MACHINE   *Equivalence (n)*

CONSTRAINTS $n \in NAT1$

SEES   *Bool_TYPE*

DEFINITIONS $A \;\widehat{=}\; 1 \,..\, n$

VARIABLES R

INVARIANT

$R \in A \leftrightarrow A \land$
$\mathsf{id}\,(\,A\,) \subseteq R \land$

$R \subseteq R^{-1} \wedge$
$(R \circ R) \subseteq R$

INITIALISATION $R := \text{id}(A)$

OPERATIONS
   $make\_singletons \quad \widehat{=} \quad R := \text{id}(A) ;$
   $b \longleftarrow join\_if\_not\_equivalent(i,j) \quad \widehat{=}$
      PRE $i \in A \wedge j \in A$ **THEN**
        IF $(i,j) \notin R$ **THEN**
          $b := TRUE \parallel R := (R \cup \{(i,j),(j,i)\})^*$
        ELSE
          $b := FALSE$
        END
      END

END

The invariant of the machine states the three defining properties of an equivalence relation: reflexivity, symmetry and transitivity. The consistency proof of this specification requires it to be shown that after each operation R stays an equivalence relation. This comes down to manipulating some algebraic identities on relations. For instance, the proof that $(R \cup \{(i,j),(j,i)\})^*$ is still a symmetric relation goes as follows:

$$((R \cup \{(i,j),(j,i)\})^*)^{-1} \subseteq ((R \cup \{(i,j),(j,i)\})^{-1})^* \subseteq (R \cup \{(i,j),(j,i)\})^*$$

Now we can base the implementation of *Weighted_Forest* on the *Equivalence* machine that we have just introduced. To implement the operations *nr_edges* and *cost_edges* we introduce two implementation variables[3] *count* and *sum* related to the set of edges E by the refinement invariant $count = \text{card}(E) \wedge sum = cost(E)$:

IMPLEMENTATION   *Weighted_Forest_I*

REFINES   *Weighted_Forest*

SEES   *Weighted_Graph*

IMPORTS   *Equivalence* (n)

CONCRETE_VARIABLES   *count , sum*

INVARIANT
   $R = (E \cup E^{-1})^* \wedge$
   $count \in 0 \mathbin{..} \text{card}(Edges) \wedge count = \text{card}(E) \wedge$
   $sum \in 0 \mathbin{..} cost(Edges) \wedge sum = cost(E)$

INITIALISATION
   BEGIN $make\_singletons ; count := 0 ; sum := 0$ **END**

OPERATIONS

---

[3] The **CONCRETE_VARIABLES** clause introduced recently in the B-method [2] avoids the tedium of encapsulating implementation variables into basic abstract machines.

$none\_selected$ $\widehat{=}$
   BEGIN $make\_singletons$ **;** $count := 0$ **;** $sum := 0$ **END ;**
$add\_edge\_if\_no\_cycle(u , v , w)$ $\widehat{=}$
   VAR b **IN**
      $b \longleftarrow join\_if\_not\_equivalent (u , v)$ **;**
      IF $b = TRUE$ **THEN**
         $count := count + 1$ **;** $sum := sum + w$
      END
   END ;
$cnt \longleftarrow nr\_edges$ $\widehat{=}$ $cnt := count$ **;**
$total \longleftarrow value\_sum$ $\widehat{=}$ $total := sum$
END

The refinement proof associated to this implementation will show that, assuming the refinement invariant $R = (E \cup E^{-1})^*$, the tests of the two conditionals $E \cup \{(u,v)\} \in Forest$ and $(u,v) \notin R$ are equivalent, and also that the new values of E and R are still related by the refinement invariant:

$$(R \cup \{(u,v),(v,u)\})^* = (E \cup \{(u,v)\} \cup (E \cup \{(u,v)\})^{-1})^*$$

When we want to prove that sum and $count$ are correctly updated inside the $join\_if\_not\_equivalent$ we rely on the precondition of the abstract operation which ensures that $(u,v) \in Edges - E$.

3.4.2 Representatives of Equivalence Classes

Now we can proceed further with the refinement of $Equivalence$. The next step in the direction of Tarjan's Union-Find algorithm is to consider a representative of each connected set, by introducing a total function $repr \in A \to A$. The refinement invariant will state that two elements are equivalent if and only if they have the same representative:

$$R = \{x,y \mid x \in A \land y \in A \land repr(x) = repr(y)\}$$

Let also $class(r) \widehat{=} repr^{-1}[\{r\}]$ denote the class of equivalence of r. When implementing the operation $join\_if\_not\_equivalent$ one would have to make a non-deterministic choice between mapping all the elements of the class of ri to rj or the other way around. At this stage we do not want to be more specific on this issue but, as we will see later, a choice based on efficiency concerns will be made at the implementation level.

A new abstract machine $Representatives$ is introduced in order to encapsulate the $repr$ function and its abstract operations, as shown below. Besides the initialisation of all sets as singletons, we need one operation for retrieving the representative of an element and another one for computing the union of two classes when knowing their representatives:

MACHINE $Representatives (n)$
CONSTRAINTS $n \in NAT1$
VARIABLES $repr$

DEFINITIONS

$A \ \widehat{=} \ 1..n$;
$Representatives \ \widehat{=} \ \mathsf{ran}\,(\,repr\,)$;
$class(\,r\,) \ \widehat{=} \ repr^{-1}\,[\,\{\,r\,\}\,]$

INVARIANT

$repr \in A \rightarrow A \wedge Representatives \lhd repr = \mathsf{id}\,(\,Representatives\,)$;

INITIALISATION $repr := \mathsf{id}\,(\,A\,)$

OPERATIONS

$make\_singletons \ \widehat{=} \ repr := \mathsf{id}\,(\,A\,)$;
$ri \longleftarrow find\_repr(\,i\,) \ \widehat{=}$
    PRE $i \in A$ **THEN** $ri := repr\,(\,i\,)$ **END** ;
$union\_sets(\,ri\,,\,rj\,) \ \widehat{=}$
    PRE $ri \in Representatives \wedge rj \in Representatives \wedge ri \neq rj$ **THEN**
        $repr := repr \nleftarrow class\,(\,ri\,) \times \{\,rj\,\}$ [] $repr := repr \nleftarrow class\,(\,rj\,) \times \{\,ri\,\}$
    END

    END

The invariant $Representatives \lhd repr = \mathsf{id}(Representatives)$ ensures that each
representative is mapped to itself by the $repr$ function. When proving that $union\_sets$
preserves this invariant, we distinguish two cases corresponding to the two branches
in the non-deterministic choice. As the two proofs are similar we will present only
the case where the new value of $repr$ is $repr' = repr \nleftarrow class(rj) \times \{ri\}$. In this case,
$ran(repr') = ran(repr) - \{rj\}$ so rj is not a representative anymore. The proof is
completed by remarking that all the other representatives are still mapped to themselves.

The precondition of the operation $union\_sets$, stating that its arguments should
be two different representatives, eliminates the need for an internal **IF** test. So it is
only at this stage that we are able to split the "test-and-set" operation into a "test"
one and a "set" one. An implementation of $Equivalence$, importing the previously
introduced $Representatives$ machine, follows below:

IMPLEMENTATION $Equivalence\_I$

REFINES $Equivalence$

SEES $Bool\_TYPE$

IMPORTS $Representatives\,(\,n\,)$

PROMOTES $make\_singletons$

INVARIANT $R = \{\,x\,,\,y \ | \ x \in A \wedge y \in A \wedge repr\,(\,x\,) = repr\,(\,y\,)\,\}$

OPERATIONS

$b \longleftarrow join\_if\_not\_equivalent(\,ii\,,\,jj\,) \ \widehat{=}$
    VAR $ri\,,\,rj$ **IN**
        $ri \longleftarrow find\_repr\,(\,ii\,)$; $rj \longleftarrow find\_repr\,(\,jj\,)$;
        IF $ri \neq rj$ **THEN**
            $union\_sets\,(\,ri\,,\,rj\,)$; $b := TRUE$
        ELSE

$$b := FALSE$$
> **END**
> **END**

END

When proving the refinement we need to show that the two tests $(i,j) \notin R$ and $repr(i) \neq repr(j)$ are equivalent, which is just a reformulation of the refinement invariant. Another proof obligation is

$$(R \cup \{(i,j),(j,i)\})^* = \{(x,y) \mid repr'(x) = repr'(y)\}$$

where $repr'$ denotes $repr \mathbin{\lhd\mkern-9mu-} class(rj) \times \{ri\}$. The proof of this property relies on the fact that only two cases are possible. First, if x and y were in the same class induced by R, then they are still mapped to the same representative by $repr'$. In the second case, x may be in the class of i and y in the class of j or vice versa, so both will share ri as a common representative.

3.4.3 Tree Representation of Disjoint Sets

The essential idea behind Tarjan's Union-Find algorithm is that mapping all the members of the class of ri to rj might be too costly, so instead one could map only ri to rj and let all the elements from the class of ri implicitly inherit rj as representative.

This leads us naturally to a tree representation of each connected set, such that the representative of an element is given by the root of the tree to which it belongs. More precisely, we introduce a *parent* function mapping every non-root element to its parent in the tree. To avoid mapping the roots to some error element, we can declare *parent* as a partial function.

The refinement invariant relating *repr* and *parent* needs to state that *repr* is obtained by iterating *parent* until reaching a root element. If

$$roots \mathrel{\widehat{=}} A - \mathrm{dom}(parent)$$
$$ancestors(i) \mathrel{\widehat{=}} parent^*[\{i\}]$$

where *roots* denotes the set of elements where *parent* is undefined and $ancestors(i)$ denotes the set of nodes that can be reached from i following *parent* links, then *repr* maps each node i to an ri such that $ri \in roots \cap ancestors(i)$.

Two more optimisations, *path compression* and *weight balancing* have been proposed by Tarjan in order to obtain an almost linear time complexity. At this development layer we shall consider only path compression as it requires only algorithmic refinement. Weight balancing deals with data refinement, as it requires another change of variable, and will be introduced in the final implementation.

The idea behind the first optimisation is to compress systematically the paths to the root of the elements examined at each *find_repr* operation. More exactly, after performing *find_repr(i)*, for every node j on the path from i to its root ri, ri should be set as the direct parent of j. Formally, this can be expressed as *parent* := $parent \mathbin{\lhd\mkern-9mu-} (ancestors(i) - \{ri\}) \times \{ri\}$.

When encapsulating *parent* into a new abstract machine, *Union_Find* one might choose to include the optimisation above as part of the *find_root* operation, or to make it available in the interface as an operation on its own. The second solution proves to be more flexible, since it lets the user decide whether it is worthwhile to perform path compression, depending on the ratio between the number of *union_sets* and *find_repr* operations. The resulting abstract machine is:

MACHINE   *Union_Find (n)*

CONSTRAINTS $n \in 1 .. MaxScalar$

VARIABLES   *parent*

DEFINITIONS

> $A \; \widehat{=} \; 1..n$;
> $roots \; \widehat{=} \; A - \mathsf{dom} \, (\, parent \,)$;
> $ancestors \, (i) \; \widehat{=} \; parent^{*} \, [\, \{ \, i \, \} \,]$;
> $descendants \, (i) \; \widehat{=} \; (parent^{-1})^{*} \, [\, \{ \, i \, \} \,]$

INVARIANT

> $parent \in A \rightarrowtail A \land parent^{+} \cap \mathsf{id} \, (\, A \,) = \{ \}$

INITIALISATION $parent := \{ \}$

OPERATIONS

> $make\_singletons \; \widehat{=} \; parent := \{ \}$;
> $ri \longleftarrow find\_root(\, i \,) \; \widehat{=}$
> > **PRE** $i \in A$ **THEN** $ri :\in ancestors \, (\, i \,) \cap roots$ **END** ;
> $compress\_path(\, i \,, ri \,) \; \widehat{=}$
> > **PRE** $i \in A \land ri \in ancestors \, (\, i \,) \cap roots$ **THEN**
> > > $parent := parent \lhdminus (ancestors \, (\, i \,) - \{ \, ri \, \}) \times \{ \, ri \, \}$
> > **END** ;
> $union\_sets(\, ri \,, rj \,) \; \widehat{=}$
> > **PRE** $ri \in roots \land rj \in roots \land ri \neq rj$ **THEN**
> > > $parent \, (\, ri \,) := rj \quad [] \quad parent \, (\, rj \,) := ri$
> > **END**
> **END**

The invariant $parent^{+} \cap \mathsf{id}(A) = \{ \}$ states that *parent* is really a tree representation as it induces no cycle. As we shall see later, this property ensures in turn the feasibility of the *find_root* operation, since from every node one can follow upwards only a finite number of *parent* links.

The invariant is trivially preserved by the operation *find_root* as it does not modify the *parent* function. In the case of *compress_path*, let

$$parent1 = parent \lhdminus (ancestors(i) - \{ri\}) \times \{ri\}$$

denote the new parent function. From $(ancestors(i) - \{ri\}) \times \{ri\} \subseteq parent^{+}$, we can infer that $parent1^{+} \subseteq parent^{+}$, which implies that $parent1^{+} \cap \mathsf{id}(A) = \{ \}$. To prove that *union_sets* preserves the invariant of the machine, note that making rj the parent of ri cannot induce a cycle. Otherwise this cycle would necessarily include the link $ri \mapsto rj$, but could not go further because rj itself has no parent.

Now we can base the implementation of the abstract machine *Representatives* on the machine *Union_Find*, by promoting the operations *make_singletons* and *union_sets* and refining *find_repr* as a call to *find_root* followed by a call to *compress_path*:

IMPLEMENTATION   *Representatives_I*

REFINES   *Representatives*

IMPORTS   *Union_Find (n)*

PROMOTES   *make_singletons , union_sets*

INVARIANT

  $repr = \{ i , ri \mid i \in A \land ri \in A \land ri \in ancestors (i) \cap roots \}$

OPERATIONS

  $ri \longleftarrow find\_repr(i)$ $\widehat{=}$
    BEGIN
      $ri \longleftarrow find\_root (ri) ; compress\_path (i , ri)$
    END

END

The refinement invariant makes it obvious that *find_root* returns the correct *ri*. On the other hand the modification of *parent* performed by *compress_path* keeps the *repr* function unchanged as all the nodes on the path from *i* to *ri* remain in the same tree of root *ri*.

The refinement proof for the *union_sets* operation consists of two parts. First, the refinement weakens the precondition of the abstract operation, since we have that *Representatives* $\subseteq$ *roots* (in fact the two sets are equal, as follows from the refinement invariant). Second, $class(ri)$ is equal to $descendants(ri)$, the set of nodes in the tree of root *ri*, so making *rj* the parent of *ri* is equivalent to moving the elements in $class(ri)$ to $class(rj)$, and this is exactly the meaning of $repr := repr < + class(ri) \times \{rj\}$.

3.4.4 Weight Balancing

The algorithm described above has bad worst-case performance because the trees formed could be degenerate. In order to avoid this, a second optimisation tries to balance the trees created by *union_sets* operations. When a tree rooted at *ri* is to be merged with a tree rooted at *rj* it makes sense to choose as a new root the node with more descendants.

To illustrate the way this optimisation is applied, we present in Fig. 3.4 the successive stages in the Union-Find algorithm, when applying *union_sets* for each of the edges introduced in Fig. 3.2. Weight balancing is applied here at steps c) and e), while at steps b) and d) the merged trees have the same number of descendants. Note as well that due to the reduced size of the example, path compression plays no role here, as it is only after the last step that we have a tree of depth 2.

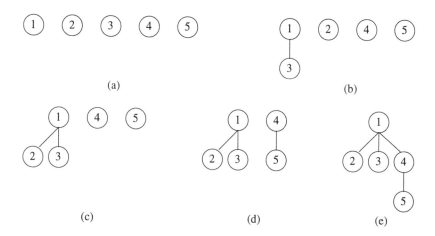

Fig. 3.4. Intermediate Stages in the Union-Find Algorithm

Weight balancing is easily implemented by maintaining the size of each tree (number of descendants of the root) as the *parent* of a root. This value should be encoded as a negative number so that the root node can be detected when travelling up the tree.

Calling *father* the new function, let us define its positive part as

$$pos \;\widehat{=}\; father \rhd 1..n$$

the function obtained by restricting *father*'s range to positive values. In the same way, define the negative part of father as

$$neg \;\widehat{=}\; father \rhd -n..-1$$

Let also

$$descendants(i) \;\widehat{=}\; (parent^{*})^{-1}[\{i\}]$$

denote the set of elements in the subtree of root i, as defined in the *Union_Find* machine. Then the refinement invariant will state that $pos = parent$ and moreover, that $neg = \lambda i.(i \in roots \,|\, -card(descendants(i)))$.

IMPLEMENTATION   *Union_Find_I*

REFINES   *Union_Find*

CONCRETE_VARIABLES   *father*

DEFINITIONS

$pos \;\widehat{=}\; father \rhd 1..n \,;$
$neg \;\widehat{=}\; father \rhd -n..1 \,;$
$singleton\_trees \;\widehat{=}\;$
    VAR i **IN**
      $i := 0 \,;$

```
        WHILE    i < n   DO
            i := i + 1 ; father ( i ) := −1
        INVARIANT
            i ∈ 0 .. n ∧ 1 .. i ◁ father = ( 1 .. i ) × { − 1 }
        VARIANT    n − i
        END
    END
```

INVARIANT

father ∈ 1 .. n → − n .. n ∧
pos = parent ∧
neg = λ i . (i ∈ roots | − card (descendants (i)))

INITIALISATION   singleton_trees

OPERATIONS

make_singletons   ≙   singleton_trees ;

ri ⟵ find_root(i)   ≙
```
    BEGIN
        ri := i ;
        WHILE    father ( ri ) > 0    DO
            ri := father ( ri )
        INVARIANT
            ri ∈ ancestors ( i ) ∧ pos = parent ∧
            neg = λ i . ( i ∈ roots  |  − card ( descendants ( i ) ) )
        VARIANT    card ( ancestors ( ri ) )
        END
    END ;
```

compress_path(i , ri)   ≙
```
    VAR    j , dad    IN
        j := i ; dad := father ( j ) ;
        WHILE    dad > 0    DO
            father ( j ) := ri ; j := dad ; dad := father ( j )
        INVARIANT
            j ∈ ancestors ( i ) ∧ dad = father ( j ) ∧
            pos = parent ◁ ( ancestors ( i ) − ancestors ( j ) ) × { ri } ∧
            neg = λ i . ( i ∈ roots  |  − card ( descendants ( i ) ) )
        VARIANT    card ( ancestors ( j ) )
        END
    END ;
```

union_sets(ri , rj)   ≙
```
    VAR    sum    IN
        sum := father ( ri ) + father ( rj ) ;
        IF    father ( ri ) < father ( rj )    THEN
            father ( rj ) := ri ; father ( ri ) := sum
        ELSE
            father ( ri ) := rj ; father ( rj ) := sum
        END
    END
```

END

The initialisation consists of a bounded loop which sets each array element of *father* to -1. This corresponds to having each element forming a tree on its own. The invariant and variant of the loop are trivial ones.

The implementation of the *find_root* operation computes *ri* by going up from *i* following the *father* links. As this pass does not modify *father* the corresponding loop invariant includes the still valid refinement invariant together with the fact that the current node is an ancestor of *i*. From this property and the fact that at the exit of the loop $ri \in roots$ (since $father(ri) < 0$) we infer that the final value of *ri* is in $ancestors(i) \cap roots$. We conclude that the computation of *ri* is correctly implemented by this loop.

The operation *compress_path* performs a second pass on the path from *i* to *ri*, setting *ri* as a direct father of all the nodes encountered on the way. The invariant of the loop states that the negative part of *father* is unchanged and that the nodes from *i* to *j* examined so far have been already adopted as direct sons of *ri*. When entering the loop, $ancestors(j) = ancestors(i)$, so the invariant is trivially true. At the exit of the loop $j = ri$ so $ancestors(j) = \{ri\}$, which proves that this is a valid implementation of the abstract operation.

The termination proof of both loops uses as variant the number of ancestors of the current node. This quantity is strictly decreased when following *father* links because *father* induces no cycle: $father^+ \cap id(1..n) = \{\}$. This property follows easily from the refinement invariant as *parent* itself induces no cycle.

Finally, weight balancing is implemented in the operation *union_sets* by comparing $father(ri)$ with $father(rj)$ (considering that both are negative numbers) and setting $father(ri) + father(rj)$ as the count field of the "winning" root. One can easily verify that both *pos* and *neg* are correctly updated, according to the refinement invariant.

A global overview of this section is given in Fig. 3.5, picturing all the steps in the refinement from *Weighted_Forest* to *Union_Find_1*.

3.5 Heap Algorithms

At this point, we still have to complete a last branch in the refinement tree (see Fig. 3.3): the implementation of the machine *Min_Weight_Edge*. We are looking here for a data structure allowing the insertion of elements into a set and also the finding and deletion of the smallest element of the set. A data structure providing for these two operations is called a *priority queue*. In this section we show how to implement *Min_Weight_Edge* as a priority queue and also use heaps [83] as an efficient implementation of priority queues.

3.5.1 Priority Queues

Actually, the *min_weight_edge* operation is required to return not only the minimum weight but also the edge for which this minimum is reached. For this reason, the

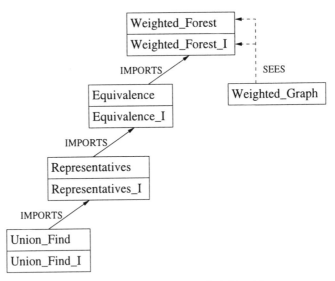

Fig. 3.5. The Refinement Path Leading to the Union-Find Algorithm

specification of priority queues will consider a function $valq : Queue \rightarrow NAT$ instead of a set. This constraint will also be reflected at the implementation level, as one would have to move around the indexes in the set *Queue* rather than the values themselves.

The indexes in the set *Queue* will be drawn from the interval $1 \mathinner{.\,.} m$ where m is a parameter of the specification representing the maximal size of the priority queue. Actually, this makes *valq* a partial function on $1 \mathinner{.\,.} m$. The insertion and deletion of elements in the queue will extend, respectively restrict, *valq* and its domain *Queue*, thus preserving the invariant $valq : Queue \rightarrow NAT$. These operations can be elegantly expressed with primitives like domain overriding ($\lhd$) and codomain restriction ($\vartriangleleft$):

MACHINE   *Priority_Queue (m)*

CONSTRAINTS $m \in NAT1$

VARIABLES   *Queue , valq*

INVARIANT $Queue \in \mathbb{P} \, (\, 1 \mathinner{.\,.} m \,) \wedge valq \in Queue \rightarrow NAT$

INITIALISATION $Queue := \{\} \parallel valq := \{\}$

OPERATIONS
    empty_queue $\widehat{=}$ $Queue := \{\} \parallel valq := \{\}$;
    insert_queue(k , w) $\widehat{=}$
        PRE $k \in (\, 1 \mathinner{.\,.} m \,) - Queue \wedge w \in NAT$ **THEN**
            $Queue := Queue \cup \{ \, k \, \} \parallel valq \, (\, k \,) := w$
        END ;
    $k , w \longleftarrow remove\_queue$ $\widehat{=}$
        PRE $Queue \neq \{\}$ **THEN**

ANY i **WHERE** $i \in Queue \land valq\,(\,i\,) = \mathsf{min}\,(\,\mathsf{ran}\,(\,valq\,)\,)$ **THEN**
    $k := i \;\|\; w := valq\,(\,i\,) \;\|$
    $Queue := Queue - \{\,k\,\} \;\|\; valq := \{\,i\,\} \lhd valq$
  END
 END

END

We have preferred to introduce *Queue* as a variable instead of a definition $Queue \,\widehat{=}\, \mathsf{dom}(valq)$. This makes the specification more readable as *Queue* has an interesting meaning on its own. Although it might seem inconvenient to state explicitly how *Queue* is updated by each operation, one should note that in the case of a definition both the "specifier" and the "prover" would have to redo this work anyway.

In order to reduce the problem of finding a minimum weight edge to the more general one of implementing a priority queue, we have to abstract from the particular nature of the set of edges. This can be achieved by decomposing the function $weight \in Edges \to NAT$ into the three functions: $node1, node2 \in 1..m \to Nodes$ and $valq \in 1..m \to NAT$, where $m = \mathsf{card}(Edges)$, such that the direct product $nodes = node1 \otimes node2$ is a bijection, $nodes \in 1..m \rightarrowtail Edges$, and $valq$ "mirrors" $weight$ on $1..m$: $valq = weight \circ nodes$.

An implementation of *Min_Weight_Edge* based on this representation is given below. The iteration primitives provided in the interface of the abstract machine *Weighted_Graph* are used in *all_unprocessed* to read the edges one by one. Adding a new edge requires the insertion of a new value in each of the three functions. The operation *min_weight_edge* returns the edge $(node1(k), node2(k))$ and its weight w, where k and w are the results returned by the call of *remove_queue*.

IMPLEMENTATION   *Min_Weight_Edge_I*

REFINES   *Min_Weight_Edge*

IMPORTS   *Weighted_Graph* , *Priority_Queue* (m)

CONCRETE_VARIABLES   *node1, node2*

DEFINITIONS
  $m \;\widehat{=}\; \mathsf{card}\,(\,Edges\,)$ **;**
  $nodes \;\widehat{=}\; node1 \otimes node2$ **;**
  read_edges $\;\widehat{=}\;$
  VAR k, b, u, v, w **IN**
    all_unread **;** *empty_queue* **;** $k := 0$ **;** $b \longleftarrow$ *no_more_edges* **;**
    WHILE $b = FALSE$ **DO**
      $k := k + 1$ **;** $u, v, w \longleftarrow$ *read_edge* **;** $b \longleftarrow$ *no_more_edges* **;**
      insert_queue (k, w) **;** *node1* (k) := u **;** *node2* (k) := v
    INVARIANT
      $k \in 0..m \land Queue = 1..k \,\land$
      $Queue \lhd nodes \in Queue \rightarrowtail Read \,\land$
      $valq = Queue \lhd (\,weight \circ nodes\,) \,\land$
      $(b = TRUE \Leftrightarrow Read = Edges)$
    VARIANT $m - k$
    END

END

INVARIANT

$node1 \in 1 .. m \rightarrow Nodes \wedge node2 \in 1 .. m \rightarrow Nodes \wedge$
$nodes \in 1 .. m \twoheadrightarrow Edges \wedge$
$valq = Queue \lhd (weight \circ nodes) \wedge$
$Unprocessed = nodes [Queue]$

INITIALISATION $read\_edges$

OPERATIONS

$all\_unprocessed \quad \widehat{=} \quad read\_edges \; ;$
$u , v , w \longleftarrow min\_weight\_edge \quad \widehat{=}$
    VAR k **IN**
        $k , w \longleftarrow remove\_queue \; ; u := node1 (k) \; ; v := node2 (k)$
    END

END

Note that *Weighted_Graph* is imported here and not seen, as we need more than read-only access to its components. However, this is the only place where this machine is imported, such that we satisfy the constraint required for a machine that is seen to be imported at most once somewhere in the development.

3.5.2 Indirect Heaps

Several approaches could be taken to implement a priority queue. We might first consider using an unordered list since inserting new elements would take constant time. But finding the smallest element would necessitate a scan of the entire list. A second suggestion would be to use a sorted list which is stored sequentially. This would allow the retrieval the smallest element in constant time, but an insertion could require moving all the elements in the list.

What we want is a data structure allowing both operations to be performed efficiently. A *heap* [83] is a tree with the property that the value at each node is guaranteed to be smaller than the values of the nodes below it. In this representation it is possible to perform insertions and deletions in logarithmic time (in the size of the heap).

The definition of the heap implies that the smallest value is at the root of the tree. After removing this value, the others have to be moved around in order to reestablish the heap property. In the same way, inserting a new value into an already existing heap, can be performed by moving this value until it reaches a position satisfying the heap property.

As we have anticipated in the previous section, we will not move around the values of *valq* but the indexes of *Queue*, which means that we will actually use an indirect heap. The idea of arranging the nodes in *Queue* to form a tree can be formalised by requiring an one-to-one correspondence between *Queue* and a finite set *Heap* of positions in the tree.

We will then refine *Queue* and *valq* by two new variables *Index* and *valh* with the trivial refinement invariant $Queue = Index \wedge valq = valh$. We will also introduce two other refinement variables *Heap* and *indh* such that $Heap \in \mathbb{P}(1..m)$ and *indh* is a bijective function: $indh \in Heap \rightarrowtail\!\!\!\rightarrow Index$.

As taking into account the tree structure will even further complicate the specification, we encapsulate the four variables above into a machine on its own, *Heap_Data*, and later include this machine in the complete heap specification. We have here again another example of *design for provability* as the invariants relating the four variables will be proved locally in *Heap_Data* and reused at the global level.

MACHINE   *Heap_Data (m)*

CONSTRAINTS $m \in NAT1$

DEFINITIONS $A \,\,\hat{=}\,\, 1..m$

VARIABLES   *Heap , Index , valh , indh*

INVARIANT

$Heap \in \mathbb{P}(A) \wedge Index \in \mathbb{P}(A) \wedge$
$indh \in Heap \rightarrowtail\!\!\!\rightarrow Index \wedge valh \in Index \rightarrow NAT$

INITIALISATION $Heap , Index , valh , indh := \{\} , \{\} , \{\} , \{\}$

OPERATIONS

 $emptyh \,\,\hat{=}\,\,\,\, Heap , Index , valh , indh := \{\} , \{\} , \{\} , \{\}$;
 $swap(i , j) \,\,\hat{=}$
  PRE $i \in Heap \wedge j \in Heap$ **THEN**
   $indh := indh \triangleleft\!\!- \{ i \mapsto indh (j) , j \mapsto indh (i) \}$
  END ;
 $inserth(k , w , node) \,\,\hat{=}$
  PRE $k \in A - Index \wedge w \in NAT \wedge node \in A - Heap$ **THEN**
   $Heap := Heap \cup \{ node \} \,\,\|\,\, indh (node) := k \,\,\|$
   $Index := Index \cup \{ k \} \,\,\|\,\, valh (k) := w$
  END ;
 $copy\_and\_remove(root , leaf) \,\,\hat{=}$
  PRE $root \in Heap \wedge leaf \in Heap$ **THEN**
   $Heap := Heap - \{ leaf \} \,\,\|$
   $indh := \{ leaf \} \triangleleft\!\!- (indh \triangleleft\!\!- \{ root \mapsto indh (leaf) \}) \,\,\|$
   $Index := Index - \{ indh (root) \} \,\,\|\,\, valh := \{ indh (root) \} \triangleleft\!\!- valh$
  END

END

As suggested by its name, *Heap_Data* contains the data manipulated by the heap, together with the various operations on this data. Unlike the other operations, *copy_and_remove* might look out of place in this interface. However, a simple *copy* operation would have violated the invariant $indh \in Heap \rightarrowtail\!\!\!\rightarrow Index$. Also, a simple *remove* operation with an arbitrary argument would have been too difficult to implement. As it will turn out later, removal is simple only for a particular leaf. The consistency proof of the *Heap_Data* machine being similar in many respects to that of *Priority_Queue*, we will not further insist on it.

Note that the value of *valh* that occurs at a tree position i is $valh(indh(i))$. This composition of functions will be used so often that it is useful to declare an abbreviation $key \mathrel{\widehat{=}} valh \circ indh$. Since $swap$ exchanges $indh(i)$ and $indh(j)$ without modifying $valh$, it has the indirect effect of exchanging $key(i)$ and $key(j)$. We can think of $swap$ as an exchange operation for the abstract array key as in the case of an usual heap and not an indirect one.

Now we can move to the complete heap specification by introducing the underlying tree structure in the form of a distinguished node $root \in A$ and a function $father \in A - \{root\} \to A$ mapping each other node to its parent in the tree. Both $father$ and $root$ will be declared as constants since they are not supposed to be modified by the heap operations. A convenient formulation of the tree property is $descendants(root) = A$, where $descendants(i) \mathrel{\widehat{=}} (father^{-1})^*[\{i\}]$ since it implies that there is one path from each node to the root. Together with the heap property which states that the values of key decrease on each ascending path, this guarantees that the minimum value will be reached in the root of the tree.

The heap property on a set S of positions in the heap can be expressed as:

$$heap(S) \mathrel{\widehat{=}} \forall (i, j).(i \in S \land j \in S \land (i, j) \in father^+ \Rightarrow key(i) \le key(j))$$

This formalisation relates arbitrarily distant positions in S. An alternative is to focus on the relationship between a node and its immediate neighbours. Suppose we define:

$$upgood(i) \mathrel{\widehat{=}} i \ne root \Rightarrow key(father(i)) > key(i)$$
$$downgood(i) \mathrel{\widehat{=}} sons(i) \ne \{\} \Rightarrow key(i) > \min(key[sons(i)])$$

where $sons(i)$ stands for $father^{-1}[\{i\}]$. Then, the following properties hold:

$$heap(A) \Leftrightarrow \forall i.(i \in A \Rightarrow upgood(i) \land downgood(i))$$
$$heap(A - \{hole\}) \land upgood(hole) \land downgood(hole) \Rightarrow heap(A)$$

The second property, where A stands for $1 .. m$, gives a sufficient condition for fixing a "hole" violating the heap property. Such a hole can appear when inserting or deleting a node from the tree, and can be removed by swapping it with a neighbouring position, as explained below.

A hole in the heap, would necessarily satisfy $upgood$ or $downgood$:

$$heap(A - \{hole\}) \Rightarrow upgood(hole) \lor downgood(hole)$$

Suppose that it satisfies $downgood$. If $upgood$ is also satisfied, then the hole vanishes. Otherwise we can move the hole upwards by swapping it with its father. Then one can prove that the new hole obtained by $hole := father(hole)$ still satisfies $heap(A - \{hole\}) \land downgood(hole)$. Thus we can repeatedly move the hole along an upward path until it vanishes.

Now, suppose we have a hole that satisfies $upgood$. If $downgood$ is also satisfied, then the hole vanishes. Otherwise we can move the hole downwards by swapping it with one of its children $son \in sons(hole)$ such that the condition $key(son) = \min(key[sons(hole)])$ holds. The new hole obtained by $hole := son$ still satisfies the condition $heap(A - \{hole\}) \land upgood(hole)$. Thus we can repeatedly move the hole along an downward path until it vanishes.

This reasoning leads to the following heap specification:

MACHINE   *Indirect_Heap (m)*

CONSTRAINTS   *m* ∈ *NAT1*

SEES   *Bool_TYPE*

INCLUDES   *Heap_Data (m)*

ABSTRACT_CONSTANTS   *root , father*

PROPERTIES

root ∈ *A* ∧ *father* ∈ *A* − { *root* } → *A* ∧
descendants (*father*) = *A*

VARIABLES   *hole*

DEFINITIONS

sons (*i*) ≙ *father* $^{-1}$ [{ *i* }] **;**
descendants (*i*) ≙ (*father* $^{-1}$) * [{ *i* }] **;**
ancestors (*i*) ≙ *father* * [{ *i* }] **;**
key ≙ *valh* ∘ *indh*) **;**
upgood (*i*) ≙ *i* ≠ *root* ⇒ *key* (*father* (*i*)) > *key* (*i*) **;**
downgood (*i*) ≙ *sons* (*i*) ≠ {} ⇒ *key* (*i*) > min (*key* [*sons* (*i*)]) **;**
heap (*S*) ≙ ∀ (*i* , *j*) . (*i* ∈ *S* ∧ *j* ∈ *S* ∧ (*i* , *j*) ∈ *father* $^{+}$ ⇒ *key* (*i*) ≤ *key* (*j*))

INVARIANT

hole ∈ *A* ∧ (*Heap* ≠ {} ⇒ *hole* ∈ *Heap*) ∧
heap(*Heap* − { *hole* })

INITIALISATION   *hole* := *root*

OPERATIONS

empty_heap ≙ **BEGIN**   *emptyh* ∥ *hole* := *root*   **END ;**
insert_heap(*k* , *w*) ≙
    PRE   *k* ∈ *A* − *Index* ∧ *w* ∈ *NAT* ∧ *heap*(*Heap*)   **THEN**
        ANY   *new*   **WHERE**
        new ∈ *A* − *Heap* ∧
        (*Heap* ≠ {} ⇒ *father* (*new*) ∈ *Heap*) ∧
        (*Heap* = {} ⇒ *new* = *root*)
        THEN
        inserth (*k* , *w* , *new*) ∥ *hole* := *new*
        END
    END ;
bb ⟵ *higher* ≙ *bb* := bool (¬ *upgood* (*hole*)) **;**
up_heap ≙
    PRE   ¬ *upgood* (*hole*)   **THEN**
    swap (*hole* , *father* (*hole*)) ∥ *hole* := *father* (*hole*)
    END ;
k , *w* ⟵ *remove_heap* ≙
    PRE   *Heap* ≠ {} ∧ *heap*(*Heap*)   **THEN**
    k := *indh* (*root*) ∥ *w* := *key* (*root*) ∥ *hole* := *root* ∥
    ANY   *leaf*   **WHERE**   *leaf* ∈ *Heap* − ran (*father*)   **THEN**
    copy_and_remove (*root* , *leaf*)
    END
    END ;

b , son ⟵ $lower$ $\widehat{=}$
   ANY min_son **WHERE**
      $min\_son \in NAT \wedge$
      $(sons(hole) \neq \{\} \Rightarrow$
                  $min\_son \in sons(hole) \wedge key\,(\,min\_son\,) = \min\,(\,key\,[\,sons(hole)\,]\,)\,)$
   THEN
      $b := \mathsf{bool}\,(\,\neg\,downgood\,(hole)\,)$ ‖ $son := min\_son$
   END ;
$down\_heap(\,son\,)$ $\widehat{=}$
   PRE $\neg\,downgood\,(hole) \wedge son \in sons(hole)$
                  $\wedge\,key\,(\,son\,) = \min\,(\,key\,[\,sons(hole)\,]\,)$ **THEN**
      $swap\,(\,son\,,\,hole\,)$ ‖ $hole := son$
   END

END

The interface of *Indirect_Heap* provides operations for moving up and down the tree (*up_heap* and *down_heap*) and for testing the opportunity to move (*higher* and *lower*). Additionally we have two other operations allowing the insertion (*insert_heap*) or removal (*remove_heap*) of elements from the heap.

Inserting a new element in the heap comes down to hooking it as a son of an already existing node, or placing it in the root if the heap is empty. In either case, the new element is a potential hole that satisfies *downgood* since it has no sons. However, to make sure that it is the only hole we require as a precondition that the heap property holds everywhere, *heap(Heap)*, before performing *insert_heap*.

Removing the minimum element, situated in the root of the tree, leaves us with two subtrees that are both heaps. To preserve the tree shape we proceed in a more roundabout manner by choosing a leaf, copying its value in the root and removing the leaf. Now the root is a potential hole that satisfies *upgood*, since it has no parent. Again, to make sure that there were no previous holes, we require *heap(Heap)* as a precondition of *remove_heap*.

The invariant of the machine states that only *hole* might possibly violate the heap property. Proving that the invariant is preserved by *up_heap* and *down_heap* relies subtly on the fact that the heap property, although violated by *hole*, still holds in the "grandfather" relationship between *sons(hole)* and *father(hole)*.

Other potential invariants like *downgood(heap)* or *upgood(heap)* are not valid here, since at this level we ignore the current moving direction and whether the hole has already vanished or not. They would appear as loop invariants in the traversal operations where a given moving direction is fixed.

Inserting an element into an already existing heap can proceed by adding the element as a leaf, thus creating a potential hole, and then swapping it with its father, grandfather, and so on, until it is greater or equal to one of these values.

Fig. 3.6 illustrates[4] the building of a heap from the weights of the edges of the graph in Fig. 3.1(a). We suppose that the edges are read in the order $(1,2),(1,3),(1,4),(2,3),(2,5),(3,4),(3,5),(4,5)$ which gives the following order for

---

[4] The use of complete binary trees in this example anticipates the last refinement decision, to be introduced in the next section.

their weights: 2, 1, 6, 1, 5, 4, 4, 3. For the sake of simplicity, each node i is labeled only with its value $key(i) = valh(indh(i))$. At each stage, the node emphasised by a bold circle contains the value inserted at that stage, value that has been moved upwards until satisfying the heap property.

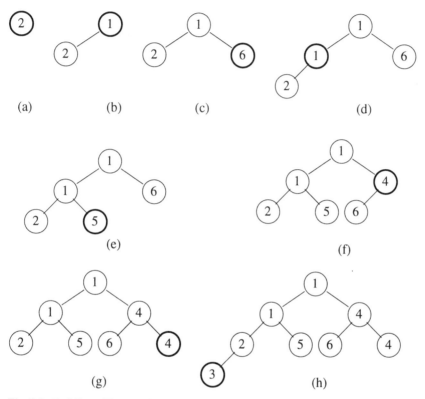

Fig. 3.6. Building a Heap by Successive Insertions

To delete the minimum element of a heap we start by calling *remove_heap*, thus creating a hole in the root of the tree, as explained above. Then we move the hole downwards by successive calls of *down_heap* as long as one of the sons has a smaller value than the hole.

As an example, the heap constructed above can be emptied by repeated deletions of the minimum element, as shown in Fig. 3.7. At each stage, the node emphasised by a bold circle contains the value of the leaf that has been copied into the root and moved down all the way until satisfying the heap property.

The actual loops performing the traversals of the tree on insertions and deletions of heap elements occur in the implementation of *Priority_Queue*:

IMPLEMENTATION   *Priority_Queue_1*

REFINES   *Priority_Queue*

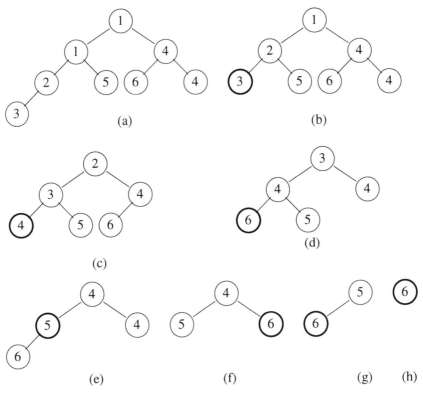

Fig. 3.7. Removing the Elements of the Heap

IMPORTS   *Indirect_Heap (m)*

INVARIANT

 Queue = Index ∧ valq = valh ∧ heap (Heap)

OPERATIONS

 empty_queue   ≙   *empty_heap* **;**

 insert_queue(kk , ww)   ≙

  VAR   *bb*   **IN**

   insert_heap (kk , ww) **;** *bb* ⟵ *higher* **;**

   WHILE   *bb = TRUE*   **DO**

    up_heap **;** *bb* ⟵ *higher*

   INVARIANT

    downgood (hole) ∧ (bb = TRUE ⟺ ¬ upgood (hole)) ∧

    Index = Index ∪ { kk } ∧ valh = valq ⩤ { kk ↦ ww }

   VARIANT   *card (ancestors (hole))*

   END

  END ;

 kk , ww ⟵ *remove_queue*   ≙

  VAR   *bb , son*   **IN**

   kk , ww ⟵ *remove_heap* **;** *bb , son* ⟵ *lower* **;**

WHILE $bb = TRUE$ **DO**
   $down\_heap (son) \ ; bb , son \longleftarrow lower$
INVARIANT
   $upgood (hole) \wedge (bb = TRUE \Leftrightarrow \neg downgood (hole)) \wedge$
   $(bb = TRUE \Rightarrow$
         $son \in sons(hole) \wedge val (son) = \mathsf{min} (val [sons(hole)])) \wedge$
   $kk = indh (root) \wedge ww = valq (kk) \wedge$
   $Index = Index - \{ kk \} \wedge valh = \{ indh (root) \} \lhd valh$
VARIANT $\mathsf{card} (descendants (hole))$
END
  END

END

The refinement invariant relates *Queue* and *valq* to *Index* and *valh*. It also states that the heap property holds everywhere between two priority queue operations, which in turn guarantees that the value *kk* returned by *remove_queue* satisfies $valq(kk) = min(valq[Queue]))$.

We already know from the invariant of *Indirect_Heap* that the heap property might be violated only in one node, $heap(Heap - \{hole\})$. This is another instance of the "design for provability" paradigm, as we have proven locally as much as we could. The only thing left to prove now is that the heap property holds on *hole* as well at the exit of each loop. For this it is sufficient to prove that *hole* satisfies both *upgood* and *downgood* at the exit of the loop.

When performing an insertion, *downgood* is initially established by *insert_heap* since a leaf has no sons, and then it is preserved as a loop invariant by each call of *up_heap*. Similarly, when deleting an element, *upgood* is established initially by *remove_heap* since the root has no parent, and then it is preserved as a loop invariant by each call of *down_heap*. In both cases the invariant of the loop and the negation of the loop test, that is *upgood(hole)* and *downgood(hole)*, hold at the exit of the loop.

3.5.3 Complete Binary Trees

In the specification of heaps we did not impose any particular constraint on the shape of the tree. One is free to choose whatever shape seems most desirable as long as the heap property is satisfied. A key decision in the implementation of heaps is to consider complete binary trees, as explained below.

The binary tree of depth *d* which has exactly $2^d - 1$ nodes is called a *full* binary tree of depth *d*. A very elegant sequential representation for full binary trees results from sequentially numbering the nodes, starting with the root on level one, then going to the nodes on level two and so on. Nodes on any level are numbered from left to right. A binary tree with *r* nodes and depth *d* is *complete* if and only if its nodes correspond to the nodes which are numbered 1 to *r* in the full binary tree of depth *d*. In a complete tree leaf nodes occur on at most two adjacent levels. As a consequence, the worst case performance of insertions and deletions will be logarithmic in the size of the heap.

The nodes of a complete tree may be compactly stored in a one dimensional array. Navigating in the tree is easy due to the regular numbering of nodes: the father of the node numbered i is given by $i/2$ (where $/$ stands for the integer division), while its left and the right children of i are given by $2*i$, respectively $2*i+1$. Actually, *root* and *father*(i), that have been previously declared as abstract constants, will be tacitly replaced by 1 and $i/2$ and thus refined away. The rigid structure of complete binary trees represented as arrays does limit their utility as data structures, but there is just enough flexibility to allow the implementation of efficient priority queue algorithms.

In this representation, the set *Heap* can be identified with the interval $1 .. sizeh$ where *sizeh* is an implementation variable denoting the size of the heap. This way, inserting or removing heap elements comes down to incrementing or decrementing *sizeh*.

The functions *indh* and *valh* will be refined by two arrays *index* and *value*, equal to *indh* and *valh* on the interval $1 .. sizeh$:

$$indh = Heap \lhd index$$
$$valh = Heap \lhd value$$

Another implementation variable *current* is introduced to refine *hole* with the trivial refinement invariant *hole* = *current*. One can remark that *index*(*current*) and *value*(*index*(*current*)) stay the same whenever *current* is swapped with one of its neighbours. In order to save some array accesses it is worth introducing two other variables, *ind_current* and *val_current*, to denote the two quantities above. This results in the following implementation of *Indirect_Heap*:

IMPLEMENTATION   *Indirect_Heap_1*

REFINES   *Indirect_Heap*

VARIABLES

  sizeh , *index* , *value* , *current* , *val_current* , *ind_current*

INVARIANT

  $sizeh \in 0 .. mm \wedge Heap = 1 .. sizeh \wedge$
  $index \in 1 .. mm \rightarrow 1 .. m \wedge indh = Heap \lhd index \wedge$
  $value \in 1 .. mm \rightarrow NAT \wedge valh = Heap \lhd value \wedge$
  $current \in 1 .. mm \wedge hole = current \wedge$
  $ind\_current \in 1 .. mm \wedge val\_current \in NAT \wedge$
  $(sizeh > 0 \Rightarrow ind\_current = index (current) \wedge val\_current = value (ind\_current))$

INITIALISATION $sizeh := 0$

OPERATIONS

  $empty\_heap \ \hat{=} \ sizeh := 0 \ ;$
  $insert\_heap(kk , ww) \ \hat{=}$
    BEGIN
      $sizeh := sizeh + 1 \ ; \ index (sizeh) := kk \ ; \ value (kk) := ww \ ;$
      $current := sizeh \ ; \ ind\_current := kk \ ; \ val\_current := ww$
    END ;

$bb \longleftarrow higher \quad \widehat{=}$
  BEGIN
    $bb := FALSE$;
    IF $current > 1$ **THEN**
      IF $value\,(\,current\,/\,2\,) > val\_current$ **THEN**
        $bb := TRUE$
      END
    END
  END ;
$up\_heap \quad \widehat{=}$
  VAR dad **IN**
    $dad := current\,/\,2$; $index\,(\,current\,) := index\,(\,dad\,)$;
    $index\,(\,dad\,) := ind\_current$; $current := dad$
  END ;
$kk\,,\,ww \longleftarrow remove\_heap \quad \widehat{=}$
  BEGIN
    $kk := index\,(\,1\,)$; $ww := value\,(\,kk\,)$;
    $index\,(\,1\,) := index\,(\,sizeh\,)$; $sizeh := sizeh - 1$;
    $current := 1$; $ind\_current := index\,(\,1\,)$; $val\_current := value\,(\,ind\_current\,)$
  END ;
$bb\,,\,son \longleftarrow lower \quad \widehat{=}$
  VAR $min\_val\,,\,right\_val$ **IN**
    $son := 2 \times current$; $bb := FALSE$;
    IF $son \leq sizeh$ **THEN**
      $min\_val := value\,(\,index\,(\,son\,)\,)$;
      IF $son < sizeh$ **THEN**
        $right\_val := value\,(\,index\,(\,son + 1\,)\,)$;
        IF $right\_val < min\_val$ **THEN**
          $son := son + 1$; $min\_val := right\_val$
        END
      END ;
      IF $min\_val < val\_current$ **THEN**
        $bb := TRUE$
      END
    END
  END ;
$down\_heap(\,son\,) \quad \widehat{=}$
  BEGIN
    $index\,(\,current\,) := index\,(\,son\,)$; $index\,(\,son\,) := ind\_current$; $current := son$
  END

END

Note that the structure of the implementation does not necessarily follow the structure of the specification. In our case the specification was decomposed into *Heap_Data* and *Indirect_Heap*, while the implementation *Indirect_Heap_I* imports no other machine.

The initialisation sets *sizeh* to 0 and leaves all other variables uninitialised[5], since their values are not constrained by the invariant in this case.

---

[5] However, the B-Toolkit raises a warning about uninitialised variables.

The non-determinism in the choice of a leaf in the operations *insert_heap* and *remove_heap* is eliminated by choosing systematically the last leaf numbered *sizeh*. This decision, together with the incrementing, respectively decrementing, of *sizeh* allows to preserve the invariant $Heap = 1 .. sizeh$.

The operations *higher* and *lower* are implemented by rather complex control structures formed of several nested conditionals. Isolating these control structures as operations on their own, instead of embedding them directly in *Priority_Queue_I*, proves to be another example of *design for provability*. Indeed, the control complexity induced by the two calls of both *higher* and *lower* in the traversal loops and by the loops themselves would have led to a combinatorial explosion in the number of proof obligations to discharge.

Fig. 3.8 gives an overview of the refinement steps performed in this section.

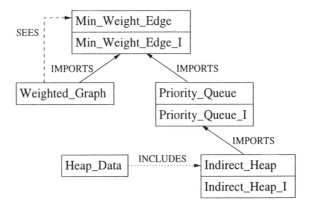

Fig. 3.8. The Refinement Path Leading to the Implementation of Heaps

3.6 Discussion

In this chapter we have presented a complete formal development of Kruskal's algorithm for solving the minimum spanning tree problem. The abstract specification of the problem was first refined by an informal implementation of Kruskal's algorithm. We have then proposed a decomposition of this implementation into two simpler subsystems, each one providing its own functionality. In turn, this allows independent designs of the two subsystems to be built: disjoint sets are implemented by the Union-Find algorithm, and priority queues are implemented as heaps. An overview of the complete development, regrouping Figs. 3.3, 3.5 and 3.8, is given in Fig. 3.9.

In spite of its relative small size (1127 lines of B and 360 proof obligations) this case study manages to exhibit some of the problems encountered when developing industrial applications in B. A significant difference between our case study and

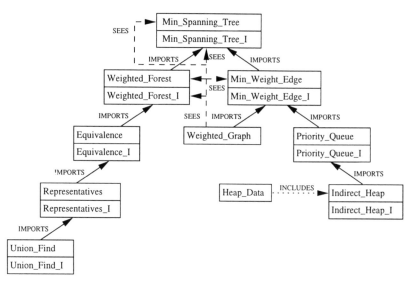

Fig. 3.9. Overview of the Complete Development

safety-critical applications is that the complexity lies rather in the data structures and the algorithms than in the size and the control structure of the application.

We have exemplified how the well-understood set-theoretical notation of B can be used to model the various data structures. In particular, note that the transitive closure operator on relations (and in particular functions) has been extensively used in formalising paths in graphs (respectively trees). The large basis of facts on set theory available in the prover makes it easier to reason on the properties of the data structures employed. One has the choice of taking a more or less rigorous approach to proof. For instance, to prove the consistency of the *Equivalence* machine, we can just assume a lemma stating that the transitive closure of a symmetric relation is still symmetric, instead of proving this lemma from basic principles by induction on the number of iterations on the relation.

The algorithmic complexity is dealt with by breaking difficult verification steps into a number of smaller and more manageable ones. Several instances of the *design for provability* paradigm have been exemplified during the development, where by making careful use of the structuring mechanisms of B, one can limit the number of proof obligations associated to each verification step.

In this respect, one of the most interesting lessons is that an explosion in the number of proof obligations might be due to performing both algorithmic and data refinement in one refinement step. In this case, one should introduce algorithmic refinement before data refinement and not the other way around. This strategy has been applied in the implementations *Min_Spanning_Tree_I* and *Priority_Queue_I* where the algorithmic refinement introduced by the **WHILE** loops is simpler to verify in terms of an abstract data representation than a concrete one.

We conclude by analysing the interest that computer scientists in general might have in formal methods. The firm mathematical foundations of formal methods and the toolkits supporting them might justify their use as an effective tool in algorithm design. One would then benefit not only from a rich specification language to express various problems, but also a machine-checked notation for the early stages of the design. These stages usually captured in algorithms textbooks by some kind of informal pseudo-code can be written formally by exploiting the liberty of mixing non-executable abstract constructs with executable concrete ones.

Going through the formalisation of the pseudo-code might require considerably more effort on the part of the algorithm designer, especially when trying to cope with the various visibility constraints of the encapsulation constructs. However, this effort might pay off in enforcing a certain discipline of design.

As an option, one might consider carrying out informal proofs of the algorithms in the way that these proofs are presented in textbooks. One would just have to formalise the various invariants and try the automatic proof facilities. Examining the unproved proof obligations might then reveal possible flaws in the design of the algorithm.

4. The B Bank

Martin Büchi

4.1 Introduction

In this chapter we develop a simple banking application with cashier and automated teller machine (ATM) functionality. The cashier can register new customers, create accounts for them, and accept deposits. At the ATM, the customer can withdraw money, query the balance, and change her secret personal identification number (PIN).

We illustrate the combination of structured and formal methods by using object-oriented modelling techniques in the analysis. The communication from B with the environment is exemplified through the development of base machines for persistent storage of objects, string handling, and for interfacing with the Web through HTML and the common gateway interface. The latter permits us to build a uniform graphical interface for both the cashier station and the ATM (Fig. 4.1).

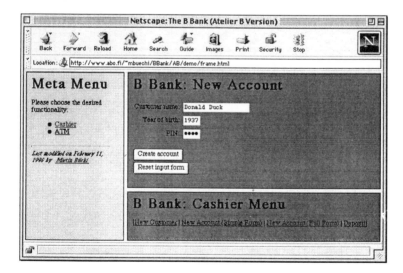

Fig. 4.1. Screenshot of the Final Application

Our aim is to carefully explain design decisions as they come up and to motivate our choices. We stress differences to classical imperative languages and development methods for them.

The sources for both Atelier B and the B-Toolkit can be fetched from the book's Web site. The final application being Web-based, it can also be run over the Internet from the book's Web page without the need for installation.

We start out by rewriting the informal requirements in structured plain English, as is commonly done in practice. This first design document helps to eliminate misunderstandings between the customer and the designer and is often part of a contract. We then proceed to a semi-formal object model using the Unified Modeling Language (UML) [31]. In this step we make the first design decisions by identifying objects, relations, and attributes. This intermediate step bridges the gap between requirement specification and B machine.

Our initial B specification *Bank* encompasses the basic functionality on an abstract level. This is the machine which we animate to find design errors. On top we build a robust graphical user interface. Underneath, we build a foundation for objects and persistent storage. This combination of top-down and bottom up development, where we start with a machine describing the functionality on an abstract level, is very common in B.

On top of the central machine *Bank* we construct a robust interface *RobustBank* with trivial preconditions and error reporting. Using this robust interface and a base machine wrapping a common-gateway interface library, we build a Web-based graphical user interface for our development.

A program consists of an algorithm and communication with the environment. Only the algorithm can be directly implemented in B. Communication is performed using base machines which give a B representation of a resource. A base machine is a machine which is specified in B, but hand coded in C, or another classical language for which a compiler exists. We illustrate the development of a base machine for interfacing with the Web in Sect. 4.7.

The implementation of *RobustBank* shows the principle of structural refinement. An implementation is based on a number of more basic machines, which are in turn based on either more basic or base machines. We discuss the difference between specification and implementation structure. Using a library machine for two-dimensional arrays and a base machine for file access we develop a framework for persistent objects. Another base machine provides persistent strings.

Fig. 4.2 gives an overview of the development process, including section numbers for quick reference. An overview of the implementation of *Bank* will be given in Fig. 4.12.

In the discussion we address the question of proofs in B. What types of properties about our system can we prove within B?

Steria's Atelier B in version 3.2 [79] has been used in this case study. Sect. 4.11 explains the differences in the implementation for B-Core's B-Toolkit 3.4.2 [59]. We briefly discuss a number of interesting differences in the language implementations and provided library constructs.

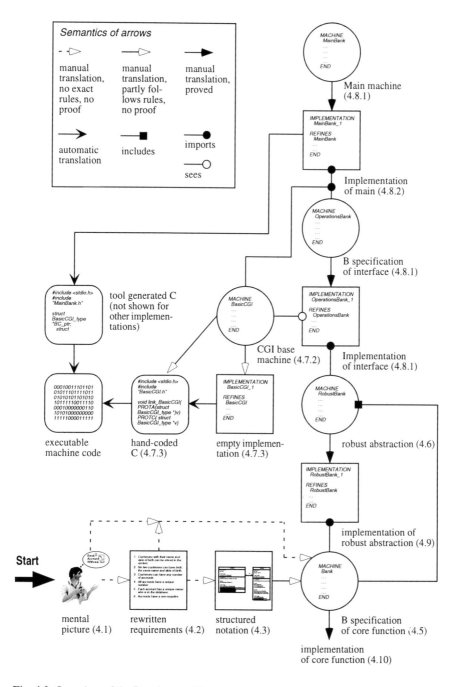

Fig. 4.2. Overview of the Development Process

4.2 Rewriting the Requirements

We start out by making the requirements of the initial application more precise. Such a complete rewrite by the developer of the customer's requirements in a common language provides for a common understanding. It can also eliminate many errors typically introduced by going directly from a mental picture to a specification, or even worse an implementation. Requirements state only what must be achieved, but not how it must be done. Fig. 4.3, an excerpt of Fig. 4.2, shows where in the development process we are.

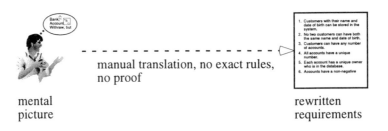

manual translation, no exact rules,
no proof

mental   rewritten
picture   requirements

Fig. 4.3. Requirement Analysis

The system should provide for:

1. Customers with their name and date of birth can be stored in the system.
2. No two customers can have both the same name and date of birth.
3. Customers can have any number of accounts.
4. All accounts have a unique number.
5. Each account has a unique owner who is in the database.
6. Accounts have a non-negative balance.
7. Accounts have a secret PIN.

The cashier can perform the following transactions:

8. The cashier can enter new customers into the system by providing their name and year of birth.
9. The cashier can create new accounts with a zero balance providing a customer identification and an initial PIN. The latter can be entered by the customer.
10. The cashier can accept deposits knowing only the number of the account. The secret PIN is not needed for deposits.

The customer can perform the following operation at the ATM, which all require the account number — entered manually rather than read from a chip or magnetic card in our simulation — and the matching secret PIN:

11. The customer can make a withdrawal of at most the current balance.
12. The customer can query the current balance.

13. The customer can change the secret PIN by providing both the old, currently valid, and the new pin. The latter becomes immediately valid and the old PIN can no longer be used.

The user interface should be Web-based and provide access to all the above listed functions of the system. For brevity, we refrain from listing the user interface requirements here. We return to the topic in Sect. 4.8. A more detailed explanation of requirement analysis can be found in software engineering books, such as [70, 77].

4.3 Structured Models

In the next step, analysis, we produce structured models from the problem statement. The structured notations help to produce specifications which are correct with respect to the user requirements. This step is performed manually, following some heuristics. However, it lacks formal rules and, therefore, also a proof. This step could be skipped, going directly to a B specification. However, this would be a rather big step and, hence, also a source of errors. The benefits of integrating formal and structured methods are becoming recognised by many researchers [35, 37]. The IEC 65A 122 standard for safety-critical software also recommends the use of both structured and formal methods for software of the highest integrity level [41]. Often customers can be taught to read structured diagrammatic notations, but not formal AMN specifications. This intermediate step provides a more concise foundation for discussion than the natural language requirements.

The desire to capture all aspects of a problem using graphical models has led to a proliferation of different diagram types. We abstain from using all these — often not very useful — diagrams and do not attempt to capture everything in a graphical notation. We regard graphical models as complimentary to the textual specifications. Not opting for an automatic translation from the graphical model, we can give true abstractions, which quickly convey the main aspects, rather than cluttering the models with implementation details.

For our case study only static structure diagrams are relevant. The large amount of information captured in static structure diagrams is widely acknowledged [43]. Dynamic models are not applicable, because all operations are modeless, for example, the customer enters the account number, the PIN, and the desired amount all at once before asking the system to perform the withdrawal. A functional model would not provide much insight, as all transactions are made against a single database.

We have chosen the Unified Modeling Language (UML) [31]. Fig. 4.4 reminds us again, where in the development process we are.

4.3.1 Class Diagrams

The class diagram shows the static data structure of the real-world system and organises it into workable pieces. It describes real-world object classes and their relationships to each other.

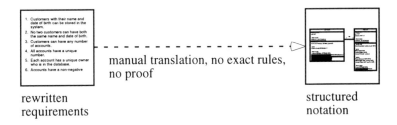

manual translation, no exact rules,
no proof

rewritten
requirements

structured
notation

Fig. 4.4. Structured Notation

In our case we identify Customer and Account as object classes (Fig. 4.5). Our simple data dictionary defines them as follows: A Customer is the holder of zero or more accounts. An Account is an entity in our bank against which transactions can be made.

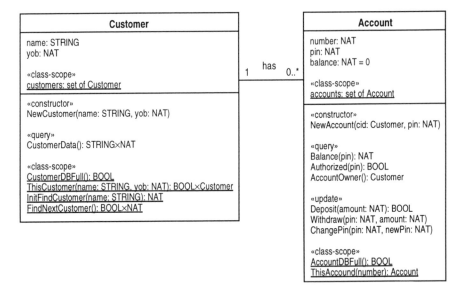

Fig. 4.5. Object Model

Next, we enumerate the attributes, that is, the properties, and the operations of the individual classes. Each Customer has a name and a year of birth (yob). In addition to the instance-scope attributes, of which each instance has its own copy, class Customer has the class-scope attribute customers, the set of all customers in the system. Class-scope members are underlined in the diagram. The class Customer has a single constructor and a single query function. The product type STRING×NAT indicates that CustomerData returns both the name and the year of birth of a customer. It also has class-scope operations to inquire whether the database is full, to retrieve a customer, and to find all customers with a certain name.

Each Account has a number, a pin, and a balance, which is initially 0. Remember that requirement 4 states that number is an identifier. In entity-relationship models, this would typically be expressed by underlining the attribute — a notation which is used for class-scope attributes in UML. Entity relationship models representing sets, each class must have an identifier. However, in object-oriented systems we can have several objects with the same values for all their attributes. Objects have a system-generated unique identifier. Hence, unlike in multisets, objects with identical attribute values can actually be distinguished. In our example, we do not have multiple objects with identical values for their attributes. A notation for indicating identifiers in class diagrams would add information.

Class Account also has a class-scope attribute accounts, the set of all accounts in the system. Account has a single constructor. The query functions permit the user to query the balance, check whether a pin is valid, and get the owner of an account. The update operations provide functionality to make a deposit or withdrawal and to change the PIN. The class-scope operations allow the user to check whether the database is full and to retrieve an account by its number.

Finally we catalogue the associations, that is, the dependencies between objects. A customer may have any number of accounts; each account has exactly one owner. This association is expressed by the line between the two classes in Fig. 4.5. The multiplicity is expressed using intervals. The '1' next to Customer says that each account is owned by exactly one customer. The '0..*' next to Account expresses that a customer may have any number of accounts. The label has names the association.

4.4 System Design

From the analysis of the system we progress to system design. System design is the high-level strategy for solving the problem and building a solution. During system design, we partition the system into subsystems, decide on what external hard- and software components we use, and establish a conceptual policy.

We start with the middle layer capturing the desired functionality (Fig. 4.6). On top of the basic functionality layer we build a robust abstraction which performs error checking and returns error codes, rather than relying on non-trivial preconditions. The top layer gives us the desired system in the form of a Web interface as defined by the problem statement. Its second foundation is the common gateway interface (CGI) subsystem, which consists of an off-the-shelf CGI library and a B wrapper. The CGI subsystem interfaces to the Web server. The latter communicates via TCP/IP with the Web browsers running on the ATM and the cashier's terminal.

In order to implement the core data, we build a subsystem which supports persistent objects and strings. The former in turn is based on two more basic subsystems, one giving us objects and a second one providing access to the file system. The two bottom layers represent the available resources, namely the hardware and the operating system.

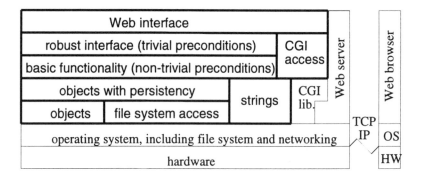

Fig. 4.6. System Design

An alternative would have been to rely on a database management system for persistent storage, giving us such standard features as transaction management, distribution, and crash recovery. We have chosen not to do so in order to maximize the ratio of formally verified software and limit the external dependencies of this case study.

4.5 B Specification

Having outlined the system architecture, we continue by translating the structured model to a B specification, giving the middle layer of basic functionality. First we translate our object model according to fixed rules which gives the state space of the machine and the signature of the operations. Then we add the initialisation and the specification of the operations with help of the rewritten requirements. Fig. 4.7 points again to our current position in the development process.

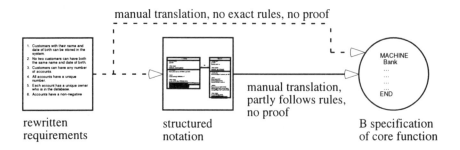

Fig. 4.7. Transformation to B Specification

4.5.1 State

For each object class we introduce a set containing all possible instances. This gives us the sets *CUSTOMER* and *ACCOUNT*. For technical reasons, detailed in Sect. 4.11, we define them as subsets of *NAT* rather than as *SETS*. The cardinalities of the sets, delimiting the maximal number of customers and accounts in the system, are given by the machine parameters *maxCustomers* and *maxAccounts*.

MACHINE
    Bank(maxCustomers, maxAccounts)

CONSTRAINTS
    $maxCustomers \in 1 .. 100000 \land maxAccounts \in 1 .. 200000$

SEES
    StrTokenType

DEFINITIONS
    $CUSTOMER == 0 .. maxCustomers\text{-}1; ACCOUNT == 0 .. maxAccounts\text{-}1$

Furthermore we introduce the two class-scope variables of Fig. 4.5 *customers* ($\subseteq$ *CUSTOMER*) and *accounts* ($\subseteq$ *ACCOUNT*), which denote the sets of customers and accounts in the system.

Mandatory attributes are modelled as total functions from the set of actual customers, respectively accounts, to the value of the attribute. This gives us variables *customerName*, *customerYob*, *accountNumber*, *accountPin*, and *accountBalance*. Identifiers, for example, *accountNumber* and the product of *customerName* and *customerYob*, are injections, capturing the fact that no two objects with the same values for these attributes can exist.

The seen machine *StrTokenType* defines the set *STRTOKEN* representing strings and the empty string constant *EmptyStringToken* ($\in$ *STRTOKEN*). The rationale behind string tokens will be explained in Sect. 4.7.1.

The relation has can be translated to the total function *accountOwner* from *accounts* to *customer*. It is a function, rather than a general relation, because the maximum multiplicity of Customer is 1; furthermore, it is total because the minimum multiplicity is also 1. The variable *foundCustomers* is used for the implementation of the search-by-name operations for customers as described below.

The last state component is the concrete (also called visible) variable *fileOpen*. It indicates whether the database has been successfully internalised from disk and, thus, whether the machine can actually be used. The difference between a normal (also called abstract or hidden) variable and a concrete variable is that the latter is implemented unchanged and can, therefore, be directly accessed by implementations that import *Bank*.

VARIABLES
    customers, customerName, customerYob,
    accounts, accountNumber, accountPin, accountBalance, accountOwner,
    foundCustomers

CONCRETE_VARIABLES
  fileOpen
INVARIANT
  customers ⊆ *CUSTOMER* ∧
  customerName ∈ *customers* → *STRTOKEN* ∧ *customerYob* ∈ *customers* → **NAT** ∧
  customerName ⊗ *customerYob* ∈ *customers* ↣ (*STRTOKEN* × **NAT**) ∧
  accounts ⊆ *ACCOUNT* ∧
  accountNumber ∈ *accounts* ↣ **NAT** ∧ *accountPin* ∈ *accounts* → **NAT** ∧
  accountBalance ∈ *accounts* → **NAT** ∧ *accountOwner* ∈ *accounts* → *customers* ∧
  fileOpen ∈ **BOOL** ∧ *foundCustomers* ⊆ *customers*

4.5.2 Functionality

In the beginning, there are no customers or accounts in the database. Hence, the initialisation assigns the empty set to the sets *customers* and *accounts* and, therefore, also to the functions representing the attributes and relations. As the database has not yet been read from disk *fileOpen* is *FALSE*. We could have designed the system so that internalisation from disk is part of initialisation. Because internalisation can fail, if, for example, the file has been corrupted, a variable indicating its success would have to be set during initialisation and checked by the higher level abstraction. Hence, we would not gain anything. We introduce the abbreviation *RESET* as the same code occurs again later.

DEFINITIONS
  RESET ==
    customers := {} || *customerName* := {} || *customerYob* := {} ||
    accounts := {} || *accountNumber* := {} || *accountPin* := {} ||
    accountBalance := {} || *accountOwner* := {} ||
    fileOpen := **FALSE** || *foundCustomers* := {}

INITIALISATION
  RESET

The first operation *NewCustomer* creates a new customer object and sets its *name* and *yob* attributes. In order to concentrate on the actual functionality, rather than error checking and reporting, the precondition not only gives a type to the parameters, but also states that there must not be any customer with both the same name and year of birth present in the database, that the database must not be full, and that internalisation (see below) must have succeeded. If these conditions are met, an arbitrary new customer object is selected using the *ANY*-clause. This object is added to *customers* and its *name* and *yob* attributes are set. Note that *customerName(newCustomer)* := *name* is an abbreviation for *customerName* := *customerName* ∪ {*newCustomer* ↦ *name*}.

  NewCustomer(*name*, *yob*) =
    PRE
      name ∈ *STRTOKEN* ∧ *yob* ∈ **NAT** ∧

$(name, yob) \notin \mathbf{ran}(customerName \otimes customerYob) \wedge$
$customers \neq CUSTOMER \wedge fileOpen = \mathbf{TRUE}$
THEN
  ANY *newCustomer* **WHERE**
    $newCustomer \in CUSTOMER - customers$
  THEN
    $customers := customers \cup \{newCustomer\} ~\|$
    $customerName(newCustomer) := name ~\| customerYob(newCustomer) := yob$
  END
END;

Any client of *NewCustomer* must be able to verify the precondition. For this purpose we introduce operations *ThisCustomer* and *CustomerDBFull*. Operation *ThisCustomer* checks whether a customer denoted by her *name* and *yob* is present. If this is the case, the operation returns result code *TRUE* and the ID of the customer. Otherwise, the result code is set to *FALSE*. The result code alone would suffice to check the existence; the operation is more general for purposes we shall see later on.

$found, cid \leftarrow \mathbf{ThisCustomer}(name, yob) =$
  PRE $name \in STRTOKEN \wedge yob \in \mathbf{NAT} \wedge fileOpen = \mathbf{TRUE}$ **THEN**
    IF $(name, yob) \in \mathbf{ran}(customerName \otimes customerYob)$ **THEN**
      $cid := (customerName \otimes customerYob)^{-1} (name, yob) ~\| found := \mathbf{TRUE}$
    ELSE
      $cid :\in CUSTOMER ~\| found := \mathbf{FALSE}$
    END
  END;

In practice, databases are assumed to have infinite capacity and their administrators are supposed to add secondary storage as the available storage gets filled. However, the number of incidents of database and buffer overflow problems clearly shows that we should not trust this assumption in a safety-critical system. Operation *CustomerDBFull* allows us to check whether the database is full and, herewith, verify the precondition *customers* $\neq$ *CUSTOMER* of *NewCustomer*. Note that we could prove the invariant of machine *Bank* to be preserved without this precondition. In the case it would not hold, the *ANY*-statement would have to choose an element from the empty set and would therefore be magic. Hence, we could not find any implementation using a finite set *CUSTOMER* which would either always find an unused member or execute magic.

$is \leftarrow \mathbf{CustomerDBFull} =$
  PRE $fileOpen = \mathbf{TRUE}$ **THEN**
    $is := \mathbf{bool}(customers = CUSTOMER)$
  END;

Operation *NewCustomer* can only be performed if the internalisation of the database from disk has succeeded. This condition is expressed by the last conjunct of the precondition: *fileOpen = TRUE*. A more pragmatic solution would be to assume that any client of *Bank* will terminate with an error message if internalisation fails and not make any calls to *NewCustomer*. However, replacing the formal precondition with this informal assumption would lead to unprovable obligations.

Operation *CustomerData* is an instance-scope operation which returns the name and year of birth of a customer. Self, the identity of the object, is modelled as a normal parameter *cid*. The identity of a customer object can be retrieved using *ThisCustomer*. Atelier B requires the additional typing $cid \in CUSTOMER$.

> *name, yob* ← **CustomerData**(*cid*) =
> **PRE** $cid \in customers \land cid \in CUSTOMER \land fileOpen = $ **TRUE THEN**
>   *name* := *customerName*(*cid*) || *yob* := *customerYob*(*cid*)
> **END**;

The find operations give the set of all customers with a certain name. First, operation *InitFindCustomer* must be called. It returns the number of matches and assigns the matching customers to *foundCustomers*. Operation *FindNextCustomer* then returns the matching customers one by one.

> *nof* ← **InitFindCustomer**(*name*) =
> **PRE** $name \in STRTOKEN \land fileOpen = $ **TRUE THEN**
> $nof, foundCustomers \in (foundCustomers = customerName^{-1} [\{name\}] \land$
> $nof = \mathbf{card}(foundCustomers))$
> **END**;
>
> *found, yob* ← **FindNextCustomer** =
> **PRE** *fileOpen* = **TRUE THEN**
>   **IF** $foundCustomers \neq \{\}$ **THEN**
>   **ANY** *cust* **WHERE** $cust \in foundCustomers$ **THEN**
>   *found* := **TRUE** || *yob* := *customerYob*(*cust*)||
>   *foundCustomers* := *foundCustomers*-{*cust*}
>   **END**
>   **ELSE** *found* := **FALSE** || $yob :\in$ **NAT**
>   **END**
> **END**;

The triple *NewAccount*, *ThisAccount*, and *AccountDBFull* is similar to the corresponding operations on customers. Operation *NewAccount* expects as parameters the ID of an existing customer and an initial secret PIN. By making the PIN a parameter we favour the scenario where the customer enters the desired PIN when the cashier creates the account. If the ATM card and the PIN are mailed to the customer, a random PIN must be generated in one of the above layers. Operation *AccountOwner* returns the owner of an account.

> *number* ← **NewAccount**(*cid, pin*) =
> **PRE**
> $cid \in customers \land cid \in CUSTOMER \land pin \in$ **NAT** $\land$
> $accounts \neq ACCOUNT \land fileOpen = $ **TRUE**
> **THEN**
>   **ANY** *newAccount, newNumber* **WHERE**

$newAccount \in ACCOUNT$ - $accounts \land$
$newNumber \in \textbf{NAT} \land newNumber \notin \textbf{ran}(accountNumber)$
THEN
$accounts := accounts \cup \{newAccount\} \;||$
$accountNumber(newAccount) := newNumber \;||$
$accountPin(newAccount) := pin \;||\; accountBalance(newAccount) := 0 \;||$
$accountOwner(newAccount) := cid \;||\; number := newNumber$
END
END;

$found, aid \leftarrow \textbf{ThisAccount}(number) =$
PRE $number \in \textbf{NAT} \land fileOpen = \textbf{TRUE}$ **THEN**
  IF $number \in \textbf{ran}(accountNumber)$ **THEN**
    $aid := accountNumber^{-1}(number) \;||\; found := \textbf{TRUE}$
  ELSE $aid :\in ACCOUNT \;||\; found := \textbf{FALSE}$
  END
END;

$is \leftarrow \textbf{AccountDBFull} =$
PRE $fileOpen = \textbf{TRUE}$ **THEN**
  $is := \textbf{bool}(accounts = ACCOUNT)$
END;

$cid \leftarrow \textbf{AccountOwner}(aid) =$
PRE $aid \in accounts \land aid \in ACCOUNT \land fileOpen = \textbf{TRUE}$ **THEN**
  $cid := accountOwner^{-1}(aid)$
END;

The operation *Balance* requires the account's PIN. The PIN is only used in the precondition to verify the legitimacy of the client, but not in the body of the operation. Specifying that the entered PIN must match the stored PIN in the precondition, forces us to prove that *Balance* is always called with the correct PIN. Unfortunately, this implies that the parameter *pin* is also present in the actual implementation where it is not used at all. To gain additional security, especially if the upper software levels are not fully proved, the correctness of the PIN could actually be verified in the implementation — contrarily to the standard practice of not verifying preconditions in implementations. Logically, it would be sound to allow implementations to have only a subset of the parameters of the corresponding machine, but in practice this would mean that the client's C code would depend not only on the interface defined by the machine, but also on the actual implementation. The alternative would be to drop the *pin* parameter altogether and trust in the clients always calling an authorisation operation, such as *Authorized*, first. However, such a condition would not create any proof obligations and would, therefore, not be verifiable within B. A model checking solution to the latter approach is documented in [26].

$bal \leftarrow \textbf{Balance}(aid, pin) =$
PRE
  $aid \in accounts \land aid \in ACCOUNT \land$
  $pin \in \textbf{NAT} \land accountPin(aid) = pin \;\land fileOpen = \textbf{TRUE}$
THEN
  $bal := accountBalance(aid)$
END;

is ← **Authorized**(*aid*, *pin*) =
PRE
    aid ∈ *accounts* ∧ *aid* ∈ *ACCOUNT* ∧ *pin* ∈ **NAT** ∧ *fileOpen* = **TRUE**
THEN
    is := **bool**(*accountPin*(*aid*) = *pin*)
END;

We can enforce that withdrawals and balance queries can only be performed with the correct PIN. On the other hand, secrecy not being a property of behaviors, we cannot ensure it in B. Nothing can prevent an implementation to output secret pins onto a device, the state of which is not captured by the B specification.

The operation *Deposit* credits the amount to the specified account. It cannot verify that the money is actually given to the bank; this is the duty of the cashier.

We have to make sure that the addition *accountBalance(aid)* + *amount* does not create an overflow. There are a number of approaches to this problem:

- One possibility is to blindly assume that no one will ever have this much money and leave the addition unguarded. This will, however, rightfully leave us with an undischargable proof obligation. Even if our assumption holds, a typing error by a cashier could crash the system. The latter could again be caught by a check for a maximum amount in the interface, leaving only a sequence of similar mis-entries as problematic.
- We could strengthen the precondition of *Deposit* with *accountBalance(aid)* < *maxint - amount* and offer an additional operation *MaximalDeposit* returning the biggest possible deposit on a given account. Such an operation could, however, be abused to query the balance without the secret PIN from another software layer. Whether such guarding between software layers is needed in a closed system is debatable. After all, no customer of the bank could abuse this loophole at an ATM. Only programmers writing clients could. Note that introducing such a loophole would not create any unprovable proof obligations in B. We cannot express a property like 'client machines cannot infer the balance without knowledge of the secret PIN' in B.
- The third possibility is to let *Deposit* indicate whether the operation has succeeded or not. This cannot as easily be abused to query the balance, because if the operation succeeds a transaction is performed and the money must actually be transferred. Hence, this solution is chosen.

status ← **Deposit**(*aid*, *amount*) =
PRE
    aid ∈ *accounts* ∧ *aid* ∈ *ACCOUNT* ∧ *amount* ∈ **NAT** ∧ *amount* > 0 ∧
    fileOpen = **TRUE**
THEN
    IF *accountBalance*(*aid*) < **MAXINT** - *amount* **THEN**
    accountBalance(*aid*) := *accountBalance*(*aid*) + *amount* ‖ *status* := **TRUE**
    ELSE *status* := **FALSE**
    END
END;

Withdraw(*aid, pin, amount*) =
  PRE
    aid ∈ *accounts* ∧ *aid* ∈ *ACCOUNT* ∧ *pin* ∈ **NAT** ∧ *amount* ∈ **NAT** ∧
    accountPin(*aid*) = *pin* ∧ *amount* ≤ *accountBalance*(*aid*) ∧
    fileOpen = **TRUE**
  THEN
    accountBalance(*aid*) := *accountBalance*(*aid*) - *amount*
  END;
ChangePin(*aid, pin, newPin*) =
  PRE
    aid ∈ *accounts* ∧ *aid* ∈ *ACCOUNT* ∧ *pin* ∈ **NAT** ∧ *accountPin*(*aid*) = *pin* ∧
    newPin ∈ **NAT** ∧ *fileOpen* = **TRUE**
  THEN
    accountPin(*aid*) := *newPin*
  END;

Operations *Withdraw* and *ChangePin* follow the same pattern as *Deposit*.

The two final operations *Open* and *Close* concern persistency. An image of the set of customers, accounts, and strings (see below) is stored in the files designated by the parameters *customerFileName*, *accountFileName*, and *stringFileName* between program runs. *Open* is meant to read an arbitrary state satisfying the invariant from secondary storage. If *Open* succeeds, the result code *status* and the status flag *fileOpen* are set to *TRUE*. Note that the new state must satisfy the invariant, even if *status* is *FALSE*. In practice, *status* = *FALSE* means that the aforementioned files do not contain the image of a legal state or that the files cannot be properly accessed. *Close* writes the current state of the machine to the three files.

  status ← **Open**(*customerFileName, accountFileName, stringFileName*) =
  PRE
    customerFileName ∈ *STRING* ∧ *accountFileName* ∈ *STRING* ∧
    stringFileName ∈ *STRING* ∧ *fileOpen* = **FALSE**
  THEN
    ANY *customersInit, customerNameInit, customerYobInit,*
      accountsInit, accountNumberInit, accountPinInit,
      accountBalanceInit, accountOwnerInit, st
    WHERE
    customersInit ⊆ *CUSTOMER* ∧
    customerNameInit ∈ *customersInit* → *STRTOKEN* ∧
    customerYobInit ∈ *customersInit* → **NAT** ∧
    customerNameInit ⊗ *customerYobInit* ∈ *customersInit* ↣ (*STRTOKEN* × **NAT**)
      ∧ *accountsInit* ⊆ *ACCOUNT* ∧
    accountNumberInit ∈ *accountsInit* ↣ **NAT** ∧
    accountPinInit ∈ *accountsInit* → **NAT** ∧
    accountBalanceInit ∈ *accountsInit* → **NAT** ∧
    accountOwnerInit ∈ *accountsInit* → *customersInit* ∧
    st ∈ **BOOL**
    THEN
    customers := *customersInit* || *customerName* := *customerNameInit* ||
    customerYob := *customerYobInit* ||
    accounts := *accountsInit* || *accountNumber* := *accountNumberInit* ||
    accountPin := *accountPinInit* || *accountBalance* := *accountBalanceInit* ||

$$accountOwner := accountOwnerInit \parallel$$
$$foundCustomers := \{\} \parallel fileOpen := st \parallel status := st$$
END
END;
$status \leftarrow$ **Close** =
PRE *fileOpen* = **TRUE THEN**
RESET $\parallel$ *status* $:\in$ **BOOL**
END
END

In B we can only reason about a single program run. We could express as an invariant with auxiliary variables the condition that calling *Close*, then arbitrarily modifying the state, and thereafter calling *Open* should be *skip* on the base state space, if both result codes indicate success. This could be expressed by *Close* creating a snapshot of the current state in a set of auxiliary variables. However, we cannot infer from this that externalisation and internalisation actually work. A meta-language statement (*Close*; *Open*) = *skip* is easier to understand than a similar condition encoded as an invariant. Hence, it might be desirable to have a formal meta language with an associated proof tool for expressing such properties in B, as is done, for example, by the Refinement Calculator [16] for the refinement calculus.

Machine *Bank*, encapsulating the basic functionality, is animated to test whether it satisfies the stated requirements and also to check whether the latter are what we actually want. The proofs for this machine ascertain that the initialisation establishes the invariant and that the operations preserve it. However, the step from the rewritten requirements and the structured notation to the formal B specification cannot be formally proven, as indicated by the arrows in Fig. 4.7.

4.5.3 Discussion

The account number is a unique identifier for accounts. Hence, instead of introducing the system-generated object identifiers *customers* ($\subseteq$ *CUSTOMER*) we could have used account numbers as identifiers, simplifying the specification. The other attributes would then have been functions with domain *accountNumber* rather than *accounts*. In the implementation, we could have still used system-generated identifiers, in order to make references to accounts independent of the chosen pattern for account numbers and to use a generic support machine for persistent objects. The two specifications can be proved to be equivalent by mutual refinement (Exercise 4.3). We decided not to make the simplification in order to better illustrate the general scheme.

In our example, we have only used very simple UML class models. We sketch here briefly the translation of some more advanced elements.

Optional attributes can be modelled by partial functions. Attributes of maximal cardinality greater than one, as allowed in entity-relationship diagrams, can be expressed as general relations. Binary relations between classes with maximum cardinality greater one for both classes are expressed as general relations in B.

Subtypes can be expressed as a subsets. Hence, polymorphism can be expressed in B as 'soft types'. However, dynamic binding must be expressed as case statements. Hence, only closed (complete) systems can be given a B translation. Furthermore, all classes with cyclic references must be specified in the same machine. The transformation is difficult because B prohibits the calling of operations from the same module and the use of sequencing in machines. B is well-suited for the translation of a certain class of object-oriented models.

The combination of B and OMT [69] object models, the predecessors of UML class models, has been pioneered by Lano [47, 46]. Different translations of object diagrams into B have been proposed [28, 76]; the B-Toolkit even offers a tool for automatic translation (Sect. 4.11).

A simple translation of statecharts to B is also given by Lano [47]. A more thorough treatment can be found in Sekerinski [74]. Exercise 4.2 uses dynamic modelling to add online banking with a login to our application.

4.6 Robust Abstraction

To keep the specification simple, the initial machine *Bank* uses non-trivial preconditions rather than elaborate error handling. We could build a graphical user interface directly upon it. However, we opt for an intermediate layer, providing roughly the same functionality but with verification of parameters. Herewith, we effectively split up the task at hand. We avoid duplication of parameter checking for transactions which can be performed in different manners, for example by a cashier or at an ATM, using different interfaces.

We have to decide whether we want to include *Bank* into the robust interface *RobustBank* or not. If we want to reason about the behaviour on the robust level or if we want to be able to do such reasoning on even higher levels, we have to include *Bank*. If, on the other hand, all interesting invariant conditions are provable on the lower level, the inclusion would not make sense. Without including *Bank* we cannot specify under which conditions the operation actually succeeds and which parameters lead to which status code. However, we are guaranteed termination, which means that the corresponding implementation can only call the lower level implementation if the latter's precondition is satisfied. The advantage of the underspecification is that the implementation is also allowed to return an error in cases not explicitly captured by the specification, arising from practical implementation issues. We decide to include *Bank* to be able to perform more reasoning; the alternative approach will be illustrated on the next level up, the user interface layer. Below is the specification of *RobustNewCustomer* in the case where *Bank* would not be included.

> *result* ← **RobustNewCustomer**(*name, yob*) =
> **PRE** *name* ∈ *STRING* ∧ *yob* ∈ **NAT THEN**
> *result* :∈ {*success, db_full, db_error, customer_already_present*}
> **END**

Although specification and implementation structuring are largely independent in B, the above decision has some practical consequences. If we include *Bank* in *RobustBank*, the latter becomes the focus of refinement and implementation. We only need to implement *Bank* if we opt for importing it in the implementation of *RobustBank*. In the alternate approach of non-inclusion, we implicitly assume that *Bank* is imported in the implementation of the robust level and that the corresponding operations are called.

MACHINE
   RobustBank(maxCustomers, maxAccounts)

CONSTRAINTS
   $maxCustomers \in 1 .. 100000 \land maxAccounts \in 1 .. 200000$

INCLUDES
   BK.Bank(maxCustomers, maxAccounts)

SEES
   StrTokenType

DEFINITIONS
   $CUSTOMER == 0 .. maxCustomers-1; ACCOUNT == 0 .. maxAccounts-1$

SETS
   RESULT = {*success, dbFull, dbError, customerAlreadyPresent,*
      unknownCustomer, negativeAmount, amountTooBig, unknownAccount,
      AmountGreaterThanBalance, WrongPin}

We rename *Bank* in the includes clause so that references to its identifiers must be fully qualified, which increases readability. Note that sets, elements of enumerated sets, and constants do not participate in the renaming.

The robust operations are overly specific with respect to the reported result codes. For example in the case of *RobustNewCustomer* the specification prescribes the result code to be *dbFull* rather than *customerAlreadyPresent* in the case where both are applicable, for example the database is full and the customer passed as parameter is already in the database. This approach is simpler, but constrains the implementation. Exercise 4.6 investigates the more general specification.

OPERATIONS
   result ← **RobustNewCustomer**(*name, yob*) =
      PRE *name* ∈ *STRTOKEN* ∧ *yob* ∈ **NAT THEN**
         IF *BK.fileOpen* = **TRUE THEN**
            IF *BK.customers* ≠ *CUSTOMER* **THEN**
               IF (*name,yob*) ∉ **ran**(*BK.customerName* ⊗ *BK.customerYob*) **THEN**
                  result := *success* || *BK.NewCustomer*(*name, yob*)
               ELSE *result* := *customerAlreadyPresent*
               END
            ELSE *result* := *dbFull*
            END
         ELSE *result* := *dbError*
         END
      END;

Since a machine is only allowed to change its local state, it is imperative that changes to *Bank*'s state are performed using the latter's operations. However, query operations such as *RobustBalance* could be specified directly and one could argue that it is pointless to write query operations in machines which are included in others. If, however, we have convinced ourselves on the level of *Bank* that any access of an account's balance requires the corresponding PIN, this claim is automatically preserved if we only use operations of *Bank* and do not read its variables directly. This approach also facilitates change. Assume that we introduce a log in *Bank* recording all operations and, thereby, transform *RobustBalance* into a state modifying operation. The operation approach does not require any changes on the robust level indicating better modular continuity. However, since in B we specify behaviour and not call-sequences — as in the realm of component software [15] —, we still might have to adapt the implementation of the robust level, if the implementation does not call the same operation.

> *result, nof* ← **RobustInitFindCustomer**(*name*) =
>   **PRE** *name* ∈ *STRTOKEN* **THEN**
>   **IF** *BK.fileOpen* = **TRUE THEN**
>   *nof* ← *BK.InitFindCustomer*(*name*) || *result* := *success*
>   **ELSE** *result* := *dbError* || *nof* :∈ **NAT**
>   **END**
>   **END**;
>
> *found, yob* ← **RobustFindNextCustomer** =
>   **IF** *BK.fileOpen* = **TRUE THEN** *found, yob* ← *BK.FindNextCustomer*
>   **ELSE** *found* := **FALSE** || *yob* := 0
>   **END**;
>
> *result, number* ← **RobustNewAccount**(*name, yob, pin*) =
>   **PRE** *name* ∈ *STRTOKEN* ∧ *yob* ∈ **NAT** ∧ *pin* ∈ **NAT THEN**
>   **IF** *BK.fileOpen* = **TRUE THEN**
>   **IF** *BK.accounts* ≠ *ACCOUNT* **THEN**
>   **IF** (*name,yob*) ∈ **ran**(*BK.customerName* ⊗ *BK.customerYob*) **THEN**
>   *result* := *success* ||
>   *number* ← *BK.NewAccount*((*BK.customerName* ⊗ *BK.customerYob*) $^{-1}$
>   (*name, yob*), *pin*)
>   **ELSE** *result* := *unknownCustomer* || *number* :∈ **NAT**
>   **END**
>   **ELSE** *result* := *dbFull* || *number* :∈ **NAT**
>   **END**
>   **ELSE** *result* := *dbError* || *number* :∈ **NAT**
>   **END**
>   **END**;
>
> *result, bal* ← **RobustBalance**(*number, pin*) =
>   **PRE** *number* ∈ **NAT** ∧ *pin* ∈ **NAT THEN**
>   **IF** *BK.fileOpen* = **TRUE THEN**
>   **IF** *number* ∈ **ran**(*BK.accountNumber*) **THEN**
>   **IF** *pin* = *BK.accountPin*(*BK.accountNumber* $^{-1}$ (*number*)) **THEN**
>   *bal* ← *BK.Balance*(*BK.accountNumber* $^{-1}$ (*number*), *pin*) ||
>   *result* := *success*
>   **ELSE** *result* := *WrongPin* || *bal* :∈ **NAT**

```
      END
    ELSE result := unknownAccount || bal :∈ NAT
    END
  ELSE result := dbError || bal :∈ NAT
  END
END;
```

$result, name, yob \leftarrow$ **RobustOwner**(*number*) =
  PRE *number* ∈ **NAT THEN**
    IF *BK.fileOpen* = **TRUE THEN**
      IF *number* ∈ **ran**(*BK.accountNumber*) **THEN**
        name := *BK.customerName*(*BK.accountOwner* $^{-1}$ (*BK.accountNumber* $^{-1}$
          (*number*))) ||
        yob := *BK.customerYob*(*BK.accountOwner* $^{-1}$ (*BK.accountNumber* $^{-1}$
          (*number*))) ||
        result := *success*
      ELSE
        result := *unknownAccount* || *name* :∈ *STRTOKEN* || *yob* :∈ **NAT**
      END
    ELSE
      result := *dbError* || *name* :∈ *STRTOKEN* || *yob* :∈ **NAT**
    END
  END;

$result, dd \leftarrow$ **RobustDeposit**(*number*, *amount*) =
  PRE *number* ∈ **NAT** ∧ *amount* ∈ **NAT THEN**
    IF *BK.fileOpen* = **TRUE THEN**
      IF *number* ∈ **ran**(*BK.accountNumber*) **THEN**
        IF *amount* > 0 **THEN**
          IF *BK.accountBalance*(*BK.accountNumber* $^{-1}$ (*number*)) <
            MAXINT - *amount* **THEN**
          $dd \leftarrow$ *BK.Deposit*(*BK.accountNumber* $^{-1}$ (*number*), *amount*) ||
          result := *success*
          ELSE *result* := *amountTooBig* || *dd* :∈ **BOOL**
          END
        ELSE *result* := *negativeAmount* || *dd* :∈ **BOOL**
        END
      ELSE *result* := *unknownAccount* || *dd* :∈ **BOOL**
      END
    ELSE *result* := *dbError* || *dd* :∈ **BOOL**
    END
  END;

$result \leftarrow$ **RobustWithdraw**(*number*, *pin*, *amount*) =
  PRE *number* ∈ **NAT** ∧ *pin* ∈ **NAT** ∧ *amount* ∈ **NAT THEN**
    IF *BK.fileOpen* = **TRUE THEN**
      IF *number* ∈ **ran**(*BK.accountNumber*) **THEN**
        IF *pin* = *BK.accountPin*(*BK.accountNumber* $^{-1}$ (*number*)) **THEN**
          IF *amount* > 0 **THEN**
            IF *amount* ≤ *BK.accountBalance*(*BK.accountNumber* $^{-1}$ (*number*))
              THEN
            BK.Withdraw(*BK.accountNumber* $^{-1}$ (*number*), *pin*, *amount*) ||
            result := *success*
            ELSE *result* := *AmountGreaterThanBalance*
            END

    ELSE *result := negativeAmount*
    END
   ELSE *result := WrongPin*
   END
  ELSE *result := unknownAccount*
  END
 ELSE *result := dbError*
 END
END;

result ← **RobustChangePin**(*number, pin, newPin*) =
 PRE *number* ∈ **NAT** ∧ *pin* ∈ **NAT** ∧ *newPin* ∈ **NAT** **THEN**
  IF *BK.fileOpen* = **TRUE THEN**
   IF *number* ∈ **ran**(*BK.accountNumber*) **THEN**
    IF *pin* = *BK.accountPin*(*BK.accountNumber* $^{-1}$ (*number*)) **THEN**
    BK.ChangePin(*BK.accountNumber* $^{-1}$ (*number*), *pin, newPin*) ||
    result := success
    ELSE *result := WrongPin*
   END
   ELSE *result := unknownAccount*
   END
  ELSE *result := dbError*
  END
 END;

status ← **RobustOpen**(*customerFileName, accountFileName, stringFileName*) =
 PRE
  customerFileName ∈ *STRING* ∧ *accountFileName* ∈ *STRING* ∧
  stringFileName ∈ *STRING*
 THEN
  IF *BK.fileOpen* = **FALSE THEN**
   status ← *BK.Open*(*customerFileName, accountFileName, stringFileName*)
  ELSE *status := **FALSE***
  END
 END;

status ← **RobustClose** =
 IF *BK.fileOpen* = **TRUE THEN**
  status ← *BK.Close*
 ELSE *status := **FALSE***
 END
END

4.7 Base Machines

Before we can build a graphical user interface on top of the robust abstraction, we need to build support for the desired input and output mechanisms. A program consists of two parts: computation and interaction with the environment. The algorithmic aspects of a program can be expressed in B, whereas the input and output must be coded in a traditional language. B does not contain direct language support for communication with the environment, because input and output is very much dependent on the target architecture (Web, X Windows, disk, audio, etc.).

The B development can be interfaced in two ways with its environment: using base machines or using a main program written in a classical programming language which calls the B development. A base machine is a machine the implementation of which is written in a classical programming language rather than in B. A specification of the desired functionality is given as a regular B machine so that it can be used by other B constructs. The actual implementation, not being expressible in B, is programmed directly in the desired classical language, for example, C or Ada. The alternative approach is to use B to create a service subsystem, a subroutine library, and write the main program which interfaces with the environment and calls the B subsystem in a classical programming language. The two approaches can also be combined, for example, we could write a base machine for file access and still write the main program interfacing with the Web in C. In fact, since only scalars and one-dimensional array are implementable directly in B0 and all other data structures use library machines, which in turn are built on base machines, few interesting developments are possible without base machines at all.

We decided to use base machines rather than writing the main program directly in a classical programming language. Base machines can be reused for other developments. From this perspective, it would be logical to have a standard library of base machines. However, the typical domain of B being embedded systems with custom interfaces, such a library would not be generally usable. Nevertheless, it would be desirable to have for educational purposes.

In many industrial applications, especially in those that build on existing components, B is only used to create the most safety-critical algorithmic part in the middle, building on well-tested databases for persistent storage and complex graphical user interfaces. This often suitable compromise requires a great amount of discipline to be exercised to avoid parts of the algorithm being expressed outside B. We have chosen the all-B approach to illustrate its feasibility.

4.7.1 Strings in Atelier B

Atelier B has a type *STRING* for constant character chains. *STRING* can be used for passing a message like "Hello world" to a terminal output machine or, in our case, to pass the names of the dump files. However, there is no support for non-literal strings as needed for customers' names. Atelier B does not permit objects of variable length, such as strings, to be passed between operations. Because there is no support for constant-length strings either, we are forced to either use tokens as references to the actual strings, which are stored in a base machine, or pass strings character-by-character with multiple calls. We opt for tokens. Machine *StrTokenType* defines a type of string tokens.

MACHINE
   StrTokenType
SETS

STRTOKEN
CONCRETE_CONSTANTS
EmptyStringToken
PROPERTIES
EmptyStringToken $\in$ *STRTOKEN*
END

Note that the set *STRTOKEN* is abstract. Therefore, normal B machines cannot simply 'create new string tokens' as would have been the case if we had used a subset of the *NAT* instead. The fact that *STRTOKEN* is valued to a subset of *NAT* in the implementation only helps the C-translator, but cannot be exploited in constructs which see or import *StrTokenType*.

Since string tokens can be compared with '=', we need to have an injection from tokens to strings. To ensure this, only one single machine called *BasicString* is allowed to generate tokens. Input base machines return tokens, not strings. Fig. 4.8 (left side) illustrates string I/O, with *BasicCGI* as an example of an I/O machine. Implementation *MainBank_1* requests a string to be input. *BasicCGI* reads a string from the Web, enters the string in *BasicString* and in return receives a token, which it returns to its client *MainBank_1*. Note that the operations for entering new strings and retrieving strings by token are not specified on the B level, but are only present in the hand-coded C implementation.

The rest of this subsection discusses additional aspects of passing objects of variable size in B. The material is of general interest, but is not necessary for understanding the case study. Hence, it can be skipped on a first reading.

Unfortunately, the token solution has a shortcoming: We cannot ensure in B that no other base machine generates tokens. For example a random base machine could have a machine parameter of set type and provide an operation which returns arbitrary elements of that set. Instantiated with *STRTOKEN*, this machine could generate tokens for which *BasicString* has no corresponding string. We must also ensure that whenever string tokens are externalised, the corresponding strings are also saved.

The obvious, but for other reasons undesirable, remedy to the first problem would be to introduce a set *legalTokens* $\subseteq$ *STRTOKEN* in *BasicString*. Any input operation would then have to modify *legalTokens*. However, only the constructs that includes/imports *BasicString*, but no others that only see *BasicString*, have access to state modifying operations of *BasicString*.[1] As a consequence, input from any source would have to be implemented in a single base machine, contradicting modularity. For example, base machines for input from the Web and from a terminal could not simply be combined by importing both, but would have to be textually merged.

---

[1] This single writer and multiple readers restriction is due to the visibility of variables of included/imported machines in the invariant of the including/importing implementation. Multiple writers could invalidate each other's invariants.

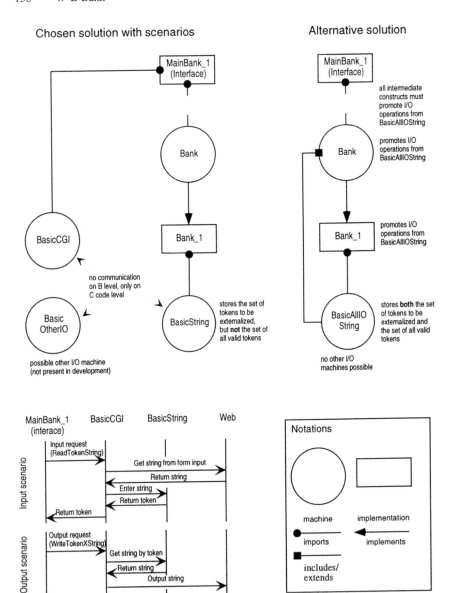

Fig. 4.8. Alternatives for Input/Output and String Storage

The single-writer restriction would complicate the design even if we would limit ourselves to a single input/output (I/O) machine. If we would not want to externalise all strings, but only a selected subset (the names of the customers) that we need again in future program runs, then implementation *Bank_1* would also need write access to *BasicString*'s state because *Bank_1* would have to control the externalisation process. All components accessing *BasicString* in write mode would have to be parents in a straight line, each imported by the next. Hence, the single I/O machine would have to import *BasicString*, respectively be merged into a single machine to also avoid the behind the scene passing of strings. Implementation *Bank_1* would then have to import this machine *BasicAllIOString*. The real inelegance would be that the I/O operations which are accessed from the interface layer would have to be promoted by the specifications *Bank* and *RobustBank*. A similar pollution of the specifications of *Bank* would occur if externalisation of strings were to be controlled by the interface layer and *Bank* would have to provide operations to query the set of strings to be externalised.

Because of the need to combine all I/O into a single I/O machine and the cluttering of specifications with implementation aspects, we do not choose this solution. Rather we accept that we cannot maintain in B a set of all valid tokens. Fig. 4.8 illustrates the two alternatives. The specification of *BasicString* is given on page 161.

4.7.2 Machine *BasicCGI*

In order to input and output data to the Web, we need a machine to access the common gateway interface (CGI), which we call *BasicCGI*. CGI is a standard for interfacing external applications with information servers, such as Web servers. A plain hypertext markup language (HTML) document that the Web daemon retrieves is static, which means it exists in a constant state: a text file that doesn't change. A CGI program, on the other hand, is executed in real-time, so that it can output dynamic information. The user fills out a form in the browser and sends the data to the server which executes the CGI program. The CGI program processes the input, modifies the local database, and generates an output which is sent back to the user's browser for display.

MACHINE
  BasicCGI
SEES
  StrTokenType

OPERATIONS
  status, num ← **ReadNat**(*name*) =
    PRE *name* ∈ *STRING* **THEN**
      status :∈ **BOOL** || *num* :∈ **NAT**
    END;

In an HTML form every field has a unique name. Operation *ReadNat* inputs a natural number value of a field, designated by its name, from a form. Since the user can enter an arbitrary number into a given field, we can only assure that *num* is a natural number. The browser, the server, and the connection between them being outside the realm of our specification, we cannot specify that the reported value is actually the one entered by the user. An implementation which always returns 0, independently of the users input would, therefore, be formally correct. Neither can we specify under which circumstances the result code indicates success. Actually, an implementation which always fails would also be correct. The intended meaning of the operation is only captured by its name and the natural language description. The only property guaranteed by the formal specification is termination.

Whether we use result codes or not depends upon how we can react to failure. Consider, for example, a measuring device with an input sensor and a disk to store the values as its only output device. If the disk fails, we can also stop execution. In this case an abstraction specifying the disk as reliable leads to a simpler system. Alternatively, we might specify the disk as unreliable, but simply ignore the result codes in the higher layers, leading to unprovable obligations. On the other hand, if we can react to failure by, for example, storing the current state on a spare disk and showing an error message on the screen, return codes are desirable. In non safety-critical systems, operations with a very high success probability are often assumed to be fully reliable, because little can be done in case of failure and the resulting system is much simpler.

To be more precise, the return codes in our example indicate whether the Web server has indicated an error or not. If, for example, the underlying hardware has malfunctioned in a way not traced by the operating system or Web server, for example, a communication error resulting in a correct checksum, the error goes unnoticed. Building up a system from components, we specify each component separately and reason about the whole system using composition rules assuming the implementations to adhere to the specification. If a specification is too weak, the corresponding component cannot be used intelligently. Although more truthful, a specification saying that the CGI functions might have failed even if the result indicates success, is useless, because we cannot build on it. Risk estimates using probabilistic reasoning would need to complement a development in B [80, 58, 57].

Operation *ReadTokenString* reads a string from a form field. As described above, the string is stored in machine *BasicString* and only a token is returned. If the string contained in the field is longer than *maxLength*, the operations returns failure.

> *status*, *str* ← **ReadTokenString**(*name*, *maxLength*) =
> **PRE** *name* ∈ *STRING* ∧ *maxLength* ∈ **NAT THEN**
>   *status* :∈ **BOOL** || *str* :∈ *STRTOKEN*
> **END**;

The remaining five operations are concerned with outputting a new document in response to the user's request. Each document has a MIME (Multipurpose Internet Message Extension) type which tells the browser the format of the remaining data stream. In our case, the type is always "text/html". Operation *WriteLiteralContent-Type* lets us send the MIME type to the browser. Parameter *mimeType* is of type *STRING* as a constant literal string is envisaged to be used as an actual parameter.

> **WriteLiteralContentType**(*mimeType*) =
> **PRE** *mimeType* ∈ *STRING* **THEN skip END**;

In HTML, certain characters such as '<' are reserved for markup purposes. Additionally, 8-bit characters must be encoded using either their mnemonic or their decimal codes in the Latin-1 character set. For example, the letter 'ü' can be encoded as either 'ü' or as ' ü'. Operation *WriteLiteralString* outputs a string without any conversions; hence, the string can contain HTML tags, but special characters must already be encoded. Operation *WriteLatin1TokenString* converts a string from the Latin-1 character set to its HTML encoding.

> **WriteLiteralString**(*str*) =
> **PRE** *str* ∈ *STRING* **THEN skip END**;
>
> **WriteLatin1TokenString**(*str*) =
> **PRE** *str* ∈ *STRTOKEN* **THEN skip END**;

In arguments to CGI programs, certain reserved characters as well as 8-bit characters must be encoded as their hexadecimal codes in the Latin-1 character set. The letter 'ü', for example, is represented as '%FC'. Since such argument strings may not contain any spaces, the latter are converted to '+'s. This type of conversion is performed by operation *WriteURLString* before outputting its argument.

> **WriteURLTokenString**(*str*) =
> **PRE** *str* ∈ *STRTOKEN* **THEN skip END**;
>
> **WriteNat**(*num*) =
> **PRE** *num* ∈ **NAT THEN skip END**
> **END**

The actual output operations are specified as skip as the output is not part of the state captured by the B specification. Although the output operations can also fail in practice, we have chosen the less safe, but more convenient approach of specifying them as reliable.

A partial modelling of the output would also have practical consequences. The operations of *BasicCGI* might be called from different implementation constructs. As long as the operations are inquiry operations they can be called from implementations which see *BasicCGI*. If, on the other hand, the output operations modify the state, the lowest machine in the hierarchy using *BasicCGI* must import the latter and promote the operations.

Machine *BasicCGI* does not enforce its output to be correct HTML, for example, there is no check for matching markup tags. Although desirable, such checks would make the machine much more cumbersome to use as tags could not be embedded in strings and the machine would have to be updated to use new HTML tags.

4.7.3 Implementing *BasicCGI*

To implement *BasicCGI* we first write an 'empty' B implementation the C translation of which gives us a C code skeleton conforming to the coding standards of Atelier B's translator. This skeleton is then filled in with the actual code. The implementation *BasicCGI_1* contains only the minimal information to conform to B and be translatable. We have to value every set and constant, initialize concrete variables of the specification, and list all the operations. Operations are simply specified as skip, if they have no return parameters and otherwise as dummy assignments to the return parameters. We do not prove anything about this empty implementation. Note that *BasicCGI_1* sees *BasicString* to force the latter being imported somewhere in the development.

> **IMPLEMENTATION**
>   *BasicCGI_1*
> **REFINES**
>   *BasicCGI*
> **SEES**
>   *StrTokenType, BasicString*
> **OPERATIONS**
>   *status, num* ← **ReadNat**(*name*) =
>   **BEGIN**
>   *status* := **TRUE**; *num* := 0
>   **END**;
>   *status, str* ← **ReadTokenString**(*name, maxLength*) =
>   **BEGIN**
>   *status* := **TRUE**; *str* := *EmptyStringToken*
>   **END**;
>   **WriteLiteralContentType**(*mimeType*) = **skip**;
>   **WriteLiteralString**(*str*) = **skip**;
>   **WriteURLTokenString**(*str*) = **skip**;
>   **WriteLatin1TokenString**(*str*) = **skip**;
>   **WriteNat**(*num*) = **skip**
> **END**

Rather than implementing CGI access from scratch we build upon the public domain ANSI C library cgic version 1.05 from Thomas Boutell [13]. This library provides for comfortable parsing of form input. The second included header file *trad_ctx.h* defines some macros such as *PROTx* to make the source code portable between ANSI C and K&R compilers.

In a project, a machine can be imported several times with different instance names. Different instances represent different data. Implementing a base machine, we have to decide whether multiple instantiation is permitted or not. If, for example, a base machine represents a physical device such as an LED only one copy of the corresponding base machine should be included in a development. If a base machine does not allow for multiple instantiations, we have to verify that the project adheres to this rule. The restriction cannot be expressed in AMN; depending upon the target language and the translator it is possible to write C code which fails to compile, respectively link if the rule is violated. If, as in our case, this is not possible, manual inspection is necessary. On the other hand, if we allow multiple instantiations, the state of an instantiation must be included into the struct *BasicX_type*. As discussed above, we do not need to make our machine *BasicCGI* instanciable, even if we use it from more than one implementation construct. Hence, we opt for this simpler approach which also corresponds more closely to the reality we model. Our third base machine *BasicFile* (Sect. 4.10.4) illustrates multiple instantiation. The hand-coded additions and modifications are set in italics in the C source files.

```
#include"cgic.h"
#ifndef trad_ctx_include_def
   #include "trad_ctx.h"
#endif

/* Links to machines from the SEES clause */
#ifndef StrTokenType_include_def
   #include "StrTokenType.h"
#endif

/* Structure associated to component (instance record) */
struct BasicCGI_type {
   int BasicCGI_init_already_done;
} ;

#define BasicCGI_include_def

/* Reference to machines from the SEES clause */
EXTERN struct StrTokenType_type *StrTokenType_ptr;

/* Prototypes of translated operations */
EXTERN void link_BasicCGI PROTF((struct BasicCGI_type *v));

EXTERN void init_BasicCGI PROTF((struct BasicCGI_type *v));

/* Type of name changed manually from INT32 to char* */
EXTERN void ReadNat_BasicCGI PROTF((struct BasicCGI_type *v,
   INT32 *status, INT32 *num, char *name));

/* The other operations can be found on the book's Web page. */
```

In its original implementation, cgic provides itself a main function and expects the user to write a function called *cgiMain* which is called after initialisation. By changing a handful of lines as indicated in the online source code, we turn cgic's *main* function into a function *cgiInit* which we call from *init_BasicCGI*. The specifications does not allow the initialisation to fail. In practice, if the initialisation fails we write a message to *stderr* and abort execution. Since we cannot perform any transaction anyhow, abortion at startup is the simplest solution. The operations are simply calls to the corresponding procedures of cgic, respectively *fprintf* commands.

```
#include <stdio.h>
#include "BasicCGI.h"
#include "BasicString.h"

void link_BasicCGI(PROTA(struct BasicCGI_type *)v)
    PROTC(struct BasicCGI_type *v)
{}

void init_BasicCGI(PROTA(struct BasicCGI_type *)v)
    PROTC(struct BasicCGI_type *v)
{
  if (StrTokenType_ptr->StrTokenType_init_already_done &&
      (v->BasicCGI_init_already_done==0)) {
    if(cgiInit()!=0){
      fprintf(stderr, "Initialization of BasicCGI failed.\n"); exit(-1);
    }
    v->BasicCGI_init_already_done=1;
  }
}


void ReadNat_BasicCGI(PROTA(struct BasicCGI_type *)v, PROTA(INT32 *)status,
      PROTA(INT32 *)num, PROTA(char *)name)
    PROTC(struct BasicCGI_type *v) PROTC( INT32 *status)
      PROTC(INT32 *num) PROTC(char *name)
{
  int s;

  s=cgiFormInteger(name, num, 0);
  if((s==0)&&(*num>=0)) {
    *status=TRUE;
  } else {
    *num=0; *status=FALSE;
  }
}
```

/* The other operations can be found on the book's Web page. */

We prove in B that all calls to operations of *BasicCGI* satisfy the respective preconditions. Hence, there is no need to write checks for the preconditions in the C code of *BasicCGI*. The hand-coded C implementation is a refinement of its B specification. The validity of the refinement has to be asserted using normal verification techniques, for example, testing and third party code inspection.

We make a separate project out of *BasicCGI*, *BasicString*, and *StrTokenType* to facilitate reuse in other projects. This also prevents us from accidentally overwriting the hand-coded implementation. The files *cgic.c* and *cgic.h* must be manually added to the Makefile, copied from the data base to the code directory. Additionally, the target *BasicCGI* must be removed from the Makefile, as we only want to create a library and make would produce an error because of the missing *main* function.

For didactic reasons, we have presented the implementation of the base machine directly following its specification. In practice, we often write the implementation only after we have actually used its specification in other constructs and, thereby, convinced ourselves of its appropriateness. The disadvantage of this is that the specification might not be implementable on the target system, causing a rework of all dependent constructs.

4.8 User Interface

The user interface presents an entry mask to the user, parses the input with the help of *BasicCGI*, sends the request to the robust interface *RobustBank*, and presents the results using again the CGI machine. We first prototype this interaction using static HTML code with normal links between the pages rather than calls to our CGI application. Once we are satisfied with the look and feel, we write the user interface

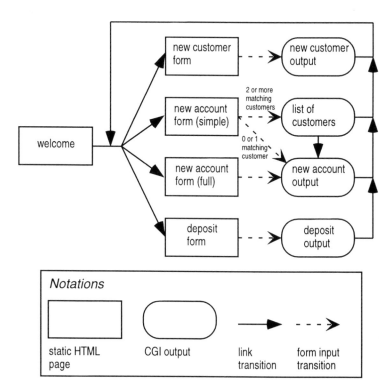

Fig. 4.9. Cashier Interaction

which generates the same HTML code based upon CGI requests. Static information, such as the input forms, remains in the form of normal HTML files.

The cashier is presented with a menu on the bottom of her terminal, from which she can choose a form to enter a new customer, create a new account for an existing customer, or make a deposit. In the 'new customer' form, the cashier enters the name and year of birth of the customer and clicks on a button to send the data to the CGI application. In response, the cashier gets a screen saying that the operation has succeeded or that an error has occurred. These messages are all generated by the same CGI program, but for prototyping we need to create different HTML pages. After reading the output message, the cashier clicks on another menu choice.

When creating a new account, the cashier has the option of entering both the customer's name and year of birth or only the name. If there is only one customer with the given name in the system, an account is created. On the other hand, if there is more than one customer with this name, the cashier is presented with a list. She then simply clicks on the desired customer to create the account. In the latter case, the links contain all the parameters, which would usually be entered into the form by the cashier. For example for customer 'Garfield', born in '1978', and PIN '2001' the URL of the link would be 'http://.../cgi-bin/AB/MainBank?command=1&name=Garfield&yob=1978&pin=2001'. The CGI

```
<HTML>
  <HEAD><TITLE>B Bank: New Customer</TITLE></HEAD>
  <BODY BGCOLOR="#228B22">
    <H1>B Bank: New Customer</H1>
    <FORM ACTION="http://www.tucs.abo.fi/cgi-bin/mbuechi/AB/MainBank"
        METHOD="POST">
      <INPUT TYPE="HIDDEN" NAME="command" VALUE="0">
      <TABLE BORDER="0">
        <TR ALIGN="Center" VALIGN="Middle">
          <TD ALIGN="RIGHT">Customer name:</TD>
          <TD ALIGN="LEFT"><INPUT NAME="name" SIZE="18"></TD>
        </TR>
        <TR ALIGN="Center" VALIGN="Middle">
          <TD ALIGN="RIGHT">Year of birth:</TD>
          <TD ALIGN="LEFT"><INPUT NAME="yob" SIZE="4"></TD>
        </TR>
      </TABLE>
      <P>
        <INPUT TYPE="submit" VALUE="Add customer"><BR>
        <INPUT TYPE="reset" VALUE="Reset input form">
      </P>
    </FORM>
  </BODY>
</HTML>
```

Fig. 4.10. HTML Source Code of 'New Customer' Form

program doesn't have to store any temporary information. 'Deposit' leads to simple one-step interaction sequences like 'new customer', as depicted in Fig. 4.9.

For brevity's sake, we do not list all the HTML pages. We assume the reader to be familiar with basic HTML. In Fig. 4.10, the *FORM* tag introduces the actual entry form. Its attribute *ACTION* states the URL of the CGI program, to which the input data is sent upon pressing the submit button. The input field 'name' takes the customer name. Rather than creating a separate CGI application for each entry form, we use a hidden input field 'command' which selects the desired operation. The CGI program is our final B applications, which we copy to the CGI directory of the Webserver and give the suitable execution rights.

The user interaction at the ATM and the corresponding HTML pages are similar. On a standard ATM, the account number is read from a card. To run our simulation without any special hardware, the user is also requested to enter the account number. A typical ATM interface is modal, that is, one first inserts the card, then enters the PIN, and finally performs the desired transaction. In our simulation, the user is requested to enter all information in a single modeless dialog. Exercise 4.2 shows how to model a modal interface using the idea of links generated by the program.

In order to make navigation easier in the simulation, we add a frame set with a meta menu which lets us easily switch between the cashier terminal and the ATM, displayed with different background colour in the right-hand side frame.

4.8.1 Main Program

To keep the size of the individual operations small, we create one operation per transaction type. Since in B operations from the same construct cannot be called, we divide the user interface into two machines. Machine *MainBank* contains the main program. It reads the 'command' field and calls the selected operation of machine *OperationsBank*, which does the actual work.

We do not duplicate the state on the user interface level in *OperationsBank*, as we do not want to perform any reasoning. Hence, the specification of the transaction operations is simply skip.

MACHINE
  OperationsBank
OPERATIONS

  NewCustomer = skip;
  NewAccount = skip;
  Deposit = skip;
  Withdraw = skip;
  Balance = skip;
  ChangePin = skip;
  Error(*number*) =
    PRE *number* ∈ **NAT THEN skip END**;

status ← **Open**(*customerFileName, accountFileName, stringFileName*) =
  PRE
    customerFileName ∈ *STRING* ∧ *accountFileName* ∈ *STRING* ∧
    stringFileName ∈ *STRING*
  THEN
    status :∈ **BOOL**
  END;
  status ← **Close** =
  BEGIN
    status :∈ **BOOL**
  END
END

The machine *MainBank* is also stateless. The specification of its single operation *main* is skip, guaranteeing only termination. Since the persistent state, existing beyond a single program run, cannot be modelled, skip is in fact the only reasonable specification for a main program.

MACHINE
  MainBank

OPERATIONS
  main = **skip**
END

4.8.2 Implementations

The implementation *MainBank_1* first opens the database. Then it reads the value of the 'command' input field, calls the selected operation, and closes the database.

IMPLEMENTATION
  MainBank_1

REFINES
  MainBank

IMPORTS
  BC.BasicCGI, OB.OperationsBank , StrTokenType

OPERATIONS
  main =
  VAR *dbst, st, res* **IN**
    dbst ← *OB.Open*("/tmp/customer", "/tmp/account", "/tmp/strings");
    IF *dbst* = **TRUE THEN**
      st, res ← *BC.ReadNat*("command");
      IF *st* = **TRUE THEN**
        CASE *res* **OF**
          EITHER 0 **THEN** *OB.NewCustomer*
          OR 1 **THEN** *OB.NewAccount*

              OR 2 **THEN** *OB.Deposit*
              OR 3 **THEN** *OB.Withdraw*
              OR 4 **THEN** *OB.Balance*
              OR 5 **THEN** *OB.ChangePin*
              ELSE *OB.Error*(0)
              END
            END
          ELSE *OB.Error*(1)
          END;
           dbst ← *OB.Close*
          ELSE *OB.Error*(2)
          END
        END
     END

The implementation *OperationsBank_1* imports *RobustBank*. The operation *NewCustomer* first outputs the header of the result screen, which is independent of the outcome of the operation. Then it reads the value of the 'name' field, calls *RobustNewCustomer* and presents the result.

The loop in operation *NewAccount* shows the advantage of not just using B to create a subroutine library. In this case, loops on the user interface level would not be proved to terminate. For brevity's sake, some operations are omitted in the listing below. They can, as all other constructs, be found on the book's Web page.

IMPLEMENTATION
   OperationsBank_1

REFINES
   OperationsBank

IMPORTS
   RB.RobustBank(100, 200)

SEES
   BC.BasicCGI

CONCRETE_CONSTANTS
   False1

PROPERTIES
   False1 ∈ **BOOL** ↣ **NAT**

VALUES
   False1 = {(**TRUE** ↦ 0), (**FALSE** ↦ 1)}

DEFINITIONS
   CASHIER_HEADER(*title*) == *HEADER*(*title*, "#228B22");
   ATM_HEADER(*title*) == *HEADER*(*title*, "#DC143C");
   HEADER(*title,color*) == (
   BC.WriteLiteralContentType("text/html");
   BC.WriteLiteralString("<HTML>\n<HEAD><TITLE>B Bank: ");
   BC.WriteLiteralString(*title*); *BC.WriteLiteralString*("</TITLE></HEAD>\n");
   BC.WriteLiteralString("<BODY BGCOLOR="); *BC.WriteLiteralString*(*color*);

```
BC.WriteLiteralString(">\n<H1>B Bank: ");
  BC.WriteLiteralString(title); BC.WriteLiteralString("</H1>\n"));
FOOTER == BC.WriteLiteralString("</BODY></HTML>\n");
DB_FULL_MSG == BC.WriteLiteralString("<P>Sorry. The database is full.</P>");
DB_ERR_MSG ==
  BC.WriteLiteralString("<P>Sorry. The databse is not working.</P>");
UNK_ACC_MSG(num) == (
  BC.WriteLiteralString("<P>Account "); BC.WriteNat(num);
  BC.WriteLiteralString(" is not in database.</P>"));
CGI_SCRIPT == "http://www.tucs.abo.fi/cgi-bin/mbuechi/AB/MainBank";
MAX_NAME_LENGTH == 256
```

OPERATIONS

NewCustomer =
  VAR *st, name, yob, result* **IN**
    CASHIER_HEADER("New Customer");
    st, name ← BC.**ReadTokenString**("name", *MAX_NAME_LENGTH*);
    IF *st* = **TRUE THEN**
      st, yob ← BC.*ReadNat*("yob");
      IF *st* = **TRUE THEN**
        result ← *RB.RobustNewCustomer(name, yob)*;
        CASE *result* **OF**
          EITHER *success* **THEN**
            BC.WriteLiteralString("<P>Customer ");
            BC.WriteLatin1TokenString(name);
            BC.WriteLiteralString(" ("); *BC.WriteNat(yob)*;
            BC.WriteLiteralString(") has been added.</P>")
          OR *customerAlreadyPresent* **THEN**
            BC.WriteLiteralString("<P>Customer ");
            BC.WriteLatin1TokenString(name);
            BC.WriteLiteralString(" ("); *BC.WriteNat(yob)*;
            BC.WriteLiteralString(") is already in database.</P>")
          OR *dbFull* **THEN DB_FULL_MSG**
          OR *dbError* **THEN DB_ERR_MSG**
          END
        END
      ELSE *BC.WriteLiteralString*("<P>Could not get year of birth.</P>")
      END
    ELSE *BC.WriteLiteralString*("<P>Could not get name.</P>")
    END;
    FOOTER
  END;

NewAccount =
  VAR *st, name, yob, pin, result, number, nof, found, ii* **IN**
    CASHIER_HEADER("New Account");
    st, name ← BC.**ReadTokenString**("name", *MAX_NAME_LENGTH*);
    IF *st* = **TRUE THEN**
      st, pin ← BC.**ReadNat**("pin");
      IF *st* = **TRUE THEN**
        st, yob ← BC.**ReadNat**("yob");
        IF *st* = **FALSE THEN**
          result, nof ← RB.**RobustInitFindCustomer**(*name*);
          IF *result* = *success* **THEN**
```
```

```
IF nof = 0 THEN
  BC.WriteLiteralString("<P>Customer ");
  BC.WriteLatin1TokenString(name);
  BC.WriteLiteralString(" is not in database.</P>")
ELSIF nof = 1 THEN
  found, yob ← RB.RobustFindNextCustomer;
  st := TRUE
ELSE BC.WriteLiteralString("<P>Choose from list:</P><UL>");
  ii := 0; found, yob ← RB.RobustFindNextCustomer;
  WHILE found = TRUE DO
    BC.WriteLiteralString("<LI><A HREF=");
    BC.WriteLiteralString(CGI_SCRIPT);
    BC.WriteLiteralString("?command=1&name=");
    BC.WriteURLTokenString(name);
    BC.WriteLiteralString("&yob=");
    BC.WriteNat(yob);
    BC.WriteLiteralString("&pin=");
    BC.WriteNat(pin);
    BC.WriteLiteralString(">");
    BC.WriteLatin1TokenString(name); BC.WriteLiteralString(" (");
    BC.WriteNat(yob); BC.WriteLiteralString(")</A></L>");
    found, yob ← RB.RobustFindNextCustomer
  INVARIANT
    yob ∈ NAT
  VARIANT
    card(RB.BK.foundCustomers)+1-False1(found)
  END;
  BC.WriteLiteralString("</UL>")
END
  ELSE DB_ERR_MSG
  END
END;
IF st = TRUE THEN
  result, number ← RB.RobustNewAccount(name, yob, pin);
  CASE result OF
    EITHER success THEN
      BC.WriteLiteralString("<P>New account number ");
      BC.WriteNat(number);
      BC.WriteLiteralString(" has been created for customer ");
      BC.WriteLatin1TokenString(name);
      BC.WriteLiteralString(" ("); BC.WriteNat(yob);
      BC.WriteLiteralString(").</P>")
    OR unknownCustomer THEN
      BC.WriteLiteralString("<P>Customer ");
      BC.WriteLatin1TokenString(name);
      BC.WriteLiteralString(" ("); BC.WriteNat(yob);
      BC.WriteLiteralString(") is not in database.</P>")
    OR dbFull THEN DB_FULL_MSG
    OR dbError THEN DB_ERR_MSG
    END
  END
END
ELSE BC.WriteLiteralString("<P>Could not get pin.</P>")
```

```
    END
  ELSE BC.WriteLiteralString("<P>Could not get name.</P>")
  END;
FOOTER
END;
```

Deposit =
```
  VAR st, number, amount, result, dd, name, yob IN
    CASHIER_HEADER("Deposit");
    st, number ← BC.ReadNat("number");
    IF st = TRUE THEN
      st, amount ← BC.ReadNat("amount");
      IF st = TRUE THEN
        result, dd ← RB.RobustDeposit(number, amount);
        CASE result OF
          EITHER success THEN
            BC.WriteLiteralString("<P>A deposit of ");
            BC.WriteNat(amount);
            BC.WriteLiteralString(" has been made on account ");
            BC.WriteNat(number);
            result, name, yob ← RB.RobustOwner(number);
            IF result = success THEN
              BC.WriteLiteralString(" belonging to ");
              BC.WriteLatin1TokenString(name);
              BC.WriteLiteralString(" ("); BC.WriteNat(yob);
              BC.WriteLiteralString(")")
            END;
            BC.WriteLiteralString(".</P>")
          OR negativeAmount THEN
            BC.WriteLiteralString("<P>Amount must be greater than 0.</P>")
          OR amountTooBig THEN
            BC.WriteLiteralString("<P>Amount too big. ")
            BC.WriteLiteralString("No deposit has been made.</P>")
          OR unknownAccount THEN UNK_ACC_MSG(number)
          OR dbError THEN DB_ERR_MSG
          END
        END
      ELSE BC.WriteLiteralString("<P>Could not get amount.</P>")
      END
    ELSE BC.WriteLiteralString("<P>Could not get number.</P>")
    END;
    FOOTER
  END;
```

/* Operations Withdraw, Balance, and ChangePin and Error omitted. Check the book's Web page. */

```
    status ← Open(customerFileName, accountFileName, stringFileName) =
      status ← RB.RobustOpen(customerFileName, accountFileName, stringFileName);

    status ← Close =
      status ← RB.RobustClose

END
```

4.9 Implementation of the Robust Abstraction

The missing piece is the implementation of the robust layer *RobustBank*. We have to make a choice as to whether we want to import *Bank* in the implementation *RobustBank_1* or whether we want to build directly on lower level abstractions.

Often, a more abstract specification is included into the robust level and a similar, more concrete specification is imported in the implementation. The machine that is included in the specification should be as abstract as possible to avoid overspecification. The machine that is imported in the implementation should be quite concrete to make it more useful. The use of two different constructs solves this dilemma. However, in our case we can include, respectively import the same ma-

Same machine Bank is both included and imported (chosen path)

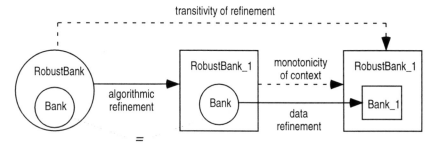

More abstract construct AbstractBank is included in specification,
more concrete construct ConcreteBank is imported in implementation (rejected alternative)

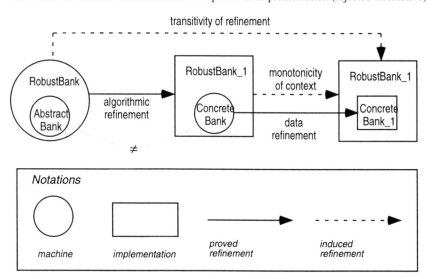

Fig. 4.11. Import of Included Machine vs. Import of More Concrete Construct

chine *Bank* in both the specification and the implementation, avoiding a proliferation of constructs. In the alternative case *Bank*, respectively a more abstract version *AbstractBank*, would have been used only in the specification, but would not have to be refined to an implementation. Fig. 4.11 shows the two options.

Importing an already included machine without renaming, respectively renaming it identically both times, constitutes an algorithmic refinement. The identity mapping invariant is implicitly added.

The operations first check whether the parameters and the current state satisfy the preconditions of the corresponding operations in *Bank* and then call them, or report an error if the conditions do not hold.

IMPLEMENTATION
RobustBank_1(maxCustomers, maxAccounts)

REFINES
RobustBank

IMPORTS
BK.Bank(maxCustomers, maxAccounts)

SEES
StrTokenType

OPERATIONS

$result \leftarrow$ **RobustNewCustomer**(*name,yob*) =
VAR *status, cid* **IN**
  IF *BK.fileOpen* = **TRUE THEN**
    status $\leftarrow$ *BK.CustomerDBFull*;
    IF *status* = **FALSE THEN**
      status, cid $\leftarrow$ *BK.ThisCustomer(name,yob)*;
      IF *status* = **FALSE THEN**
        BK.NewCustomer(name,yob); *result* := *success*
      ELSE *result* := *customerAlreadyPresent*
      END
    ELSE *result* := *dbFull*
    END
  ELSE *result* := *dbError*
  END
END;

$result, nof \leftarrow$ **RobustInitFindCustomer**(*name*) =
IF *BK.fileOpen* = **TRUE THEN**
  nof $\leftarrow$ *BK.InitFindCustomer(name)*; *result* := *success*
ELSE
  result := *dbError*; *nof* := 0
END;

$found, yob \leftarrow$ **RobustFindNextCustomer** =
IF *BK.fileOpen* = **TRUE THEN**
  found, yob $\leftarrow$ *BK.FindNextCustomer*
ELSE
  found := **FALSE**; *yob* := 0
END;

```
result, number ← RobustNewAccount(name, yob, pin) =
  VAR status, cid IN
    number := 0;
    IF BK.fileOpen = TRUE THEN
      status ← BK.AccountDBFull;
      IF status = FALSE THEN
        status, cid ← BK.ThisCustomer(name, yob);
        IF status = TRUE THEN
          number ← BK.NewAccount(cid, pin); result := success
        ELSE result := unknownCustomer
        END
      ELSE result := dbFull
      END
    ELSE result := dbError
    END
  END;
result, bal ← RobustBalance(number, pin) =
  VAR status, aid IN
    bal := 0;
    IF BK.fileOpen = TRUE THEN
      status, aid ← BK.ThisAccount(number);
      IF status = TRUE THEN
        status ← BK.Authorized(aid, pin);
        IF status = TRUE THEN
          bal ← BK.Balance(aid, pin); result := success
        ELSE result := WrongPin
        END
      ELSE result := unknownAccount
      END
    ELSE result := dbError
    END
  END;
result, name, yob ← RobustOwner(number) =
  VAR status, aid, cid IN
    yob := 0;
    IF BK.fileOpen = TRUE THEN
      status, aid ← BK.ThisAccount(number);
      IF status = TRUE THEN
        cid ← BK.AccountOwner(aid);
        name, yob ← BK.CustomerData(cid);
        result := success
      ELSE
        result := unknownAccount; name := EmptyStringToken; yob := 0
      END
    ELSE
      result := dbError; name := EmptyStringToken; yob := 0
    END
  END;
```

/* Operations RobustBalance, RobustOwner, RobustDeposit, RobustWithdraw, and RobustChangePin omitted. Check on the book's Web page. */

```
status ← RobustOpen(customerFileName, accountFileName, stringFileName) =
  IF BK.fileOpen = FALSE THEN
```

> $status \leftarrow BK.Open(customerFileName, accountFileName, stringFileName)$
> **ELSE** $status :=$ **FALSE**
> **END**;
>
> $status \leftarrow$ **RobustClose** =
> **IF** $BK.fileOpen =$ **TRUE THEN**
> $status \leftarrow BK.Close$
> **ELSE** $status :=$ **FALSE**
> **END**
>
> **END**

4.10 Implementation of *Bank*

Our next task is to refine *Bank* to an implementation, because we have chosen to import it into *RobustBank*. In Sect. 4.4 we have already outlined the basic structure of this implementation. Now we have to take a closer look at our requirements on one hand and the available resources, that is, the B library machines and the operating system of the target computer, on the other. This is the gap we have to bridge.

The data structures we need to implement are object classes with attributes as well as relations. We need to be able to create new objects, read and modify their attributes, and externalise and internalise them. All our attributes are of types *NAT* and *STRTOKEN*. If we provide a possibility to reference string tokens with natural numbers, strings, respectively references to string tokens can also be stored like *NAT*s. Functional relations (*accountOwner*) can also be modelled as *NAT* attributes if *NAT* is also chosen as the identifier type for objects.

Atelier B provides a base machine *BASIC_ARRAY_RGE* for two dimensional array. This could be used to store objects with their *NAT* attributes by letting the first index select the object and the second the desired attribute or vice versa. If the number of fields is known, we could alternatively use a number of one-dimensional arrays which can be directly implemented in B0.

A simple machine for file access named *BASIC_FILE_VAR*, originating from the data-base example of the B Book [2], is also provided. This machine permits objects with attributes of identical type to be stored and retrieved from file. Using it to externalise strings would be very cumbersome. Also, it does not provide for persistency between program runs as the name of the file is generated at random. Neither does it perform any error handling; file system errors cause it to abort.

We could implement *Bank* directly on our own base machines *BasicFile* and *BasicString* and on *BASIC_ARRAY_RGE*. However, it seems to be wiser to introduce a middle layer, which encapsulates general support for objects. This simplifies the implementation of *Bank* and gives us a reusable subsystem. It also frees us from hardwiring whether we want to internalise the complete database at startup or whether we only want to keep the currently accessed object in the main memory.

We implement *Bank* using a machine *Object* providing the aforementioned support for objects and *BasicString*. The specification still leaves it open whether the complete database is kept in main memory or not. In the implementation we can no longer postpone the decision. We decide to read the whole database at startup; the other solution for a similar object-support machine is developed by Abrial in the aforementioned data-base example. Fig. 4.12 shows the structure of the intended development with section numbers for reference. We create a separate project for the object support and string machines to facilitate reuse.

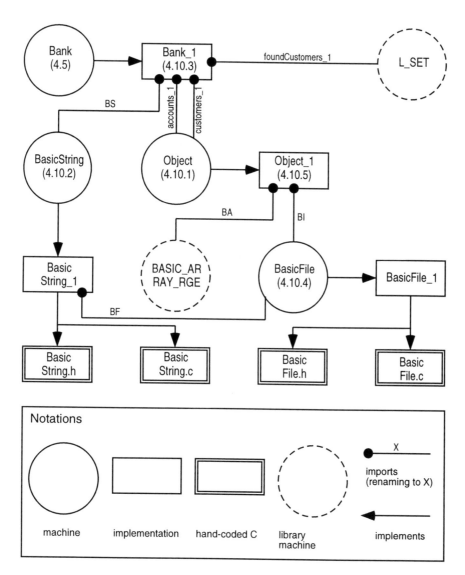

Fig. 4.12. Implementation of *Bank*

We proceed in a top-down fashion. We first identify the required functionality for implementing *Bank*, specify the necessary machines *Object* and *BasicString*, and then implement *Bank*. We then repeat the same sequence of steps for *Object* and *BasicString*.

4.10.1 Machine *Object*

As stated above, *Object* must be able to store a set of objects, each having a given number of attributes of identical type. We need to create new objects, modify and read their fields, search for an object by the value of one of its fields, and check whether the database is full or not.

Object has four parameters. The first parameter *maxNofObjs* denotes the maximal number of objects, which the machine can store. As discussed in Sect. 4.5, such an upper bound is needed in a safety-critical system in order to avoid overflows. The question remains, however, how we should constrain the maximal value of objects. This value is determined by the available main memory storing the objects and the available disk space for externalisation. This contradicts our aim to make the specification independent of the target computer. Even if we know our target architecture, the available memory at run time depends also upon which other processes are running and how many instantiations of the *Object* machine are present. Obviously, we cannot formally prove the instantiations to work for any value — except for 0. Such a proof would not be within B. In practice, we have to reason for the complete system that the chosen instantiations are permissible for the given resources. We implement our machine so that it allocates all the required memory at startup. Although failure during initialisation also violates the specification, it is usually less harmful than at run time. For the second resource, the disk storage, we take the more optimistic and less safe assumption that the disk always has at least as much free space as we have main memory.

MACHINE
   Object(maxNofObjs, nofFields, VALUE, valueElement)

CONSTRAINTS
   maxNofObjs ∈ **NAT1** ∧ *nofFields* ∈ **NAT1** ∧ *valueElement* ∈ *VALUE*

DEFINITIONS
   FIELD == 0 .. *nofFields*-1; *OBJECT* == 0 .. *maxNofObjs*-1

VARIABLES
   object, objectSequence, field, foundObjects

CONCRETE_VARIABLES
   fileOpen

INVARIANT
   object ⊆ *OBJECT* ∧ **card**(*object*) ≤ *maxNofObjs* ∧
   objectSequence ∈ **perm**(*object*) ∧ *field* ∈ *FIELD* → (*object* → *VALUE*) ∧
   fileOpen ∈ **BOOL** ∧ *foundObjects* ⊆ *object*

INITIALISATION

$object := \{\} \parallel objectSequence := [] \parallel field := FIELD \times \{ \{\} \} \parallel$
$fileOpen := \textbf{FALSE} \parallel foundObjects := \{\}$

The second parameter *nofFields* takes the number of fields per object. It would be desirable to use a machine parameter of set type to designate the fields rather than the integer range $0 .. nofFields\text{-}1$. Using such a branded type, certain errors could be flagged by the type checker rather than resulting in unprovable obligations at a later stage of the development. The reason why we do not use a machine parameter of set type is that it is not possible in B to iterate over an arbitrary set in an implementation as will be required in the implementation of *Object*. An iterator base machine cannot be implemented either because of an unfortunate C encoding decision in Atelier B.

The third parameter *VALUE* is the domain of the fields. The fourth parameter *valueElement* takes an arbitrary element of *VALUE*. It is required for the deterministic initialisation of a concrete variable of type *VALUE* in the implementation *Object_1*.

OPERATIONS

$obj \leftarrow \textbf{CreateObject}(initValue) =$
PRE
  $initValue \in VALUE \wedge \textbf{card}(object) < maxNofObjs \wedge fileOpen = \textbf{TRUE}$
THEN
  ANY $newObj, objSeq$ **WHERE**
    $newObj \in OBJECT - object \wedge objSeq \in \textbf{perm}(object \cup \{newObj\})$
  THEN
    $object := object \cup \{newObj\} \parallel objectSequence := objSeq \parallel$
    $field := \lambda\, ii.(ii \in FIELD \mid field(ii) \cup \{newObj \mapsto initValue\}) \parallel$
    $obj := newObj$
  END
END;

$vv \leftarrow \textbf{GetField}(oo, ff) =$
PRE $oo \in \textbf{NAT} \wedge oo \in object \wedge ff \in FIELD\;\; \wedge fileOpen = \textbf{TRUE}$ **THEN**
  $vv := field(ff)(oo)$
END;

$\textbf{SetField}(oo, ff, vv) =$
PRE
  $oo \in \textbf{NAT} \wedge oo \in object \wedge$
  $ff \in FIELD \wedge vv \in VALUE\;\; \wedge fileOpen = \textbf{TRUE}$
THEN
  $field(ff)(oo) := vv \parallel foundObjects :\in \mathcal{P}\,(object)$
END;

$is \leftarrow \textbf{Full} =$
PRE $fileOpen = \textbf{TRUE}$ **THEN**
  $is := \textbf{bool}(\textbf{card}(object) = maxNofObjs)$
END;

$nof \leftarrow \textbf{NofObjects} =$
PRE $fileOpen = \textbf{TRUE}$ **THEN**
  $nof := \textbf{card}(object)$
END;

Operation *GetSequenceObj* permits the traversal of all objects. For this purpose we have introduced the variable *objectSequence*, which is always a permutation of the set of objects. Operation *CreateObject* reshuffles the sequence to allow for more implementation freedom. Exercise 4.5 shows how this, without the provision for deleting objects overly general specification, allows the simple addition of object deletion.

$obj \leftarrow$ **GetSequenceObj**(*index*) =
PRE
    $index \in$ **NAT** $\land$ $index+1 \in$ **dom**(*objectSequence*) $\land$ *fileOpen* = **TRUE**
THEN $obj := objectSequence(index+1)$
END;

The find operations follow the same pattern as their correspondences in *Bank*.

InitFind(*ff, vv*) =
    PRE $ff \in FIELD \land vv \in VALUE \land fileOpen = $ **TRUE THEN**
        $foundObjects := field(ff)^{-1}[\{vv\}]$
    END;
$found, oo \leftarrow$ **FindNext** =
    PRE $fileOpen = $ **TRUE THEN**
        IF $foundObjects \neq \{\}$ **THEN**
            ANY obj **WHERE** $obj \in foundObjects$ **THEN**
                $found, oo, foundObjects := $ **TRUE**, $obj, foundObjects - \{obj\}$
            END
        ELSE $found := $ **FALSE** $||$ $oo :\in OBJECT$
        END
    END;

Internalizing objects with references to other objects (relations), we have to be able to verify whether the references denote valid objects. Operation *InDomain* serves this purpose.

$is \leftarrow$ **InDomain**(*obj*) =
    PRE $obj \in$ **NAT** $\land$ $fileOpen = $ **TRUE THEN**
        $is := $ **bool**($obj \in object$)
    END;

If the file denoted by parameter *name* of *Open* does not exist a new file is created.

$status \leftarrow$ **Open**(*fileName*) =
    PRE $fileName \in STRING$ **THEN**
        ANY $obj, objSeq, st$ **WHERE**
            $obj \subseteq OBJECT \land$ **card**(obj) $\leq maxNofObjs \land$
            $objSeq \in$ **perm**(obj) $\land st \in$ **BOOL**
        THEN
            $object := obj || objectSequence := objSeq || foundObjects :\in \mathcal{P}(obj) ||$
            $field :\in FIELD \rightarrow (obj \rightarrow VALUE) || status := st || fileOpen := st$
        END
    END;

```
status ← Close =
  PRE fileOpen = TRUE THEN
    fileOpen := FALSE || status :∈ BOOL
  END

END
```

4.10.2 Machine *BasicString*

As explained in Sect. 4.7.1, machine *BasicString* stores all strings in the system. Because of the single writer restriction, this cannot be reflected in the B specification. The latter only represents the mapping from natural number indices to string tokens and the registration of strings to be externalised.

Machine *BasicString* can store at most *maxNofStrings* persistent strings. Operation *AddString* can be specified without any precondition that enough memory is available for a string of a certain size as the memory allocation has already taken place upon token generation.

```
MACHINE
  BasicString(maxNofStrings)

CONSTRAINTS
  maxNofStrings ∈ NAT1
SEES
  StrTokenType
VARIABLES
  regStrings, bsFileOpen
INVARIANT
  regStrings ∈ NAT ⤔ STRTOKEN ∧ card(regStrings) ≤ maxNofStrings ∧
  bsFileOpen ∈ BOOL
INITIALISATION
  regStrings := {} || bsFileOpen := FALSE
OPERATIONS
  index ← AddString(ss) =
    PRE
      ss ∈ STRTOKEN ∧ card(regStrings) ≠ maxNofStrings ∧
      bsFileOpen = TRUE
    THEN
      IF ss ∈ ran(regStrings) THEN index := regStrings⁻¹ (ss)
      ELSE
        ANY newId WHERE newId ∈ NAT-dom(regStrings) THEN
          index, regStrings := newId, regStrings ∪ {(newId ↦ ss)}
        END
      END
    END;
  is ← IsFull =
    is := bool(card(regStrings)=maxNofStrings);
```

$bb \leftarrow$ **InDomain**(*index*) =
  PRE *index* $\in$ **NAT THEN**
    $bb :=$ **bool**(*index* $\in$ **dom**(*regStrings*))
  END;
$ss \leftarrow$ **GetString**(*index*) =
  PRE
    index $\in$ **NAT** $\wedge$ *index* $\in$ **dom**(*regStrings*) $\wedge$ *bsFileOpen* = **TRUE**
  THEN
    $ss :=$ *regStrings*(*index*)
  END;
found, *index* $\leftarrow$ **FindString**(*ss*) =
  PRE *ss* $\in$ *STRTOKEN* **THEN**
    IF *ss* $\in$ **ran**(*regStrings*) **THEN**
      found, *index* := **TRUE**, *regStrings* $^{-1}$ (*ss*)
    ELSE
      found := **FALSE** $\|$ *index* :$\in$ **NAT**
    END
  END;

status, *nof* $\leftarrow$ **BsOpen**(*fileName*) =
  PRE *fileName* $\in$ *STRING* **THEN**
    ANY *res*, *regStringsInit* **WHERE**
      res $\in$ **BOOL** $\wedge$ *regStringsInit* $\in$ **NAT** $\rightarrowtail$ *STRTOKEN* $\wedge$
      card(*regStringsInit*) $\leq$ *maxNofStrings*
    THEN
      regStrings := *regStringsInit* $\|$ *bsFileOpen* := *res* $\|$
      status := *res* $\|$ *nof* := **card**(*regStringsInit*)
    END
  END;
status $\leftarrow$ **BsClose** =
  PRE *bsFileOpen* = **TRUE THEN**
    bsFileOpen := **FALSE** $\|$ *status* :$\in$ **BOOL**
  END
END

The empty implementation as well as the hand-coded C source are available from the book's Web page.

4.10.3 Implementation *Bank_1*

Using *Object*, *BasicString*, and *L_SET* we can now implement *Bank*. We instantiate the *Object* machine twice to implement the customer and account objects. Library machine *L_SET* is used for temporary storage of the not yet retrieved set of customers from the find operations.

IMPLEMENTATION
  Bank_1(*maxCustomers*, *maxAccounts*)

REFINES
  Bank

IMPORTS
BASIC_BOOL, *BASIC_ARITHMETIC*,
BS.BasicString(*maxCustomers*),
customers_1.Object(*maxCustomers*, 2, **NAT**, 0),
accounts_1.Object(*maxAccounts*, 4, **NAT**, 0),
foundCustomers_1.L_SET(*maxCustomers*, **NAT**)

SEES
StrTokenType

Constant *False1* is introduced for expressing variant functions in operations *ThisCustomer* and *InitFindCustomer*.

CONCRETE_CONSTANTS
False1

PROPERTIES
$False1 \in$ **BOOL** $\rightarrowtail$ **NAT**

VALUES
$False1 = \{(\textbf{TRUE} \mapsto 0), (\textbf{FALSE} \mapsto 1)\}$

During internalisation, we have to check whether all references from accounts to customers captured by *accountOwner* reference existing customers and whether all references to strings from *customerName* are in the domain of the internalised strings. Hence, internalisation fails if it fails in one of the three instantiated machines or the consistency check fails. Rather than resetting the already internalised parts if an error is detected, the linking invariant separates two cases. If internalisation succeeded, the state is represented by the state of the imported machines. Otherwise, it is the initial state. Implementation *Bank_1* is a data refinement of machine *Bank* as specified by the linking invariant.

DEFINITIONS
$customerName\_1 == 0$;
$customerYob\_1 == 1$;
$accountNumber\_1 == 0$;
$accountPin\_1 == 1$;
$accountBalance\_1 == 2$;
$accountOwner\_1 == 3$

CONCRETE_VARIABLES
nextAccountNumber_1

INVARIANT
$nextAccountNumber\_1 \in$ **NAT** $\wedge$
$((fileOpen = \textbf{TRUE}) \Rightarrow$
$customers = customers\_1.object \wedge$
$(\forall ll.(ll \in accounts\_1.object \Rightarrow$
$customerName(ll) = BS.regStrings(customers\_1.field(customerName\_1)(ll)))) \wedge$
$customers\_1.field(customerName\_1) \in accounts\_1.object \rightarrowtail \textbf{dom}(BS.regStrings) \wedge$
$\textbf{card}(BS.regStrings) \leq \textbf{card}(customers) \wedge$
$customerYob = customers\_1.field(customerYob\_1) \wedge$

$accounts = accounts\_1.object \land$
$accountNumber = accounts\_1.field(accountNumber\_1) \land$
$accountPin = accounts\_1.field(accountPin\_1) \land$
$accountBalance = accounts\_1.field(accountBalance\_1) \land$
$accountOwner = accounts\_1.field(accountOwner\_1) \land$
$(\forall ll.(ll \in accounts\_1.object \Rightarrow$
$\quad customers\_1.field(accountNumber\_1)(ll) < nextAccountNumber\_1)) \land$
$nextAccountNumber\_1 < \textbf{MAXINT} - maxAccounts + \textbf{card}(accounts) \land$
$customers\_1.fileOpen = \textbf{TRUE} \land$
$accounts\_1.fileOpen = \textbf{TRUE} \land$
$BS.bsFileOpen = \textbf{TRUE} \land$
$foundCustomers = \textbf{ran}(foundCustomers\_1.set\_vrb)) \land$
$((fileOpen = \textbf{FALSE}) \Rightarrow$
$\quad customers = \{\} \land customerName = \{\} \land customerYob = \{\} \land$
$\quad accounts = \{\} \land accountNumber = \{\} \land$
$\quad accountPin = \{\} \land accountBalance = \{\} \land$
$\quad accountOwner = \{\} \land$
$\quad foundCustomers = \{\})$

INITIALISATION

$nextAccountNumber\_1 := 0; fileOpen := \textbf{FALSE}$

OPERATIONS

NewCustomer(*name*, *yob*) =
  VAR *cid*, *ii* **IN**
    $cid \leftarrow$ **customers_1.CreateObject**(0);
    $ii \leftarrow$ **BS.AddString**(*name*);
    customers_1.SetField(*cid*, *customerName_1*, *ii*);
    customers_1.SetField(*cid*, *customerYob_1*, *yob*)
  END;

name, *yob* $\leftarrow$ **CustomerData**(*cid*) =
  VAR *sn* **IN**
    $sn \leftarrow$ **customers_1.GetField**(*cid*, *customerName_1*);
    name $\leftarrow$ **BS.GetString**(*sn*);
    yob $\leftarrow$ **customers_1.GetField**(*cid*, *customerYob_1*)
  END;

is $\leftarrow$ **CustomerDBFull** =
  BEGIN
    is $\leftarrow$ **customers_1.Full**;
    IF *is*=**FALSE THEN**
      is $\leftarrow$ **BS.IsFull**
    END
  END;

found, *cid* $\leftarrow$ **ThisCustomer**(*name*, *yob*) =
  VAR *sindex*, *curYob* **IN**
    $cid := 0; curYob := 0;$
    found, *sindex* $\leftarrow$ **BS.FindString**(*name*);
    IF *found* = **TRUE THEN**
      customers_1.InitFind(*customerName_1*, *sindex*);
      found, *cid* $\leftarrow$ **customers_1.FindNext**;
      IF *found*=**TRUE THEN**
        curYob $\leftarrow$ **customers_1.GetField**(*cid*, *customerYob_1*)

```
        END;
        WHILE (found = TRUE) ∧ (yob ≠ curYob) DO
          found, cid ← customers_1.FindNext;
          IF found = TRUE THEN
            curYob ← customers_1.GetField(cid, customerYob_1)
          END
        INVARIANT
          cid ∈ 0 .. maxCustomers-1 ∧
          (yob ≠ curYob ⇒
            yob ∉ customerYob[customerName ⁻¹ [{name}]-
                customers_1.foundObjects]) ∧
          (found = FALSE ⇒ customers_1.foundObjects= {} ) ∧
          (found = TRUE ⇒ (cid ∈ customerName ⁻¹ [{name}] ∧
              curYob = customerYob(cid))) ∧
          (yob = curYob ⇒ (cid = (customerName ⊗ customerYob) ⁻¹ (name,yob) ∧
              found = TRUE))
        VARIANT
          card(customers_1.foundObjects) + 1 - False1(found)
        END
      END
    END;
  nof ← InitFindCustomer(name) =
    VAR found, index, sindex IN
      foundCustomers_1.CLR_SET;
      nof := 0;
      found, sindex ← BS.FindString(name);
      IF found = TRUE THEN
        customers_1.InitFind(customerName_1, sindex);
        found, index ← customers_1.FindNext;
        WHILE found = TRUE DO
          foundCustomers_1.INS_SET(index);
          nof := nof + 1;
          found, index ← customers_1.FindNext
        INVARIANT
          (found = TRUE ⇒
            customerName ⁻¹ [{name}] = ran(foundCustomers_1.set_vrb) ∪
              customers_1.foundObjects ∪ {index}) ∧
          (found = FALSE ⇒
            customerName ⁻¹ [{name}] = ran(foundCustomers_1.set_vrb) ∧
            customers_1.foundObjects = {} ) ∧
          nof = card(foundCustomers_1.set_vrb)
        VARIANT
          card(customers_1.foundObjects)+1-False1(found)
        END
      END
    END;
  found, yob ← FindNextCustomer =
    VAR nof, cid IN
      nof ← foundCustomers_1.CARD_SET;
      IF nof = 0 THEN
        found := FALSE;
        yob := 0
```

```
    ELSE
      found := TRUE;
      cid ← foundCustomers_1.VAL_SET(1);
      foundCustomers_1.RMV_SET(cid);
      yob ← customers_1.GetField(cid, customerYob_1)
    END
  END;
```

We assign consecutive account numbers to newly created accounts, where *next-AccountNumber* contains the next account number which is the greatest number in the system plus one. We do, however, not blindly trust that the internalised file adheres to this convention, that is, we do not simply set *nextAccountNumber* to number of accounts plus one, which would lead to an undischargable proof obligation.

```
number ← NewAccount(cid, pin) =
  VAR aid IN
    aid ← accounts_1.CreateObject(0);
    accounts_1.SetField(aid, accountNumber_1, nextAccountNumber_1);
    accounts_1.SetField(aid, accountPin_1, pin);
    accounts_1.SetField(aid, accountBalance_1, 0);
    accounts_1.SetField(aid, accountOwner_1, cid);
    number := nextAccountNumber_1;
    nextAccountNumber_1 := nextAccountNumber_1 + 1
  END;

bal ← Balance(aid, pin) =
  bal ← accounts_1.GetField(aid, accountBalance_1);

is ← Authorized(aid, pin) =
  VAR actualPin IN
    actualPin ← accounts_1.GetField(aid, accountPin_1);
    is := bool(pin = actualPin)
  END;

cid ← AccountOwner(aid) =
  cid ← accounts_1.GetField(aid, accountOwner_1);

status ← Deposit(aid, amount) =
  VAR bal, xx IN
    bal ← accounts_1.GetField(aid, accountBalance_1);
    xx := MAXINT - amount;
    IF bal < xx THEN
      accounts_1.SetField(aid, accountBalance_1, bal+amount);
      status := TRUE
    ELSE
      status := FALSE
    END
  END;
```

Operation *Deposit* introduces the local variable *xx* only because in B0 the arguments of a comparison cannot contain arithmetic expressions.

/* Operations Withdraw, ChangePin, AccountDBFull, and ThisAccount omitted. Check on the book's Web page. */

status ← **Open**(*customerFileName*, *accountFileName*, *stringFileName*) =
 VAR *nofAccounts, ii, aid, owner, nbr, nofStrings, nofCustomers, cid* **IN**
 fileOpen := **FALSE**;
 nextAccountNumber_1 := 0;
 status ← *customers_1.Open*(*customerFileName*);
 IF *status* = **TRUE THEN**
  status ← *accounts_1.Open*(*accountFileName*);
  IF *status* = **TRUE THEN**
   nofAccounts ← *accounts_1.NofObjects*;
   ii := 0;
   WHILE (*ii* < *nofAccounts*) ∧ (*status* = **TRUE**) **DO**
    aid ← *accounts_1.GetSequenceObj*(*ii*);
    owner ← *accounts_1.GetField*(*aid, accountOwner_1*);
    status ← *customers_1.InDomain*(*owner*);
    nbr ← *accounts_1.GetField*(*aid, accountNumber_1*);
    IF *nbr* ≥ *nextAccountNumber_1* **THEN**
     VAR *xx, yy* **IN**
     xx := **MAXINT** - *nbr*;
     yy := *maxAccounts* - *nofAccounts* + 1;
     IF *xx* < *yy* **THEN**
      status := **FALSE**
     ELSE
      nextAccountNumber_1 := *nbr* + 1
     END
    END
   END;
   ii := *ii* + 1
   INVARIANT
   ii ∈ 0 .. *nofAccounts* ∧
   (*status* = **TRUE** ⇒
    (∀ *kk*.(*kk* ∈ **ran**(1 .. *ii* ◁ *accounts_1.objectSequence*) ⇒
    accounts_1.field(*accountNumber_1*)(*kk*) < *nextAccountNumber_1*)) ∧
    nextAccountNumber_1 < **MAXINT** - *maxAccounts* + *nofAccounts*)
   VARIANT
   nofAccounts - *ii*
   END;
   IF *status* = **TRUE THEN**
    nofCustomers ← *customers_1.NofObjects*;
    status, nofStrings ← *BS.BsOpen*(*stringFileName*);
    IF (*status* = **TRUE**) ∧ (*nofStrings*<*nofCustomers*) **THEN**
     ii := 0;
     WHILE (*ii* < *nofCustomers*) ∧ (*status* = **TRUE**) **DO**
      cid ← *customers_1.GetSequenceObj*(*ii*);
      nbr ← *customers_1.GetField*(*cid, customerName_1*);
      status ← *BS.InDomain*(*nbr*);
      ii := *ii* + 1
     INVARIANT
     ii ∈ 0 .. *nofCustomers* ∧
     (∀ *kk*.(*kk* ∈ 0 .. *ii*-1 ⇒
     customers_1.field(*customerName_1*)(*kk*) ∈ **dom**(*BS.regStrings*)))
     VARIANT
     nofCustomers - *ii*
     END

```
            ELSE
               status := FALSE
            END
          END;
          fileOpen := status
        END
      END
    END;
  status ← Close =
    BEGIN
      status ← customers_1.Close;
      IF status = TRUE THEN
        status ← accounts_1.Close;
        IF status = TRUE THEN
          status ← BS.BsClose
        END
      END;
      nextAccountNumber_1 := 0;
      fileOpen := FALSE
    END
END
```

4.10.4 Machine *BasicFile*

In order to permanently store objects on disk, as required for the implementation of
Object, we need a base machine to access the file system, which we call *BasicFile*.
It should let us open a file in different modes, access the file, and provide operations
to delete a file and check for the existence of a file. We want to store both natural
numbers as well as elements of a given set, passed as a machine parameter. An
instance of *BasicFile* represents a single file.

The variables *fileName* and *fileMode* denote the name and mode of the currently
open file. The name of the file has been specified as an arbitrary string, although
certain characters might not be permitted in file names and certain names might
denote special resources.

MACHINE
  BasicFile(VALUE)

SETS
  FILE_MODE = {*READ_WRITE, TRUNCATE_WRITE, READ, WRITE*}

DEFINITIONS
  READ_MODE == {*READ_WRITE, READ*};
  WRITE_MODE == {*READ_WRITE, TRUNCATE_WRITE, WRITE*}

VARIABLES
  fileMode, fileOpen

INVARIANT
  fileMode ∈ *FILE_MODE* ∧

fileOpen ∈ **BOOL**

INITIALISATION
  fileMode :∈ *FILE_MODE* || *fileOpen* := **FALSE**

OPERATIONS
  status ← **Open**(*fileName*, *mode*) =
    PRE *fileName* ∈ *STRING* ∧ *mode* ∈ *FILE_MODE* **THEN**
      ANY *rr* **WHERE** *rr* ∈ **BOOL THEN**
        fileMode := *mode* || *fileOpen* := *rr* || *status* := *rr*
      END
    END;

  status ← **Close** =
    PRE *fileOpen* = **TRUE THEN**
      fileOpen := **FALSE** || *status* :∈ **BOOL**
    END;

  status ← **Delete**(*fileName*) =
    PRE *fileName* ∈ *STRING* **THEN**
      status :∈ **BOOL**
    END;

  exists ← **FileExists**(*fileName*) =
    PRE *fileName* ∈ *STRING* **THEN**
      exists :∈ **BOOL**
    END;

The read operations are specified as returning an arbitrary value, not linking write and read at all. Such a specification would be very difficult to capture in B, too cumbersome to apply in reasoning in clients, and impossible to satisfy in the implementation.

  status ← **WriteNat**(*num*) =
    PRE *num* ∈ **NAT** ∧ *fileOpen* = **TRUE** ∧ *fileMode* ∈ *WRITE_MODE* **THEN**
      status :∈ **BOOL**
    END;

  status, *num* ← **ReadNat** =
    PRE *fileOpen* = **TRUE** ∧ *fileMode* ∈ *READ_MODE* **THEN**
      status :∈ **BOOL** || *num* :∈ **NAT**
    END;

  status ← **WriteVal**(*val*) =
    PRE *val* ∈ *VALUE* ∧ *fileOpen* = **TRUE** ∧ *fileMode* ∈ *WRITE_MODE* **THEN**
      status :∈ **BOOL**
    END;

  status, *val* ← **ReadVal** =
    PRE *fileOpen* = **TRUE** ∧ *fileMode* ∈ *READ_MODE* **THEN**
      status :∈ **BOOL** || *val* :∈ *VALUE*
    END
END

The C implementation, which is based on the code skeleton generated from the empty B implementation, consists mostly of straightforward calls of the corresponding functions of *stdio.h*. The procedure *ReadVal_BasicFile* also checks whether the read value actually represents an element of the machine parameter *VALUE*. Unfortunately, Atelier B's C translator only passes the upper bound of the representing integer range in the ill-named parameter *size_VALUE* in the initialisation. This suffices for enumerated sets that are represented as consecutive integer constants starting from 0. However, for instantiations of *VALUE* with integer ranges with a lower bound other than 0 we cannot test whether the read value is below the indicated range. The sources of *BasicFile_1.imp*, *BasicFile.h*, and *BasicFile.c* can be found online.

4.10.5 Implementation *Object_1*

Using the base machine *BasicFile* and the library machine *BASIC_ARRAY_RGE* we can now implement *Object* and, herewith, finish the development.

BASIC_ARRAY_RGE models a two dimensional array with the total function $arr\_rge \in RANGE \rightarrow (INDEX \rightarrow VALUE)$, where *INDEX*, *VALUE*, and *RANGE* are machine parameters. We instantiate *RANGE* with the set of fields and *INDEX* with the object numbers. For example, $arr\_rge(0)(7)$ denotes the 0th field of the 7th object. We use the variable *nofObjs_1* to denote the number of objects and link it to *object* with $object = 0 .. nofObjs\_1\text{-}1$. This gives us also the linking invariant for *field* as $\forall ii.(ii \in FIELD \Rightarrow field(ii) = 0 .. nofObjs\_1\text{-}1 \lhd arr\_rge(ii))$.

IMPLEMENTATION
  Object_1(maxNofObjs, nofFields, VALUE, valueElement)

REFINES
  Object

IMPORTS
  BI.BasicFile(VALUE),
  BA.BASIC_ARRAY_RGE(0 .. maxNofObjs-1, VALUE, 0 .. nofFields-1)

DEFINITIONS
  $FIELD == 0 .. nofFields\text{-}1;\ OBJECT == 0 .. maxNofObjs\text{-}1;$
  $READ\_MODE == \{READ\_WRITE, READ\};$
  $WRITE\_MODE == \{READ\_WRITE, TRUNCATE\_WRITE, WRITE\}$

CONCRETE_VARIABLES
  nofObjs_1, findField, findValue, findMax, findNext

INVARIANT
  $nofObjs\_1 \in 0 .. maxNofObjs \wedge object = 0 .. nofObjs\_1\text{-}1 \wedge$
  $\textbf{size}(objectSequence) = nofObjs\_1 \wedge$
  $(\forall ii.(ii \in 0 .. nofObjs\_1\text{-}1 \Rightarrow objectSequence(ii+1) = ii)) \wedge$
  $(\forall ii.(ii \in FIELD \Rightarrow field(ii) = 0 .. nofObjs\_1\text{-}1 \lhd (BA.arr\_rge(ii)))) \wedge$
  $(fileOpen = \textbf{TRUE} \Rightarrow (BI.fileOpen = \textbf{TRUE} \wedge BI.fileMode \in WRITE\_MODE)) \wedge$
  $findField \in FIELD \wedge findValue \in VALUE \wedge$
  $findMax \in \text{-}1 .. nofObjs\_1\text{-}1 \wedge findNext \in 0 .. nofObjs\_1 \wedge$

$foundObjects = (field(findField)^{-1}[\{findValue\}]) \cap findNext \mathbin{..} findMax$

INITIALISATION
  $nofObjs\_1 := 0; fileOpen := \textbf{FALSE};$
  $findField := 0; findValue := valueElement; findMax := -1; findNext := 0$

OPERATIONS
  $obj \leftarrow$ **CreateObject**$(initValue) =$
    VAR fld **IN**
      $fld := 0;$
      WHILE $fld < nofFields$ **DO**
        $BA.STR\_ARR\_RGE(fld, nofObjs\_1, initValue);$
        $fld := fld + 1$
      INVARIANT
        $fld \in 0 \mathbin{..} nofFields \wedge$
        $(\forall ii.(ii \in FIELD \Rightarrow field(ii) = 0 \mathbin{..} nofObjs\_1\text{-}1 \lhd (BA.arr\_rge(ii)))) \wedge$
        $(\forall ii.(ii \in 0 \mathbin{..} fld\text{-}1 \Rightarrow BA.arr\_rge(fld)(nofObjs\_1) = initValue))$
      VARIANT
        $nofFields - fld$
      END;
      $obj := nofObjs\_1; nofObjs\_1 := nofObjs\_1 + 1$
    END;

  $vv \leftarrow$ **GetField**$(oo, ff) =$
    $vv \leftarrow BA.VAL\_ARR\_RGE(ff, oo);$

  SetField$(oo, ff, vv) =$
    $BA.STR\_ARR\_RGE(ff, oo, vv);$

  $is \leftarrow$ **Full** $=$
    IF $nofObjs\_1 = maxNofObjs$ **THEN** $is := \textbf{TRUE}$
    ELSE $is := \textbf{FALSE}$
    END;

  $nof \leftarrow$ **NofObjects** $=$
    $nof := nofObjs\_1;$

  $obj \leftarrow$ **GetSequenceObj**$(index) =$
    $obj := index;$

  InitFind$(ff, vv) =$
    BEGIN
      $findField := ff; findValue := vv; findMax := nofObjs\_1\text{-}1; findNext := 0$
    END;

  $found, oo \leftarrow$ **FindNext** $=$
    VAR $val, maxObj, findStart$ **IN**
      $found := \textbf{FALSE}; oo := 0;$
      IF $findNext \leq findMax$ **THEN**
        $val \leftarrow BA.VAL\_ARR\_RGE(findField, findNext);$
        $findStart := findNext;$
        WHILE $(findNext < findMax) \wedge (val \neq findValue)$ **DO**
          $findNext := findNext + 1;$
          $val \leftarrow BA.VAL\_ARR\_RGE(findField, findNext)$
        INVARIANT
          $findNext \in 0 \mathbin{..} findMax \wedge$
          $(\forall ll.(ll \in findStart \mathbin{..} findNext\text{-}1 \Rightarrow BA.arr\_rge(findField)(ll) \neq findValue)) \wedge$

```
        val = BA.arr_rge(findField)(findNext)
      VARIANT
        findMax-findNext
      END;
      IF val = findValue THEN
        found := TRUE; oo := findNext
      END;
        findNext := findNext + 1
    END
  END;

is ← InDomain(obj) =
    is := bool(obj < nofObjs_1);

status ← Open(fileName) =
  VAR st, ii, fld, vv IN
    status ← BI.FileExists(fileName);
    IF status = TRUE THEN
      status ← BI.Open(fileName, READ);
    IF status = TRUE THEN
      status, nofObjs_1 ← BI.ReadNat;
      IF (status = TRUE) ∧ (nofObjs_1 ≤ maxNofObjs) THEN
        ii := 0;
        WHILE (status = TRUE) ∧ (ii < nofObjs_1) DO
          fld := 0;
          WHILE (status = TRUE) ∧ (fld < nofFields) DO
            status, vv ← BI.ReadVal;
            BA.STR_ARR_RGE(fld, ii, vv);
            fld := fld + 1
          INVARIANT
            fld ∈ 0 .. nofFields
          VARIANT
            nofFields - fld
          END;
          ii := ii + 1
        INVARIANT
          ii ∈ 0 .. nofObjs_1
        VARIANT
          nofObjs_1 - ii
        END;
        IF status = TRUE THEN
          status ← BI.Close;
          IF status = TRUE THEN
            status ← BI.Open(fileName, TRUNCATE_WRITE)
          END
        END
      ELSE
        nofObjs_1:=0;
        status := FALSE
      END
    ELSE
      nofObjs_1 := 0
    END
  ELSE
    nofObjs_1 := 0; status ← BI.Open(fileName, TRUNCATE_WRITE)
```

```
        END;
        findMax := -1; findNext := 0;
        fileOpen := status
    END;
status ← Close =
    VAR ss, ii, fld, vv IN
        ss ← BI.WriteNat(nofObjs_1);
        IF ss = TRUE THEN
            ii := 0;
            WHILE (ss = TRUE) ∧ (ii < nofObjs_1) DO
                fld := 0;
                WHILE (ss = TRUE) ∧ (fld < nofFields) DO
                    vv ← BA.VAL_ARR_RGE(fld, ii);
                    ss ← BI.WriteVal(vv);
                    fld := fld + 1
                INVARIANT
                    fld ∈ 0 .. nofFields
                VARIANT
                    nofFields - fld
                END;
                ii := ii + 1
            INVARIANT
                ii ∈ 0 .. nofObjs_1
            VARIANT
                nofObjs_1 - ii
            END
        END;
        IF ss = TRUE THEN
            status ← BI.Close
        ELSE
            status := FALSE; ss ← BI.Close
        END;
        fileOpen := FALSE
    END
END
```

At this point we can translate the complete project.

4.11 B-Toolkit Implementation

In this section we list some of the changes necessary to port the case study from
Atelier B to the B-Toolkit. The point of this section is to illustrate the large differences between the two tools —even on the language level!— which make porting
a non-trivial task. The magnitude of such a port can be compared to the translation
of an X Window program written in K&R C to ANSI C on the Apple Macintosh:
both require some little changes on the language level and the use of a different
base library. The rest of this section is mainly targeted at B-Toolkit users who are
interested in a description of the adaptations made in the B-Toolkit version of the
ATM.

4.11.1 Differences in the Supported Language

The following 'syntactic' differences can be compensated for with simple rewrites:

- In the B-Toolkit, machine parameters are not repeated in refinements and implementations.
- In the B-Toolkit, lowercase machine parameters are implicitly constrained to be of type *SCALAR*.
- Ordered pairs must be written as $(a \mapsto b)$ rather than (a, b) in the B-Toolkit, whereas both notations are allowed in Atelier B.
- Sets and constants are valued in the *PROPERTIES* clause; there is no special values *VALUES* clause as in Atelier B.
- The constant *MAXINT*, the greatest representable natural number, is not predefined in the B-Toolkit.
- In the B-Toolkit, the subset $0 .. MAXINT$ is denoted by *SCALAR* rather than *NAT*. The type *SCALAR* is defined in machine *Scalar_TYPE*, which must be imported if scalars are used.
- In the B-Toolkit, booleans are defined as enumerated type in the library machine *Bool_TYPE*, which must be imported if booleans are used.
- In the B-Toolkit, strings are defined as sequences in the library *String_TYPE*, which must be imported if strings are used.
- In the B-Toolkit, there can only be one *DEFINITION* clause per construct. Definitions are visible in the whole construct, not just from the syntactic introduction point on forward as in Atelier B. Parameters of definitions are restricted to single-letter identifiers (jokers). Definitions containing the parallel operator ('||') must be parenthesised.
- In the B-Toolkit, renamed variables must be parenthesised if the inverse is taken.
- In the B-Toolkit, the *bool(P)* operator, which converts the value of a condition to a *BOOL*, is not available in implementations. An if-clause must be used instead.
- The B-Toolkit C translator does not accept arithmetic expressions as actual parameters. The values of arithmetic expressions must be evaluated and stored in local variables, which can then be passed as parameters.
- The C translator does not accept read access to output parameters, even if they have been properly initialized. Local variables, which are at the end of the operation assigned to the output parameters, must be used within the operation in place of output parameters appearing on the right hand side of assignments or in conditions.
- Whereas the Atelier B translator creates only few name clashes, which lead to errors at link time, its correspondent in the B-Toolkit cannot even handle operations on different layers with identical names. Hence, one is forced to invent new names and, thereby, pollute the name space.

The following differences make porting from the Atelier B to the B-Toolkit difficult:

- The B-Toolkit does not support dot renaming in implementations. This means that renamed textual copies of multiple used constructs must be made. In our case, *Object* and all the constructs it needs would have to be textually present with different name prefixes. This also requires identical proofs to be performed for each copy. This restriction in the B-Toolkit is due to the fact that all constructs are single instance only which is also exhibited by the C translator putting implementation data into global variables rather than instantiation records. On the level of base machines, which reside in the standard library, textual renaming is performed automatically upon configuration. The team library does not provide for renaming.

- In the B-Toolkit all constants are abstract, whereas Atelier B has both concrete and abstract constants. The B-Toolkit translator decides which constants can be used in implementations.

- Concrete variables and variables in implementations are not supported. All global variables, such as *nextAccountNumber_1*, must be implemented using library machines. Sets which are both included and imported lead to name clashes. Different renaming does not help because sets do not participate in renaming. Hence, sets must be factored out into separate machines which are only seen in the specification. Third-party constructs which do not respect this design pattern, such as the library machines in B-Toolkit prior to version 4, can, therefore, not be easily extended as extension is performed by both including and importing the same machine.

The following differences would make porting from the B-Toolkit to Atelier B difficult. Some of these 'additional features' are used in the B-Toolkit version:

- Machines can contain the *VAR* clause. Hence, we can use it to hide the return parameter *dd* from *Deposit* in *RobustDeposit*.

- Machine parameters are visible in the *PROPERTIES* clause. Hence, we could model the set *CUSTOMER* of machine *Bank* as an abstract set with cardinality *maxCustomers* and value it to *CUSTOMER = 0..maxCustomers-1* in the implementation. To rule out any circular definitions, Atelier B does not permit this in accordance with [2, Chapter 12.1.7].

- The B-Toolkit allows strings to be passed as parameters. Hence, there is no need to introduce string tokens. Strings being sequences implies that functions such as *size* are applicable. Porting a construct which makes use of this from B-Toolkit would be difficult. In general, string support in the B-Toolkit is better. Unfortunately, B-Toolkit's C translator creates fixed length arrays for local string variables and does not perform any overflow tests.

- Sets of imported or seen machines can be used in the instantiation of other machines.

- Set machine parameters can be instantiated with 'unions' ('$\cup$') of sets. This is not described in the B Book [2]; it could be understood as type sums. Unfortunately, on the implementation level, where sets are represented as (initial) intervals of natural numbers, operations on such sets are based on the natural number projections only, leading, in our opinion, to ill-typed expressions and wrong results. Thus, for sets *COLORS = {red, blue, green}* and *FRUITS = {apple, banana, grape}* we can calculate *{red, blue} $\cap$ {banana, grape} = {blue} = {banana}* as both *blue* and *banana* are represented by 2. Union of sets is used extensively by the base generator (see below).

4.11.2 Differences in the Provided Base Machines and Libraries

In the B-Toolkit, all provided library machines are base machines, whereas Atelier B comes only with a small set of base machines and numerous extensions in the form of normal B developments. In the B-Toolkit, base machines reside in the standard library (SLIB).

The B specification of base machines must be given in a separate project, otherwise the linker requires an implementation in B and does not use the hand-coded C source. After successful analysis and compilation, the configured construct along with its C implementation is copied to the SLIB, to which one needs write permission. The main differences in the C encoding are the representation of machine data in global variables rather than in instance records and the division of header information into the '.h' and a '.g' file. Note that when introducing a construct from the SLIB, the C sources are copied. Thus, if the (implementation of the) base machine is changed, it must be removed and reintroduced into projects using it.

Compilation and linking is under the control of the tool. Hence, external source files such as *cgic* cannot simply be added manually to the Makefile as in Atelier B. Instead, they need to be introduced as so-called lower-level SLIB constructs. Lower-level SLIB constructs have no B specification and can only be accessed from the C code of other SLIB constructs. Instead of a lower-level SLIB, a normal C library can be created out of the legacy code and included manually in a normal SLIB construct.

4.11.3 Adapting the Development

The B-Toolkit implementation takes the above listed language differences into account. Additionally, supplied base machines have been used in place of the self-developed persistent object machines. The B-Toolkit provides base machines for objects and string objects. Library machine *Bank_str_obj*, where *Bank* is the rename prefix for the instanciation, provides for string objects, like our own base machine *BasicString*. *Rename_ffnc_obj* provides for two dimensional arrays; it replaces *Object* of our Atelier B development. We introduce two copies called *CUSTOMER_ffnc_obj* and *ACCOUNT_ffnc_obj* for storing customers and accounts respectively.

In combination with machine *file_dump*, the multiple object machines also provide for persistency. A file is opened with *file_dump* into which all machines can externalise their state. Unfortunately, the code contains no error or consistency checking. Atelier B's library also contains a machine *BASIC_SAVE* which roughly corresponds to *file_dump*; however, it does not function anymore and the corresponding procedures have been removed from the B specification of the other library machines.

4.11.4 Automatic Translation of Object Models

The B-Toolkit acknowledges the fact that object models can be automatically translated to B machines. From a textual description of the object model a set of machines and corresponding implementations is generated. The base description (Fig. 4.13) lists global variables (customers and accounts) as well as the object classes (CUSTOMER and ACCOUNT) with their attributes and the relations. Relations can be expressed asymmetrically by being part of one of the participating object classes, as done in the example, or as separate entities.

From the base construct, a list of operations on the global variables and on objects of the listed classes is generated. After optional manual filtering of the operations' list, a set of machines and implementations is generated. The implementations are based on constructs from the standard library described above. Based on Bank-Foundation it would then be possible to implement Bank. Editing the generated machines and implementations directly is not recommended because of the lack of backward propagation to the base construct; it would result in breaking the link and the possibility to regenerate the constructs after changing the base.

It is doubtful whether using the base generation tool would be justified in our case. Even if certain aspects are actually formally proved and the code is automatically generated, added complexity is a source for errors. Manual reuse of those library constructs that are actually needed seems to be better suited in our case.

```
SYSTEM
  BankFoundation

IS

  GLOBAL
    customers : SET(CUSTOMER)[100];
    accounts : SET(ACCOUNT)[200]
  END;

  BASE
    CUSTOMER
  MANDATORY
    name : STRING [256]; yob : NAT
  END;

  BASE
    ACCOUNT
  MANDATORY
    number : NAT; pin : NAT;
    balance : NAT; owner : CUSTOMER
  END

END
```

Fig. 4.13. Base Construct for Automatic Generation

The B-Toolkit comes with three small data base like examples, called **PERSON1**, **PERSON2**, and **PERSON3**, which illustrate the differences between the manual use of the standard library constructs and the application of the base generator.

4.12 Discussion

4.12.1 Related Work

The B Book [2] contains a much smaller example of a database application. The database example as well as an ATM case study are included in the Atelier B distribution. The documentation of the ATM, which is in French only, provides an exemplary requirement specifications, a traceability matrix, and a set of test scenarios. On the other hand, it lacks a description of the construction process as well as a detailed explanation of the produced code. The ATM relies on a Tcl/Tk graphical interface as main program and delegates more work to unverified base machines.

A comprehensive B bibliography is maintained by the B users group on the Web at http://estas1.inrets.fr:8001/ESTAS/BUG/WWW/BUGhome/BUGhome.html.

4.12.2 Metrics

Fig. 4.14 provides some metrics of the development. The empty implementations of the base machines, the hand-coded C sources, and the HTML pages are not included.

4.12.3 What Have We Proved?

We would like to conclude with a few remarks on proofs. What have we actually proved in our development? We have proved that all operations of the machines respect their invariants and that the implementations are refinements of their specifications, provided that the B theory is correct, the tools generated all necessary obligations, and the tools did not discharge any false obligations.

What haven't we proved? We haven't proved that the specification corresponds to the informal requirements; especially, that we have captured all requirements as invariants. Furthermore, we haven't proved that the hand-coded base machines actually satisfy their specifications. We are also at the mercy of the B to C translator, the C compiler, and the used computers with their operating systems.

In conclusion, the many unprovable and unproved aspects even of a formal development in B are a clear sign, that good engineering practices, including animation, peer code review, and testing, are also important in a 'proved' development.

4.13 Exercises

Exercise 4.1 (Search operations). Give the cashier the possibility to display all customers who have their 20th birthday this year and are entitled to a present. Use the pattern of *SetFindCustomer* and *FindNextCustomer* of machine *Bank*.

Machines

	total length	obvious proof obligations	proof obligations	percent auto proved
MainBank	9 lines	3	0	100
OperationsBank	49 lines	19	0	100
RobustBank	239 lines	101	10	100
Bank	288 lines	394	49	95
Object	171 lines	125	17	100
BasicFile	102 lines	26	0	100
BasicString	98 lines	41	6	100
BasicCGI	72 lines	15	0	100
StrTokenType	14 lines	1	0	100
Total	1042 lines	725	82	98

Implementations (without base machines)

	total length	obvious proof obligations	proof obligations	percent auto proved
MainBank_1	52 lines	16	4	100
OperationsBank_1	334 lines	1028	285	99
RobustBank_1	206 lines	856	27	85
Bank_1	305 lines	526	643	71
Object_1	204 lines	291	230	70
StrTokenType_1	10 lines	3	2	100
Total	1111 lines	2720	1191	78

Fig. 4.14. Statistics of the Development

Exercise 4.2 (Online banking). Extend the bank so that customers can transfer money from one account to another over the Internet. The customer logs in using the account number, a password, and a one time code. The latter can for simplicity be chosen to be the login number. After login, the customer can make any number of transfers from her accounts to any accounts. The session is terminated by an explicit logout or after a fixed timeout. Withdrawals must now also be authorisable using the customer's password rather than the secret PINs of the individual accounts. Tool generated forms, similar to the lists generated by 'new account', which contain hidden information, like the 'command' field, can be used so that the password and one time code must only be entered once. For the timeout, a base machine giving the time must be added and the time when a one time code was first used must be stored on disk between program runs.

Exercise 4.3 (Simplified specification of accounts). As noted in Sect. 4.5.3, account numbers being unique they could be used as object identifiers for accounts in machine *Bank*. Remove the sets *ACCOUNT* and *accounts*, change the type of *accountNumber* to *NAT* and the domain of the other account attributes to *account-Number*, and constrain the cardinality of *accountNumber* to *maxAccounts*. Introduce the current specification as a refinement of the new one. Optionally, introduce the simplified specification as refinement of the current specification to gain an equivalence proof by mutual refinement.

Exercise 4.4 (Subtyping). Use subtyping modelled by subsetting to introduce two kinds of accounts. Savings accounts which get interest and cheque accounts without interest, but with the advantage that they allow overdrafts up to a certain limit.

Exercise 4.5 (Deleting customers and accounts). Provide for the deletion of customers and accounts. Be careful not to allow the deletion of accounts with non zero balance and of customers with accounts. Which invariants of the current system depend on the fact that deletion of customers and accounts is not possible?

Exercise 4.6 (Non-deterministic choice of error codes). If several preconditions of a transaction are not satisfied, the robust operations prescribes exactly which result code must be returned. For example, if *RobustNewAccount* is called with a non-existent customer when the account data base is full, *dbFull* rather than *unknownCustomer* must be reported. Respecify the robust operations so that the choice of the reported violated condition is arbitrary, thus avoiding overspecification.

Part II

Reactive Systems

5. Parallel Programming with the B Method

Michael Butler, Marina Waldén

5.1 Introduction

In later chapters we shall use B AMN to design examples of so-called *reactive systems*. Reactive systems are systems that maintain an on-going interaction with their environment. Reactive systems may also be composed of parallel interacting subsystems. Examples of such systems include plant controllers and electronic mail services. The action system formalism, introduced by Back and Kurki-Suonio [5], provides a framework for designing reactive systems by providing ways of modelling on-going interaction, techniques for parallel decomposition of systems and, of course, techniques for refining systems.

As we have already seen, a system is specified in B AMN as an abstract machine consisting of a state and some operations acting on that state. This is essentially the same structure as an action system, which describes the behaviour of a parallel reactive system in terms of some state variables and the atomic actions (i.e., operations) that can make changes to the state. The operations of both B machines and action systems are described using notations based on Dijkstra's guarded command language [22]. Action systems are used to construct parallel and distributed systems in a stepwise manner as described by Back and Sere [7]. Stepwise refinement of action systems is formalised within the refinement calculus [7] based on the weakest-precondition calculus of Dijkstra. As B machines are also refined in a stepwise manner relying on this calculus, we can refine action systems within the B-Method. Thus action systems and B AMN are quite similar and, as we shall see in this and subsequent chapters, applying the action system notions of parallelism within B AMN is straightforward and it allows us to design parallel reactive systems using B AMN.

Different views as to what constitutes the observable behaviour of an action system may be taken. In this chapter, we consider a *state-based* view of action systems. In the state-based view, action systems have a local and a global state. An action system interacts with the environment, i.e., other action systems, via its global state. It is, thus, only the global state that is visible to and accessible to the environment. In the *event-based* view, action systems only have internal state and they interact with the environment via shared actions. A state-based view is also taken in Chapters 6 and 7, while an event-based view is studied in Chapter 8.

In this chapter we give a brief introduction to action systems and describe how they can be embedded in the B-Method. We also study action systems extended with procedures. We show how action systems can be composed into parallel systems. Finally, we compare the proof obligations of action system refinement and refinement within the B-Method.

5.2 Actions and Action Systems

We consider the action system framework and its embedding in the B-Method giving a brief introduction to action systems.

5.2.1 Action Systems in B AMN

We write the general form of an action system A as an Abstract Machine Specification:

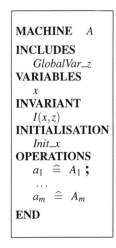

MACHINE A

INCLUDES
    GlobalVar_z
VARIABLES
    x
INVARIANT
    $I(x,z)$
INITIALISATION
    Init_x
OPERATIONS
    $a_1 \ \widehat{=} \ A_1$;
    . . .
    $a_m \ \widehat{=} \ A_m$

END

Here the variables z are the *global* variables and x are the *local* variables. Each variable is associated with some domain of values. The set of possible assignments of values to the state variables constitutes the state space. The data invariant of A is given as $I(x,z)$. The initialisation statement *Init_x* assigns initial values to the local variables x. The global variables z are used for interaction with the environment, i.e., other action systems. Each action A_i is a statement on the state variables and is named a_i.

Since the global variables should be available to more than one action system, we need to treat them differently from the local variables. The global variable z of the action system A is included as a machine, *GlobalVar_z*, in the abstract machine specification A. A separate machine should exist for each global variable. An action system can then include exactly those global variables it refers to. In the machine *GlobalVar_z* we declare the global variable z and give its properties in the *invariant* clause:

```
MACHINE      GlobalVar_z
VARIABLES
    z
INVARIANT
    T(z)
INITIALISATION
    Init_z
OPERATIONS
    assign_z(y) ≙ PRE T(y) THEN z := y END
END
```

The variable z is assigned via an operation $assign\_z(y)$, where the value y to be assigned to z is given as the parameter. All assignments to z in an action A_i in the action system A are replaced by calls to $assign\_z$ in the corresponding operations in the machine specification A.

If a global variable z is a read-only variable in the action system A and is of type natural number or set, it can alternatively be given as parameters in the machine A, $A(z)$, with their properties in the *constraints*-clause.

The behaviour of an action system is that of Dijkstra's guarded iteration statement [22] on the state variables: the initialisation statement is executed first; thereafter, as long as there are enabled actions, one action at a time is non-deterministically chosen and executed. When none of the actions are enabled, the action system terminates.

If two actions are independent, i.e., they do not have any variables in common, they can be executed in parallel. Their parallel execution is then equivalent to executing the actions one after the other, in either order. More on these topics and further references can be found elsewhere [5, 7, 8].

5.2.2 Actions in B AMN

Actions will be specified as statements in the generalised substitution notation of B AMN. The semantics of generalised substitutions is defined using weakest-precondition formulae: for statement S and postcondition P, the formula $[S]P$ characterises those initial states from which S is guaranteed to terminate in a state satisfying P. The formula $[S]false$ represents those initial states from which S is guaranteed to establish any postcondition; to see this, we have that for any P,

$$false \Rightarrow P.$$

Now, since $[S]$ is monotonic, we have

$$[S]false \Rightarrow [S]P.$$

We say that S behaves miraculously in an initial state satisfying $[S]false$, since it can establish any postcondition. For example, the statement

SELECT *false* **THEN** *T* **END**

is miraculous in any initial state since

$$[\textbf{SELECT } false \textbf{ THEN } T \textbf{ END}]false = true.$$

We take the view that a statement is "enabled" only in those initial states in which it behaves non-miraculously. The condition under which a statement S is enabled is called its *guard*, written $gd(S)$, where

$$gd(S) \; \hat{=} \; \neg \, [S]false.$$

From this we get the following rules for calculating the guards of *guarded statements*, *unbounded* and *bounded choice statements*, as well as *assignment statements*:

$$gd(\, \textbf{SELECT } G \textbf{ THEN } S \textbf{ END} \,) = G \wedge gd(S)$$
$$gd(\, \textbf{ANY } x \textbf{ WHERE } P \textbf{ THEN } S \textbf{ END} \,) = (\exists x. \; P \wedge gd(S))$$
$$gd(\, \textbf{CHOICE } S \textbf{ OR } T \textbf{ END} \,) = gd(S) \vee gd(T)$$
$$gd(\, x := E \,) = true.$$

For example, we get

$$gd(\, \textbf{ANY } x \textbf{ WHERE } x \in a \textbf{ THEN } a := a \setminus \{x\} \textbf{ END} \,)$$
$$= (\exists x. \; x \in a \wedge true)$$
$$= a \neq \{\}.$$

which means that this unbounded choice statement is enabled only when $a \neq \{\}$.

A common form of an action is **SELECT** *G* **THEN** *S* **END**, where the *guard* G is a boolean expression on some state variables and the *body* S is a statement on these variables. We say that this action is enabled in a state when its guard G evaluates to *true* and S is enabled. The action is a guarded statement which has the weakest precondition,

$$[\textbf{SELECT } G \textbf{ THEN } S \textbf{ END}]P \; \hat{=} \; G \Rightarrow [S]P.$$

The syntax of an action interpreted as an operation in the B-Method is:

$$Operation\_name \; \hat{=} \; \textbf{PRE } P \textbf{ THEN } (\textbf{SELECT } G \textbf{ THEN } S \textbf{ END}) \textbf{ END}$$

where the precondition P mostly has the value *true* and can then be left out.

Fig. 5.1 decribes a simple action system that sorts five natural number variables. Each action swaps adjacent pairs of variables if the value of the lower one is greater than the value of the higher one. Eventually the variables will end up sorted in ascending order and all the actions will be disabled.

```
MACHINE     Sort
VARIABLES
    x1,x2,x3,x4,x5
INVARIANT
    x1 ∈ NAT ∧ x2 ∈ NAT ∧ x3 ∈ NAT ∧ x4 ∈ NAT ∧ x5 ∈ NAT
OPERATIONS
    Swap₁  ≙  SELECT x1 > x2 THEN x1,x2 := x2,x1 END ;
    Swap₂  ≙  SELECT x2 > x3 THEN x2,x3 := x3,x2 END ;
    Swap₃  ≙  SELECT x3 > x4 THEN x3,x4 := x4,x3 END ;
    Swap₄  ≙  SELECT x4 > x5 THEN x4,x5 := x5,x4 END
END
```

Fig. 5.1. An Action System that Sorts Five Variables

5.3 Procedures Within Action Systems

In order to express communication and synchronisation within action systems composed in parallel, as described in Sect. 5.4, we use action systems extended with procedures [6, 7].

5.3.1 Procedures

Let us first study the procedures in the action systems. A procedure is declared by giving a *procedure header*, p, as well as a *procedure body*, P. The call on a parameterless procedure $p \mathrel{\widehat{=}} P$ within the statement S is determined by the substitution:

$$S' = S[P/p].$$

Thus, the body P of the procedure p is substituted for each call on the procedure in the statement S, i.e. the statement is expanded.

The procedures can also pass parameters. There are three different mechanisms of parameter passing for procedures: *call-by-value*, *call-by-result* and *call-by-value-result*. Call-by-value is denoted as $p(f)$, call-by-result as $f \leftarrow p$ and call-by-value-result as $f' \leftarrow p(f)$, where f is a parameter. This is actually the B mechanism. We note that the value-result parameter f is renamed to f' on the lefthand side in the declaration. Procedures with parameters can be expanded in the same way as procedures without parameters. Let $y',z \leftarrow p(x,y) \mathrel{\widehat{=}} P$ be a procedure declaration, where x, y and z are formal parameters. A call on p with the actual parameters a, b and c can then be expanded in the following way

$$S' = S[P'/b,c \leftarrow p(a,b)],$$

where P' is the statement

VAR x,y,y',z **IN** $x := a$ **;** $y := b$ **;** P **;** $b := y'$ **;** $c := z$ **END.**

Furthermore, we permit the procedure bodies to have guards that are not equivalent to *true*. If an action calls a procedure that is not enabled, the system acts as if the calling action never was enabled. Thus, the enabledness of the whole statement is determined by the enabledness of the procedure. The calling action and the procedure are executed as a single atomic entity. This can easily be seen by an example. Let us consider the action

$$A \mathrel{\widehat{=}} \textbf{SELECT } a \textbf{ THEN } S_1 \textbf{ ; } P \textbf{ ; } S_2 \textbf{ END}$$

and the procedure declaration

$$P \mathrel{\widehat{=}} \textbf{SELECT } b \textbf{ THEN } T \textbf{ END}.$$

Expanding the action A then gives the following action:

$$\textbf{SELECT } a \wedge \neg([S_1]\neg b) \textbf{ THEN } S_1 \textbf{ ; } T \textbf{ ; } S_2 \textbf{ END},$$

when S_1, T and S_2 are considered to be always enabled. The guard of the action A is, thus, $gd(A) = a \wedge \neg([S_1]\neg b)$.

In an action system a global procedure declaration can model the receiving of a message, while a procedure call on an imported procedure can be seen as sending a message. Since the calling action and the procedure are executed as a single atomic entity, they are synchronised. Thus, by using this extended action system framework we can also model synchronisation and communication via procedures.

5.3.2 Procedures within Abstract Machines

An *action system A* with procedures is of the form

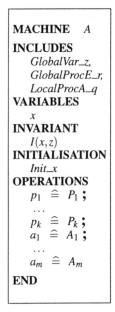

on the state variables x and z, where the variables x and z are the local and the global variables, respectively, as before. The data invariant is given as $I(x,z)$. The procedures r are the imported procedures of A. They are declared in another action system and called from within A. Together with the exported procedures p, which are declared in A, but called from other action systems, they form the global procedures. The local procedures q are both declared and called within A. The local procedures are assumed to be distinct from the global ones.

A procedure without parameters is interpreted as a statement in B AMN in the same way as an action with the precondition *true*. Procedures with input parameters have a non-trivial precondition. For example, the procedure $y',z \leftarrow p(x,y) \ \hat{=} \ P$ of an action system is in B AMN given as:

$$y',z \longleftarrow p(x,y) \ \hat{=} \ \textbf{PRE } T(x,y) \textbf{ THEN } P \textbf{ END}$$

where $T(x,y)$ gives the types of the input parameters x and y. Again the parameter on the lefthand side is renamed.

The global procedures p are given in the same abstract machine as the actions. The local procedures q, on the other hand, are introduced in a separate machine:

> **MACHINE**   *LocalProc_q*
> **OPERATIONS**
> $q_1 \ \hat{=} \ Q_1$;
>   ...
> $q_l \ \hat{=} \ Q_l$
> **END**

This is due to the fact that if an operation A calls an operation B, then A and B cannot be operations of the same machine due to restrictions in the B-Method. Since the local procedures are called from actions in A, they cannot themselves be located in A. The exported global procedures p, on the other hand, are assumed to be called from another machine. The global procedures r that are called in the actions of A, but not declared in A, are introduced by including the machine *GlobalProcE_r*:

> **MACHINE**   *GlobalProcE_r*
> **OPERATIONS**
> $r \ \hat{=} \ $ skip
> **END**

where their headers are given. Since the bodies of these procedures are not of interest to us, they can be given as skip or remain undefined. These procedures are declared in some other system E composed in parallel with A in the manner described in the next section.

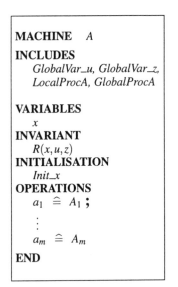

Fig. 5.2. The Action Systems A and B in B AMN

5.4 Parallel Composition

Action systems can be composed to form parallel systems [7]. The parallel composition of the action systems A and B is written $A \parallel B$. This composition is formed by merging the variables and actions of the subsystems A and B. The local state variables of the subsystems have to be distinct. This can, however, easily be achieved by renaming before forming the composition.

Let us now consider the action systems A and B given in B AMN in Fig. 5.2, where the variable lists x and y contain no common variables. The global variables and the procedures are defined as previously. The parallel composition $A \parallel B$ of A and B is then defined as the abstract machine AB in Fig. 5.3. The common global variable z of A and B will also be a global variable of the parallel composition $A \parallel B$. Similarily the global procedures of A declared in *GlobalProcA* are considered as global procedures of $A \parallel B$, even if they are exported procedures of A and imported procedures of B. For the rest the variables, the invariant and the initialisation, as well as the operations in A and B are simply merged to form $A \parallel B$.

The invariant of $A \parallel B$ is the conjunction of the invariants of the subsystems A and B. This imposes, however, an extra requirement on the operations of the subsystems. The operations A_i should preserve the invariant S, while the operations B_j should preserve invariant R. This is mainly a restriction on the assignments to the common global variables z in the operations A_i and B_j. These proof obligations are an extension of the normal proof obligations prescribed by the B-Method. In the B-Method, a machine cannot be included in several different machines simultaneously. Since machines A and B of Fig. 5.3 share *GlobalVar_z* and *GlobalProcA*,

```
MACHINE    AB
INCLUDES
    GlobalVar_u, GlobalVar_v, GlobalVar_z,
    LocalProcA, GlobalProcA,
    LocalProcB, GlobalProcB
VARIABLES
    x, y
INVARIANT
    R(x, u, z) ∧ S(y, v, z)
INITIALISATION
    Init_x || Init_y
OPERATIONS
    a₁  ≙  A₁ ;
    ⋮
    aₘ  ≙  Aₘ ;
    b₁  ≙  B₁ ;
    ⋮
    bₙ  ≙  Bₙ
END
```

Fig. 5.3. The Parallel Composition of Action Systems A and B

they cannot be part of the same development in the B-Method and proof obligations requiring that they preserve each other's invariants would not be necessary. However, we wish them to be part of the same development and hence need to check that they do preserve each other's invariants.

The global variables are here included as separate machines. In cases where they are read-only, they could also be declared as parameters of the machines. Consider the machines A and B with their global variables u, z and v, z in Fig. 5.2. Let us first assume z to be a read-only variable in A, but not in B. The parallel composition of $A(z)$ and B then gives the same result AB as in Fig. 5.3. In cases where z is read-only in both components, i.e., we would have $A(z)$ and $B(z)$, their parallel composition would be the machine $AB(z)$. As the final case we consider the global variable u of A to be read-only. We then have that the parallel composition of $A(u)$ and B yields the machine $AB(u)$.

We can note that the global procedures of A in Fig. 5.2 are given in a separate machine *GlobalProcA* instead of in the *operations*-clause. A similar approach is taken in B. Additionally we assume that B calls the global procedures of A including these procedures in B. The global procedures are, here, given in separate machines, since some of them will be called locally in the composed machine AB. This approach is necessary in the B-Method whenever we consider more than one action system at a time and these action systems call the global procedures of each other.

MACHINE   *SortA*

INCLUDES   *GlobalVar_x3*

VARIABLES
  $x1, x2$
INVARIANT
  $x1 \in NAT \land x2 \in NAT$
OPERATIONS
  $Swap_1$ $\widehat{=}$ **SELECT** $x1 > x2$ **THEN** $x1, x2 := x2, x1$ **END** ;
  $Swap_2$ $\widehat{=}$ **SELECT** $x2 > x3$ **THEN** $x2, x3 := x3, x2$ **END**

END

MACHINE   *SortB*

INCLUDES   *GlobalVar_x3*

VARIABLES
  $x4, x5$
INVARIANT
  $x4 \in NAT \land x5 \in NAT$
OPERATIONS
  $Swap_3$ $\widehat{=}$ **SELECT** $x3 > x4$ **THEN** $x3, x4 := x4, x3$ **END** ;
  $Swap_4$ $\widehat{=}$ **SELECT** $x4 > x5$ **THEN** $x4, x5 := x5, x4$ **END**

END

Fig. 5.4. Parallel Sort

As an example of parallel composition, consider the two action systems *Sort1* and *Sort2* of Fig. 5.4. The parallel composition of these is similar to the single system *Sort* of Fig. 5.1 except that $x3$ is global in *Sort1* $\parallel$ *Sort2*.

5.5 Refining Action Systems

Specification machines usually contain abstract data structures that are not directly implementable in a programming language. *Data refinement* is used in order to bring abstract specifications towards implementations by replacing the local variables of the abstract machine with concrete variables that are more easily implemented. A general discussion on data refinement is given in Chapter 1.

5.5.1 Data Refinement of Actions

An abstraction invariant $R(x, x', z)$ relating the abstract variables x and the concrete variables x', as well as the global variables z, is used to replace abstract statements with concrete statements. If S is a statement on the variables x, z, S' is a statement on the variables x', z, and $R(x, x', z)$ is the abstraction invariant, then we write

$$S \sqsubseteq_R S'$$

for "S is data-refined by S' under abstraction invariant R".

5.5.2 Refinement of Action Systems

We may refine an action system A with an action system A', where A and A' have corresponding actions and global state, but possibly different local variables. Let the abstract action system A have the variables x and z, and the refined action system A' have the variables x' and z. The variables x are the abstract local variables that are data refined into the concrete local variables x'. They are invisible to the environment. The global variables z, on the other hand, form the interface to the environment and are left unchanged.

In Fig. 5.5 the abstract action system A and its refinement A' are shown as abstract machines with the refinement relation $R(x, x', z)$. The machines for the global variables and the local procedures are as before. In the refinement machine A' the local procedures q are refined. We have also renamed the global variable z to z' due to restrictions in the B-Method and include the modified machine $GlobalVar\_z'$. However, in the *invariant* clause we state that the global variables z and z' really are the same, $z = z'$. For ease of reference, we let $R'(x, x', z, z')$ denote the whole abstraction invariant $R(x, x', z) \wedge z = z'$.

Let us now study the refinement rule:

Definition 5.1. *For the abstract action system* A *and the concrete action system* A' *in Fig. 5.5,* A *is refined by* A' *with abstraction invariant* $R'(x, x', z, z')$*, denoted* A $\sqsubseteq_{R'}$ A'*, provided each of the conditions below hold.*

1. $Init\_x \sqsubseteq_{R'} Init\_x'$
2. $P_i \sqsubseteq_{R'} P'_i$,   for $i = 1, \ldots, k$
3. $A_i \sqsubseteq_{R'} A'_i$,   for $i = 1, \ldots, m$
4. $R' \wedge gd(P_i) \Rightarrow gd(P'_i)$,   for $i = 1, \ldots, k$.
5. $R' \wedge gd(A_i) \Rightarrow gd(A'_i)$,   for $i = 1, \ldots, m$.

Conditions 1, 2 and 3 ensure that the initialisation and each operation, i.e., each global procedure and action, of A' is a refinement of its counterpart in A, and are referred to as data-refinement conditions. These are precisely the conditions that define refinement of machines in B AMN [2]. Conditions 4 and 5 ensure that a global procedure or an action in A' is only enabled, if the corresponding global procedure or action in A is enabled, and are referred to as progress conditions. In order to be able to prove these two conditions within the B-Method extra operations need to be introduced into the machines of the action systems. This is discussed later in Chapter 7. The refinement of the local procedures q is proved via Conditions 3 and 5 for the actions by expanding the procedure calls in the actions as explained in Sect. 5.3.1.

MACHINE A	REFINEMENT A'
	REFINES
	A
INCLUDES	INCLUDES
$GlobalVar\_z$,	$GlobalVar\_z'$
$LocalProc\_q$	$LocalProc\_q'$
VARIABLES	VARIABLES
x	x'
INVARIANT	INVARIANT
$I(x,z)$	$R(x,x',z) \wedge z = z'$
INITIALISATION	INITIALISATION
$Init\_x$	$Init\_x'$
OPERATIONS	OPERATIONS
$p_1 \;\widehat{=}\; P_1\;;$	$p_1 \;\widehat{=}\; P_1'\;;$
$\vdots$	$\vdots$
$p_k \;\widehat{=}\; P_k\;;$	$p_k \;\widehat{=}\; P_k'\;;$
$a_1 \;\widehat{=}\; A_1\;;$	$a_1 \;\widehat{=}\; A_1'\;;$
$\vdots$	$\vdots$
$a_m \;\widehat{=}\; A_m$	$a_m \;\widehat{=}\; A_m'$
END	END

Fig. 5.5. An Abstract Action System A and its Refinement A' in B AMN

Intuitively, $A \sqsubseteq_R A'$ means that any observable behaviour of A' is also an observable behaviour of A. Back and von Wright have investigated this notion more formally in [9]. There, the observable behaviour of an action system is modelled as a set of *state-traces*, where a state-trace is a finite or infinite sequence of states representing a possible evolution of the state of a system. Action system A is refined by A' when the state-traces of A' are a subset of the state-traces of A. Back and von Wright show that the refinement rule of Definition 5.1 is sound in this model, since the rule implies state-trace refinement. This state-trace approach is similar to the approach of Abadi and Lamport [1] to modelling reactive systems.

5.5.3 Refinement and Parallel Composition

The conditions in Definition 5.1 are sufficient to guarantee correct data refinement between action systems that are executed in isolation. The action system A might, however, occur in parallel composition with another action system B. If action system A is refined by A', $A \sqsubseteq_R A'$, for some abstract relation R, then $A \parallel B$ is refined by $A' \parallel B$ under the same relation R. The context B has then to be taken into account in the refinement rule. We have that $A \parallel B \sqsubseteq_R A' \parallel B$, if the following holds for every action B in B:

$$R \wedge [B]true \Rightarrow [B]R.$$

Thus, the context B should not interfere with the action system A and it should preserve the abstract relation R.

5.6 Discussion

In this chapter we gave a brief introduction to action systems and described how they can be embedded in the B-Method. The structure of an action system corresponds closely to the structure of a B machine. We saw that the action system notions of shared global variables and shared global procedures can be modelled within the B framework. The only extension we needed was the extra proof obligation on parallel systems requiring that they preserve each other's invariants.

Some examples of parallel composition and refinement will be given in later chapters.

6. Production Cell

Emil Sekerinski [1]

6.1 Introduction

This chapter is about specifying and implementing a control program for a production cell using action systems in AMN. The production cell consists of five machines: two conveyor belts, an elevating and rotating table, a two-arm robot, and a press. The machines are equipped with a total of 18 sensors for determining the positions of the machines and for sensing the transported plates and a total of eight actuators for setting the motors.

The production cell is a typical example of a *discrete control system*. In reality, all machines evolve continuously. However, at certain points the change of their state is notified to the control program, which may react to this change. Hence, the evolution of the system can be sufficiently represented as a sequence of steps. This means that discrete control systems can be modelled with (discrete) action systems. This chapter presents a general approach to developing control programs for discrete systems in AMN, and illustrates this with the complete development of a control program for a production cell.

6.1.1 Specifying Control Systems with Action Systems

When concerned with the correctness of the control program, or controller for short, we note that it cannot be judged on its own but rather depends on the expected behaviour of the controlled plant as well. Hence, for formally verifying the correctness of a controller, the behaviour of the plant, here in the form of the five production cell machines, has to be specified as well.

For discrete control systems, the plant can be modelled as an action system with only actions, which become enabled as the system evolves, and the controller as an action system with only procedures, which are called by the plant. The controller procedures are understood as "interrupt procedures" which are called upon certain sensor changes. The controller reads the sensors and sets the actuators. In turn, the plant reads the actuators and sets the sensors (see Fig. 6.1). In this model, different components of the plant may evolve concurrently, but the controller has no concurrent activity in parallel to the plant: the controller only reacts "instantaneously" to events from the plant. This can be justified as the controller procedures are rather

---

[1] Work done at Åbo Akademi, Finland.

simple and can be executed sufficiently fast compared to the evolution of the plant such that their execution time is negligible. This is an assumption for modelling control systems which can often, although not always, be made. If it does not hold, the model of the controller has to include execution times, which is beyond the scope of this chapter (this is studied, for example, in [29]).

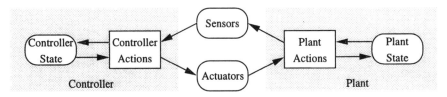

Fig. 6.1. Model of a Discrete Control System

6.1.2 Structure of the Development

The approach taken here is to start with a model of the *whole* production cell system as an action system in AMN. This model describes the behaviour of the whole system, i.e. the mechanical plant and the controller. Next, plant and controller are separated in a refinement step, in the sense that their parallel composition refines the initial specification. The plant specification describes the assumptions about the behaviour of the plant; it is not further refined. It can be used for checking whether the actual plant does indeed satisfy these assumptions. Finally, in a second refinement step, the controller is implemented.

The controller is developed by first viewing each machine as a system in isolation and modelling each machine as an action system in AMN (Sec. 6.3). Next, the controllers of all machine are derived by separating controller and plant in a refinement step (Sec. 6.4). Then, the specification of the whole production cell is constructed using the specifications of the individual machines (Sec. 6.5). Finally, the controller of the whole system is derived (Sec. 6.6), reusing the previously derived controllers of the machines. In this way, the specifications and controllers of the machines become reusable for other plants.

This chapter gives an example of an action system in AMN with a comparatively large number of actions, but with simple bodies involving only simple data structures. The whole variety of structuring facilities of AMN are used. No loop introduction or other more complicated algorithmic refinement steps are needed. The whole development, including the proofs, is carried out with Atelier B.

The generated code for the controller can be connected to a graphical simulation of the production cell. For this, some additional code is needed for reading sensor values and writing actuator settings. This code, as well as the graphical simulation, can be obtained from the book's World Wide Web page.

For an understanding of the approach, this chapter can be read selectively by focusing on specific machines. Most of the issues of developing a control program for a single machine can be studied with the feed belt. A simple interaction between two machines is that of the feed belt and the table. The robot is an example of a machine with a structured state space and involved internal safety requirements as well as an involved interaction with other machines. Finally, the deposit belt is an example of a machine where the state cannot be fully observed but which still can be treated with the same technique.

6.2 The Production Cell

The production cell consists of five interacting machines, a conveyor belt (the feed belt), an elevating and rotating table, a robot with two orthogonal arms, a press, and another conveyor belt (the deposit belt), arranged as in Fig. 6.2.

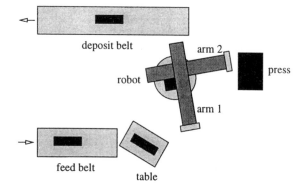

Fig. 6.2. Top View of the Production Cell

The task of the production cell is to press metal plates which arrive on the feed belt and to place them on the deposit belt. The following actions happen in sequence while a metal plate traverses through the cell:

- The feed belt conveys the plate onto the table.
- The table elevates and rotates the plate to a position where the first robot arm can grip the plate.
- The first robot arm grips the plate, the robot rotates counterclockwise and feeds the press.
- The press forges the plate and opens again.
- The robot, after rotating clockwise, unloads the press with its second arm.
- The robot turns counterclockwise and releases the metal plate over the deposit belt.
- The deposit belt conveys the plate to its end.

All machines act in parallel thus allowing several plates to be processed concurrently. The robot is equipped with two arms in order to maximise throughput of the production cell: the robot is supposed to fetch a plate from the table while another plate is still being pressed such that the press can be quickly unloaded and loaded again. The control program has to ensure that

- the metal plates are processed properly, i.e. all metal plates are transported properly and pressed exactly once and
- safety requirements of the machines are guaranteed, i.e. the machines do not move beyond end positions and do not collide.

We give a description of the "logical" properties of the machines, leaving out details such as their geometry and speed, as well as the interface to the sensors and actuators.

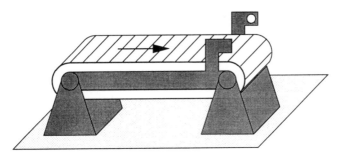

Fig. 6.3. The Feed Belt

The Feed Belt. The feed belt transports plates placed on its left end to its right end and then to the table (see Fig. 6.3). A photo-electric cell goes "on" when a plate arrives at the right end and goes "off" when it leaves the belt (and thus has moved onto the table). The motor for the belt may be switched on and off: it has to be on while waiting for a new plate and has to be switched off when a plate is at the end of the belt but cannot be delivered onto the table.

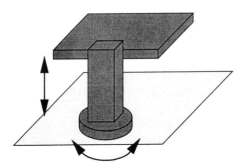

Fig. 6.4. The Table

The Table. The table lifts a single plate to the height of the robot and rotates the plate clockwise such that it is orthogonal to the first robot arm. (The latter is needed because the robot arms have no rotating grippers.)

The table (see Fig. 6.4) has two reversing electric motors, one for elevating and one for rotating. Mechanical sensors indicate whether the table is at its left, right, upper, and lower end position, respectively. The table must not move beyond its end position. We assume that initially the table is in its lower left position.

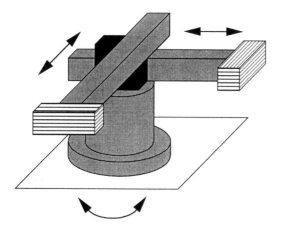

Fig. 6.5. The Robot

The Robot. The robot has two orthogonal arms on a rotating base (see Fig. 6.5). Both robot arms may extend and retract by reversing electric motors. Both arms have three sensor positions, an inner, middle, and outer position, respectively. These arm positions are reported by mechanical sensors.

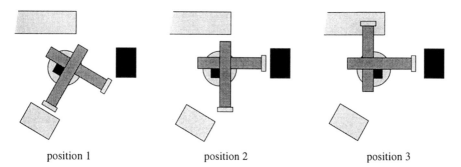

position 1   position 2   position 3

Fig. 6.6. The Three Robot Positions, with Both Arms of the Robot Retracted

The base has a reversing motor for rotation. The three relevant positions of the base are indicated by a mechanical sensor for each position (see Fig. 6.6).

1. In position 1, arm 1 has to extend to middle position for fetching a metal plate from the table.

2. In position 2, arm 2 has to extend to its outer position for picking a metal plate from the press.
3. In position 3, arm 1 has to extend to its outer position for loading the press and the arm 2 has to extend to its middle position for placing a metal plate on the deposit belt.

While rotating the robot, both arms have to be retracted to their inner position. Neither the robot base nor the robot arms must move beyond their respective end positions.

Electromagnetic grippers at the end of each arm can hold a metal plate as long as they are switched on. We assume that initially the robot base is at position 3, arm 1 is at its inner position and arm 2 is at its middle position, and both grippers are off.

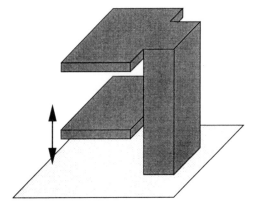

Fig. 6.7. The Press

The Press. The press has a platform on which the metal plates are placed by the robot (see Fig. 6.7). It closes by moving its platform up and opens by moving the platform down by a reversing motor. Due to the different heights of the robot arms, different positions have to be taken for loading and unloading the press: it is un-loaded by robot arm 2 in lower end position and loaded by robot arm 1 in middle position. Three mechanical sensors indicating the lower, middle and upper position, respectively.

Since the press platform and the robot arms may collide, the following safety requirements have to be guaranteed. Firstly, when the robot is in position 3, robot arm 1 may extend only if the platform is in loading (middle) position. Secondly, when the robot is in position 2, robot arm 2 may extend only if the platform is in unloading (lower) position. The platform may move only after the respective robot arm has retracted to its inner position again. Of course, the platform must not move beyond its upper and lower end position. We assume that initially the press is at its lower position and is empty.

The Deposit Belt. The deposit belt transports plates placed by the robot on its right end to its left end. A photo-electric cell goes "on" when a plate arrives at the left end and goes "off" when it has been removed (by a person or some other machine). The motor for the belt may be switched on and off: it has to be off while waiting for a new plate to be placed by the robot or while a plate is at its end. It has to be switched on when a plate is placed on it and no other plate is at the belt's end. A new plate may only be placed on the belt if there is no other plate on the belt or one plate is at the end of the belt; in both cases the belt motor must be off.

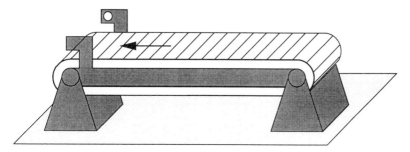

Fig. 6.8. The Deposit Belt

6.3 Specification of the Machines

For a modular specification of the production cell, first the behaviour of each machine is specified separately as an AMN machine. The following principles are applied:

- All possible machine states are identified and are represented by variables of appropriate types.
- Each relevant sensor change is mapped to one action.
- Possibly additional actions for the interaction of the machine with its environment are introduced.
- Safety requirements of the machines are expressed in the respective invariants.

A schema of the machine specification is given in Fig. 6.9. We interpret these machine specifications as action systems where all operations are actions. When a parameterised action is selected, the parameters will have some arbitrary value which is determined by the machine's environment. Alternatively, non-determinism of the environment can be modelled by a non-deterministic choice within the action. If the machines are viewed in isolation, these two mechanisms are equivalent. However, these actions are later composed to larger actions where this non-determinism is reduced. This composition can be more conveniently expressed when the non-determinism is controlled by parameters.

When looking at machine specifications in isolation, the names of the actions are irrelevant. However, later for the production cell specification, the actions will be referred to by their names for composing larger actions.

MACHINE   *Machine*

VARIABLES

   machine state

INVARIANT

   variable types ∧
   safety requirements

INITIALISATION

   machine state initialisation

OPERATIONS

   Action (parameters)   ≙
      SELECT   *guard*   **THEN**
         machine state change
      END ;

   . . .

END

Fig. 6.9. Schema for Machine Specifications

At this stage, only the safety requirements concerning the individual production cell machines can be expressed. Safety requirements concerning the interaction of the machines are expressed when constructing the specification of the whole production cell.

6.3.1 The Feed Belt

For an abstract model of the feed belt, we identify the following states:

Running The belt is running with no part at the sensor.
Stopped The belt is stopped with a part at the sensor.
Delivering The belt is running but with a part at the sensor.

The type of the feed belt state is defined in a separate AMN machine:

MACHINE   *FeedBeltTypes*
SETS
   $FEEDBELT = \{ Running , Stopped , Delivering \}$
END

The belt is initialised to state *Running*. From *Running* it may go to state *Delivering* or first to *Stopped* and then to *Delivering*. From state *Delivering*, the belt goes to state *Running* again. The transitions between the states are caused by actions *EndReached* and *PartLeft*, which correspond to sensor changes, and by the action *ContinueDelivery*, which represents an interaction with the environment:

MACHINE   *FeedBelt*
SEES   *FeedBeltTypes*
VARIABLES
   belt
INVARIANT
   belt $\in$ *FEEDBELT*
INITIALISATION
   belt := *Running*
OPERATIONS

EndReached A part reaches the end of the belt; for this, the belt must have been running. The parameter *halt* indicates whether the belt has to be stopped or can be kept running.

EndReached (*halt*) $\widehat{=}$
   PRE   *halt* $\in$ *BOOL*   **THEN**
      SELECT   *belt* = *Running* $\land$ *halt* = *TRUE*   **THEN**
        belt := *Stopped*
      WHEN   *belt* = *Running* $\land$ *halt* = *FALSE*   **THEN**
        belt := *Delivering*
      END
   END ;

ContinueDelivery The environment is ready to accept the part at the end of the belt.

ContinueDelivery $\widehat{=}$
   SELECT   *belt* = *Stopped*   **THEN**   *belt* := *Delivering*   **END ;**

PartLeft The part on the belt has left the belt; for this, the belt must have been delivering.

PartLeft $\widehat{=}$
   SELECT   *belt* = *Delivering*   **THEN**   *belt* := *Running*   **END**
END

6.3.2 The Table

For an abstract model of the table, we represent its elevating state and its rotating state. Concerning the elevating state, the table is in exactly one of the following states:

AtUpper , *AtLower* The table is at its upper or lower sensor position, respectively.
MovingUp , *MovingDown* The table is moving upwards or downwards, respectively.

Concerning the rotating state, the table is in exactly one of the following states:

AtLeft , *AtRight* The table is at its left (counterclockwise) or right (clockwise) sensor position, respectively.

RotatingRight , *RotatingLeft* The table is rotating to the right (clockwise) or to the left (counterclockwise) sensor position, respectively.

The type of the elevating and rotating state of the table is defined in a separate AMN machine:

MACHINE   *TableTypes*
SETS

$ELEV = \{$ *AtUpper* , *MovingUp* , *AtLower* , *MovingDown* $\}$ **;**
$ROT = \{$ *AtLeft* , *RotatingRight* , *AtRight* , *RotatingLeft* $\}$

END

We assume that the table is initially in state *AtLower* and *AtLeft*. From there, it goes to state *MovingUp* and *RotatingRight* simultaneously, and from there to state *AtUpper* and *AtRight* in either order. From there, the table goes to state *MovingDown* and *RotatingRight* simultaneously, and from these back again to *AtLower* and *AtLeft* in either order.

The actions *PartPlaced* and *PartTaken* represent interactions with the environment, the actions *UpReached*, *DownReached*, *RightReached*, and *LeftReached* correspond to sensor changes.

MACHINE   *Table*
SEES   *TableTypes*
VARIABLES

elev , *rot*

INVARIANT

$elev \in ELEV \wedge rot \in ROT$

INITIALISATION

$elev := AtLower \;\|\; rot := AtLeft$

OPERATIONS

PartPlaced A part is placed on the table; for this, the table must be in lower left position.

PartPlaced $\hat{=}$
    SELECT $elev = AtLower \wedge rot = AtLeft$ **THEN**
      $elev := MovingUp \;\|\; rot := RotatingRight$
    END ;

PartTaken A part is removed from the table; for this, the table must be in upper right position.

PartTaken $\hat{=}$
    SELECT $elev = AtUpper \wedge rot = AtRight$ **THEN**

$elev := MovingDown \;\|\; rot := RotatingLeft$
END ;

UpReached The table reaches its upper sensor position. For this, the table must have been moving upwards. The parameter *moveBack*, determined by the table's environment, indicates whether the table stays in its upper end position or moves back to lower left end position.

$UpReached\,(\,moveBack\,)\quad\widehat{=}$
    PRE $moveBack \in BOOL$ **THEN**
        SELECT $elev = MovingUp \wedge moveBack = TRUE$ **THEN**
            $elev := MovingDown \;\|\; rot := RotatingLeft$
        WHEN $elev = MovingUp \wedge moveBack = FALSE$ **THEN**
            $elev := AtUpper$
        END
    END ;

DownReached The table reaches its lower sensor position. For this, the table must have been moving downwards.

$DownReached\quad\widehat{=}$
    SELECT $elev = MovingDown$ **THEN** $elev := AtLower$ **END ;**

RightReached The table reaches its right sensor position. For this, the table must have been moving rightwards. The parameter *moveBack*, determined by the table's environment, indicates whether the table stays in its right end position or moves back to lower left end position.

$RightReached\,(\,moveBack\,)\quad\widehat{=}$
    PRE $moveBack \in BOOL$ **THEN**
        SELECT $rot = RotatingRight \wedge moveBack = TRUE$ **THEN**
            $elev := MovingDown \;\|\; rot := RotatingLeft$
        WHEN $rot = RotatingRight \wedge moveBack = FALSE$ **THEN**
            $rot := AtRight$
        END
    END ;

LeftReached The table reaches its left sensor position. For this, the table must have been moving leftwards.

$LeftReached\quad\widehat{=}$
    SELECT $rot = RotatingLeft$ **THEN** $rot := AtLeft$ **END**
END

We did not assume anything about the relative speeds of rotating and elevating. If it was guaranteed by the mechanics that the table reaches its right and left end position before its upper and lower end position, respectively, we could model this by changing the action *UpReached* and *DownReached* as follows:

UpReached (*moveBack*) $\hat{=}$
    PRE   *moveBack* $\in$ *BOOL*   **THEN**
       SELECT   *elev* = *MovingUp* $\wedge$ *rot* = *AtRight* $\wedge$ *moveBack* = *TRUE*   **THEN**
          elev := *MovingDown* $\|$ *rot* := *RotatingLeft*
       WHEN   *elev* = *MovingUp* $\wedge$ *rot* = *AtRight* $\wedge$ *moveBack* = *FALSE*   **THEN**
          elev := *AtUpper*
       END
    END ;

DownReached $\hat{=}$
    SELECT   *elev* = *MovingDown* $\wedge$ *rot* = *AtLeft*   **THEN**   *elev* := *AtLower*
    END ;

The advantage of strengthening the specification in this way is that the logic of the controller may get simplified. The disadvantage is that the resulting controller can only be used if this assumption about the mechanics is indeed guaranteed. Since in our case we cannot make such an assumption anyway, we proceed with the more general specification.

6.3.3 The Robot

For an abstract model of the robot, we model the state of the robot base and the state of each of the two robot arms with their grippers. The robot base is either:

AtPos1 , *AtPos2* , *AtPos3* The robot base is at sensor position 1, 2, or 3, respectively.
RotatingFwdToPos2 The robot base is rotating from position 1 counterclockwise to position 2.
RotatingFwdToPos3 The robot base is rotating from position 2 counterclockwise to position 3.
RotatingBackToPos2 The robot base is rotating from position 3 clockwise to position 2.
RotatingBackToPos1 The robot base is rotating from position 2 clockwise to position 1.

The robot arms are in exactly one of following states:

AtInner , *AtMiddle* The robot arm is at its inner or middle sensor position, respectively. Note that there is a sensor for the outer position, but the arms do not rest there, they immediately retract again. Hence there is no need to represent it.
ExtendingToMiddle The robot arm is extending from its inner to its middle sensor position.
ExtendingToOuter The robot arm is retracting from its middle to its outer sensor position.
RetractingToMiddle The robot arm is retracting from its outer to its middle sensor position.
RetractingToInner The robot arm is retracting from its middle to its inner sensor position.

MACHINE *TwoArmRobotTypes*

SETS

ROBOTBASE = { *AtPos1* , *RotatingFwdToPos2* , *AtPos2* , *RotatingFwdToPos3* , *AtPos3* , *RotatingBackToPos2* , *RotatingBackToPos1* } **;**

ROBOTARM = { *AtInner* , *ExtendingToMiddle* , *RetractingToInner* , *AtMiddle* , *ExtendingToOuter* , *RetractingToMiddle* }

END

The grippers of the robot arms either hold or don't hold a part, which is represented by the boolean variables *arm1Holding* and *arm2Holding*, respectively.

In order to generalise the specification of the robot, we refer to the other machines in a more general way, rather than assuming the particular machines of the production cell. The robot loads and unloads a processing unit, here the press, by performing following sequence of moves cyclically:

- After a part becomes available in position 1, arm 1 fetches the part, arm 1 retracts to innermost position, and the robot turns to position 2.
- When processing finishes while in position 2, arm 2 extends to its outermost position, fetches the part, retracts to its innermost position, and the robot turns to position 3.
- When the processing unit becomes again ready for being loaded while in position 3, arm 1 extends to its outermost position, releases the part it holds, and retracts to its innermost position. Also, arm 2 extends and, when the deposit (which is here a belt) becomes ready, releases its part. When both arms are free and retracted, the robot turns to position 1 and extends arm 1 to its middle position.

We assume that initially the robot is in position 3, arm 1 is at its inner position, arm 2 is at its middle position, and both grippers are released. To initiate the cycle, first arm 2 has to retract to its inner position.

The actions *PartAvailable*, *ProcessingFinished*, *ProcessingReady*, *DepositReady* represent interactions with the environment, the actions *Pos1Reached*, *Pos2Reached* *Pos3Reached*, *Arm1InReached*, *Arm1MiddleReached*, *Arm1OutReached*, *Arm2In-Reached*, *Arm2MiddleReached*, and *Arm2OutReached* correspond to sensor changes.

MACHINE *TwoArmRobot*

SEES *TwoArmRobotTypes*

VARIABLES

base , *arm1* , *arm2* , *arm1Holding* , *arm2Holding*

INVARIANT

base ∈ *ROBOTBASE* ∧ *arm1* ∈ *ROBOTARM* ∧ *arm2* ∈ *ROBOTARM* ∧ *arm1Holding* ∈ *BOOL* ∧ *arm2Holding* ∈ *BOOL* ∧

Safety Requirement Arm 1 must not be extended beyond its middle position at robot position 1 and must not extend at all at robot position 2. Arm 2 must not be extended at all at robot position 1 and must not be extended beyond its middle position at robot position 3.

$(base = AtPos1 \Rightarrow arm1 \in \{ \, ExtendingToMiddle \, , AtMiddle \, , RetractingToInner \, \} \,) \wedge$
$(base = AtPos1 \wedge arm1 \in \{ \, ExtendingToMiddle \, , AtMiddle \, \} \Rightarrow$
    $arm1Holding = FALSE \,) \wedge$
$(base = AtPos1 \wedge arm1 = RetractingToInner \Rightarrow arm1Holding = TRUE \,) \wedge$
$(base = AtPos1 \Rightarrow arm2 = AtInner \wedge arm2Holding = FALSE \,) \wedge$

$(base = AtPos2 \Rightarrow arm1 = AtInner \wedge arm1Holding = TRUE \,) \wedge$
$(base = AtPos2 \Rightarrow arm2 \in \{ \, AtInner \, , ExtendingToMiddle \, , ExtendingToOuter \, ,$
    $RetractingToMiddle \, , RetractingToInner \, \} \,) \wedge$
$(base = AtPos2 \wedge arm2 \in \{ \, AtInner \, , ExtendingToMiddle \, , ExtendingToOuter \, \} \Rightarrow$
    $arm2Holding = FALSE \,) \wedge$
$(base = AtPos2 \wedge arm2 \in \{ \, RetractingToMiddle \, , RetractingToInner \, \} \Rightarrow$
    $arm2Holding = TRUE \,) \wedge$

$(base = AtPos3 \Rightarrow arm1 \in \{ \, AtInner \, , ExtendingToMiddle \, , ExtendingToOuter \, ,$
    $RetractingToMiddle \, , RetractingToInner \, \} \,) \wedge$
$(base = AtPos3 \wedge arm1 \in \{ \, ExtendingToMiddle \, , ExtendingToOuter \, \} \Rightarrow$
    $arm1Holding = TRUE \,) \wedge$
$(base = AtPos3 \wedge arm1 \in \{ \, RetractingToMiddle \, , RetractingToInner \, \} \Rightarrow$
    $arm1Holding = FALSE \,) \wedge$
$(base = AtPos3 \Rightarrow arm2 \in \{ \, ExtendingToMiddle \, , AtMiddle \, , RetractingToInner \, ,$
    $AtInner \, \} \,) \wedge$
$(base = AtPos3 \wedge arm2 \in \{ \, ExtendingToMiddle \, , AtMiddle \, \} \Rightarrow$
    $arm2Holding = TRUE \,) \wedge$
$(base = AtPos3 \wedge arm2 \in \{ \, RetractingToInner \, , AtInner \, \} \Rightarrow$
    $arm2Holding = FALSE \,) \wedge$

Safety Requirement The robot must rotate only with both arms retracted.

$(base = RotatingFwdToPos2 \Rightarrow arm1 = AtInner \wedge arm1Holding = TRUE \,) \wedge$
$(base = RotatingFwdToPos2 \Rightarrow arm2 = AtInner \wedge arm2Holding = FALSE \,) \wedge$

$(base = RotatingFwdToPos3 \Rightarrow arm1 = AtInner \wedge arm1Holding = TRUE \,) \wedge$
$(base = RotatingFwdToPos3 \Rightarrow arm2 = AtInner \wedge arm1Holding = TRUE \,) \wedge$

$(base = RotatingBackToPos2 \Rightarrow arm1 = AtInner \,) \wedge$
$(base = RotatingBackToPos2 \Rightarrow arm2 = AtInner \,) \wedge$

$(base = RotatingBackToPos1 \Rightarrow arm1 = AtInner \wedge arm2Holding = FALSE \,) \wedge$
$(base = RotatingBackToPos1 \Rightarrow arm2 = AtInner \wedge arm2Holding = FALSE \,)$

INITIALISATION

$base := AtPos3 \, \|$
$arm1 := AtInner \, \| \, arm2 := RetractingToInner \, \|$
$arm1Holding := FALSE \, \| \, arm2Holding := FALSE$

OPERATIONS

PartAvailable A part becomes available for being transported to processing and the robot is ready to take it, i.e. the robot is in position 1 and arm 1 is extended to middle position. Then arm 1 retracts to its inner position, holding the part.

$PartAvailable \quad \widehat{=}$
    SELECT $\quad base = AtPos1 \wedge arm1 = AtMiddle \quad$ **THEN**
        $arm1 := RetractingToInner \, \| \, arm1Holding := TRUE$

END ;

ProcessingFinished Processing of a part has finished and the robot is ready for taking it, i.e. the robot is in position 2 and arm 2 is retracted. Then arm 2 extends.

ProcessingFinished ≘
    SELECT $base = AtPos2 \wedge arm2 = AtInner$ **THEN**
       $arm2 := ExtendingToMiddle$
    END ;

ProcessingReady A part may be processed and the robot is ready for placing it, i.e. the robot is in position 3 and arm 1 is retracted and holds a part. Then arm 1 extends to its outer position via its middle position.

ProcessingReady ≘
    SELECT $base = AtPos3 \wedge arm1 = AtInner \wedge arm1Holding = TRUE$ **THEN**
       $arm1 := ExtendingToMiddle$
    END ;

DepositReady The next machine becomes ready for further transporting a part and the robot is in position 3 and arm 2 is in middle position. As stated in the invariant, arm 2 holds a (processed) part in this position. Arm 2 then releases the part and retracts to its inner position.

DepositReady ≘
    SELECT $base = AtPos3 \wedge arm2 = AtMiddle$ **THEN**
       $arm2 := RetractingToInner \parallel arm2Holding := FALSE$
    END ;

Pos1Reached The robot base reaches position 1 while rotating backward. Then the rotating motor stops and arm 1 extends in order to pick up an unprocessed part.

Pos1Reached ≘
    SELECT $base = RotatingBackToPos1$ **THEN**
       $base := AtPos1 \parallel arm1 := ExtendingToMiddle$
    END ;

Pos2Reached The robot base reaches position 2. This happens while either the robot base rotates forward from position 1 or rotates backward from position 3. In case it reaches position 2 from position 1, it stops and if *unload* is true, arm 2 extends to the outer position via the middle position. In case the base rotates back from position 3, it continues to rotate to position 1.

Pos2Reached (unload) ≘
    PRE $unload : BOOL$ **THEN**
       SELECT $base = RotatingFwdToPos2$ **THEN**
          $base := AtPos2 \parallel$
          IF $unload = TRUE$ **THEN** $arm2 := ExtendingToMiddle$ **END**
       WHEN $base = RotatingBackToPos2$ **THEN**

$base := RotatingBackToPos1$
      END
END ;

Pos3Reached The robot base reaches position 3 while rotating forward from position 2. Arm 2 extends to its middle position and, as stated in the invariant, holds a part. If *load* is true, arm 1 extends as well in order to release the unprocessed part it holds.

$Pos3Reached$ ($load$) $\widehat{=}$
      PRE $load : BOOL$ **THEN**
            SELECT $base = RotatingFwdToPos3$ **THEN**
                  $base := AtPos3$ ||
                  IF $load = TRUE$ **THEN** $arm1 := ExtendingToMiddle$ **END** ||
                  $arm2 := ExtendingToMiddle$
            END
      END ;

Arm1InReached Arm 1 reaches its inner position while retracting from its middle position position. This happens either in robot position 1 after arm 1 has picked up a part, or in position 3 after arm 1 has released a part. In position 1 the robot starts to rotate forward to position 2, and in position 3 the robot starts to rotate backward to position 1 via position 2, provided robot arm 2 is retracted as well.

$Arm1InReached$ $\widehat{=}$
      SELECT $arm1 = RetractingToInner \wedge base = AtPos1$ **THEN**
            $arm1 := AtInner$ || $base := RotatingFwdToPos2$
      WHEN $arm1 = RetractingToInner \wedge base = AtPos3$ **THEN**
            $arm1 := AtInner$ ||
            IF $arm2 = AtInner$ **THEN** $base := RotatingBackToPos2$ **END**
      END ;

Arm1MiddleReached Arm 1 reaches its middle position. This happens while either the base is at position 1 and arm 1 is extending to its middle position, or while the base is at position 3 and arm 1 is extending to its outer position via its middle position, holding a part, or while the base is in position 3 and arm 1 is retracting from its outer position. As follows from the invariant, arm 1 is extending to and retracting from its outer position only when the robot base in at position 3. When extending in position 1, the parameter *fetchPart* determines whether there is a part available for fetching. If so, arm 1 grabs it and retracts again, otherwise it stops there.

$Arm1MiddleReached$ ($fetchPart$) $\widehat{=}$
      PRE $fetchPart \in BOOL$ **THEN**
            SELECT $arm1 = ExtendingToMiddle \wedge base = AtPos1$ **THEN**
                  IF $fetchPart = FALSE$ **THEN** $arm1 := AtMiddle$
                  ELSE $arm1 := RetractingToInner$ || $arm1Holding := TRUE$
                  END
            WHEN $arm1 = ExtendingToMiddle \wedge base = AtPos3$ **THEN**
                  $arm1 := ExtendingToOuter$
            WHEN $arm1 = RetractingToMiddle$ **THEN**
                  $arm1 := RetractingToInner$
            END

END ;

Arm1OutReached Arm 1 reaches its outer position. As follows from the invariant, the robot must be at position 3 and arm 1 must be holding a part. Then arm 1 releases the part and retracts to its inner position.

Arm1OutReached $\;\; \widehat{=}$
    SELECT $arm1 = ExtendingToOuter$ **THEN**
        $arm1 := RetractingToMiddle \;\parallel\; arm1Holding := FALSE$
    END ;

Arm2InReached Arm 2 reaches its inner position. This happens in robot position 2 after picking up a processed part or in robot position 3 after releasing the processed part. In position 2 the robot starts to rotate forward to position 3. In position 3, the robot starts to rotate backward to position 1 via position 2, provided arm 1 is retracted as well.

Arm2InReached $\;\; \widehat{=}$
    SELECT $arm2 = RetractingToInner \wedge base = AtPos2$ **THEN**
        $arm2 := AtInner \;\parallel\; base := RotatingFwdToPos3$
    WHEN $arm2 = RetractingToInner \wedge base = AtPos3$ **THEN**
        $arm2 := AtInner \;\parallel$
        IF $arm1 = AtInner \wedge arm1Holding = FALSE$ **THEN**
            $base := RotatingBackToPos2$
        END
    END ;

Arm2MiddleReached Arm 2 reaches its middle position, while either the base is at position 3 and arm 2 extends to its middle position, while the base is at position 2 and arm 2 extends to its outer position via the middle position, or while arm 2 retracts from its outer position. According to the invariant, the base is in this case at position 2. When extending in position 3 and the parameter *depositPart* is true, the processed part is released and the arm retracts again, otherwise it stops there.

Arm2MiddleReached (depositPart) $\;\; \widehat{=}$
    PRE $depositPart \in BOOL$ **THEN**
        SELECT $arm2 = ExtendingToMiddle \wedge base = AtPos3$ **THEN**
            IF $depositPart = FALSE$ **THEN** $arm2 := AtMiddle$
            ELSE $arm2 := RetractingToInner \;\parallel\; arm2Holding := FALSE$
            END
        WHEN $arm2 = ExtendingToMiddle \wedge base = AtPos2$ **THEN**
            $arm2 := ExtendingToOuter$
        WHEN $arm2 = RetractingToMiddle$ **THEN**
            $arm2 := RetractingToInner$
        END
    END ;

Arm2OutReached Arm 2 reaches its outer position. According to the invariant, the base is in position 3. Arm 2 picks up a part and retracts again.

Arm2OutReached $\;\; \widehat{=}$

      SELECT   *arm2 = ExtendingToOuter*   **THEN**
         arm2 := RetractingToMiddle ‖ *arm2Holding := TRUE*
      END
END

6.3.4 The Press

For an abstract model of the press, the press is in exactly one of the following states:

AtUnloading , *AtLoading* The press is at its lower sensor position for unloading or at its middle sensor position for loading, respectively. Note that there is a sensor for the upper position in which the press is closed, but the press does not rest there, it immediately opens again. Hence there is no need to represent it.

MovingToLoading , *MovingToUnloading* The press is moving upwards from its lower position to its middle position or moving downwards from its middle position to its lower position, respectively.

Pressing , *Opening* The press is moving upwards from its middle sensor position to its upper position or moving downwards from its upper sensor position to its middle position, respectively.

MACHINE   *PressTypes*
SETS

   PRESS = { *AtUnloading* , *MovingToLoading* , *AtLoading* , *Pressing* , *Opening* ,
     MovingToUnloading }

END

The press goes cyclically from state *AtLoading*, after being loaded, to states *Pressing*, *Opening*, *MovingToUnloading*, and *AtUnloading*, where after the part has been taken it goes to states *MovingToLoading* and *AtLoading* again. We assume that the table is initially in its middle position and may have a pressed part available; to initiate the cycle, the press has to move to its unloading position.

The actions *PartPlaced* and *PartTaken* represent interactions with the environment, the actions *DownReached*, *MiddleReached*, and *UpReached* correspond to sensor changes.

MACHINE   *Press*
SEES   *PressTypes*
VARIABLES

   press

INVARIANT

   press ∈ *PRESS*

INITIALISATION

   press := MovingToUnloading

OPERATIONS

PartPlaced A part is placed in the press and the press may close. For this, the press must be in its middle, loading position.

$PartPlaced$ $\,\widehat{=}$
    SELECT $\quad press = AtLoading$ **THEN** $press := Pressing$ **END** ;

PartTaken A part is fetched from the press and the press may move towards the middle position (for getting loaded again). For this, the press must be in its lower unloading position.

$PartTaken$ $\,\widehat{=}$
    SELECT $\quad press = AtUnloading$ **THEN** $press := MovingToLoading$
    END ;

DownReached The press reaches the lower sensor position. For this, the press must be below the middle position and must have been moving downwards. The press motor is then stopped such that the press can be unloaded.

$DownReached$ $\,\widehat{=}$
    SELECT $\quad press = MovingToUnloading$ **THEN** $press := AtUnloading$
    END ;

MiddleReached The press reaches the middle sensor position. This happens when either the press is above the middle position and moves downwards or is below the middle position and moves upwards. In the first case, the press continues to move downwards and in the second case the press stops for being loaded.

$MiddleReached$ $\,\widehat{=}$
    SELECT $\quad press = MovingToLoading$ **THEN** $press := AtLoading$
    WHEN $\quad press = Opening$ **THEN** $press := MovingToUnloading$
    END ;

UpReached The press reaches the upper sensor position. For this, the press must be above the middle position and must have been moving upwards. Then the motor is reversed for opening the press again.

$UpReached$ $\,\widehat{=}$
    SELECT $\quad press = Pressing$ **THEN** $press := Opening$ **END**
END

6.3.5 The Deposit Belt

For an abstract model of the deposit belt, the deposit belt is in exactly one of the following states:

Empty The belt is stopped and there are no parts on it.

Transporting The belt is running with one part being transported.

Available The belt is stopped with a part at the end.

AvailableAndPlaced The belt is stopped with a part at the end and a second part is at the front of the belt.

MACHINE *DepositBeltTypes*

SETS

> *DEPOSITBELT* = { *Empty* , *Transporting* , *Available* , *AvailableAndPlaced* }

END

We assume that the belt is initially in state *Empty*. From there, it goes to states *Transporting* and then to *Available*. From state *Available*, the belt goes either to state *Empty* or to state *AvailableAndPlaced* and from there to state *Transporting*. The transitions between these states are caused by the action *PartPlaced*, which represents an interaction with the environment, or the actions *EndReached* and *PartTaken*, which correspond to sensor changes:

MACHINE *DepositBelt*

SEES *DepositBeltTypes*

VARIABLES

> *belt*

INVARIANT

> *belt* $\in$ *DEPOSITBELT*

INITIALISATION

> *belt* := *Empty*

OPERATIONS

PartPlaced A part is placed on the front of the belt, provided no part is already there. The belt starts to transport if no part is at the end of the belt.

> *PartPlaced* $\widehat{=}$
> **SELECT**   *belt* = *Empty*   **THEN**   *belt* := *Transporting*
> **WHEN**   *belt* = *Available*   **THEN**   *belt* := *AvailableAndPlaced*
> **END** ;

EndReached A part reaches the end of the belt. The belt is then stopped, with a part available at its end.

> *EndReached* $\widehat{=}$
> **SELECT**   *belt* = *Transporting*   **THEN**   *belt* := *Available*   **END** ;

PartTaken The part at the end of the belt is taken. If another part is placed on the front of the belt, the belt starts to run.

PartTaken $\quad \widehat{=}$
    SELECT   *belt = Available*   **THEN**   *belt := Empty*
    WHEN   *belt = AvailableAndPlaced*   **THEN**   *belt := Transporting*
    END

END

6.4 Derivation of the Machine Controllers

The next step is to decompose each machine into a plant and a controller. A general approach is as follows:

- The plant is represented as an action system in AMN with local variables and with actions. The controller is represented as an action system with local variables and procedures.
- Actuators and sensors become global variables to the plant and controller and are put in separate AMN machines. The actuators are read by the plant and set via operation calls by the controller. The sensors are read by the controller and set via operation calls by the plant. For this, the plant includes the sensors and sees the actuators. Dually, the controller includes the actuators and sees the sensors.
- The abstract machine is refined by the parallel composition of the plant and controller, with the actuators and sensors made local to the parallel composition. The abstraction invariant relates the abstract machine state to the plant state, the controller state and to the sensors and actuators. By having possibly different plant and controller states we can take into account that the controller may have only *partial observability* of the plant and may need to keep track of the plant evolution in its own way.
- The actions of the plant refine the corresponding actions of the machine: the guards are now expressed in terms of the plant variables, sensors, and actuators; the bodies of the actions model the evolution of the machine by changing the plant state and the sensors and then calling the corresponding controller procedures, like interrupt procedures. For this, the plant includes the controller and refines the abstract machine specification.

The general decomposition schema for this approach is shown in Fig. 6.10. If a plant action does not require a reaction of the controller, the corresponding call can be omitted. Also, if the actuators can not only be set but also read, appropriate procedures in the actuator machine can be added. Having the actuators and sensors encapsulated in separate machines allows to abstract from the details of a particular communication mechanism, which depends on the underlying hardware and operating environment, e.g. memory mapped I/O or calls to send and receive operations.

Since this is a refinement step, the invariance properties of each machine are inherited automatically: the controller, when "applied" to the plant, guarantees all previously shown safety requirements.

Although our goal is to produce controllers for the machines, we get as a byproduct specifications of the physical plant as well. These specifications are not going to

REFINEMENT   *MachinePlant*
REFINES   *Machine*
INCLUDES   *MachineCtrl , MachineSensors*
VARIABLES
  plant state
INVARIANT
  variable types ∧
  refinement invariant for plant variables,
  controller variables, actuators, sensors
INITIALISATION
  plant state and sensors initialisation

OPERATIONS
  Action (parameters)   ≙
    SELECT   *refined guard*   **THEN**
      plant state and sensors change **;**
      ActionCtrl (parameters)
    END ;

  . . .

END

MACHINE   *MachineCtrl*
INCLUDES   *MachineActuators*
SEES   *MachineSensors*
VARIABLES
  controller state
INVARIANT
  variable types
INITIALISATION
  controller state and actuators
  initialisation

OPERATIONS
  ActionCtrl (parameters)   ≙
    controller state and
    actuators change **;**

  . . .

END

MACHINE   *MachineSensors*
VARIABLES
  sensors
INVARIANT
  variable types
INITIALISATION
  sensors :∈ *any value*

OPERATIONS
  SetSensor (ss)   ≙
    sensor := ss **;**

  . . .

END

MACHINE   *MachineActuators*
VARIABLES
  actuators
INVARIANT
  variable types
INITIALISATION
  actuators :∈ *any value*

OPERATIONS
  SetActuator (aa)   ≙
    actuator := aa **;**

  . . .

END

Fig. 6.10. General Decomposition Schema for Plant and Controller

be implemented in AMN, but can be used to check whether the physical plant does indeed conform to these specifications.

This schema, although generally applicable, has the disadvantage that, when the system gets large the abstraction invariant can get rather complex. For the production cell machines, we can employ a variation of this schema, shown in Fig. 6.11 and Fig. 6.12. This schema helps in composing the production cell controller of the machine controller by keeping the abstraction invariants local to the controllers. It also incorporates two further simplifications:

- The decomposition into plant and controller and the introduction of sensors and actuators is split into two successive refinement steps. The first refinement step does not involve data refinement and yields an abstract specification of the plant and the controller. The second refinement step refines the controller by introducing the sensors and actuators with an abstraction invariant. Thus, the sensors and actuators become local variables of the controller rather than its global variables as in the general schema.
- As the machines are equipped with enough sensors, each controller can keep track of the plant state. Thus, we can identify the controller and plant state with the abstract machine state. In the decomposition step, we keep it in *CONCRETE_-VARIABLES* in the controller (which is included in the plant). This way, the plant and later the combined controller of the production cell can read those variables.
- Since all sensors are binary, all sensor changes can be signalled to the controller by a controller call for each sensor value. There is no need to represent the sensors explicitly in AMN machines.
  A difference to the general schema is that we only get an abstract plant specification, not one which involves the sensors and actuators.

In this schema, the machine controllers (Fig. 6.11) now appear to be similar to the original machine specification (Fig. 6.9). However, there is one significant difference: the operations in the controller are procedures with preconditions whereas the operations in the machines are actions with guards. Thus, in a subsequent refinement step the preconditions of the controller procedures may be weakened or eliminated.

For the refinement of the abstract machines to the plants, the conditions for action system refinement as given in Chapter 5 have to hold. Of the four conditions given in Definition 5.1, the first three (the initialisations are data-refined, the procedures are data-refined, and the actions are data-refined) are those of AMN refinement and checked by the tools. The fourth condition (under the abstraction invariant the guard of each abstract action implies the guard of the refining action) holds in our scheme trivially since the guards remain unchanged.

The following three types for actuator values are used:

MACHINE   *ActuatorTypes*

SETS

  $MOTOR = \{ RUN , HALT \}$;
  $REVMOTOR = \{ FWD , BACK , STOP \}$;
  $GRIPPER = \{ HOLD , RELEASE \}$

REFINEMENT   *MachinePlant*

REFINES   *Machine*

INCLUDES   *MachineCtrl*

OPERATIONS

   Action (parameters) $\hat{=}$
     SELECT   *guard*   **THEN**
      ActionCtrl (parameters)
     END ;

   . . .

END

MACHINE   *MachineCtrl*

CONCRETE_VARIABLES

   machine state

INVARIANT

   variable types

INITIALISATION

   machine state initialisation

OPERATIONS

   ActionCtrl (parameters) $\hat{=}$
     PRE   *guard*   **THEN**
      machine state change
     END ;

   . . .

END

Fig. 6.11. Decomposition Schema for the Production Cell Machines

---

IMPLEMENTATION   *MachineCtrlImp*

REFINES   *MachineCtrl*

IMPORTS   *MachineActuators*

INVARIANT

   refinement invariant for actuators

INITIALISATION

   machine state and
   actuators initialisation

OPERATIONS

   ActionCtrl (parameters) $\hat{=}$
     machine state change and
     actuator setting **;**

   . . .

END

MACHINE   *MachineActuators*

VARIABLES

   actuators

INVARIANT

   variable types

INITIALISATION

   actuators $:\in$ *any value*

OPERATIONS

   SetActuator (aa) $\hat{=}$
     actuator := aa **;**

   . . .

END

Fig. 6.12. Refinement Schema for the Controllers of the Production Cell

END

6.4.1 The Feed Belt

The first refinement step decomposes *FeedBelt* into *FeedBeltPlant* and *FeedBeltCtrl*. The refinement of the action *EndReached* relies on the fact that

> **SELECT** $belt = Running \wedge halt = TRUE$ **THEN**
> $belt := Stopped$
> **WHEN** $belt = Running \wedge halt = FALSE$ **THEN**
> $belt := Delivering$
> **END**

is equivalent to:

> **SELECT** $belt = Running$ **THEN**
>   **IF** $halt = TRUE$ **THEN** $belt := Stopped$
>   **ELSE** $belt := Delivering$
>   **END**
> **END**

The resulting code is:

MACHINE   *FeedBeltCtrl*

SEES   *FeedBeltTypes*

CONCRETE_VARIABLES

   belt

INVARIANT

   $belt \in FEEDBELT$

INITIALISATION

   $belt := Running$

OPERATIONS

   $EndReachedCtrl\ (\ halt\ )\quad \widehat{=}$
      PRE $halt \in BOOL \wedge belt = Running$ **THEN**
         IF $halt = TRUE$ **THEN** $belt := Stopped$
         ELSE $belt := Delivering$
         END
      END ;

   $ContinueDeliveryCtrl\quad \widehat{=}$
      PRE $belt = Stopped$ **THEN** $belt := Delivering$ **END** ;

   $PartLeftCtrl\quad \widehat{=}$
      PRE $belt = Delivering$ **THEN** $belt := Running$ **END**

END

REFINEMENT   *FeedBeltPlant*

REFINES   *FeedBelt*

SEES   *FeedBeltTypes*

INCLUDES   *FeedBeltCtrl*

OPERATIONS

EndReached (*halt*) $\hat{=}$
    PRE   *halt* ∈ *BOOL*   **THEN**
        SELECT   *belt* = *Running*   **THEN**   *EndReachedCtrl* (*halt*)   **END**
    END ;

ContinueDelivery =
    SELECT   *belt* = *Stopped*   **THEN**   *ContinueDeliveryCtrl*   **END** ;

PartLeft =
    SELECT   *belt* = *Delivering*   **THEN**   *PartLeftCtrl*   **END**

END

The second refinement step introduces in the controller the actuator *motor* of type *MOTOR* for the feed belt motor. It is set to *RUN* if the feed belt is *Running* or *Delivering* and is be set to *HALT* if the feed belt is *Stopped*. Also, in this refinement step the preconditions are eliminated.

MACHINE   *FeedBeltActuators*

SEES   *ActuatorTypes*

VARIABLES

    motor

INVARIANT

    motor ∈ *MOTOR*

INITIALISATION

    motor :∈ *MOTOR*

OPERATIONS

SetMotor (*mm*) $\hat{=}$
    PRE   *mm* ∈ *MOTOR*   **THEN**   *motor* := *mm*   **END**

END

IMPLEMENTATION   *FeedBeltCtrlImp*

REFINES   *FeedBeltCtrl*

SEES   *FeedBeltTypes* , *ActuatorTypes*

IMPORTS   *FeedBeltActuators*

INVARIANT

    (*belt* ∈ { *Running* , *Delivering* } ⇒ *motor* = *RUN*) ∧
    (*belt* = *Stopped* ⇒ *motor* = *HALT*)

INITIALISATION

    belt := *Running* ; *SetMotor* (*RUN*)

OPERATIONS

EndReachedCtrl (*halt*) $\hat{=}$
    IF   *halt* = *TRUE*   **THEN**   *belt* := *Stopped* ; *SetMotor* (*HALT*)
    ELSE   *belt* := *Delivering*

END ;

ContinueDeliveryCtrl $\widehat{=}$
    BEGIN   *belt* := *Delivering* **;** *SetMotor* (*RUN*)   **END ;**

PartLeftCtrl $\widehat{=}$
    belt := *Running*

END

6.4.2 The Table

The first refinement step decomposes *Table* into *TablePlant* and *TableCtrl*. Like above, SELECT statements with multiple branches are transformed into SELECT statements with a single guard and body.

MACHINE   *TableCtrl*

SEES   *TableTypes*

CONCRETE_VARIABLES

   elev , *rot*

INVARIANT

   $elev \in ELEV \wedge rot \in ROT$

INITIALISATION

   elev := *AtLower* $\parallel$ *rot* := *AtLeft*

OPERATIONS

PartPlacedCtrl $\widehat{=}$
    PRE $elev = AtLower \wedge rot = AtLeft$ **THEN**
      elev := *MovingUp* $\parallel$ *rot* := *RotatingRight*
    END ;

PartTakenCtrl $\widehat{=}$
    PRE $elev = AtUpper \wedge rot = AtRight$ **THEN**
      elev := *MovingDown* $\parallel$ *rot* := *RotatingLeft*
    END ;

UpReachedCtrl (*moveBack*) $\widehat{=}$
    PRE $moveBack \in BOOL \wedge elev = MovingUp$ **THEN**
      IF $moveBack = TRUE$ **THEN**
        elev := *MovingDown* $\parallel$ *rot* := *RotatingLeft*
      ELSE   *elev* := *AtUpper*
      END
    END ;

DownReachedCtrl $\widehat{=}$
    PRE $elev = MovingDown$ **THEN**   *elev* := *AtLower*   **END ;**

RightReachedCtrl (*moveBack*) $\widehat{=}$
    PRE $moveBack \in BOOL \wedge rot = RotatingRight$ **THEN**
      IF $moveBack = TRUE$ **THEN**
        elev := *MovingDown* $\parallel$ *rot* := *RotatingLeft*
      ELSE   *rot* := *AtRight*
      END
    END ;

LeftReachedCtrl $\hat{=}$
    PRE   *rot = RotatingLeft*   **THEN**   *rot := AtLeft*   **END**

END

REFINEMENT   *TablePlant*

REFINES   *Table*

SEES   *TableTypes*

INCLUDES   *TableCtrl*

OPERATIONS

PartPlaced $\hat{=}$
    SELECT   *elev = AtLower ∧ rot = AtLeft*   **THEN**   *PartPlacedCtrl*   **END ;**

PartTaken $\hat{=}$
    SELECT   *elev = AtUpper ∧ rot = AtRight*   **THEN**   *PartTakenCtrl*   **END ;**

UpReached (moveBack) $\hat{=}$
    PRE   *moveBack ∈ BOOL*   **THEN**
        SELECT   *elev = MovingUp*   **THEN**   *UpReachedCtrl (moveBack)*
        END
    END ;

DownReached $\hat{=}$
    SELECT   *elev = MovingDown*   **THEN**   *DownReachedCtrl*   **END ;**

RightReached (moveBack) $\hat{=}$
    PRE   *moveBack ∈ BOOL*   **THEN**
        SELECT   *rot = RotatingRight*   **THEN**   *RightReachedCtrl (moveBack)*
        END
    END ;

LeftReached $\hat{=}$
    SELECT   *rot = RotatingLeft*   **THEN**   *LeftReachedCtrl*   **END**

END

The second refinement step introduces in the controller the actuators *elevMotor* and *rotMotor* of type *REVMOTOR* for elevating and rotating the table, respectively. The actuator *elevMotor* is set to *FWD* if the table is *MovingUp*, to *BACK* if the table is *MovingDown*, and to *STOP* if the table is *AtLower* or *AtUpper* position. The actuator *rotMotor* is set analogously. Also, in this refinement step the preconditions are eliminated.

MACHINE   *TableActuators*

SEES   *ActuatorTypes*

VARIABLES

   elevMotor , rotMotor

INVARIANT

   elevMotor ∈ REVMOTOR ∧ rotMotor ∈ REVMOTOR

INITIALISATION

   elevMotor :∈ REVMOTOR ‖ *rotMotor :∈ REVMOTOR*

OPERATIONS

$SetElevMotor\ (\ em\ )\quad \widehat{=}$
   PRE $em \in REVMOTOR$ **THEN** $elevMotor := em$ **END** ;

$SetRotMotor\ (\ rm\ )\quad \widehat{=}$
   PRE $rm \in REVMOTOR$ **THEN** $rotMotor := rm$ **END**

END

IMPLEMENTATION $TableCtrlImp$

REFINES $TableCtrl$

SEES $TableTypes$, $ActuatorTypes$

IMPORTS $TableActuators$

INVARIANT

$(\ elev = MovingUp \Rightarrow elevMotor = FWD\ ) \wedge$
$(\ elev = MovingDown \Rightarrow elevMotor = BACK\ ) \wedge$
$(\ elev \in \{\ AtLower\ ,AtUpper\ \} \Rightarrow elevMotor = STOP\ ) \wedge$
$(\ rot = RotatingRight \Rightarrow rotMotor = FWD\ ) \wedge$
$(\ rot = RotatingLeft \Rightarrow rotMotor = BACK\ ) \wedge$
$(\ rot \in \{\ AtLeft\ ,AtRight\ \} \Rightarrow rotMotor = STOP\ )$

INITIALISATION

$elev := AtLower$; $rot := AtLeft$;
$SetElevMotor\ (\ STOP\ )$; $SetRotMotor\ (\ STOP\ )$

OPERATIONS

$PartPlacedCtrl\quad \widehat{=}$
   BEGIN
      $elev := MovingUp$; $rot := RotatingRight$;
      $SetElevMotor\ (\ FWD\ )$; $SetRotMotor\ (\ FWD\ )$
   END ;

$PartTakenCtrl\quad \widehat{=}$
   BEGIN
      $elev := MovingDown$; $rot := RotatingLeft$;
      $SetElevMotor\ (\ BACK\ )$; $SetRotMotor\ (\ BACK\ )$
   END ;

$UpReachedCtrl\ (\ moveBack\ )\quad \widehat{=}$
   IF $moveBack = TRUE$ **THEN**
      $elev := MovingDown$; $SetElevMotor\ (\ BACK\ )$;
      $rot := RotatingLeft$; $SetRotMotor\ (\ BACK\ )$
   ELSE $elev := AtUpper$; $SetElevMotor\ (\ STOP\ )$
   END ;

$DownReachedCtrl\quad \widehat{=}$
   BEGIN $elev := AtLower$; $SetElevMotor\ (\ STOP\ )$ **END** ;

$RightReachedCtrl\ (\ moveBack\ )\quad \widehat{=}$
   IF $moveBack = TRUE$ **THEN**
      $elev := MovingDown$; $SetElevMotor\ (\ BACK\ )$;
      $rot := RotatingLeft$; $SetRotMotor\ (\ BACK\ )$
   ELSE $rot := AtRight$; $SetRotMotor\ (\ STOP\ )$
   END ;

    LeftReachedCtrl $\hat{=}$
        BEGIN   *rot* := *AtLeft* **;** *SetRotMotor* (*STOP*) **END**
END

6.4.3 The Robot

The first refinement step decomposes *TwoArmRobot* into *TwoArmRobotPlant* and *TwoArmRobotCtrl*. As previously, SELECT statements with multiple branches are transformed into SELECT statements with a single guard and body. The refinement of the action *Pos2Reached* relies on the fact that

    SELECT   *base* = *RotatingFwdToPos2* **THEN**
      base := *AtPos2* || ...
    WHEN   *base* = *RotatingBackToPos2* **THEN**
      belt := *RotatingBackToPos1*
    END

is equivalent to:

    SELECT   *base* $\in$ {*RotatingFwdToPos2*, *RotatingBackToPos2* } **THEN**
    IF   *base* = *RotatingFwdToPos2* **THEN**
      base := *AtPos2* || ...
    ELSE   *belt* := *RotatingBackToPos1*
    END
    END

    Similar equivalences are used for *Arm1InReached*, *Arm1MiddleReached*, *Arm2-InReached*, and *Arm2MiddleReached*. The resulting code is:

MACHINE   *TwoArmRobotCtrl*

SEES   *TwoArmRobotTypes*

CONCRETE_VARIABLES

    base , *arm1* , *arm2* , *arm1Holding* , *arm2Holding*

INVARIANT

    base $\in$ *ROBOTBASE* $\wedge$ *arm1* $\in$ *ROBOTARM* $\wedge$ *arm2* $\in$ *ROBOTARM* $\wedge$
    arm1Holding $\in$ *BOOL* $\wedge$ *arm2Holding* $\in$ *BOOL*

INITIALISATION

    base := *AtPos3* ||
    arm1 := *AtInner* || *arm2* := *RetractingToInner* ||
    arm1Holding := *FALSE* || *arm2Holding* := *FALSE*

OPERATIONS

    PartAvailableCtrl $\hat{=}$
      PRE   *base* = *AtPos1* $\wedge$ *arm1* = *AtMiddle* **THEN**
        arm1 := *RetractingToInner* || *arm1Holding* := *TRUE*
      END **;**

    ProcessingFinishedCtrl $\hat{=}$
      PRE   *base* = *AtPos2* $\wedge$ *arm2* = *AtInner* **THEN**
        arm2 := *ExtendingToMiddle*

END ;

ProcessingReadyCtrl $\hat{=}$
  PRE   *base = AtPos3* ∧ *arm1 = AtInner* ∧ *arm1Holding = TRUE*   **THEN**
    arm1 := ExtendingToMiddle
  END ;

DepositReadyCtrl $\hat{=}$
  PRE   *base = AtPos3* ∧ *arm2 = AtMiddle*   **THEN**
    arm2 := RetractingToInner ‖ *arm2Holding := FALSE*
  END ;

Pos1ReachedCtrl $\hat{=}$
  PRE   *base = RotatingBackToPos1*   **THEN**
    base := AtPos1 ‖ *arm1 := ExtendingToMiddle*
  END ;

Pos2ReachedCtrl (unload) $\hat{=}$
  PRE   *unload* ∈ *BOOL* ∧ *base* ∈ { *RotatingFwdToPos2* , *RotatingBackToPos2* }
  THEN
    IF   *base = RotatingFwdToPos2*   **THEN**
      base := AtPos2 ‖
        IF   *unload = TRUE*   **THEN**   *arm2 := ExtendingToMiddle*   **END**
      ELSE   *base := RotatingBackToPos1*
    END
  END ;

Pos3ReachedCtrl (load) $\hat{=}$
  PRE   *load* ∈ *BOOL* ∧ *base = RotatingFwdToPos3*   **THEN**
    base := AtPos3 ‖
    IF   *load = TRUE*   **THEN**   *arm1 := ExtendingToMiddle*   **END** ‖
    arm2 := ExtendingToMiddle
  END ;

Arm1InReachedCtrl $\hat{=}$
  PRE   *arm1 = RetractingToInner*   **THEN**
    arm1 := AtInner ‖
    IF   *base = AtPos1*   **THEN**   *base := RotatingFwdToPos2*
    ELSIF   *arm2 = AtInner*   **THEN**   *base := RotatingBackToPos2*
    END
  END ;

Arm1MiddleReachedCtrl (fetchPart) $\hat{=}$
  PRE   *fetchPart* ∈ *BOOL* ∧ *arm1* ∈ { *ExtendingToMiddle* , *RetractingToMiddle* }
  THEN
    IF   *arm1 = ExtendingToMiddle* ∧ *base = AtPos1*   **THEN**
      IF   *fetchPart = FALSE*   **THEN**   *arm1 := AtMiddle*
      ELSE   *arm1 := RetractingToInner* ‖ *arm1Holding := TRUE*
      END
    ELSIF   *arm1 = ExtendingToMiddle*   **THEN**   *arm1 := ExtendingToOuter*
    ELSE   *arm1 := RetractingToInner*
    END
  END ;

Arm1OutReachedCtrl $\hat{=}$
  PRE   *arm1 = ExtendingToOuter*   **THEN**
    arm1 := RetractingToMiddle ‖ *arm1Holding := FALSE*
  END ;

Arm2InReachedCtrl $\widehat{=}$
  PRE   *arm2 = RetractingToInner*   **THEN**
    arm2 := AtInner ||
    IF   *base = AtPos2*   **THEN**   *base := RotatingFwdToPos3*
    ELSIF   *arm1 = AtInner ∧ arm1Holding = FALSE*   **THEN**
      base := RotatingBackToPos2
    END
  END ;

Arm2MiddleReachedCtrl (*depositPart*) $\widehat{=}$
  PRE   *depositPart ∈ BOOL ∧ arm2 ∈* { *ExtendingToMiddle* ,
    RetractingToMiddle }   **THEN**
    IF   *arm2 = ExtendingToMiddle ∧ base = AtPos3*   **THEN**
      IF   *depositPart = FALSE*   **THEN**   *arm2 := AtMiddle*
      ELSE   *arm2 := RetractingToInner* || *arm2Holding := FALSE*
      END
    ELSIF   *arm2 = ExtendingToMiddle*   **THEN**
      arm2 := ExtendingToOuter
    ELSE
      arm2 := RetractingToInner
    END
  END ;

Arm2OutReachedCtrl $\widehat{=}$
  PRE   *arm2 = ExtendingToOuter*   **THEN**
    arm2 := RetractingToMiddle || *arm2Holding := TRUE*
  END

END

REFINEMENT   *TwoArmRobotPlant*

REFINES   *TwoArmRobot*

SEES   *TwoArmRobotTypes*

INCLUDES   *TwoArmRobotCtrl*

OPERATIONS

PartAvailable $\widehat{=}$
  SELECT   *base = AtPos1 ∧ arm1 = AtMiddle*   **THEN**   *PartAvailableCtrl*
  END ;

ProcessingFinished $\widehat{=}$
  SELECT   *base = AtPos2 ∧ arm2 = AtInner*   **THEN**   *ProcessingFinishedCtrl*
  END ;

ProcessingReady $\widehat{=}$
  SELECT   *base = AtPos3 ∧ arm1 = AtInner ∧ arm1Holding = TRUE*   **THEN**
    ProcessingReadyCtrl
  END ;

DepositReady $\widehat{=}$
  SELECT   *base = AtPos3 ∧ arm2 = AtMiddle*   **THEN**   *DepositReadyCtrl*
  END ;

Pos1Reached $\widehat{=}$
  SELECT   *base = RotatingBackToPos1*   **THEN**   *Pos1ReachedCtrl*   **END** ;

Pos2Reached (*unload*) $\widehat{=}$

PRE $unload \in BOOL$ **THEN**
    SELECT $base \in \{\ RotatingFwdToPos2\ ,\ RotatingBackToPos2\ \}$ **THEN**
        $Pos2ReachedCtrl\ (\ unload\ )$
    END
END ;

$Pos3Reached\ (\ load\ )$ $\widehat{=}$
    PRE $load \in BOOL$ **THEN**
        SELECT $base = RotatingFwdToPos3$ **THEN** $Pos3ReachedCtrl\ (\ load\ )$
    END
END ;

$Arm1InReached$ $\widehat{=}$
    SELECT $arm1 = RetractingToInner$ **THEN** $Arm1InReachedCtrl$ **END ;**

$Arm1MiddleReached\ (\ fetchPart\ )$ $\widehat{=}$
    PRE $fetchPart \in BOOL$ **THEN**
        SELECT $arm1 \in \{\ ExtendingToMiddle\ ,\ RetractingToMiddle\ \}$ **THEN**
          $Arm1MiddleReachedCtrl\ (\ fetchPart\ )$
    END
END ;

$Arm1OutReached$ $\widehat{=}$
    SELECT $arm1 = ExtendingToOuter$ **THEN** $Arm1OutReachedCtrl$
END ;

$Arm2InReached$ $\widehat{=}$
    SELECT $arm2 = RetractingToInner$ **THEN** $Arm2InReachedCtrl$ **END ;**

$Arm2MiddleReached\ (\ depositPart\ )$ $\widehat{=}$
    PRE $depositPart \in BOOL$ **THEN**
        SELECT $arm2 \in \{\ ExtendingToMiddle\ ,\ RetractingToMiddle\ \}$ **THEN**
          $Arm2MiddleReachedCtrl\ (\ depositPart\ )$
    END
END ;

$Arm2OutReached$ $\widehat{=}$
    SELECT $arm2 = ExtendingToOuter$ **THEN** $Arm2OutReachedCtrl$ **END**
END

The second refinement step introduces the following actuators in the controller:

rotMotor This actuator of type *REVMOTOR* is for rotating the robot base. It is set to *FWD* if the base is *RotatingFwdToPos2* or *RotatingFwdToPos3*, it is set to *BACK* if the base is *RotatingBackToPos2* or *RotatingBackToPos1*, and it is set to *STOP* if the base is *AtPos1*, *AtPos2*, or *AtPos3*.

arm1Motor , *arm2Motor* These actuators of type *REVMOTOR* are for extending and retracting arm 1 and arm 2, respectively. They are set to *FWD* if the corresponding arm is *ExtendingToMiddle* or *ExtendingToOuter*, they are set to *BACK* if the corresponding arm is *RetractingToInner* or *RetractingToOuter*, and are set to *STOP* if the arm is *AtInner* or *AtMiddle*. (Recall that the arms never stay at the outer position, they retract immediately.)

arm1Gripper , *arm2Gripper* These actuators of type *GRIPPER* are set to *HOLD* if *arm1Holding* or *arm2Holding* is true, respectively, and are set to *RELEASE* otherwise.

Also, in this refinement step the preconditions are eliminated. The resulting code is:

MACHINE   *TwoArmRobotActuators*

SEES   *ActuatorTypes*

VARIABLES

   rotMotor , *arm1Motor* , *arm2Motor* , *arm1Gripper* , *arm2Gripper*

INVARIANT

   $rotMotor \in REVMOTOR \land$
   $arm1Motor \in REVMOTOR \land arm2Motor \in REVMOTOR \land$
   $arm1Gripper : GRIPPER \land arm2Gripper \in GRIPPER$

INITIALISATION

   $rotMotor :\in REVMOTOR \parallel$
   $arm1Motor :\in REVMOTOR \parallel arm2Motor :\in REVMOTOR \parallel$
   $arm1Gripper :\in GRIPPER \parallel arm2Gripper :\in GRIPPER$

OPERATIONS

   $SetRotMotor\ (\ rm\ )\quad \widehat{=}$
        PRE $rm \in REVMOTOR$ **THEN** $rotMotor := rm$ **END** ;

   $SetArm1Motor\ (\ a1\ )\quad \widehat{=}$
        PRE $a1 \in REVMOTOR$ **THEN** $arm1Motor := a1$ **END** ;

   $SetArm2Motor\ (\ a2\ )\quad \widehat{=}$
        PRE $a2 \in REVMOTOR$ **THEN** $arm2Motor := a2$ **END** ;

   $SetArm1Gripper\ (\ g1\ )\quad \widehat{=}$
        PRE $g1 \in GRIPPER$ **THEN** $arm1Gripper := g1$ **END** ;

   $SetArm2Gripper\ (\ g2\ )\quad \widehat{=}$
        PRE $g2 \in GRIPPER$ **THEN** $arm2Gripper := g2$ **END**

END

IMPLEMENTATION   *TwoArmRobotCtrlImp*

REFINES   *TwoArmRobotCtrl*

SEES   *TwoArmRobotTypes* , *ActuatorTypes*

IMPORTS   *TwoArmRobotActuators*

INVARIANT

   $(\ rotMotor = FWD\ ) \Leftrightarrow (\ base \in \{\ RotatingFwdToPos2\ ,\ RotatingFwdToPos3\ \}\ ) \land$
   $(\ rotMotor = BACK\ ) \Leftrightarrow (\ base \in \{\ RotatingBackToPos2\ ,\ RotatingBackToPos1\ \}\ ) \land$
   $(\ rotMotor = STOP\ ) \Leftrightarrow (\ base \in \{\ AtPos1\ ,\ AtPos2\ ,\ AtPos3\ \}\ ) \land$

   $(\ arm1Motor = FWD\ ) \Leftrightarrow (\ arm1 \in \{\ ExtendingToMiddle\ ,\ ExtendingToOuter\ \}\ ) \land$
   $(\ arm1Motor = BACK\ ) \Leftrightarrow (\ arm1 \in \{\ RetractingToInner\ ,\ RetractingToMiddle\ \}\ ) \land$
   $(\ arm1Motor = STOP\ ) \Leftrightarrow (\ arm1 \in \{\ AtInner\ ,\ AtMiddle\ \}\ ) \land$

   $(\ arm2Motor = FWD\ ) \Leftrightarrow (\ arm2 \in \{\ ExtendingToMiddle\ ,\ ExtendingToOuter\ \}\ ) \land$
   $(\ arm2Motor = BACK\ ) \Leftrightarrow (\ arm2 \in \{\ RetractingToInner\ ,\ RetractingToMiddle\ \}\ ) \land$
   $(\ arm2Motor = STOP\ ) \Leftrightarrow (\ arm2 \in \{\ AtInner\ ,\ AtMiddle\ \}\ ) \land$

   $(\ arm1Gripper = HOLD\ ) \Leftrightarrow (\ arm1Holding = TRUE\ ) \land$
   $(\ arm2Gripper = HOLD\ ) \Leftrightarrow (\ arm2Holding = TRUE\ )$

INITIALISATION

    base := AtPos3 ; *arm1 := AtInner* ; *arm2 := RetractingToInner* ;
    SetRotMotor (STOP) ; *SetArm1Motor (STOP)* ; *SetArm2Motor (BACK)* ;
    arm1Holding := FALSE ; *arm2Holding := FALSE* ;
    SetArm1Gripper (RELEASE) ; *SetArm2Gripper (RELEASE)*

OPERATIONS

PartAvailableCtrl $\widehat{=}$
    BEGIN
        arm1 := RetractingToInner ; *SetArm1Motor (BACK)* ;
        arm1Holding := TRUE ; *SetArm1Gripper (HOLD)*
    END ;

ProcessingFinishedCtrl $\widehat{=}$
    BEGIN   *arm2 := ExtendingToMiddle* ; *SetArm2Motor (FWD)*   **END** ;

ProcessingReadyCtrl $\widehat{=}$
    BEGIN   *arm1 := ExtendingToMiddle* ; *SetArm1Motor (FWD)*   **END** ;

DepositReadyCtrl $\widehat{=}$
    BEGIN
        arm2 := RetractingToInner ; *arm2Holding := FALSE* ;
        SetArm2Motor (BACK) ; *SetArm2Gripper (RELEASE)*
    END ;

Pos1ReachedCtrl $\widehat{=}$
    BEGIN
        base := AtPos1 ; *SetRotMotor (STOP)* ;
        arm1 := ExtendingToMiddle ; *SetArm1Motor (FWD)*
    END ;

Pos2ReachedCtrl (unload) $\widehat{=}$
    IF   *base = RotatingFwdToPos2*   **THEN**
    base := AtPos2 ; *SetRotMotor (STOP)* ;
        IF   *unload = TRUE*   **THEN**
          arm2 := ExtendingToMiddle ; *SetArm2Motor (FWD)*
        END
    ELSE   *base := RotatingBackToPos1*
    END ;

Pos3ReachedCtrl (load) $\widehat{=}$
    BEGIN
        base := AtPos3 ; *SetRotMotor (STOP)* ;
        IF   *load = TRUE*   **THEN**
          arm1 := ExtendingToMiddle ; *SetArm1Motor (FWD)*
        END ;
        arm2 := ExtendingToMiddle ; *SetArm2Motor (FWD)*
    END ;

Arm1InReachedCtrl $\widehat{=}$
    BEGIN
        arm1 := AtInner ; *SetArm1Motor (STOP)* ;
        IF   *base = AtPos1*   **THEN**
        base := RotatingFwdToPos2 ; *SetRotMotor (FWD)*
        ELSIF   *arm2 = AtInner*   **THEN**
        base := RotatingBackToPos2 ; *SetRotMotor (BACK)*
        END

END ;

Arm1MiddleReachedCtrl (fetchPart)   ≙
    IF   *arm1 = ExtendingToMiddle ∧ base = AtPos1*   **THEN**
        IF   *fetchPart = FALSE*   **THEN**
            arm1 := AtMiddle **;** *SetArm1Motor (STOP)*
        ELSE
            arm1 := RetractingToInner **;** *SetArm1Motor (BACK)* **;**
            arm1Holding := TRUE **;** *SetArm1Gripper (HOLD)*
        END
    ELSIF   *arm1 = ExtendingToMiddle*   **THEN**   *arm1 := ExtendingToOuter*
    ELSE   *arm1 := RetractingToInner*
    END ;

Arm1OutReachedCtrl   ≙
    BEGIN
        arm1 := RetractingToMiddle **;** *SetArm1Motor (BACK)* **;**
        arm1Holding := FALSE **;** *SetArm1Gripper (RELEASE)*
    END ;

Arm2InReachedCtrl   ≙
    BEGIN
        arm2 := AtInner **;** *SetArm2Motor (STOP)* **;**
        IF   *base = AtPos2*   **THEN**
            base := RotatingFwdToPos3 **;** *SetRotMotor (FWD)*
        ELSIF   *arm1 = AtInner ∧ arm1Holding = FALSE*   **THEN**
            base := RotatingBackToPos2 **;** *SetRotMotor (BACK)*
        END
    END ;

Arm2MiddleReachedCtrl (depositPart)   ≙
    IF   *arm2 = ExtendingToMiddle ∧ base = AtPos3*   **THEN**
        IF   *depositPart = FALSE*   **THEN**
            arm2 := AtMiddle **;** *SetArm2Motor (STOP)*
        ELSE
            arm2 := RetractingToInner **;** *SetArm2Motor (BACK)* **;**
            arm2Holding := FALSE **;** *SetArm2Gripper (RELEASE)*
        END
    ELSIF   *arm2 = ExtendingToMiddle*   **THEN**   *arm2 := ExtendingToOuter*
    ELSE   *arm2 := RetractingToInner*
    END ;

Arm2OutReachedCtrl   ≙
    BEGIN
        arm2 := RetractingToMiddle **;** *arm2Holding := TRUE* **;**
        SetArm2Gripper (HOLD) **;** *SetArm2Motor (BACK)*
    END

END

6.4.4 The Press

The first refinement step decomposes *Press* into *PressPlant* and *PressCtrl*. The SE-LECT statement with two branches in the action *MiddleReached* is transformed into a SELECT statements with a single guard and body.

MACHINE   *PressCtrl*

SEES   *PressTypes*

CONCRETE_VARIABLES

   press

INVARIANT

   press ∈ *PRESS*

INITIALISATION

   press := *MovingToUnloading*

OPERATIONS

   PartPlacedCtrl $\widehat{=}$
     PRE   *press* = *AtLoading*   **THEN**   *press* := *Pressing*   **END** ;

   PartTakenCtrl $\widehat{=}$
     PRE   *press* = *AtUnloading*   **THEN**   *press* := *MovingToLoading*   **END** ;

   DownReachedCtrl $\widehat{=}$
     PRE   *press* = *MovingToUnloading*   **THEN**   *press* := *AtUnloading*   **END** ;

   MiddleReachedCtrl $\widehat{=}$
     PRE   *press* ∈ { *MovingToLoading* , *Opening* }   **THEN**
     IF   *press* = *MovingToLoading*   **THEN**   *press* := *AtLoading*
     ELSE   *press* := *MovingToUnloading*
     END
     END ;

   UpReachedCtrl $\widehat{=}$
     PRE   *press* = *Pressing*   **THEN**   *press* := *Opening*   **END**

END

REFINEMENT   *PressPlant*

REFINES   *Press*

SEES   *PressTypes*

INCLUDES   *PressCtrl*

OPERATIONS

   PartPlaced $\widehat{=}$
     SELECT   *press* = *AtLoading*   **THEN**   *PartPlacedCtrl*   **END** ;

   PartTaken $\widehat{=}$
     SELECT   *press* = *AtUnloading*   **THEN**   *PartTakenCtrl*   **END** ;

   DownReached $\widehat{=}$
     SELECT   *press* = *MovingToUnloading*   **THEN**   *DownReachedCtrl*   **END** ;

   MiddleReached $\widehat{=}$
     SELECT   *press* ∈ { *MovingToLoading* , *Opening* }   **THEN**
     MiddleReachedCtrl
     END ;

   UpReached $\widehat{=}$
     SELECT   *press* = *Pressing*   **THEN**   *UpReachedCtrl*   **END**

END

The second refinement step introduces in the controller the actuator *motor* of type *REVMOTOR* for the press motor. It is set to *FWD* if the press is *Moving-ToLoading* or *Pressing*, to *BACK* if the press is *Opening* or *MovingToUnloading*, and to *STOP* if the press is *AtUnloading* or *AtLoading*. Also, in this refinement step the preconditions are eliminated.

MACHINE   *PressActuators*

SEES   *ActuatorTypes*

VARIABLES

   motor

INVARIANT

   motor ∈ *REVMOTOR*

INITIALISATION

   motor :∈ *REVMOTOR*

OPERATIONS

   SetMotor (*mm*) $\widehat{=}$
      PRE   *mm* ∈ *REVMOTOR*   **THEN**   *motor* := *mm*   **END**

END

IMPLEMENTATION   *PressCtrlImp*

REFINES   *PressCtrl*

SEES   *PressTypes* , *ActuatorTypes*

IMPORTS   *PressActuators*

INVARIANT

   (*press* ∈ { *MovingToLoading* , *Pressing* } ⇒ *motor* = *FWD*) ∧
   (*press* ∈ { *Opening* , *MovingToUnloading* } ⇒ *motor* = *BACK*) ∧
   (*press* ∈ { *AtUnloading* , *AtLoading* } ⇒ *motor* = *STOP*)

INITIALISATION

   press := *MovingToUnloading* ; *SetMotor* (*BACK*)

OPERATIONS

   PartPlacedCtrl $\widehat{=}$
      BEGIN   *press* := *Pressing* ; *SetMotor* (*FWD*)   **END** ;

   PartTakenCtrl $\widehat{=}$
      BEGIN   *press* := *MovingToLoading* ; *SetMotor* (*FWD*)   **END** ;

   DownReachedCtrl $\widehat{=}$
      BEGIN   *press* := *AtUnloading* ; *SetMotor* (*STOP*)   **END** ;

   MiddleReachedCtrl $\widehat{=}$
      IF   *press* = *MovingToLoading*   **THEN**
         press := *AtLoading* ; *SetMotor* (*STOP*)
      ELSE   *press* := *MovingToUnloading*
      END ;

   UpReachedCtrl $\widehat{=}$
      BEGIN   *press* := *Opening* ; *SetMotor* (*BACK*)   **END**

END

6.4.5 The Deposit Belt

The first refinement step decomposes *DepositBelt* into *DepositBeltPlant* and *DepositBeltCtrl*. Again, SELECT statements with multiple branches are transformed into SELECT statements with a single guard and body.

MACHINE   *DepositBeltCtrl*

SEES   *DepositBeltTypes*

CONCRETE_VARIABLES

   belt

INVARIANT

   belt ∈ *DEPOSITBELT*

INITIALISATION

   belt := *Empty*

OPERATIONS

   PartPlacedCtrl   ≙
      PRE   *belt* ∈ { *Empty* , *Available* }   **THEN**
         IF   *belt* = *Empty*   **THEN**   *belt* := *Transporting*
         ELSE   *belt* := *AvailableAndPlaced*
         END
      END ;

   EndReachedCtrl   ≙
      PRE   *belt* = *Transporting*   **THEN**   *belt* := *Available*   **END** ;

   PartTakenCtrl   ≙
      PRE   *belt* ∈ { *Available* , *AvailableAndPlaced* }   **THEN**
         IF   *belt* = *Available*   **THEN**   *belt* := *Empty*
         ELSE   *belt* := *Transporting*
         END
      END

END

REFINEMENT   *DepositBeltPlant*

REFINES   *DepositBelt*

SEES   *DepositBeltTypes*

INCLUDES   *DepositBeltCtrl*

OPERATIONS

   PartPlaced   ≙
      SELECT   *belt* ∈ { *Empty* , *Available* }   **THEN**   *PartPlacedCtrl*   **END** ;

   EndReached   ≙
      SELECT   *belt* = *Transporting*   **THEN**   *EndReachedCtrl*   **END** ;

   PartTaken   ≙
      SELECT   *belt* ∈ { *Available* , *AvailableAndPlaced* }   **THEN**

      PartTakenCtrl
   END
END

In this refinement step, the operation *PartTakenCtrl* is noteworthy: its effect depends on whether a part is placed on the front of the belt (*AvailableAndPlaced*) or not (*Available*), which is not observable by any sensor readings. Hence, it is essential that the deposit belt controller keeps track of the plant state. (For the other machines, the state is fully observable and keeping the plant state in extra variables is merely a convenience for testing the state.)

The second refinement step introduces in the controller the actuator *motor* of type *MOTOR* for the deposit belt motor. It is set to *RUN* if the deposit belt is *Transporting* and to *HALT* if the deposit belt is *Empty*, *Available*, or *AvailableAndPlaced*. Also, in this refinement step the preconditions are eliminated.

MACHINE   *DepositBeltActuators*

SEES *ActuatorTypes*

VARIABLES

   motor

INVARIANT

   motor ∈ *MOTOR*

INITIALISATION

   motor :∈ *MOTOR*

OPERATIONS

   SetMotor (*mm*) ≙
     PRE   *mm* ∈ *MOTOR*   **THEN**   *motor* := *mm*   **END**

END

IMPLEMENTATION   *DepositBeltCtrlImp*

REFINES *DepositBeltCtrl*

SEES *ActuatorTypes* , *DepositBeltTypes*

IMPORTS *DepositBeltActuators*

INVARIANT

   (*belt* = *Transporting* ⇒ *motor* = *RUN*) ∧
   (*belt* ∈ { *Empty* , *Available* , *AvailableAndPlaced* } ⇒ *motor* = *HALT*)

INITIALISATION

   belt := *Empty* ; *SetMotor* (*HALT*)

OPERATIONS

   PartPlacedCtrl ≙
     IF   *belt* = *Empty*   **THEN**   *belt* := *Transporting* ; *SetMotor* (*RUN*)
     ELSE   *belt* := *AvailableAndPlaced*
     END ;

   EndReachedCtrl ≙

BEGIN   *belt := Available* **;** *SetMotor (HALT)*   **END ;**
PartTakenCtrl $\widehat{=}$
    IF   *belt = Available*   **THEN**   *belt := Empty*
    ELSE   *belt := Transporting* **;** *SetMotor (RUN)*
    END
END

6.5 Specification of the Production Cell

The production cell is specified in terms of the specifications of the individual machines:

- All machines are included once. By this, their variables and their initialisations are inherited. For referring to the machines more easily, they are given short names by renaming.
- For each sensor change of each machine, there is one action in the production cell. In the simplest case, a production cell action "calls" the corresponding action of the machine concerned with this sensor change. In case the sensor change leads possibly to an interaction with another machine, that interaction is specified as well.
- Safety requirements concerning the interaction of the machines are expressed in the invariant.

The structure of the resulting specification is shown in Fig. 6.13. Note that the production cell is not expressed as the parallel composition of the machines, but rather by reusing the specifications of the machines through inclusion. Since the machines are included, their variables can only be changed through their operations. This ensures that the invariant of each machine is also an invariant of the production cell. In this way, the safety properties of the machines get automatically promoted to safety properties of the production cell.

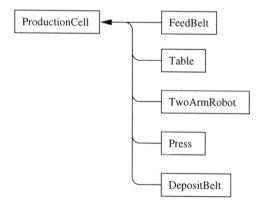

Fig. 6.13. Structure of the *ProductionCell* Specification: Arrows Stand for Inclusion

MACHINE *ProductionCell*
SEES
   FeedBeltTypes , *TableTypes* , *TwoArmRobotTypes* , *PressTypes* , *DepositBeltTypes*
INCLUDES
   FB . *FeedBelt* , *TB* . *Table* , *RB* . *TwoArmRobot* , *PR* . *Press* , *DB* . *DepositBelt*
INVARIANT

Safety Requirement Delivery from the feed belt to the table is allowed only if the table
is at lower left position.

$$(\, FB \, . \, belt = Delivering \Rightarrow TB \, . \, elev = AtLower \wedge TB \, . \, rot = AtLeft \,) \wedge$$

Safety Requirement Robot arm 1 may only extend towards the press if the press is in its
middle position. Robot arm 2 may only extend towards the press only if the press is in its
lower position.

$$(\, RB \, . \, base = AtPos3 \wedge PR \, . \, press \neq AtUnloading \Rightarrow RB \, . \, arm1 = AtInner \,) \wedge$$
$$(\, RB \, . \, base = AtPos2 \wedge PR \, . \, press \neq AtUnloading \Rightarrow RB \, . \, arm2 = AtInner \,) \wedge$$

Safety Requirement The press may only move if arm 1 is safe and if arm 2 is safe.

$$(\, RB \, . \, base = AtPos3 \wedge RB \, . \, arm1 \neq AtInner \Rightarrow PR \, . \, press = AtLoading \,) \wedge$$
$$(\, RB \, . \, base = AtPos2 \wedge RB \, . \, arm2 \neq AtInner \Rightarrow PR \, . \, press = AtUnloading \,)$$

OPERATIONS

FeedBeltEndReached A part reaches the end of the feed belt. If the table is ready for
loading, i.e. in its lower left position, the feed belt continues to run, otherwise it stops.

FeedBeltEndReached $\widehat{=}$
   FB . *EndReached* (**bool** (*TB* . *elev* $\neq$ *AtLower* $\vee$ *TB* . *rot* $\neq$ *AtLeft*)) **;**

FeedBeltPartLeft A part has left the feed belt and is placed on the table.

FeedBeltPartLeft $\widehat{=}$
   BEGIN   *FB* . *PartLeft* || *TB* . *PartPlaced*   **END ;**

TableUpReached The table reaches its upper position. If it is also in its right position, i.e.
becomes ready for unloading, and the robot is waiting for unloading the table, the robot
picks the part.

TableUpReached $\widehat{=}$
   IF   *TB* . *rot* = *AtRight* $\wedge$ *RB* . *base* = *AtPos1* $\wedge$ *RB* . *arm1* = *AtMiddle*   **THEN**
      TB . *UpReached* (*TRUE*) || *RB* . *PartAvailable*
   ELSE   *TB* . *UpReached* (*FALSE*)

END ;

TableDownReached The table reaches its lower position. If it is also in its left position, i.e. becomes ready for loading, and a part is available on the feed belt, the feed belt continues to run.

$TableDownReached \quad \hat{=}$
 BEGIN
  TB . $DownReached$ ||
  IF TB . $rot = AtLeft \wedge FB$. $belt = Stopped$ **THEN**
   FB . $ContinueDelivery$
  END
 END ;

TableRightReached The table reaches its right position. If it is also in its upper position, i.e. becomes ready for unloading, and the robot is waiting for unloading the table, the robot picks the part.

$TableRightReached \quad \hat{=}$
 IF TB . $elev = AtUpper \wedge RB$. $base = AtPos1 \wedge RB$. $arm1 = AtMiddle$ **THEN**
  TB . $RightReached$ ($TRUE$) || RB . $PartAvailable$
 ELSE TB . $RightReached$ ($FALSE$)
 END ;

TableLeftReached The table reaches its left position. If it is also in its lower position, i.e. becomes ready for loading, and a part is available on the feed belt, the feed belt continues to run.

$TableLeftReached \quad \hat{=}$
 BEGIN
  TB . $LeftReached$ ||
  IF TB . $elev = AtLower \wedge FB$. $belt = Stopped$ **THEN**
   FB . $ContinueDelivery$
  END
 END ;

RobotPos1Reached The robot base reaches position 1. The robot then continues to extend arm 1.

$RobotPos1Reached \quad \hat{=} \quad RB$. $Pos1Reached$ **;**

RobotPos2Reached The robot base reaches position 2, either while rotating forward or while rotating backward. If rotating forward and if the press is ready for unloading, the robot continues to unload it.

$RobotPos2Reached \quad \hat{=}$
 RB . $Pos2Reached$ (**bool** (PR . $press = AtUnloading$)) **;**

RobotPos3Reached The robot base reaches position 3. Arm 2 starts to extend to its middle position. If the press is ready for being loaded, the robot continues with loading the press by extending arm 1.

$RobotPos3Reached$ $\widehat{=}$ RB . $Pos3Reached$ (**bool** (PR . $press = AtLoading$)) **;**

RobotArm1InReached Robot arm 1 reaches its inner position, while the robot is either in position 1 after picking a part or position 3 after placing a part in the press. In position 1, the robot starts to rotate forward. In position 3, the press starts to process and the robot starts to rotate backward, provided arm 2 is free.

$RobotArm1InReached$ $\widehat{=}$
   BEGIN
      IF RB . $base = AtPos3$ **THEN** PR . $PartPlaced$ **END** $\|$
      RB . $Arm1InReached$
   END ;

RobotArm1MiddleReached Robot arm 1 reaches its middle position, while the robot is either in position 1 or position 3. In position 1, if the table has a part available, the part is fetched and both the robot and table continue. In position 3, the arm continues to extend or retract.

$RobotArm1MiddleReached$ $\widehat{=}$
   IF RB . $base = AtPos1 \wedge TB$. $elev = AtUpper \wedge TB$. $rot = AtRight$ **THEN**
      RB . $Arm1MiddleReached$ ($TRUE$) $\|$ TB . $PartTaken$
   ELSE RB . $Arm1MiddleReached$ ($FALSE$)
   END ;

RobotArm1OutReached Robot arm 1 reaches its outer position, while the robot is in position 3 for loading the press. The arm then releases the gripper and retracts.

$RobotArm1OutReached$ $\widehat{=}$ RB . $Arm1OutReached$ **;**

RobotArm2InReached Robot arm 2 reaches its inner position, while the robot is in position 2 (for unloading the press). The robot then rotates forward and the press moves to its loading position.

$RobotArm2InReached$ $\widehat{=}$
   BEGIN
      IF RB . $base = AtPos2$ **THEN** PR . $PartTaken$ **END** $\|$
      RB . $Arm2InReached$
   END ;

RobotArm2MiddleReached Robot arm 2 reaches its middle position, while the robot is either in position 2 (for unloading the press) or in position 3 (for depositing the part). In position 2 it continues to extend or retract, in position 3 it releases the part it is holding with arm 2, provided the deposit belt is free.

RobotArm2MiddleReached $\hat{=}$
    IF   *RB . base = AtPos3 ∧ DB . belt = Empty*   **THEN**
        RB . Arm2MiddleReached (TRUE) || *DB . PartPlaced*
    ELSE   *RB . Arm2MiddleReached (FALSE)*
    END ;

RobotArm2OutReached Robot arm 2 reaches its outer position, while the robot is in position 2 (for unloading the press). The arm then picks the part in the press and retracts.

RobotArm2OutReached $\hat{=}$ *RB . Arm2OutReached* **;**

PressDownReached The press reaches its lower position. If the robot is in position 2, the robot continues with unloading the press.

PressDownReached $\hat{=}$
    BEGIN
        PR . DownReached ||
        IF   *RB . base = AtPos2*   **THEN**   *RB . ProcessingFinished*   **END**
    END ;

PressMiddleReached The press reaches its middle position. If the robot is in position 3 and arm 1 holds an unprocessed part, the robot starts loading the press.

PressMiddleReached $\hat{=}$
    BEGIN
        IF   *PR . press = MovingToLoading ∧ RB . base = AtPos3 ∧*
            RB . arm1 = AtInner ∧ RB . arm1Holding = TRUE   **THEN**
            RB . ProcessingReady
        END ||
        PR . MiddleReached
    END ;

PressUpReached The press reaches its upper position. The press then opens again.

PressUpReached $\hat{=}$ *PR . UpReached* **;**

DepositBeltEndReached The part on the deposit belt reaches the end of the belt. The belt stops. If the robot is holding a part over the deposit belt, the part is released.

DepositBeltEndReached $\hat{=}$
    BEGIN
        DB . EndReached ||
        IF   *RB . base = AtPos3 ∧ RB . arm2 = AtMiddle*   **THEN**
            RB . DepositReady
        END
    END ;

DepositBeltPartTaken The part at the end of the deposit belt is removed. The deposit belt may continue to run if there is another part on it.

DepositBeltPartTaken $\widehat{=}$ *DB . PartTaken*
END

The actions considered so far were of the standard form **SELECT** P **THEN** S or of the more general form **SELECT** P_1 **THEN** S_1 **WHEN** P_2 **THEN** S_2 ... **END**. Here, the composed actions are of a more complex form. Still, they can be equivalently expressed in the standard form. For example, action *FeedBeltPartLeft* is defined by:

FB . PartLeft $\parallel$ *TB . PartPlaced*

Using the definitions of *PartLeft* and *PartPlaced*, this is after renaming equivalent to:

SELECT   *FB . belt = Delivering*   **THEN**   *FB . belt :=* Running   **END** $\parallel$
SELECT   *TB . elev = AtLower* $\wedge$ *TB . rot = AtLeft*   **THEN**
    TB . elev := MovingUp $\parallel$ *TB . rot := RotatingRight*
END

For the subsequent transformation, we rewrite this using the definition of **SELECT** (see Appendix):

(*FB . belt = Delivering* $\Longrightarrow$ *FB . belt :=* Running) $\parallel$
(*TB . elev = AtLower* $\wedge$ *TB . rot = AtLeft* $\Longrightarrow$
    TB . elev := MovingUp $\parallel$ *TB . rot := RotatingRight*)

(1)	$S \parallel$ skip	$= S$			
(2)	$S \parallel T$	$= T \parallel S$	(9)	$S [] S$	$= S$
(3)	$S \parallel (T \parallel U)$	$= (S \parallel T) \parallel U$	(10)	$S [] T$	$= T [] S$
(4)	$true \Longrightarrow S$	$= S$	(11)	$S [] (T [] U)$	$= (S [] T) [] U$
(5)	$(P \wedge Q) \Longrightarrow S$	$= P \Longrightarrow (Q \Longrightarrow S)$	(12)	$true \mid S$	$= S$
(6)	$(P \Longrightarrow S) \parallel T$	$= P \Longrightarrow (S \parallel T)$	(13)	$(P \wedge Q) \mid S$	$= P \mid (Q \mid S)$
		if $[T]$ *true* holds	(14)	$(P \mid S) \parallel T$	$= P \mid (S \parallel T)$
(7)	$(P \Longrightarrow S) [] T$	$= P \Longrightarrow (S [] T)$	(15)	$(P \mid S) [] T$	$= P \mid (S [] T)$
		if $[T]$ *true* holds	(16)	$P \mid (Q \Longrightarrow S)$	$= (P \Rightarrow Q) \mid (P \mid S)$
(8)	$P \Longrightarrow (Q \mid S)$	$= (P \Rightarrow Q) \mid (P \Longrightarrow S)$			

Fig. 6.14. Transformation Rules for Statements S, T, U and Predicates P, Q

Fig. 6.14 gives basic identities which can be used for merging the two actions into one. The predicate $[S]true$ characterises those states for which termination is guaranteed (the precondition) of S. In the machine *ProductionCell*, termination is guaranteed for all operations, hence this predicate holds. By applying rule (6) twice and then simplifying with rule (5), we get:

FB . belt = Delivering $\wedge$ *TB . elev = AtLower* $\wedge$ *TB . rot = AtLeft* $\Longrightarrow$
    FB . belt := Running $\parallel$ *TB . elev := MovingUp* $\parallel$ *TB . rot := RotatingRight*

Finally, this is equivalently expressed in AMN as follows, which is now the standard form for actions:

SELECT   *FB . belt = Delivering ∧ TB . elev = AtLower ∧ TB . rot = AtLeft*   **THEN**
    FB . belt := Running ‖ *TB . elev :=* MovingUp ‖ *TB . rot :=* RotatingRight
END

Using the rules in Fig. 6.14, the other actions can be transformed to standard form as well.

6.6 Derivation of the Production Cell Controller

The final step is to construct the controller of the production cell out of the controllers of the machines. This is done in two refinement steps:

- The first refinement step decomposes the production cell into a production cell plant and a production cell controller. The plant is modelled as an action system with only actions and the controller as an action system with only procedures. The plant includes the controller and refines the production cell. The controller procedures call the controllers of the machines following the pattern of how the production cell actions are composed of the actions of the machines.
- In the second refinement step the controller is implemented by eliminating those constructs which are not allowed in AMN implementations.

MACHINE   *ProductionCellCtrl*
SEES
    FeedBeltTypes , TableTypes , TwoArmRobotTypes , PressTypes , DepositBeltTypes
INCLUDES
    FB . FeedBeltCtrl , TB . TableCtrl , RB . TwoArmRobotCtrl , PR . PressCtrl ,
    DB . DepositBeltCtrl
OPERATIONS
    FeedBeltEndReachedCtrl $\widehat{=}$
        PRE   *FB . belt = Running*   **THEN**
            FB . EndReachedCtrl (**bool** *(TB . elev ≠ AtLower ∨ TB . rot ≠ AtLeft))*
        END ;

    FeedBeltPartLeftCtrl $\widehat{=}$
        PRE   *FB . belt = Delivering ∧ TB . elev = AtLower ∧ TB . rot = AtLeft*   **THEN**
            FB . PartLeftCtrl ‖ TB . PartPlacedCtrl
        END ;

    TableUpReachedCtrl $\widehat{=}$
        PRE   *TB . elev = MovingUp*   **THEN**
            IF   *TB . rot = AtRight ∧ RB . base = AtPos1 ∧ RB . arm1 = AtMiddle*
            THEN   *TB . UpReachedCtrl (TRUE) ‖ RB . PartAvailableCtrl*
            ELSE   *TB . UpReachedCtrl (FALSE)*
            END
        END ;

    TableDownReachedCtrl $\widehat{=}$
        PRE   *TB . elev = MovingDown*   **THEN**
            TB . DownReachedCtrl ‖

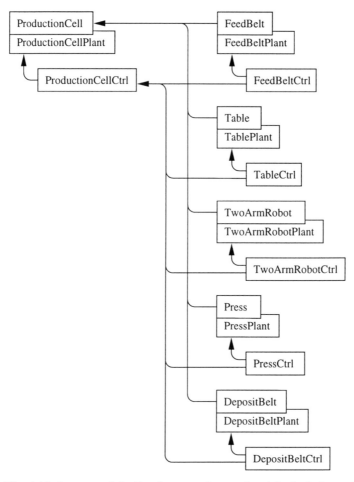

Fig. 6.15. Structure of the Development: Arrows Stand for Inclusion and Tiling Indicates Refinement

$$
\begin{aligned}
&\textbf{IF}\quad TB\,.\,rot = AtLeft \wedge FB\,.\,belt = Stopped \quad \textbf{THEN}\\
&\qquad FB\,.\,ContinueDeliveryCtrl\\
&\textbf{END}\\
&\textbf{END}\,;
\end{aligned}
$$

$TableRightReachedCtrl \;\;\widehat{=}$
    PRE $TB\,.\,rot = RotatingRight$ **THEN**
    IF $TB\,.\,elev = AtUpper \wedge RB\,.\,base = AtPos1 \wedge RB\,.\,arm1 = AtMiddle$
    THEN $TB\,.\,RightReachedCtrl\,(\,TRUE\,)\;\;\|\;\;RB\,.\,PartAvailableCtrl$
    ELSE $TB\,.\,RightReachedCtrl\,(\,FALSE\,)$
    END
    END ;

$TableLeftReachedCtrl \;\;\widehat{=}$
    PRE $TB\,.\,rot = RotatingLeft$ **THEN**

       TB . LeftReachedCtrl ‖
     IF   *TB . elev = AtLower* ∧ *FB . belt = Stopped*   **THEN**
       FB . ContinueDeliveryCtrl
     END
   END ;

RobotPos1ReachedCtrl ≙
   PRE   *RB . base = RotatingBackToPos1*   **THEN**   *RB . Pos1ReachedCtrl*
   END ;

RobotPos2ReachedCtrl ≙
   PRE   *RB . base* ∈ { *RotatingFwdToPos2* , *RotatingBackToPos2* }   **THEN**
     RB . Pos2ReachedCtrl (**bool** (*PR . press = AtUnloading*))
   END ;

RobotPos3ReachedCtrl ≙
   PRE   *RB . base = RotatingFwdToPos3*   **THEN**
     RB . Pos3ReachedCtrl (**bool** (*PR . press = AtLoading*))
   END ;

RobotArm1InReachedCtrl ≙
   PRE   *RB . arm1 = RetractingToInner* ∧
     (*RB . base = AtPos3* ⇒ *PR . press = AtLoading*)   **THEN**
     IF   *RB . base = AtPos3*   **THEN**   *PR . PartPlacedCtrl*   **END** ‖
     RB . Arm1InReachedCtrl
   END ;

RobotArm1MiddleReachedCtrl ≙
   PRE   *RB . arm1* ∈ { *ExtendingToMiddle* , *RetractingToMiddle* }   **THEN**
     IF   *RB . base = AtPos1* ∧ *TB . elev = AtUpper* ∧ *TB . rot = AtRight*   **THEN**
       RB . Arm1MiddleReachedCtrl (TRUE) ‖ *TB . PartTakenCtrl*
     ELSE   *RB . Arm1MiddleReachedCtrl (FALSE)*
     END
   END ;

RobotArm1OutReachedCtrl ≙
   PRE   *RB . arm1 = ExtendingToOuter*   **THEN**   *RB . Arm1OutReachedCtrl*
   END ;

RobotArm2InReachedCtrl ≙
   PRE   *RB . arm2 = RetractingToInner* ∧
     (*RB . base = AtPos2* ⇒ *PR . press = AtUnloading*)   **THEN**
     IF   *RB . base = AtPos2*   **THEN**   *PR . PartTakenCtrl*   **END** ‖
     RB . Arm2InReachedCtrl
   END ;

RobotArm2MiddleReachedCtrl ≙
   PRE   *RB . arm2* ∈ { *ExtendingToMiddle* , *RetractingToMiddle* }   **THEN**
     IF   *RB . base = AtPos3* ∧ *DB . belt = Empty*   **THEN**
       RB . Arm2MiddleReachedCtrl (TRUE) ‖ *DB . PartPlacedCtrl*
     ELSE   *RB . Arm2MiddleReachedCtrl (FALSE)*
     END
   END ;

RobotArm2OutReachedCtrl ≙
   PRE   *RB . arm2 = ExtendingToOuter*   **THEN**   *RB . Arm2OutReachedCtrl*
   END ;

PressDownReachedCtrl ≙

PRE PR . $press = MovingToUnloading \wedge$
(RB . $base = AtPos2 \Rightarrow RB$. $arm2 = AtInner$)
THEN
   PR . $DownReachedCtrl$ ||
   IF RB . $base = AtPos2$ **THEN** RB . $ProcessingFinishedCtrl$ **END**
END ;

PressMiddleReachedCtrl $\hat{=}$
PRE PR . $press \in \{$ $MovingToLoading$, $Opening$ $\}$ **THEN**
   IF PR . $press = MovingToLoading \wedge RB$. $base = AtPos3 \wedge$
      RB . $arm1 = AtInner$
   THEN RB . $ProcessingReadyCtrl$
   END ||
   PR . $MiddleReachedCtrl$
END ;

PressUpReachedCtrl $\hat{=}$
PRE PR . $press = Pressing$ **THEN** PR . $UpReachedCtrl$ **END** ;

DepositBeltEndReachedCtrl =
PRE DB . $belt = Transporting$ **THEN**
   DB . $EndReachedCtrl$ ||
   IF RB . $base = AtPos3 \wedge RB$. $arm2 = AtMiddle$ **THEN**
      RB . $DepositReadyCtrl$
   END
END ;

DepositBeltPartTakenCtrl $\hat{=}$
PRE DB . $belt = Available$ **THEN** DB . $PartTakenCtrl$ **END**

END

REFINEMENT   *ProductionCellPlant*

REFINES   *ProductionCell*

SEES

   FeedBeltTypes , *TableTypes* , *TwoArmRobotTypes* , *PressTypes* , *DepositBeltTypes*

INCLUDES

   ProductionCellCtrl

OPERATIONS

   FeedBeltEndReached $\hat{=}$
      SELECT FB . $belt = Running$ **THEN** $FeedBeltEndReachedCtrl$ **END** ;
   FeedBeltPartLeft $\hat{=}$
      SELECT FB . $belt = Delivering$ **THEN** $FeedBeltPartLeftCtrl$ **END** ;
   TableUpReached $\hat{=}$
      SELECT TB . $elev = MovingUp$ **THEN** $TableUpReachedCtrl$ **END** ;
   TableDownReached $\hat{=}$
      SELECT TB . $elev = MovingDown$ **THEN** $TableDownReachedCtrl$
      END ;
   TableRightReached $\hat{=}$
      SELECT TB . $rot = RotatingRight$ **THEN** $TableRightReachedCtrl$
      END ;

TableLeftReached $\hat{=}$
 SELECT *TB . rot = RotatingLeft* **THEN** *TableLeftReachedCtrl* **END ;**

RobotPos1Reached $\hat{=}$
 SELECT *RB . base = RotatingBackToPos1* **THEN** *RobotPos1ReachedCtrl*
 END ;

RobotPos2Reached $\hat{=}$
 SELECT *RB . base* $\in$ { *RotatingFwdToPos2* , *RotatingBackToPos2* } **THEN**
  RobotPos2ReachedCtrl
 END ;

RobotPos3Reached $\hat{=}$
 SELECT *RB . base = RotatingFwdToPos3* **THEN**
  RobotPos3ReachedCtrl
 END ;

RobotArm1InReached $\hat{=}$
 SELECT *RB . arm1 = RetractingToInner* **THEN** *RobotArm1InReachedCtrl*
 END ;

RobotArm1MiddleReached $\hat{=}$
 SELECT *RB . arm1* $\in$ { *ExtendingToMiddle* , *RetractingToMiddle* } **THEN**
  RobotArm1MiddleReachedCtrl
 END ;

RobotArm1OutReached $\hat{=}$
 SELECT *RB . arm1 = ExtendingToOuter* **THEN**
  RobotArm1OutReachedCtrl
 END ;

RobotArm2InReached $\hat{=}$
 SELECT *RB . arm2 = RetractingToInner* **THEN**
  RobotArm2InReachedCtrl
 END ;

RobotArm2MiddleReached $\hat{=}$
 SELECT *RB . arm2* $\in$ { *ExtendingToMiddle* , *RetractingToMiddle* } **THEN**
  RobotArm2MiddleReachedCtrl
 END ;

RobotArm2OutReached $\hat{=}$
 SELECT *RB . arm2 = ExtendingToOuter* **THEN**
  RobotArm2OutReachedCtrl
 END ;

PressDownReached $\hat{=}$
 SELECT *PR . press = MovingToUnloading* **THEN**
  PressDownReachedCtrl
 END ;

PressMiddleReached $\hat{=}$
 SELECT *PR . press* $\in$ { *MovingToLoading* , *Opening* } **THEN**
  PressMiddleReachedCtrl
 END ;

PressUpReached $\hat{=}$
 SELECT *PR . press = Pressing* **THEN** *PressUpReachedCtrl* **END ;**

DepositBeltEndReached $\hat{=}$
 SELECT *DB . belt = Transporting* **THEN** *DepositBeltEndReachedCtrl*

END ;

$DepositBeltPartTaken \quad \hat{=}$
    SELECT DB . $belt = Available$ **THEN** $DepositBeltPartTakenCtrl$
    END

END

IMPLEMENTATION $ProductionCellCtrlImp$

REFINES $ProductionCellCtrl$

SEES

    $FeedBeltTypes$, $TableTypes$, $TwoArmRobotTypes$, $PressTypes$, $DepositBeltTypes$

IMPORTS

    FB . $FeedBeltCtrl$, TB . $TableCtrl$, RB . $TwoArmRobotCtrl$, PR . $PressCtrl$,
    DB . $DepositBeltCtrl$

OPERATIONS

    $FeedBeltEndReachedCtrl \quad \hat{=}$
        IF TB . $elev \neq AtLower \vee TB$. $rot \neq AtLeft$ **THEN**
            FB . $EndReachedCtrl$ ($TRUE$)
        ELSE FB . $EndReachedCtrl$ ($FALSE$)
        END ;

    $FeedBeltPartLeftCtrl \quad \hat{=}$
        BEGIN FB . $PartLeftCtrl$ **;** TB . $PartPlacedCtrl$ **END ;**

    $TableUpReachedCtrl \quad \hat{=}$
        IF TB . $rot = AtRight \wedge RB$. $base = AtPos1 \wedge RB$. $arm1 = AtMiddle$ **THEN**
            TB . $UpReachedCtrl$ ($TRUE$) **;** RB . $PartAvailableCtrl$
        ELSE TB . $UpReachedCtrl$ ($FALSE$)
        END ;

    $TableDownReachedCtrl \quad \hat{=}$
        BEGIN
            TB . $DownReachedCtrl$ **;**
            IF TB . $rot = AtLeft \wedge FB$. $belt = Stopped$ **THEN**
                FB . $ContinueDeliveryCtrl$
            END
        END ;

    $TableRightReachedCtrl \quad \hat{=}$
        IF TB . $elev = AtUpper \wedge RB$. $base = AtPos1 \wedge RB$. $arm1 = AtMiddle$ **THEN**
            TB . $RightReachedCtrl$ ($TRUE$) **;** RB . $PartAvailableCtrl$
        ELSE TB . $RightReachedCtrl$ ($FALSE$)
        END ;

    $TableLeftReachedCtrl \quad \hat{=}$
        BEGIN
            TB . $LeftReachedCtrl$ **;**
            IF TB . $elev = AtLower \wedge FB$. $belt = Stopped$ **THEN**
                FB . $ContinueDeliveryCtrl$
            END
        END ;

    $RobotPos1ReachedCtrl \quad \hat{=} \quad RB$. $Pos1ReachedCtrl$ **;**

    $RobotPos2ReachedCtrl =$

IF   *PR . press = AtUnloading*   **THEN**   *RB . Pos2ReachedCtrl (TRUE)*
ELSE   *RB . Pos2ReachedCtrl (FALSE)*
END ;

RobotPos3ReachedCtrl   ≙
   IF   *PR . press = AtLoading*   **THEN**   *RB . Pos3ReachedCtrl (TRUE)*
   ELSE   *RB . Pos3ReachedCtrl (FALSE)*
   END ;

RobotArm1InReachedCtrl   ≙
   BEGIN
      IF   *RB . base = AtPos3*   **THEN**   *PR . PartPlacedCtrl*   **END ;**
      RB . Arm1InReachedCtrl
   END ;

RobotArm1MiddleReachedCtrl   ≙
   IF   *RB . base = AtPos1 ∧ TB . elev = AtUpper ∧ TB . rot = AtRight*   **THEN**
      RB . Arm1MiddleReachedCtrl (TRUE) ; TB . PartTakenCtrl
   ELSE   *RB . Arm1MiddleReachedCtrl (FALSE)*
   END ;

RobotArm1OutReachedCtrl   ≙   *RB . Arm1OutReachedCtrl* **;**

RobotArm2InReachedCtrl   ≙
   BEGIN
      IF   *RB . base = AtPos2*   **THEN**   *PR . PartTakenCtrl*   **END ;**
      RB . Arm2InReachedCtrl
   END ;

RobotArm2MiddleReachedCtrl   ≙
   IF   *RB . base = AtPos3 ∧ DB . belt = Empty*   **THEN**
      RB . Arm2MiddleReachedCtrl (TRUE) ; DB . PartPlacedCtrl
   ELSE   *RB . Arm2MiddleReachedCtrl (FALSE)*
   END ;

RobotArm2OutReachedCtrl   ≙
   RB . Arm2OutReachedCtrl **;**

PressDownReachedCtrl   ≙
   BEGIN
      PR . DownReachedCtrl **;**
      IF   *RB . base = AtPos2*   **THEN**   *RB . ProcessingFinishedCtrl*   **END**
   END ;

PressMiddleReachedCtrl   ≙
   BEGIN
      IF   *PR . press = MovingToLoading ∧ RB . base = AtPos3 ∧*
      RB . arm1 = AtInner
      THEN   *RB . ProcessingReadyCtrl*
      END ;
      PR . MiddleReachedCtrl
   END ;

PressUpReachedCtrl   ≙   *PR . UpReachedCtrl* **;**

DepositBeltEndReachedCtrl   ≙
   BEGIN
      DB . EndReachedCtrl **;**
      IF   *RB . base = AtPos3 ∧ RB . arm2 = AtMiddle*   **THEN**
      RB . DepositReadyCtrl

END
END ;

DepositBeltPartTakenCtrl $\hat{=}$ *DB . PartTakenCtrl*

END

6.7 Discussion

The development was done completely with Atelier B version 3.2. Table 6.1 summarises the length and the proving results for groups of AMN machines.

The entry *ActuatorTypes* comprises the AMN machines *ActuatorTypes* and *ActuatorTypesImp* (the dummy implementation). The entry *FeedBelt* comprises the AMN machines *FeedBelt*, *FeedBeltPlant*, *FeedBeltCtrl*, *FeedBeltCtrlImp*, *FeedBeltActuators*, *FeedBeltActuatorsImp* (a simple device-specific implementation), *FeedBeltTypes*, and *FeedBeltTypesImp* (the required dummy implementation). The subsequent entries are analogous. The entry *ProductionCell* comprises the AMN machines *ProductionCell*, *ProductionCellPlant*, *ProductionCellCtrl*, and *ProductionCellCtrlImp*. The implementations of *FeedBeltActuators* etc. which are required for interfacing to the actuators are left out of the table.

The obvious proof obligations are those which are discharged immediately when generated. All other proof obligations are submitted for automatic proving. Those which could not be proved automatically, were proved interactively. The numbers show a high degree of automation in the proofs and suggest that AMN, the tool support, and the chosen modelling approach are suitable for this kind of problem. However, it should be noted that all variables of the production cell range over finite types and thus a complete automation of the proofs is theoretically possible.

	total length	obvious proof obligations	proof obligations	number unproved	percent autoproved
ActuatorTypes	16 lines	8	0	0	100
FeedBelt	181 lines	69	12	0	100
Table	299 lines	191	39	0	100
TwoArmRobot	672 lines	1522	555	31	94
Press	222 lines	102	21	0	100
DepositBelt	188 lines	73	15	0	100
ProductionCell	578 lines	1770	194	23	88
Total	2157 lines	3735	836	54	94

Table 6.1. Statistics of the Development

We like to add some critical observations about using AMN. First, specifications are complicated by the fact that sequential composition is currently not allowed in AMN machines (but it is allowed in refinements and implementations). For example, it would have been simpler to define *TableUpReached* in *ProductionCell* by

TB . UpReached **;**

IF   *... robot can pick up part ...*   **THEN**
       RB . PartAvailable ∥ *TB . PartTaken*
END

for expressing that when the table reaches its upper position, it either stays there or moves back again. Since this is not allowed, the action *TB.UpReached* was given a parameter which determines whether the table should move back or not, i.e. whether the *TB.PartTaken* action should be performed as well. This leads to the situations that some actions of *Table* have such an additional parameter and some don't and is the only reason why action parameters are needed for the production cell at all. It also leads to slight code duplication. Another solution would have been to formulate the *ProductionCell* specification with sequential composition as an AMN refinement which refines some dummy AMN machine.

Secondly, guards and preconditions are treated asymmetrically in the sense that preconditions of (composed) operations have to be stated explicitly but guards don't. The *ProductionCell* actions are composed of actions of included AMN machines but the guard of the composed action is not stated explicitly. By contrast, the procedures of *ProductionCellCtrl* are composed of procedures of included AMN machines and the preconditions of the composed procedures need to be stated explicitly.

Finally, as discussed in Chapter 5, action system refinement leads to more proof obligations than those of AMN machine refinement. Although these can also be handled within AMN (see also Chapter 7), these are not generated automatically. For the production cell, this no problem since the guards of the actions were left unchanged in refinement, hence the additional proof obligation for action system refinement, the exit condition, holds trivially. However, with the proposed general refinement schema for control systems, automatic generation of these proof obligations would be helpful.

We conclude by discussing some related approaches. The traditional model of discrete event control systems, with separate specifications of the controller and the controlled system, is based on formal language theory [72]. Established and tool-supported approaches for the specification and verification of reactive systems are Statecharts [34] and Esterel [11]. Both have been applied to control systems, but typically with only the controller being specified. Statecharts and Esterel assume that the outputs of the program are in *perfect synchrony* with the inputs, i.e. the execution time is zero. This is the same assumption made here.

The distinguishing feature of the action system approach is that it allows the description of a control system on different levels of abstraction, with a number of proof obligations guaranteeing that each level is a refinement of the previous one. Here we have illustrated how this allows the initial specification to be a concise and abstract model of the control system and details of actuators and sensors to be introduced later. As also illustrated in subsequent chapters of this book, distribution can be introduced in refinement steps, thus allowing the development of distributed control systems.

Another approach to modelling control systems with action systems, where the controller is a set of actions rather than procedures, is proposed in [73]. A case study of refining a control system with action systems, where the continuous behaviour of the plant is taken into account, is presented in [17].

The production cell has been formally treated by numerous approaches [50]. A development of a control program by refinement where the machines are modelled as communicating processes is given in [27]. This allows a simpler specification of the machines but makes proofs of safety properties difficult since the machines have no state. The production cell has also been treated by an extension of AMN by traces, threads and temporal logic formulae [48].

6.8 Exercises

Exercise 6.1 (Additional Machine for Graphical Simulation). The derived controller can be used for driving a graphical simulation of the production cell, if for that purpose a sixth machine, a crane, is added. The crane takes parts on the deposit belt and puts them on the feed belt again, making the whole process cyclic. The crane has an electromagnetic gripper which may be turned on and off, a bidirectional motor for lifting and lowering the gripper, and a bidirectional motor for moving the crane forward (towards the feed belt) and backward (towards the deposit belt). Sensors are placed at the upper, the lower, the feed belt and the deposit belt end position, respectively. The crane must move between the two conveyor belts only in the upper position. For picking up a part from the deposit belt, the gripper has to be lowered, for placing a part on the feed belt the gripper has simply to be released. The graphical simulation and a description of its interface can be found on the book's Web page.

Exercise 6.2 (Avoiding Processing Delays). The specification of the robot has the following deficiency. When a part is ready in the press, the robot first waits until another part is available on the table, and only after picking up that part is the press unloaded. If the arrival of new parts on the table is delayed, unloading the press is delayed as well. Improve the specification of the robot such that the press may be unloaded immediately in these situations. When is the decision whether to unload the press or first to pick up a new part on the table made best? Would you make it dependent on the state of the table, the feed belt (which both may signal that a new part is arriving shortly), or the deposit belt (which may not allow a part to be placed on it)?

Exercise 6.3 (Faster Robot Movement). Assume that the robot may rotate and move its arms simultaneously and that the press may be loaded and unloaded with extended and rotating robot arms. Modify the robot operations and weaken the safety requirements accordingly.

Exercise 6.4 (Non-deterministic Initialisation). The plant specification assumes that all machines are in proper initial positions. A more realistic specification would allow arbitrary initial positions. Also, sensors like those on the end of the conveyor belts might report the presence of a part. Express this by appropriate non-deterministic assignments to the variables in the initialisation. To cope with non-deterministic initialisation, introduce a variable which determines whether the system is in *INIT* or *NORMAL* mode. In *INIT* mode, the only action of the machines is to go to defined positions for further operation. Make the appropriate changes. Would you introduce a mode variable for each machine or for the whole production cell? Would you insist that all safety requirements hold in initialisation mode?

Exercise 6.5 (Shutdown). The production cell specification assumes that the system is continuously running until power is switched off. Introduce a *SHUTDOWN* mode, in which all machines are stopped gracefully, and an operation *ShutDown* which enters that mode. Would you introduce a *SHUTDOWN* mode for each machine or for the whole production cell? Would you shut down all machines simultaneously or in a certain order?

Exercise 6.6 (Emergency Stop). Introduce an operation *EmergencyStop* of the production cell which immediately stops all motors but keeps the grippers switched on. How would you recover from such a situation? Do all safety requirements still hold in the case of an emergency stop?

Exercise 6.7 (Fault Detection). The preconditions of the (abstract) machine controllers express constraints under which theses procedures will be called. In case a machine breaks, these constraints might not hold. For example, if the feed belt sensor breaks, it might report that the part at the end left the belt even though the belt is not running. Make the controller more robust by checking for failures. Decide how to react to each failure: either ignore it if safe operation is still possible (assuming that the failure is transient), issue a warning on the screen and continue, or do an emergency stop. Would you also change the machine specifications and the plants? Note that a violation of a constraint may also be the consequence of an earlier failure. Also note that some abnormal situations may also occur due to human intervention, e.g. removing or placing a part.

Exercise 6.8 (Further Machine Requirements). Formalise the following safety requirements as invariance properties:

- If the table is moving upwards (downwards), it is either in its right (left) position or rotating towards it.
- Robot arm 1 is holding a part if and only if the robot is at position 1 and arm 1 is retracting to the inner position, the robot is at position 2, or the robot is at position 3 and robot arm 1 is extending to the middle or outer position.

Express and formalise similar requirements for the table turning to the left and to the right, and for robot arm 2.

Add the following variables for modelling the state of the machines more precisely: a variable indicating whether a part is on the table, and a variable whether a part is in the press. Modify all affected operations to update those variables. Formalise following requirements as invariance properties:

- If a part is on the table, it is either moving towards or at its upper right position.
- If no part in on the table, it is either moving towards or at its lower left position.
- The table is never in loading position with an part on it.
- The table is never in unloading position with no part on it.

Can you think of similar requirements for the press?

Exercise 6.9 (Additional Sensors). Assume that two additional sensors are added to the production cell, one indicating whether a part is on the table and one indicating whether a part is in the press. Use those sensors for a non-deterministic initialisation (Exercise 6.4), and for a more elaborate fault detection (Exercise 6.7).

7. Distributed Load Balancing

Marina Waldén

7.1 Introduction

We specify a load balancing algorithm using *action systems* with procedures as described in Chapter 5. A process network is considered to be associated with an action system assigning each variable to a process. Messages are passed between the processes by explicit communication. In a distributed action system each action and procedure is local to some process referring only to variables of that process.

Our goal is to give the load balancing algorithm as a distributed action system. The initial specification of the load balancing algorithm is not yet distributed. In order to refine the algorithm into a distributed action system we use the *superposition refinement method* [5, 30, 44], a powerful program modularisation and structuring method for developing action systems in a layered manner by superposing a computation on top of an existing one. We carry out three superposition steps each introducing mechanisms that take the centralised initial specification of the load balancing algorithm into a description that is completely distributed. Superposition refinement is a special case of the more general data refinement method presented in Chapter 5. We show how this refinement method is formalised within the B-Method.

7.2 Informal Problem Description

Let us now study the load balancing algorithm [33]. We consider a network of processes, where the network forms a connected graph (V,E). The edges E in the graph are the communication links between the processes V. Communication can only take place between processes directly connected by an edge and it can go in both directions. Even so, the graph is considered to be a rooted directed tree, where the edges are directed towards the root. Each process is assumed to know the identities of its direct neighbours and the number of tasks it posesses, i.e., its load.

The threshold, *top*, that states the preferable load of a process is considered to be a fixed positive number $(top > 0)$, and is a constant of the load balancing algorithm. In node i the number of tasks is denoted by $load\_i$. The tasks themselves are irrelevant for the algorithm. Initially all the loads are 0 and the tasks are arbitrary elements of the set *Tasks*.

In the load balancing system each node i receives new loads from an environment. Thus, we have a reactive system. The load balancing algorithm strives to

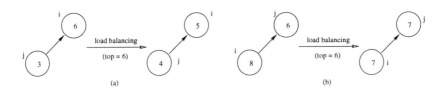

Fig. 7.1. (a) Sending Down a Task in the Tree, and (b) Sending Up a Task in the Tree

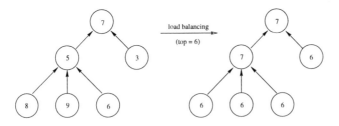

Fig. 7.2. An Example of a Network Before and After Executing the Load Balancing Algorithm

distribute the load in the system evenly among the processes. If node j has a load less than the threshold, and its father, node i, in the tree structure has a load greater than or equal to the threshold, a task can be moved down from node i to its son, node j by increasing the load of j and decreasing the load of i as in Fig. 7.1(a). On the other hand, if node i has too many tasks and its father, node j, has a load less than or equal to the threshold, a task can be sent from node i up to its father, node j, which is shown in Fig. 7.1(b). The load balancing makes it possible for a node in the tree to transfer tasks from one of its branches to another. The load balancing in a tree of nodes is then as in Fig. 7.2. Following the computation pattern above no process is idle forever, if there is enough work to be done.

The load of a node is always greater than or equal to zero during the computation as stated in the invariant:

$$(\forall i. \ i \in V. \ load\_i \geq 0).$$

This is due to the fact that initially the load of a node i is assigned 0 and during the computation the load is only decreased if it is greater than or equal to top (> 0), otherwise it is increased. The new loads sent to the load balancing system from the environment are assumed to be greater than or equal to 0.

At termination, when new loads are not sent to the system, each node either has a load greater than or equal to the threshold top or a load less than or equal to top:

$$(\forall i. \ i \in V. \ load\_i \geq top) \vee (\forall i. \ i \in V. \ load\_i \leq top).$$

7.3 Problem Specification

Let us now write the specification of the load balancing algorithm as an action system using B AMN. For better readability, we restrict the graph of our machine to a graph with two nodes, node 1 and node 2. Node 2 is considered to be the root. It is, however, easy to extend the algorithm to contain more than two nodes. By expressing the loads as functions from nodes to natural numbers, we could even have replication of nodes.

The load balancing algorithm is given as the abstract machine specification *Actions1*. The name *Actions1* refer to "the actions in step 1". Note that there is some redundancy in some of the procedures: when a procedure has parameters, the type of the parameter is restricted in a PRE-substitution. The procedure itself may have a guard given in a SELECT-substitution. Sometimes the former condition implies the latter, but here we prefer to keep this redundancy in order to be faithful to the original action systems' ideas [82], see e.g. the operation *New_Load_1P* below.

MACHINE   *Actions1* (*top*)

---

top denotes the preferable load of a process

CONSTRAINTS

   $top > 0$

SEES

   TaskProcessing

TaskProcessing contains the abstract type *TASKS* and operations for processing tasks, described below

---

VARIABLES

   load1 , *load2* , *task1* , *task2*

---

load1 and *load2* denote the number of tasks in nodes 1 and 2

task1 and *task2* denote tasks in nodes 1 and 2

INVARIANT

   $load1 \in \mathbb{N} \land load2 \in \mathbb{N} \land task1 \in TASKS \land task2 \in TASKS$

INITIALISATION

   $load1 := 0 \parallel load2 := 0 \parallel task1 :\in TASKS \parallel task2 :\in TASKS$

Initially all loads are 0 and each task variable is an arbitrary member of the abstract type *TASKS*

OPERATIONS

New loads *ll* are received from the environment via the global procedures **New_Load**

$New\_Load\_1P(\, ll \,)$ ≙
   PRE $ll \in \mathbb{N}$ **THEN**
      SELECT $ll \geq 0$ **THEN** $load1 := ll$
      END
   END ;
$New\_Load\_2P(\, ll \,)$ ≙
   PRE $ll \in \mathbb{N}$ **THEN**
      SELECT $ll \geq 0$ **THEN** $load2 := ll$
      END
   END ;

Operations to be introduced later in the refinement:

$Commit\_12$ ≙   skip **;**
$Commit\_21$ ≙   skip **;**

Bal_Loads_Down_21 sends a task from node 2 down to the child node 1 when node 2 is overloaded

---

$Bal\_Loads\_Down\_21$ ≙
   SELECT $load1 < top \wedge load2 \geq top$
   THEN $Process\_Task\_1 \, (\, task2 \,) \, \| \, load1 := load1 + 1 \, \| \, load2 := load2 - 1$
   END ;

Bal_Loads_Up_12 sends a task from node 1 up to the parent node 2 when node 1 is overloaded

---

$Bal\_Loads\_Up\_12$ ≙
   SELECT $load2 \leq top \wedge load1 > top$
   THEN $Process\_Task\_2 \, (\, task1 \,) \, \| \, load2 := load2 + 1 \, \| \, load1 := load1 - 1$
   END ;

Operations to be introduced later in the refinement:

$Release\_Nodes\_12$ ≙   skip **;**
$Release\_Nodes\_21$ ≙   skip **;**

Exit_Cond contains the exit condition of the action system for verification purposes

---

$Exit\_Cond$ ≙

SELECT $\neg$ (*load1* < *top* $\wedge$ *load2* $\geq$ *top*) $\wedge$ $\neg$ (*load2* $\leq$ *top* $\wedge$ *load1* > *top*)
THEN   skip
END

END

The types of the tasks and the operations processing them are defined in the machine *TaskProcessing* below. The operations are given as skip, since they are not of interest to us. Because of this it is enough to give the machine *TaskProcessing* in the SEES-clause of *Actions1* above. In case these operations change the state of the action system *Actions1*, the machine *TaskProcessing* would need to be given in the INCLUDES-clause of *Actions1*.

MACHINE   *TaskProcessing*
SETS

TASKS

TASKS is an abstract type of the tasks in the system

OPERATIONS

Process_Task models a task being processed without specifying how

---

$Process\_Task\_1(\ task\ )$ $\hat{=}$ **PRE** $task \in TASKS$ **THEN**   skip   **END** ;
$Process\_Task\_2(\ task\ )$ $\hat{=}$ **PRE** $task \in TASKS$ **THEN**   skip   **END**

END

We consider a variable, an action, as well as a procedure with the first index i to belong to node i. In a distributed system actions and procedures of a node refer only to variables of that node. The load balancing algorithm *Actions1* is not distributed, since variables of both node 1 and node 2 are referenced in order to evaluate the guards of the actions *Bal_Loads_Down_21* and *Bal_Loads_Up_12* of nodes 1 and 2. Furthermore, variables of both node 1 and node 2 are assigned to in these actions.

In this chapter we develop a distributed load balancing algorithm, where each node only accesses its own variables. This development is performed by superposing a set of mechanisms on the specification *Actions1* and introducing procedures in such a way that, for example, an action with references to variables of both nodes 1 and 2 can be separated into an action with references to the variables of node 1 and a procedure with references to the variables of node 2 called by this action. This will result in an algorithm where each action and procedure only refers to variables of a single node.

7.4 Superposition Refinement

We use the *superposition* method to develop the distributed load balancing algorithm. Superposition is a powerful program modularisation and structuring method for developing parallel and distributed systems [5, 30, 44]. By applying the superposition method to a program, we can increase the degree of parallelism of the program and decentralise the control in the program. We add new functionality to the algorithm while the original computation is preserved. The new functionality could, for example, be an information gathering mechanism that replaces direct access to shared variables.

The superposition method has been formalised as a program refinement rule within the refinement calculus for action systems [8]. It is a special kind of data refinement and it is expressed as below for action systems extended with procedures [75].

Let $\mathcal{A}$ and $\mathcal{A}'$ be the two action systems given in B AMN in Fig. 7.3. The global variables are the imported variables u and the exported variables z. The imported variables are assumed to be read-only variables in $\mathcal{A}$ and $\mathcal{A}'$. They are declared in some other action system. The exported variables on the other hand are declared and initialised in $\mathcal{A}$ and $\mathcal{A}'$. Since they are also accessible from other action systems, they are declared in the machine *GlobalVar_z*. The local variables x are declared in both action systems. The superposition step adds new local variables y into $\mathcal{A}'$. The purpose of these new local variables is to encode the superposed mechanism. This is done by refining the global procedures P_i and the actions A_i. Additionally some new actions B_j can be introduced.

Informally, an action system $\mathcal{A}$ is correctly data refined by another action system $\mathcal{A}'$ using the data invariant R when:

(S1) the initialisation in $\mathcal{A}'$ establishes R for any initial values on u and f, where f denotes all the formal parameters of all the global procedures declared in $\mathcal{A}$,

(S2) each body of a global procedure P_i is data refined by the corresponding procedure body P_i' using R, i.e., the procedure P_i' has the same effect on the variables x and z as P_i,

(S3) every action A_i is data refined by the corresponding A_i' using R, i.e., the action A_i' has the same effect on the variables x and z as A_i,

(S4) every action B_i is a data refinement of the empty statement skip using R, i.e., these actions cannot modify the original variables x and z,

(S5) all actions in $\mathcal{A}$ are disabled whenever all actions in $\mathcal{A}'$ are disabled when R holds, i.e., whenever the computation of $\mathcal{A}'$ terminates so does that of $\mathcal{A}$,

(S6) if a procedure P_i is enabled in $\mathcal{A}$, so is P_i' in $\mathcal{A}'$ or then actions in $\mathcal{A}'$ will enable P_i', i.e., in case $\mathcal{A}$ can continue its computation by responding to a call on P_i so can $\mathcal{A}'$ or then P_i' will become enabled in some later state, and

(S7) the computation denoted by the actions $B_1, \ldots, B_k$ terminates provided R holds, i.e., the new actions cannot by themselves introduce an infinite, non-terminating computation into the system.

The correctness of the data refinement of the local procedures q is checked in step (S3) by expanding the calling statements in the actions as described in Chapter 5.

```
┌─────────────────────────────────┐  ┌─────────────────────────────────┐
│ MACHINE    𝒜(u)                 │  │ REFINEMENT    𝒜'                │
│                                 │  │ REFINES                         │
│                                 │  │   𝒜                             │
│ INCLUDES                        │  │ INCLUDES                        │
│   GlobalVar_z,                  │  │   GlobalVar_z'                  │
│   LocalProcA_q, GlobalProcE_r   │  │   LocalProcA_q', GlobalProcE_r' │
│ VARIABLES                       │  │ VARIABLES                       │
│   x                             │  │   x,y                           │
│ INVARIANT                       │  │ INVARIANT                       │
│   I(x,z,u)                      │  │   R(x,y,z,u) ∧ z' = z           │
│ INITIALISATION                  │  │ INITIALISATION                  │
│   x := x_0                      │  │   x,y := x_0,y_0                │
│ OPERATIONS                      │  │ OPERATIONS                      │
│   P_1 ≙ SELECT gP_1             │  │   P_1 ≙ SELECT gP'_1            │
│            THEN sP_1 END ;      │  │            THEN sP'_1 END ;     │
│     ...                         │  │     ...                         │
│   P_n ≙ SELECT gP_n             │  │   P_n ≙ SELECT gP'_n            │
│            THEN sP_n END ;      │  │            THEN sP'_n END ;     │
│   A_1 ≙ SELECT gA_1             │  │   A_1 ≙ SELECT gA'_1            │
│            THEN sA_1 END ;      │  │            THEN sA'_1 END ;     │
│     ...                         │  │     ...                         │
│   A_l ≙ SELECT gA_l             │  │   A_l ≙ SELECT gA'_l            │
│            THEN sA_l END ;      │  │            THEN sA'_l END ;     │
│   B_1 ≙ skip ;                  │  │   B_1 ≙ SELECT gB_1             │
│                                 │  │            THEN sB_1 END ;      │
│     ...                         │  │     ...                         │
│   B_k ≙ skip ;                  │  │   B_k ≙ SELECT gB_k             │
│                                 │  │            THEN sB_k END ;      │
│   exit_cond ≙                   │  │   exit_cond ≙                   │
│     SELECT ¬(gA_1 ∨...∨ gA_l)   │  │     SELECT ¬(gA'_1 ∨...∨ gA'_l  │
│       THEN skip END             │  │                 ∨gB_1 ∨...∨ gB_k)│
│                                 │  │       THEN skip END             │
│ END                             │  │ END                             │
└─────────────────────────────────┘  └─────────────────────────────────┘
```

Fig. 7.3. Superposition Refinement Within the B-Method

The enabledness of the local procedures is checked within (S5). New procedures are not introduced in this refinement step. They are assumed to be introduced in a separate step where no refinements are involved.

Formally the superposition method is stated as a refinement rule as follows.

Definition 7.1 (Superposition refinement). *Consider the abstract action system $\mathcal{A}$ and the concrete action system $\mathcal{A}'$ as in Fig. 7.3. Let $g\mathcal{A}$ be the disjunction of the guards of the actions A_i, $g\mathcal{A}'$ the disjunction of the guards of the actions A'_i and $g\mathcal{B}$ the disjunction of the guards of the actions B_j. Let further f denote all the formal parameters of all the procedures P_i. Then $\mathcal{A}$ is superposition refined by $\mathcal{A}'$ using $R(x,y,z,u,f)$, denoted $\mathcal{A} \leq_R \mathcal{A}'$, if*

(S1) $R(x_0, y_0, z_0, u, f)$
(S2) $P_i \sqsubseteq_R P'_i$, for $i = 1, \ldots, n$
(S3) $A_i \sqsubseteq_R A'_i$, for $i = 1, \ldots, l$
(S4) skip $\sqsubseteq_R B_i$, for $i = 1, \ldots, k$
(S5) $R \wedge \neg(g\mathcal{A}' \vee g\mathcal{B}) \Rightarrow \neg g\mathcal{A}$
(S6) $R \wedge gP_i \Rightarrow$
$\qquad (gP'_i \vee [$ **WHILE** $\neg gP'_i$ **DO**
$\qquad\qquad$ (**CHOICE** A'_1 **OR** $\ldots$ **OR** A'_l **OR** B_1 **OR** $\ldots$ **OR** B_k
$\qquad\qquad$ **OR** (**SELECT** $\neg(g\mathcal{A}' \vee g\mathcal{B})$ **THEN** skip **END**) **END**)
$\qquad\qquad$ **END**] $TRUE$), for $i = 1, \ldots, n$
(S7) $R \Rightarrow [$ **WHILE** gB **DO** (**CHOICE** B_1 **OR** $\ldots$ **OR** B_k **END**) **END** $]$ $TRUE$

Intuitively, a superposition refinement is a data refinement. Hence, it can be justified via the general theory on data refinement. In a superposition step, no new computations are added into the set of traces of an action system, as the observable behaviour of a system w.r.t. the original variables is kept unchanged.

Generally, the data refinement of Condition (S3), $A_i \sqsubseteq_R A'_i$, holds if

$\qquad$ (A1) **PRE** gA' **THEN** sA_i **END** $\sqsubseteq_R sA'_i$ and
$\qquad$ (A2) $R \wedge gA'_i \Rightarrow gA_i$.

This follows directly from the rule of data refining one action with another as described in Chapter 5. Thus, according to (A1) A'_i has the same effect on the program variables as A_i has when R holds and, moreover, A'_i establishes R. The Condition (A2) requires that A_i is enabled whenever A'_i is enabled provided R holds. The Conditions (S2) and (S4) are defined in the same way.

The Conditions (S1) - (S3) follow directly from Definition 5.1 in Chapter 5. The refinement of the auxiliary actions B_j is expressed with the Condition (S4) and (S7). These conditions have no corresponding conditions in Definition 5.1. Condition (S5) is a modification of the Condition (4) in Definition 5.1 taking the auxiliary actions into consideration. In Definition 5.1 Conditions (2) and (4) together state that the guards of the procedures are not allowed to change during the refinement process. Condition (S6), however, allows the guards of the procedure P_i to be strengthened as long as the refined procedure P'_i will be enabled within the refined action system $\mathcal{A}'$. We can note that the superposition refinement $\mathcal{A} \leq_R \mathcal{A}'$ is the same as the data refinement $\mathcal{A} \sqsubseteq_R \mathcal{A}'$ when there are no auxiliary actions in $\mathcal{A}'$ and the guards of the procedures are not changed.

Successive superposition refinements of action systems can be modelled as follows:

$\qquad$ If $\mathcal{A}_0 \leq_{R_1} \mathcal{A}_1$ and $\mathcal{A}_1 \leq_{R_2} \mathcal{A}_2$ then $\mathcal{A}_0 \leq_{R_1 \wedge R_2} \mathcal{A}_2$.

MACHINE   *GlobalVar_z*

VARIABLES
  z

INVARIANT
  $T(z)$

INITIALISATION
  $z := z_0$

OPERATIONS
  $assign\_z(y) \cong$ **PRE** $T(y)$ **THEN** $z := y$ **END**

END

Fig. 7.4. Declaration of a Global Variable z of $\mathcal{A}$

MACHINE   *LocalProcA_q*

OPERATIONS
  $q_1 \cong$ **SELECT** gQ_1 **THEN** sQ_1 **END** ;

  $\vdots$

  $q_l \cong$ **SELECT** gQ_l **THEN** sQ_l **END**

END

Fig. 7.5. The Local Procedures of $\mathcal{A}$

7.5 Superposition Step Within the B-Method

We will now discuss how the superposition rule can be interpreted within the B-Method, in order to be able to perform the derivation of the distributed load balancing algorithm using the B-Method.

Let us consider the specification $\mathcal{A}$ and its superposition refinement $\mathcal{A}'$ given in Fig. 7.3. The invariant $R(x, y, z, u)$ used in the refinement step is considered to include the invariant $I(x, z, u)$ of the action system being refined. The exported global variable z is included as the separate machine in Fig. 7.4, while the read-only global variables u are given as parameters. The local procedures, q, and their refinements are given in the separate abstract machines *LocalProcA_q* and *LocalProcA_q'*, respectively. These machines only contain an OPERATIONS-clause where each local procedure q_i is represented as an operation as in Fig. 7.5. The imported global procedures r are introduced via the machine *GlobalProcE_r* in Fig. 7.6. Since only the headers r of these procedures are of importance to us, they are defined as skip as explained in Chapter 5.

In the B-Method all the refinements of a specification use the same operation names as the specification, which means that all operations that will exist in the final refinement also have to exist in the first specification. Since the operations $B_1, \ldots, B_k$ occur in the machine refinement $\mathcal{A}'$, they are introduced as skip-operations in the

```
MACHINE    GlobalProcE_r
OPERATIONS
    r  ≙  skip
END
```

Fig. 7.6. The Imported Global Procedures of $\mathcal{A}$

machine $\mathcal{A}$. The operation *exit_cond* is introduced in order to be able to prove Condition (S5) of the superposition rule.

Let us now study how the proof rule for superposition refinement of action systems can be performed in the B-Method. The proof obligations (B1) - (B4) of the B-Method are given in the Appendix. The first superposition Condition (S1) concerning the initialisation is equivalent to the Condition (B2). The Conditions (S2) - (S5) are implied by the Condition (B4) for the global procedures P_i, the actions A_i, the auxiliary actions B_i and the exit condition, respectively. This correspondence is discussed in more detail elsewhere [82]. The Conditions (S6) and (S7) of the superposition rule require that some extra B constructs are generated. Therefore, these conditions are treated more thoroughly below.

The Conditions (B1) and (B3) do not correspond to any of the conditions in the superposition rule. Since the invariant I is included in the invariant R due to the superposition refinement and the preconditions are equivalent, they trivially hold for the embedded action system.

7.5.1 Enabledness of Global Procedures

Let us now proceed with the Condition (S6):

$$R \wedge gP_i \Rightarrow$$
$$(gP_i' \vee [\, \textbf{WHILE } \neg gP_i' \textbf{ DO}$$
$$\quad (\textbf{CHOICE } A_1' \textbf{ OR } \dots \textbf{ OR } A_l' \textbf{ OR } B_1 \textbf{ OR } \dots \textbf{ OR } B_k$$
$$\quad \textbf{OR } (\textbf{SELECT } \neg (g\mathcal{A}' \vee g\mathcal{B}) \textbf{ THEN skip END}) \textbf{ END})$$
$$\textbf{END}]\, TRUE)$$

For the weakest precondition of the WHILE-loop we need to find a variant such that the invariant R implies that the variant is a natural number and that the variant is decreased each time one of the actions in the loop is executed. These conditions are created as proof obligations (T1) - (T5) for the WHILE-loop within the B-Method. We, thus, need to make a separate refinement step within the B-Method using a WHILE-loop to prove this condition. The proof obligations (T1) - (T5) are given in the Appendix.

When checking the enabledness of the global procedures P_i in the B-Method we create an abstract machine and a machine implementation for the Condition (S6).

```
IMPLEMENTATION    NewGlobalProc
REFINES
    OldGlobalProc
IMPORTS
    AllActionSystem
OPERATIONS
    EnableProc ≙
        VAR x, y, z, e  IN
            x := x₀ ;  y := y₀ ;  z := z₀ ;  e := e₀ ;
            IF ¬gP'ᵢ  THEN
                WHILE ¬gP'ᵢ  DO
                    x, y, z, e ⟵ AllActions(x, y, z, e)
                INVARIANT R(x, y, z, u) ∧ Rₑ(z, u, e)
                VARIANT E(e)
                END
            END
        END
END
```

Fig. 7.7. Construct in B for Checking Enabledness of Global Procedures

The abstract machine specification *OldGlobalProc* has the invariant $R \wedge gP_i$ and one operation, skip. Its machine implementation *NewGlobalProc* will then have the invariant *TRUE* and a WHILE-loop as the refined operation. The condition on the guard gP'_i is automatically generated from an IF-substitution (observe the slight redundancy in the machine, but not in the Condition (S6)). This implementation is generated considering the refined machine $\mathcal{A}'$ and is shown in Fig. 7.7.

A new expression $E(e)$ operating on the variables e is created as the variant. The invariant $R(x, y, z, u)$ of the Abstract Machine refinement $\mathcal{A}'$ is included in the invariant of the loop. The relation $R_e(z, u, e)$ gives the definition of the variant and is also included in the invariant. Furthermore, the initialisation of the refinement $\mathcal{A}'$ is the initialisation of the loop. The negation of the guard of the global procedure, $\neg gP'_i$, forms the WHILE-loop condition. Hence, a separate implementation machine is needed for each global procedure. The non-deterministic choice of the actions in the Condition (S6) is represented as a call to the operation *AllActions* in the included machine specification *AllActionSystem*. The operation *AllActions* shown in Fig. 7.8 is a SELECT-substitution containing all the operations of $\mathcal{A}'$, i.e., the non-deterministic choice of the actions in $\mathcal{A}'$.

The Condition (S6) in the superposition rule can now be expressed in terms of proof obligations generated within the B-Method:

$$(S6) \Leftrightarrow (T2) \wedge (T4).$$

The Conditions (T1), (T3), and (T5) do not directly correspond to any condition in the superposition rule. The Condition (T1) is partly proved by proving the Condition (B2) and (T3) by proving (B4) for A_i and B_i, but additionally they check that the variant establishes the invariant $R_e(z, u, e)$ in the initialisation and in the operations

$$
\begin{aligned}
&x_o, y_o, z_o \longleftarrow AllActions(x, y, z) \;\widehat{=}\\
&\quad \textbf{PRE } x, y, z \in \textit{Types } \textbf{THEN}\\
&\qquad \textbf{SELECT } gA_1' \ \ \textbf{THEN } sA_1'\\
&\qquad \textbf{WHEN } gA_2' \ \ \textbf{THEN } sA_2'\\
&\qquad\qquad\qquad \vdots\\
&\qquad \textbf{WHEN } gA_l' \ \ \textbf{THEN } sA_l'\\
&\qquad \textbf{WHEN } gB_1 \ \ \textbf{THEN } sB_1\\
&\qquad\qquad\qquad \vdots\\
&\qquad \textbf{WHEN } gB_k \ \ \textbf{THEN } sB_k\\
&\qquad \textbf{WHEN } \neg(gA_1' \vee \ldots \vee gA_l' \vee gB_1 \vee \ldots \vee gB_k)\\
&\qquad\quad \textbf{THEN } \mathsf{skip}\\
&\qquad \textbf{END}\\
&\quad \textbf{END}
\end{aligned}
$$

Fig. 7.8. The Non-Deterministic Choice Between all the Operations in the Refined Machine

A_i and B_i. Since the postcondition of the loop is considered to be *TRUE* here, the Condition (T5) holds trivially.

7.5.2 Termination of Auxiliary Actions

The last condition, (S7), of the superposition rule:

$$R \Rightarrow [\ \textbf{WHILE } gB \textbf{ DO } (\textbf{CHOICE } B_1 \textbf{ OR } \ldots \textbf{ OR } B_k \textbf{ END}) \textbf{ END}\ ]\ TRUE$$

can be checked within the B-Method in a similar way as the enabledness of the global procedures, Condition (S6). Thus, we also create an abstract machine specification and a machine implementation for the Condition (S7).

Here, the abstract machine specification has *TRUE* as the invariant and skip as the initialisation and as the only operation. The machine implementation will again have the invariant *TRUE* and a WHILE-loop as the refined operation. This refined operation, *TermOfActions*, is given in Fig. 7.9. The operation *TermOfActions* corresponds to the operation *EnableProc* previously created for the Condition (S6). We can, however, note that the WHILE-loop condition here constitutes of the disjunction of the guards of the auxiliary actions. Furthermore, the operation *AuxAction* called from the WHILE-loop gives the non-deterministic choice merely of the auxiliary actions B_i. This operation is represented as a SELECT-substitution in the same way as the operation *AllAction* for the Condition (S6).

The Condition (S7) in the superposition rule can now as the Condition (S6) be translated into terms of proof obligations generated in the B-Method by:

$$(S7) \Leftrightarrow (T2) \wedge (T4).$$

Hence, there are corresponding proof obligations in the B-Method for each Condition (S1)-(S7) in the superposition rule.

$TermOfActions \cong$
  VAR x, y, z, e **IN**
    $x := x_0$; $y := y_0$; $z := z_0$; $e := e_0$;
    WHILE $(gB_1 \vee \ldots \vee gB_k)$ **DO**
      $x, y, z, e \longleftarrow AuxActions(x, y, z, e)$
    INVARIANT $R(x, y, z, u) \wedge R_e(z, u, e)$
    VARIANT $E(e)$
    END
  END

Fig. 7.9. Operation for Checking Termination of Auxiliary Actions

7.6 Refinement Step 1: Distributing Loads

Let us now study the development of the distributed load balancing algorithm using the superposition refinement. We want to have a distributed load balancing algorithm where each action and procedure of a node refer only to the variables of that node. In order to achieve this from the machine specification *Actions1*, we have to distribute the loads as follows. We introduce the procedures *Trans_Task_1P* and *Trans_Task_2P* modelling the links between node 1 and node 2. They are called from the actions *Bal_Loads_Down_21* and *Bal_Loads_Up_12*, respectively. Let us, for example, consider the action *Bal_Loads_Down_21*. This action is modified to send a task of node 2 to the neighbouring node 1 via the procedure *Trans_Task_1P* and at the same time decrease *load2* of node 2 by one. Node 1 then increases its variable *load1* upon receiving the task via this procedure. Hence, we have the assignment to *load2* in the action *Bal_Loads_Down_21* of node 2 and the assignment to *load1* in the procedure *Trans_Task_1P* of node 1 called from the action *Bal_Loads_Down_21*, and we have distributed the variable *load*.

The local procedures *Trans_Task_1P* and *Trans_Task_2P* are introduced as the same kind of operations within the B-Method as the actions and the global procedures. Since these local procedures are called from the actions in *Actions1P*, we introduce a new machine, *Procedures1*, only containing these procedures. This machine is then included in the machine *Actions1P*. The global procedures are only called from other action systems than *Actions1P* and can therefore be operations in *Action1P*. This corresponds well to proof obligations in the superposition refinement step, where the global procedures are proved with the Conditions (S2) and (S6) and the local procedures are proved via the Conditions (S3) and (S5) for the actions. An overview of this step is given in Fig. 7.10. The refinement relation is given as a "staircase", while the arrows show which machines are included in others. The bold lines denote the current step.

The machine refinement *Actions1P* representing the global procedures and the actions of the load balancing algorithm is given below.

REFINEMENT   *Actions1P*
REFINES

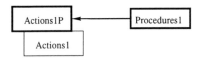

Fig. 7.10. Overview of the Derivation After the First Refinement Step

Actions1
SEES
    TaskProcessing
INCLUDES
    Procedures1

The machine *Procedures1* contains the local procedures as operations

---

VARIABLES
    load1 , *load2* , *task1* , *task2*
INVARIANT
    load1 $\in \mathbb{N} \wedge$ *load2* $\in \mathbb{N} \wedge$ *task1* $\in$ *TASKS* $\wedge$ *task2* $\in$ *TASKS*
INITIALISATION
    load1 := 0 $\|$ *load2* := 0 $\|$ *task1* :$\in$ *TASKS* $\|$ *task2* :$\in$ *TASKS*

OPERATIONS
    New_Load_1P(ll) $\;\; \widehat{=}$
      PRE   *ll* $\in \mathbb{N}$ **THEN**
          SELECT   *ll* ≥ 0 **THEN**   *load1* := *ll*
          END
      END ;
    New_Load_2P(ll) $\;\; \widehat{=}$
      PRE   *ll* $\in \mathbb{N}$ **THEN**
          SELECT   *ll* ≥ 0 **THEN**   *load2* := *ll*
          END
      END ;
    Commit_12 $\widehat{=}$ skip ;
    Commit_21 $\widehat{=}$ skip ;

Bal_Loads_Down_21 of node 2 sends *task2* to node 1 and order node 1 to change *load1* via the procedure *Trans_Task_1P*, when node 2 is overloaded

---

Bal_Loads_Down_21 $\widehat{=}$
    SELECT   *load1* $<$ *top* $\wedge$ *load2* $\geq$ *top*
    THEN   *load1* $\longleftarrow$ *Trans_Task_1P* (2 , *task2* , *load1*) ; *load2* := *load2* $-$ *1*
    END ;

Bal_Loads_Up_12 of node 1 sends *task1* to node 2 to increase *load2* via the procedure *Trans_Task_2P*

$Bal\_Loads\_Up\_12 \quad \widehat{=}$
    SELECT $load2 \le top \wedge load1 > top$
    THEN $load2 \longleftarrow Trans\_Task\_2P (1 , task1 , load2)$ **;** $load1 := load1 - 1$
    END ;
$Release\_Nodes\_12 \quad \widehat{=} \quad$ skip **;**
$Release\_Nodes\_21 \quad \widehat{=} \quad$ skip **;**
$Exit\_Cond \quad \widehat{=}$
    SELECT $\neg (load1 < top \wedge load2 \ge top) \wedge \neg (load2 \le top \wedge load1 > top)$
    THEN   skip
    END

END

The new local procedures are given as follows:

MACHINE   *Procedures1*
SEES

    TaskProcessing

OPERATIONS

The procedure **Trans_Task** processes the task, *taskm* that it receives from node *mm* and increases its load by 1

$load1\_0 \longleftarrow Trans\_Task\_1P(mm , taskm , load1) \quad \widehat{=}$
    PRE $mm = 2 \wedge taskm \in TASKS \wedge load1 \in \mathbb{N}$ **THEN**
    $Process\_Task\_1 (taskm) \parallel load1\_0 := load1 + 1$
    END ;
$load2\_0 \longleftarrow Trans\_Task\_2P(mm , taskm , load2) \quad \widehat{=}$
    PRE $mm = 1 \wedge taskm \in TASKS \wedge load2 \in \mathbb{N}$ **THEN**
    $Process\_Task\_2 (taskm) \parallel load2\_0 := load2 + 1$
    END

END

We can note that the new machine *Procedures1* does not have a state space of its own. In this machine the state space of the action system is changed via the parameters of the procedures. The variable *load1*, therefore, is still an input as well as an output parameter in the procedure call *Trans_Task_1P* in action *Bal_Loads_Down_21*, even if we claim that we have distributed its assignment completely into *Trans_Task_1P*.

Expanding the procedure calls in the two operations *Bal_Loads_Down_21* and *Bal_Loads_Up_12* in the machine refinement *Actions1P* results in the corresponding operations in the machine specification *Actions1*. We actually only write the machine in a different form, when we introduce new procedures. Thus, *Actions1P* and *Procedures1P* together is a re-written form of *Actions1*.

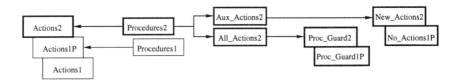

Fig. 7.11. Overview of the Derivation After the Second Refinement Step

In this step we do not introduce any auxiliary actions nor do we change the guards of the global procedures. Thus, we do not need to introduce any extra constructs in the B-Method to prove this refinement step. The five proof obligations generated for this refinement step were all trivial and were automatically discharged.

7.7 Refinement Step 2: Estimation of Neighbouring Loads

As the second refinement step we add a mechanism to estimate the loads of each neighbour. The more knowledge a node has about its neighbours the more precisely it can perform its share of the load balancing independently. Thus, this step will make the control more decentralised and distributed in the system.

The load estimation can be performed by adding the variables *estim* and *rec* to the algorithm. For example, the variable *estim12* denotes the estimate that node 1 has about the load in the neighbouring node 2. The boolean variable *rec12* has the value *TRUE*, when node 2 is committed to node 1 and node 1 has the right estimate of *load2*, otherwise it has the value *FALSE*. The values of *estim21* and *rec21* are defined in the same way. This refinement step is a superposition refinement.

Fig. 7.11 gives an overview of the load balancing system at the second refinement step. Via the machines *Actions2* and *Procedures2* we can check the refinement of the initialisation, the actions, the procedures and the exit condition. The enabledness of the procedure guards is checked via the machines *Proc_Guard1P*, *Proc_Guard2* as well as *All_Actions2* and the termination condition via the machines *No_Actions1P*, *New_Actions2* as well as *Aux_Actions2*.

7.7.1 Refinement of Actions and Procedures

Let us consider the refined load balancing algorithm in *Actions2* and *Procedures2*. Initially the estimate *estim* is 0 and the variable *rec* has the value *FALSE*. We split the load balancing into three phases in this step. In the first phase nodes 1 and 2 commit to each other for changing loads and update their estimates, *estim12* and *estim21*, to correspond to the loads *load2* and *load1*, respectively. In the second phase nodes 1 and 2 change their loads as long as there is an imbalance between them. In this phase the estimates of nodes 1 and 2 are also updated. Thus, a node will always have the right estimate of the neighbour that it is changing loads with. In the third phase when the loads are balanced between nodes 1 and 2, the commitment between them is released and they are free to commit to other neighbours. Furthermore, a node can only be given a new load from the environment, when it is not involved in load balancing with some other node.

The load balancing, the second phase, in the refined action system is handled via the old operations *Bal_Loads_Down_21* and *Bal_Loads_Up_12* as well as *Trans_Task_1P* and *Trans_Task_2P*. These are modified to update the load estimates *estim21* and *estim12*. For the first and the third phase we need to introduce the auxiliary actions *Commit* and *Release_Nodes*. Each node i should have the auxiliary actions *Commit_ij* and *Release_Nodes_ij* for each outgoing edge (i, j) and each incoming edge (j, i). In *Actions2*, where $E = \{(1,2)\}$, node 1 has one outgoing edge and node 2 has one incoming edge. Thus, the auxiliary operations are *Commit_12* and *Release_Nodes_12* of node 1, and *Commit_21* and *Release_Nodes_21* of node 2.

The refined machine *Actions2* can now be given as follows:

REFINEMENT   *Actions2*

REFINES

Actions1P

SEES

Bool_TYPE , *TaskProcessing*

INCLUDES

Procedures2

VARIABLES

load1 , *load2* , *task1* , *task2* , *estim12* , *estim21* , *rec12* , *rec21*

---

estim12 denotes the estimate that node 1 has about the load in node 2.

rec12 has the value *TRUE* when node 2 is committed to node 1, otherwise *FALSE*.

INVARIANT

$load1 \in \mathbb{N} \wedge load2 \in \mathbb{N} \wedge task1 \in TASKS \wedge task2 \in TASKS$
$\wedge\ estim12 \in \mathbb{N} \wedge estim21 \in \mathbb{N} \wedge rec12 \in BOOL \wedge rec21 \in BOOL$
$\wedge\ (\ rec12 = TRUE \Rightarrow load2 = estim12\ )$
$\wedge\ (\ rec21 = TRUE \Rightarrow load1 = estim21\ )$

Node 1 has the right estimate of the load in node 2, $(load2 = estim12)$, when node 2 is committed to node 1, $(rec12 = TRUE)$.

INITIALISATION

$load1$, $load2 := 0 , 0$ || $task1 :\in TASKS$ || $task2 :\in TASKS$
|| $estim12$, $estim21 := 0 , 0$ || $rec12$, $rec21 := FALSE , FALSE$

Initially the estimates are set to 0 and no nodes are committed.

OPERATIONS

If node 1 is not committed to any neighbour, it can receive a new load from the environment via **New_Load_1P**.

New_Load_1P(ll) $\widehat{=}$
  PRE $ll \in \mathbb{N}$ **THEN**
    SELECT $rec12 = FALSE \wedge rec21 = FALSE \wedge ll \geq 0$
    THEN $load1 := ll$
    END
  END ;
New_Load_2P(ll) $\widehat{=}$
  PRE $ll \in \mathbb{N}$ **THEN**
    SELECT $rec12 = FALSE \wedge rec21 = FALSE \wedge ll \geq 0$
    THEN $load2 := ll$
    END
  END ;

Commit_12 can be executed if
- there is an estimated imbalance between the loads of nodes 1 and 2 or
- node 2 does not have a good enough estimate of load1 or
- node 2 is already committed to node 1.
Node 1 should *not* be comitted to node 2 upon execution.
The estimate *estim21* is updated and node 1 becomes committed to node 2.
Note that $A \vee B \wedge C = (A \vee B) \wedge C$ below.

Commit_12 $\widehat{=}$
  SELECT
    Imbalance (*load1* , *estim12*) $\vee$ *BadlyEstimated* (*load1* , *estim21*)
    $\vee$ *rec12* = *TRUE* $\wedge$ *rec21* = *FALSE*
  THEN $estim21 := load1$; $rec21 := TRUE$
  END ;
Commit_21 $\widehat{=}$
  SELECT
    Imbalance (*estim21* , *load2*) $\vee$ *BadlyEstimated* (*load2* , *estim12*)
    $\vee$ *rec21* = *TRUE* $\wedge$ *rec12* = *FALSE*
  THEN $estim12 := load2$; $rec12 := TRUE$
  END ;

Bal_Loads_Down_21 can be executed when nodes 1 and 2 are committed and node 2 is overloaded. When the task, *task2*, is sent to node 1 the loads and estimates are updated in the nodes 1 and 2.

Bal_Loads_Down_21 $\widehat{=}$
  SELECT $estim21 < top \wedge load2 \geq top \wedge rec21 = TRUE$
  THEN
    $load1$, $estim12 \longleftarrow$ *Trans_Task_1P* (2 , *task2* , *load1* , *estim12* , *rec12*) ;
    $load2 := load2 - 1$; $estim21 := estim21 + 1$
  END ;

$Bal\_Loads\_Up\_12$ $\widehat{=}$
  SELECT $estim12 \leq top \wedge load1 > top \wedge rec12 = TRUE$
  THEN
      $load2$, $estim21 \longleftarrow Trans\_Task\_2P$ (1 , $task1$, $load2$, $estim21$, $rec21$) ;
      $load1 := load1 - 1$; $estim12 := estim12 + 1$
  END ;

Release_Nodes_12 can be executed if nodes 1 and 2 are committed to each other and there is no imbalance between these nodes. The nodes are released from the commitment by assigning *FALSE* to the *rec*-variables.

$Release\_Nodes\_12$ $\widehat{=}$
  SELECT $\neg$ ($Imbalance$ ($load1$, $estim12$)) $\wedge rec12 = TRUE \wedge rec21 = TRUE$
  THEN $rec12 := FALSE$; $rec21 := FALSE$
  END ;
$Release\_Nodes\_21$ $\widehat{=}$
  SELECT $\neg$ ($Imbalance$ ($estim21$, $load2$)) $\wedge rec21 = TRUE \wedge rec12 = TRUE$
  THEN $rec21 := FALSE$; $rec12 := FALSE$
  END ;
$Exit\_Cond$ $\widehat{=}$
  SELECT
      $\neg Guard\_Commit\_12 \wedge \neg Guard\_Commit\_21$
      $\wedge \neg Guard\_Bal\_Load\_Down\_21$
      $\wedge \neg Guard\_Bal\_Load\_Up\_12$
      $\wedge \neg Guard\_Release\_Nodes\_12 \wedge \neg Guard\_Release\_Nodes\_21$
  THEN   skip
  END

DEFINITIONS

$Imbalance$ (x , y) $\widehat{=}$ $x < top \wedge y \geq top \vee$ ($x > top \wedge y \leq top$) ;
$BadlyEstimated$ (x , y) $\widehat{=}$ $x > top \wedge y < top \vee$ ($x < top \wedge y > top$) $\vee$
      ($x = top \wedge y \neq top$) $\vee$ ($x \neq top \wedge y = top$) ;
$Guard\_Commit\_12$ $\widehat{=}$
      $Imbalance$ ($load1$, $estim12$) $\vee BadlyEstimated$ ($load1$, $estim21$) $\vee rec12 = TRUE$
      $\wedge rec21 = FALSE$;
$Guard\_Commit\_21$ $\widehat{=}$
      $Imbalance$ ($estim21$, $load2$) $\vee BadlyEstimated$ ($load2$, $estim12$) $\vee rec21 = TRUE$
      $\wedge rec12 = FALSE$;
$Guard\_Bal\_Load\_Down\_21$ $\widehat{=}$
      $estim21 < top \wedge load2 \geq top \wedge rec21 = TRUE \wedge rec12 = TRUE$;
$Guard\_Bal\_Load\_Up\_12$ $\widehat{=}$
      $estim12 \leq top \wedge load1 > top \wedge rec12 = TRUE \wedge rec21 = TRUE$;
$Guard\_Release\_Nodes\_12$ $\widehat{=}$
      $\neg$ ($Imbalance$ ($load1$, $estim12$)) $\wedge rec12 = TRUE \wedge rec21 = TRUE$;
$Guard\_Release\_Nodes\_21$ $\widehat{=}$
      $\neg$ ($Imbalance$ ($estim21$, $load2$)) $\wedge rec21 = TRUE \wedge rec12 = TRUE$

END

In this step we extend the invariant of *Actions1P* with the definition of the new variables, *estim* and *rec* to get the invariant of *Actions2*. Except for the types of the new variables, the invariant in *Actions2* should also state that when *rec_ij* holds, node i has the right estimate of $load\_j$:

$$(\forall i,j.\ i,j \in V \wedge ((i,j) \in E \vee (j,i) \in E).$$
$$rec\_ij = TRUE \Rightarrow load\_j = estim\_ij),$$

considering that $E = \{(1,2)\}$. In case there were more edges in E than we consider here, the invariant would also need to state that when rec_ij has the value $TRUE$, i.e., node j is committed to node i, the nodes i and j cannot be committed to any other node. This can formally be given as:

$$(\forall i,j.\ i,j \in V \wedge ((i,j) \in E \vee (j,i) \in E).\ rec\_ij = TRUE \Rightarrow$$
$$((\forall k.\ k \in V \wedge ((i,k) \in E \ \vee (k,i) \in E) \wedge k \neq j.$$
$$rec\_ik = FALSE \wedge rec\_ki = FALSE) \wedge$$
$$(\forall k.\ k \in V \wedge ((j,k) \in E \ \vee (k,j) \in E) \wedge k \neq i.$$
$$rec\_jk = FALSE \wedge rec\_kj = FALSE))).$$

The procedures *Trans_Task_1P* and *Trans_Task_2P* are turned into guarded procedures in this refinement step. Since they model a node receiving a task from a neighbouring node, the sending node must be committed to this node for the procedure to be enabled. The local procedures are given as follows:

MACHINE   *Procedures2*

SEES

   Bool_TYPE , *TaskProcessing*

OPERATIONS

Trans_Task_1P receives a task from node $mm(= 2)$ and updates the load of node 1 as well as its estimate of the load of the sender, if the sender is committed to node 1

$load1\_0$, $estim12\_0$ ⟵ *Trans_Task_1P*(mm , $taskm$, $load1$, $estim12$, $rec12$)   ≙
    PRE $mm = 2 \wedge taskm \in TASKS \wedge load1 \in \mathbb{N} \wedge estim12 \in \mathbb{N} \wedge rec12 \in BOOL$
    THEN
        SELECT $rec12 = TRUE$
        THEN
            Process_Task_1 (*taskm*) ‖
            $load1\_0 := load1 + 1$ ‖ $estim12\_0 := estim12 - 1$
        END
    END ;
$load2\_0$, $estim21\_0$ ⟵ *Trans_Task_2P*(mm , $taskm$, $load2$, $estim21$, $rec21$)   ≙
    PRE $mm = 1 \wedge taskm \in TASKS \wedge load2 \in \mathbb{N} \wedge estim21 \in \mathbb{N} \wedge rec21 \in BOOL$
    THEN
        SELECT $rec21 = TRUE$
        THEN
            Process_Task_2 (*taskm*) ‖
            $load2\_0 := load2 + 1$ ‖ $estim21\_0 := estim21 - 1$
        END

END

END

We have proven the Conditions (S1) - (S5) of the superposition refinement. Out of the 22 obligations generated, only the two concerning the operation *Exit_cond* could not be discharged automatically. By supplying the tool with some logical rules that simplify these obligations, these can also be proved. The superposition Conditions (S6) and (S7) will be treated in the following subsections.

7.7.2 Refining the Guards of the Global Procedures

A node cannot receive a new load from the environment, if it is comitted to change loads with a neighbouring node. Thus, when introducing the load estimates and splitting up the load balancing in this refinement step, the guards of the global procedures *New_Loads* are strengthened. Because of this the enabledness of the global procedures must be checked explicitly via the Condition (S6). Since the guards of the procedures *New_Load_1P* and *New_Load_2P* are identical, we only need to check one of them.

We first create the machine specification *Proc_Guard1P*. The invariant of the machine *Actions2* and the guard of the procedure *New_Load* in the machine *Actions1P* form the invariant of the new machine. In the OPERATIONS-clause there is only a skip-operation.

MACHINE   *Proc_Guard1P* (*top*)

CONSTRAINTS

   $top > 0$

SEES

   Bool_TYPE , *TaskProcessing*

VARIABLES

   load1 , *load2* , *task1* , *task2* , *estim12* , *estim21* , *rec12* , *rec21* , *ll*

INVARIANT

The invariant of *Actions2*:

This invariant is given here for verification purposes and forms the antecedent of the proof rule (S6) checking enabledness of global procedures $(R \wedge gP)$

$load1 \in \mathbb{N} \wedge load2 \in \mathbb{N} \wedge task1 \in TASKS \wedge task2 \in TASKS$
$\wedge\ estim12 \in \mathbb{N} \wedge estim21 \in \mathbb{N} \wedge rec12 \in BOOL \wedge rec21 \in BOOL$
$\wedge\ (\ rec12 = TRUE \Rightarrow load2 = estim12\ )$
$\wedge\ (\ rec21 = TRUE \Rightarrow load1 = estim21\ )$

The guard of procedure *New_Load* in *Actions1P*:

$\wedge\ ll \in \mathbb{N} \wedge ll \geq 0$

INITIALISATION

$load1\ ,\ load2 := 0\ ,\ 0\ \parallel\ task1 :\in TASKS\ \parallel\ task2 :\in TASKS\ \parallel\ ll :\in \mathbb{N}$
$\parallel\ estim12\ ,\ estim21 := 0\ ,\ 0\ \parallel\ rec12\ ,\ rec21 := FALSE\ ,\ FALSE$

Given in order to establish the invariant

OPERATIONS

Proc_Enabled to be introduced as a check for enabledness of the global procedure *New_Load*

$Proc\_Enabled\ \ \widehat{=}\ \ \mathsf{skip}$

END

Next, we create a machine implementation *Proc_Guard2* from the actions and the global procedures of the refinement machine *Actions2*. The negation of the guard of the procedure *New_Load_1P* is given as the WHILE-condition and the operation *All_Actions* in machine *All_Actions2* is called from the loop. This operation consists of a non-deterministic choice of all the actions in *Actions2*.

IMPLEMENTATION   *Proc_Guard2*

REFINES

Proc_Guard1P

SEES

Bool_TYPE , *TaskProcessing* , *Functions*

IMPORTS

All_Actions2

All_Actions2 contains all the actions of *Actions2*

OPERATIONS

$Proc\_Enabled\ \ \widehat{=}$
    VAR $load1\ ,\ load2\ ,\ estim12\ ,\ estim21\ ,\ rec12\ ,\ rec21\ ,\ ll\ ,\ C1\ ,\ C2\ ,\ C3$ **IN**

The initialisation of *Actions2*:

$load1 := 0\ \mathbf{;}\ load2 := 0\ \mathbf{;}\ estim12 := 0\ \mathbf{;}\ estim21 := 0\ \mathbf{;}$
$rec12 := FALSE\ \mathbf{;}\ rec21 := FALSE\ \mathbf{;}\ ll := 0\ \mathbf{;}$

C1 is 1 if *rec12* has the value *TRUE*, and 0 otherwise
C2 is 1 if *rec21* has the value *TRUE*, and 0 otherwise

C3 models the imbalance among the loads
These variables are updated each time the loop is executed

$C1 \longleftarrow BTS\_BOOL\,(\,rec12\,)$ **;** $C2 \longleftarrow BTS\_BOOL\,(\,rec21\,)$ **;**
$C3 \longleftarrow imbalance\,(\,load1\,,\,load2\,,\,top\,,\,estim12\,,\,estim21\,,\,rec12\,,\,rec21\,)$ **;**

IF $\neg\,(\,rec12 = FALSE \wedge rec21 = FALSE \wedge ll \geq 0\,)$ **THEN**

Perform only if the global procedure *New_Load* in *Actions2* is not directly enabled

---

WHILE $\neg\,(\,rec12 = FALSE \wedge rec21 = FALSE \wedge ll \geq 0\,)$ **DO**

Execute as long as the global procedure *New_Load* is not enabled

---

$load1\,,\,load2\,,\,estim12\,,\,estim21\,,\,rec12\,,\,rec21\,,\,C3 \longleftarrow$
$All\_Actions\,(\,load1\,,\,load2\,,\,estim12\,,\,estim21\,,\,rec12\,,\,rec21\,,\,top\,,\,C3\,)$ **;**
$C1 \longleftarrow BTS\_BOOL\,(\,rec12\,)$ **;** $C2 \longleftarrow BTS\_BOOL\,(\,rec21\,)$
INVARIANT

The invariant of *Actions2*:

$load1 \in \mathbb{N} \wedge load2 \in \mathbb{N}$
$\wedge\, estim12 \in \mathbb{N} \wedge estim21 \in \mathbb{N} \wedge rec12 \in BOOL \wedge rec21 \in BOOL$
$\wedge\,(\,rec12 = TRUE \Rightarrow load2 = estim12\,)$
$\wedge\,(\,rec21 = TRUE \Rightarrow load1 = estim21\,)$
$\wedge\, ll \in \mathbb{N}$

The properties of the variant, explained above

$\wedge\, C1 \in \mathbb{N} \wedge C2 \in \mathbb{N} \wedge C3 \in \mathbb{N}$
$\wedge\,(\,rec12 = TRUE \Rightarrow C1 = 1\,) \wedge (\,rec12 = FALSE \Rightarrow C1 = 0\,)$
$\wedge\,(\,rec21 = TRUE \Rightarrow C2 = 1\,) \wedge (\,rec21 = FALSE \Rightarrow C2 = 0\,)$
VARIANT

The variant decreases each time the loop is executed:
$(2 - (C1 + C2))$ decreases each time a node becomes committed, and
C3 decreases after each balance action and at release of commitment between two nodes

---

$2 - (\,C1 + C2\,) + C3$
      END
    END
  END
END

The non-deterministic choice of the actions in the refinement machine *Actions2* is given in the machine *All_Actions2* below. The tasks are declared within this specification machine, even if the rest of the variables are declared within the implementation machine *Proc_Guard2*. This is due to the fact that the tasks are treated in a non-deterministic manner in the derivation of the load balancing algorithm and the machine implementation does not allow non-determinism. We can observe that we do not use the implementation machine in the usual way here, but in such a way that we are able to generate the right proof obligations for proving the superposition refinement.

MACHINE   *All_Actions2*

SEES

   Bool_TYPE , *TaskProcessing*

INCLUDES

   Procedures2

VARIABLES

   task1 , *task2*

The variable *task* is treated non-deterministically and is therefore declared here

---

INVARIANT

   task1 $\in$ *TASKS* $\wedge$ *task2* $\in$ *TASKS*

INITIALISATION

   task1 $:\in$ *TASKS* $\parallel$ *task2* $:\in$ *TASKS*

OPERATIONS

All_Actions represents the non-deterministic choice among all the actions in the refined machine *Actions2*

---

load1_0 , *load2_0* , *estim12_0* , *estim21_0* , *rec12_0* , *rec21_0* , *C3_0* $\longleftarrow$
All_Actions(*load1* , *load2* , *estim12* , *estim21* , *rec12* , *rec21* , *top* , *C3*) $\hat{=}$

   PRE   *load1* $\in \mathbb{N} \wedge$ *load2* $\in \mathbb{N} \wedge$ *estim12* $\in \mathbb{N} \wedge$ *estim21* $\in \mathbb{N}$
       $\wedge$ *rec12* $\in$ *BOOL* $\wedge$ *rec21* $\in$ *BOOL* $\wedge$ *top* $\in \mathbb{N}_1 \wedge C3 \in \mathbb{N}$
   THEN

Commit_12 $[]$ *Commit_21* $[]$ *Bal_Loads_Down_21* $[]$ *Bal_Loads_Up_12*
$[]$ *Release_Nodes_12* $[]$ *Release_Nodes_21* $[]$ *Exit_Cond*

       SELECT
          Imbalance (*load1* , *estim12*) $\vee$ *BadlyEstimated* (*load1* , *estim21*)
          $\vee$ *rec12* = *TRUE* $\wedge$ *rec21* = *FALSE*
       THEN   *estim21_0* := *load1* $\parallel$ *rec21_0* := *TRUE*
       WHEN
          Imbalance (*estim21* , *load2*) $\vee$ *BadlyEstimated* (*load2* , *estim12*)

$\lor$ $rec21 = TRUE \land rec12 = FALSE$
THEN $estim12\_0 := load2 \parallel rec12\_0 := TRUE$
WHEN
$estim21 < top \land load2 \geq top \land rec21 = TRUE$
THEN
$load1\_0 , estim12\_0 \longleftarrow Trans\_Task\_1P (2 , task2 , load1 , estim12 , rec12)$
$\parallel load2\_0 := load2 - 1 \parallel estim21\_0 := estim21 + 1$
$\parallel C3\_0 := C3 - 1$
WHEN
$estim12 \leq top \land load1 > top \land rec12 = TRUE$
THEN
$load2\_0 , estim21\_0 \longleftarrow Trans\_Task\_2P (1 , task1 , load2 , estim21 , rec21)$
$\parallel load1\_0 := load1 - 1 \parallel estim12\_0 := estim12 + 1$
$\parallel C3\_0 := C3 - 1$
WHEN
$\lnot (Imbalance (load1 , estim12)) \land rec12 = TRUE \land rec21 = TRUE$
THEN $rec12\_0 := FALSE \parallel rec21\_0 := FALSE \parallel C3\_0 := 0$
WHEN
$\lnot (Imbalance (estim21 , load2)) \land rec21 = TRUE \land rec12 = TRUE$
THEN $rec21\_0 := FALSE \parallel rec12\_0 := FALSE \parallel C3\_0 := 0$
WHEN
$\lnot Guard\_Commit\_12 \land \lnot Guard\_Commit\_21$
$\land \lnot Guard\_Bal\_Load\_Down\_21$
$\land \lnot Guard\_Bal\_Load\_Up\_12$
$\land \lnot Guard\_Release\_Nodes\_12 \land \lnot Guard\_Release\_Nodes\_21$
THEN   skip
END
END

DEFINITIONS

$Imbalance (x , y) \; \hat{=} \; x < top \land y \geq top \lor (x > top \land y \leq top) \; ;$
$BadlyEstimated (x , y) \; \hat{=} \; x > top \land y < top \lor (x < top \land y > top) \lor$
$(x = top \land y \neq top) \lor (x \neq top \land y = top) \; ;$
$Guard\_Commit\_12 \; \hat{=}$
$Imbalance (load1 , estim12) \lor BadlyEstimated (load1 , estim21) \lor rec12 = TRUE$
$\land rec21 = FALSE \; ;$
$Guard\_Commit\_21 \; \hat{=}$
$Imbalance (estim21 , load2) \lor BadlyEstimated (load2 , estim12) \lor rec21 = TRUE$
$\land rec12 = FALSE \; ;$
$Guard\_Bal\_Load\_Down\_21 \; \hat{=}$
$estim21 < top \land load2 \geq top \land rec21 = TRUE \land rec12 = TRUE \; ;$
$Guard\_Bal\_Load\_Up\_12 \; \hat{=}$
$estim12 \leq top \land load1 > top \land rec12 = TRUE \land rec21 = TRUE \; ;$
$Guard\_Release\_Nodes\_12 \; \hat{=}$
$\lnot (Imbalance (load1 , estim12)) \land rec12 = TRUE \land rec21 = TRUE \; ;$
$Guard\_Release\_Nodes\_21 \; \hat{=}$
$\lnot (Imbalance (estim21 , load2)) \land rec21 = TRUE \land rec12 = TRUE$

END

In the variant, $(2 - (C1 + C2)) + C3$, of the WHILE-loop we state that the system becomes more balanced each time the balancing actions *Bal_Loads_Down_21* and *Bal_Loads_Up_12* are executed. The variable *C3* represents this decreasing imbalance in the following way. It is decreased by one after each balancing operation and, furthermore, by three after the commitment between the nodes has been released. This is expressed in the machine *Functions*.

MACHINE   *Functions*
SEES
   Bool_TYPE

OPERATIONS

The variable *C3* is part of the loop variant for the load balancing algorithm. It records the decrease in the imbalance of the system during execution. When a commitment is released it is decreased by 3.

$C3 \longleftarrow$ *imbalance*(*load1* , *load2* , *top* , *estim12* , *estim21* , *rec12* , *rec21*) $\widehat{=}$

   PRE   *load1* $\in \mathbb{N} \wedge$ *load2* $\in \mathbb{N} \wedge$ *top* $\in \mathbb{N}_1$
         $\wedge$ *estim12* $\in \mathbb{N} \wedge$ *estim21* $\in \mathbb{N} \wedge$ *rec12* $\in BOOL \wedge$ *rec21* $\in BOOL$
   THEN
      IF   *load1* $>$ *top* $\wedge$ *load2* $\leq$ *top*   **THEN** $C3 := 3 + ($ *top* $-$ *load2* $)$
      ELSIF   *load1* $<$ *top* $\wedge$ *load2* $\geq$ *top*   **THEN** $C3 := 3 + ($ *top* $-$ *load1* $)$
      ELSIF $\neg$ (*load1* $=$ *estim21*) $\vee \neg$ (*load2* $=$ *estim12*)
         $\vee$ *rec12* $= TRUE \vee$ *rec21* $= TRUE$ **THEN** $C3 := 3$
      ELSE $C3 := 0$
      END
   END

END

   The 59 proof obligations generated for the machine *Proc_Guards2* form the enabledness condition for the global procedure *New_Load* in the machine refinement *Actions2*. Of these proof obligations only 10 could not be discharged automatically. The definition of the variant gives the extra rules needed to discharge these proof obligations.

7.7.3 Termination of Auxiliary Actions

The termination of the auxiliary actions *Commit* and *Release_Nodes* needs to be checked with Condition (S7) in order for *Actions2* to be a superposition refinement of *Actions1P*. This condition is checked within the B-Method by first creating a machine *No_Actions1P* to represent the non-existence of the auxiliary actions of *Actions2* in *Actions1P*.

MACHINE   *No_Actions1P* (*top*)
CONSTRAINTS
   top > 0

OPERATIONS

Aux_Actions_Term models the termination of no auxiliary actions in *Actions1P*

$Aux\_Actions\_Term \quad \widehat{=} \quad$ skip

END

Furthermore, we create the implementation machine *New_Actions2* to model the termination of the auxiliary actions in *Actions2*. The same invariant and variant are used here as previously when checking the guards of the global procedures.

IMPLEMENTATION   *New_Actions2*

REFINES

No_Actions1P

SEES

Bool_TYPE , *Functions*

IMPORTS

Aux_Actions2

Aux_Actions2 contains the auxiliary actions of *Actions2*

OPERATIONS

$Aux\_Actions\_Term \quad \widehat{=}$
   VAR   *load1* , *load2* , *estim12* , *estim21* , *rec12* , *rec21* , *C1* , *C2* , *C3*   **IN**

The initialisation of *Actions2*:

   $load1 := 0 \; ; \; load2 := 0 \; ; \; estim12 := 0 \; ; \; estim21 := 0 \; ;$
   $rec12 := FALSE \; ; \; rec21 := FALSE \; ;$

C1 is 1 if *rec12* has the value *TRUE*, and 0 otherwise
C2 is 1 if *rec21* has the value *TRUE*, and 0 otherwise
C3 models the imbalance among the loads
These variables are updated each time the loop is executed

   $C1 \longleftarrow BTS\_BOOL \; (\; rec12 \;) \; ; \; C2 \longleftarrow BTS\_BOOL \; (\; rec21 \;) \; ;$
   $C3 \longleftarrow imbalance \; (\; load1 \; , load2 \; , top \; , estim12 \; , estim21 \; , rec12 \; , rec21 \;) \; ;$

   WHILE $Guard\_Commit\_12 \; \vee \; Guard\_Commit\_21 \; \vee$
      $Guard\_Release\_Nodes\_12 \; \vee \; Guard\_Release\_Nodes\_21$ **DO**

Execute as long as one of the auxiliary actions are enabled

   $estim12 \; , estim21 \; , rec12 \; , rec21 \; , C3 \longleftarrow$
   $Aux\_Actions \; (\; load1 \; , load2 \; , estim12 \; , estim21 \; , rec12 \; , rec21 \; , top \; , C3 \;) \; ;$
   $C1 \longleftarrow BTS\_BOOL \; (\; rec12 \;) \; ; \; C2 \longleftarrow BTS\_BOOL \; (\; rec21 \;)$
   INVARIANT

The invariant of *Actions2*:

$load1 \in \mathbb{N} \wedge load2 \in \mathbb{N}$
$\wedge\ estim12 \in \mathbb{N} \wedge estim21 \in \mathbb{N} \wedge rec12 \in BOOL \wedge rec21 \in BOOL$
$\wedge\ (\ rec12 = TRUE \Rightarrow load2 = estim12\ )$
$\wedge\ (\ rec21 = TRUE \Rightarrow load1 = estim21\ )$

The properties of the variant, as explained above:

$\wedge\ C1 \in \mathbb{N} \wedge C2 \in \mathbb{N} \wedge C3 \in \mathbb{N}$
$\wedge\ (\ rec12 = TRUE \Rightarrow C1 = 1\ ) \wedge (\ rec12 = FALSE \Rightarrow C1 = 0\ )$
$\wedge\ (\ rec21 = TRUE \Rightarrow C2 = 1\ ) \wedge (\ rec21 = FALSE \Rightarrow C2 = 0\ )$
VARIANT

The variant decreases each time the loop is executed:
$(2 - (C1 + C2))$ decreases each time a node becomes committed and
$C3$ decreases at release of commitment between two nodes

$2 - (\ C1 + C2\ ) + C3$
END
END

DEFINITIONS
Imbalance $(\ x, y\ ) \ \hat{=} \ x < top \wedge y \geq top \vee (\ x > top \wedge y \leq top\ )$ **;**
BadlyEstimated $(\ x, y\ ) \ \hat{=} \ x > top \wedge y < top \vee (\ x < top \wedge y > top\ ) \vee$
    $(\ x = top \wedge y \neq top\ ) \vee (\ x \neq top \wedge y = top\ )$ **;**
Guard_Commit_12 $\ \hat{=}$
    Imbalance $(\ load1, estim12\ ) \vee BadlyEstimated (\ load1, estim21\ ) \vee rec12 = TRUE$
    $\wedge\ rec21 = FALSE$ **;**
Guard_Commit_21 $\ \hat{=}$
    Imbalance $(\ estim21, load2\ ) \vee BadlyEstimated (\ load2, estim12\ ) \vee rec21 = TRUE$
    $\wedge\ rec12 = FALSE$ **;**
Guard_Release_Nodes_12 $\ \hat{=}$
    $\neg\ (\ Imbalance\ (\ load1, estim12\ )\ ) \wedge rec12 = TRUE \wedge rec21 = TRUE$ **;**
Guard_Release_Nodes_21 $\ \hat{=}$
    $\neg\ (\ Imbalance\ (\ estim21, load2\ )\ ) \wedge rec21 = TRUE \wedge rec12 = TRUE$

END

The non-deterministic choice of the auxiliary operations in the refinement machine *Actions2* is given in the machine *Aux_Actions2* below.

MACHINE   *Aux_Actions2*
SEES

Bool_TYPE

OPERATIONS

Aux_Actions represents the non-deterministic choice of all the auxiliary actions in the refined machine *Actions2*

---

estim12_0 , *estim21_0* , *rec12_0* , *rec21_0* , *C3_0* ⟵
Aux_Actions(*load1* , *load2* , *estim12* , *estim21* , *rec12* , *rec21* , *top* , *C3*)   ≙

    PRE   *load1* ∈ ℕ ∧ *load2* ∈ ℕ ∧ *estim12* ∈ ℕ ∧ *estim21* ∈ ℕ
        ∧ *rec12* ∈ *BOOL* ∧ *rec21* ∈ *BOOL* ∧ *top* ∈ ℕ$_1$ ∧ *C3* ∈ ℕ
    THEN

Commit_12 ⏮ *Commit_21* ⏮ *Release_Nodes_12* ⏮ *Release_Nodes_21*

        SELECT
            Imbalance (*load1* , *estim12*) ∨ *BadlyEstimated* (*load1* , *estim21*)
            ∨ *rec12* = *TRUE* ∧ *rec21* = *FALSE*
        THEN   *estim21_0* := *load1* ∥ *rec21_0* := *TRUE*
        WHEN
            Imbalance (*estim21* , *load2*) ∨ *BadlyEstimated* (*load2* , *estim12*)
            ∨ *rec21* = *TRUE* ∧ *rec12* = *FALSE*
        THEN   *estim12_0* := *load2* ∥ *rec12_0* := *TRUE*
        WHEN
            ¬ (*Imbalance* (*load1* , *estim12*)) ∧ *rec12* = *TRUE* ∧ *rec21* = *TRUE*
        THEN   *rec12_0* := *FALSE* ∥ *rec21_0* := *FALSE* ∥ *C3_0* := 0
        WHEN
            ¬ (*Imbalance* (*estim21* , *load2*)) ∧ *rec21* = *TRUE* ∧ *rec12* = *TRUE*
        THEN   *rec21_0* := *FALSE* ∥ *rec12_0* := *FALSE* ∥ *C3_0* := 0
        END
      END
  DEFINITIONS
  Imbalance (*x* , *y*) ≙ *x* < *top* ∧ *y* ≥ *top* ∨ (*x* > *top* ∧ *y* ≤ *top*) **;**
  BadlyEstimated (*x* , *y*) ≙ *x* > *top* ∧ *y* < *top* ∨ (*x* < *top* ∧ *y* > *top*) ∨
    (*x* = *top* ∧ *y* ≠ *top*) ∨ (*x* ≠ *top* ∧ *y* = *top*)
END

The 28 proof obligations generated by the B-Toolkit imply the Condition (S7) in the superposition rule. By also discharging these proof obligations we have proved the superposition step completely. For this construct only three of the generated proof obligations could not be discharged automatically. According to the definition of the variant they are, however, trivially true and can be discharged with the help of the interprover.

7.7.4 Introducing New Procedures

The auxiliary actions *Commit_12* and *Release_Nodes_12* of node 1 assign variables of both node 1 and node 2, i.e., the variables with the first index 1 and 2. Since the actions of each node in a distributed system should only assign variables of the node

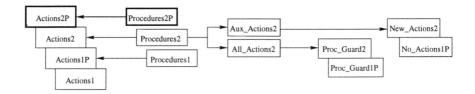

Fig. 7.12. Overview of the Derivation After the new Procedures are Introduced in the Second Refinement Step

itself, we create two new procedures *Trans_Load* and *Release_Refl* for each node in the network. The procedure *Trans_Load* models a link for sending loads between nodes, while the procedure *Release_Refl* synchronises the release of a commitment between two nodes. All the assignments to the variables of for example node 2 in the auxiliary actions *Commit_12* and *Release_Nodes_12* of node 1 are moved to the procedures *Trans_Load_2P* and *Release_Refl_2P*, respectively. These assignments are replaced by calls to the procedures in the corresponding actions. Hence, we have taken yet another step towards a distributed system.

The actions are now given in the machine *Actions2P* and the procedures in the machine *Procedures2P*. Fig. 7.12 shows how these machines are related to the previously developed system.

REFINEMENT   *Actions2P*

REFINES

  Actions2

SEES

  Bool_TYPE , *TaskProcessing*

INCLUDES

  Procedures2P

VARIABLES

  load1 , *load2* , *task1* , *task2* , *estim12* , *estim21* , *rec12* , *rec21*

INVARIANT

  load1 $\in \mathbb{N} \wedge$ *load2* $\in \mathbb{N} \wedge$ *task1* $\in$ *TASKS* $\wedge$ *task2* $\in$ *TASKS*
  $\wedge$ *estim12* $\in \mathbb{N} \wedge$ *estim21* $\in \mathbb{N} \wedge$ *rec12* $\in$ *BOOL* $\wedge$ *rec21* $\in$ *BOOL*
  $\wedge$ (*rec12* = *TRUE* $\Rightarrow$ *load2* = *estim12*)
  $\wedge$ (*rec21* = *TRUE* $\Rightarrow$ *load1* = *estim21*)

INITIALISATION

  load1 , *load2* := 0 , 0 || *task1* :$\in$ *TASKS* || *task2* :$\in$ *TASKS*
  || *estim12* , *estim21* := 0 , 0 || *rec12* , *rec21* := *FALSE* , *FALSE*

OPERATIONS

  New_Load_1P(*ll*) $\hat{=}$
    PRE   *ll* $\in \mathbb{N}$ **THEN**
      SELECT   *rec12* = *FALSE* $\wedge$ *rec21* = *FALSE* $\wedge$ *ll* ≥ 0
      THEN   *load1* := *ll*

END
END ;
New_Load_2P(ll) $\hat{=}$
PRE $ll \in \mathbb{N}$ **THEN**
   SELECT   *rec12 = FALSE* $\wedge$ *rec21 = FALSE* $\wedge$ *ll* $\geq$ *0*
   THEN   *load2 := ll*
   END
END ;

Commit_12 transfers the load of node 1 to node 2 for updating via procedure
Trans_Load_2P

Commit_12 $\hat{=}$
  SELECT
    Imbalance (load1 , estim12) $\vee$ *BadlyEstimated (load1 , estim21)*
    $\vee$ *rec12 = TRUE*
  THEN   *estim21 , rec21* $\longleftarrow$ *Trans_Load_2P (1 , load1 , rec21)*
  END ;
Commit_21 $\hat{=}$
  SELECT
    Imbalance (estim21 , load2) $\vee$ *BadlyEstimated (load2 , estim12)*
    $\vee$ *rec21 = TRUE*
  THEN   *estim12 , rec12* $\longleftarrow$ *Trans_Load_1P (2 , load2 , rec12)*
  END ;
Bal_Loads_Down_21 $\hat{=}$
  SELECT   *estim21 < top* $\wedge$ *load2* $\geq$ *top* $\wedge$ *rec21 = TRUE*
  THEN
    load1 , estim12 $\longleftarrow$ *Trans_Task_1P (2 , task2 , load1 , estim12 , rec12)* ;
    load2 := load2 $-$ *1* ; *estim21 := estim21* $+$ *1*
  END ;
Bal_Loads_Up_12 $\hat{=}$
  SELECT   *estim12* $\leq$ *top* $\wedge$ *load1 > top* $\wedge$ *rec12 = TRUE*
  THEN
    load2 , estim21 $\longleftarrow$ *Trans_Task_2P (1 , task1 , load2 , estim21 , rec21)* ;
    load1 := load1 $-$ *1* ; *estim12 := estim12* $+$ *1*
  END ;

Release_Nodes_12 releases the commitment in node 1 and requests node 2 to do the same
via procedure *Release_Refl_2P*

Release_Nodes_12 $\hat{=}$
  SELECT $\neg$ *(Imbalance (load1 , estim12))* $\wedge$ *rec12 = TRUE*
  THEN   *rec12 := FALSE* ; *rec21* $\longleftarrow$ *Release_Refl_2P (1 , rec21)*
  END ;
Release_Nodes_21 $\hat{=}$
  SELECT $\neg$ *(Imbalance (estim21 , load2))* $\wedge$ *rec21 = TRUE*
  THEN   *rec21 := FALSE* ; *rec12* $\longleftarrow$ *Release_Refl_1P (2 , rec12)*
  END ;

Exit_Cond $\widehat{=}$
    SELECT
        $\neg$ *Guard_Commit_12* $\wedge$ $\neg$ *Guard_Commit_21*
        $\wedge$ $\neg$ *Guard_Bal_Load_Down_21*
        $\wedge$ $\neg$ *Guard_Bal_Load_Up_12*
        $\wedge$ $\neg$ *Guard_Release_Nodes_12* $\wedge$ $\neg$ *Guard_Release_Nodes_21*
    THEN   skip
    END

DEFINITIONS

Imbalance (x, y) $\widehat{=}$ $x < top \wedge y \geq top \vee (x > top \wedge y \leq top)$;
BadlyEstimated (x, y) $\widehat{=}$ $x > top \wedge y < top \vee (x < top \wedge y > top) \vee$
$(x = top \wedge y \neq top) \vee (x \neq top \wedge y = top)$;
Guard_Commit_12 $\widehat{=}$
    Imbalance (*load1* , *estim12*) $\vee$ *BadlyEstimated* (*load1* , *estim21*) $\vee$ *rec12* = *TRUE*
    $\wedge$ *rec21* = *FALSE* ;
Guard_Commit_21 $\widehat{=}$
    Imbalance (*estim21* , *load2*) $\vee$ *BadlyEstimated* (*load2* , *estim12*) $\vee$ *rec21* = *TRUE*
    $\wedge$ *rec12* = *FALSE* ;
Guard_Bal_Load_Down_21 $\widehat{=}$
    estim21 < *top* $\wedge$ *load2* $\geq$ *top* $\wedge$ *rec21* = *TRUE* $\wedge$ *rec12* = *TRUE* ;
Guard_Bal_Load_Up_12 $\widehat{=}$
    estim12 $\leq$ *top* $\wedge$ *load1* > *top* $\wedge$ *rec12* = *TRUE* $\wedge$ *rec21* = *TRUE* ;
Guard_Release_Nodes_12 $\widehat{=}$
    $\neg$ (*Imbalance* (*load1* , *estim12*)) $\wedge$ *rec12* = *TRUE* $\wedge$ *rec21* = *TRUE* ;
Guard_Release_Nodes_21 $\widehat{=}$
    $\neg$ (*Imbalance* (*estim21* , *load2*)) $\wedge$ *rec21* = *TRUE* $\wedge$ *rec12* = *TRUE*

END

The new procedures *Trans_Load* and *Release_Refl* are added to the procedures in *Procedures2* to form the machine *Procedures2P*.

MACHINE   *Procedures2P*

SEES

Bool_TYPE , *TaskProcessing*

OPERATIONS

load1_0 , *estim12_0* $\longleftarrow$ *Trans_Task_1P*(*mm* , *taskm* , *load1* , *estim12* , *rec12*) $\widehat{=}$
    PRE   *mm* = 2 $\wedge$ *taskm* $\in$ *TASKS* $\wedge$ *load1* $\in$ $\mathbb{N}$ $\wedge$ *estim12* $\in$ $\mathbb{N}$ $\wedge$ *rec12* $\in$ *BOOL*
    THEN
        SELECT   *rec12* = *TRUE*
        THEN
            Process_Task_1 (*taskm*) $\|$
            load1_0 := *load1* + 1 $\|$ *estim12_0* := *estim12* $-$ 1
        END
    END ;
load2_0 , *estim21_0* $\longleftarrow$ *Trans_Task_2P*(*mm* , *taskm* , *load2* , *estim21* , *rec21*) $\widehat{=}$
    PRE   *mm* = 1 $\wedge$ *taskm* $\in$ *TASKS* $\wedge$ *load2* $\in$ $\mathbb{N}$ $\wedge$ *estim21* $\in$ $\mathbb{N}$ $\wedge$ *rec21* $\in$ *BOOL*
    THEN
        SELECT   *rec21* = *TRUE*
        THEN
            Process_Task_2 (*taskm*) $\|$
            load2_0 := *load2* + 1 $\|$ *estim21_0* := *estim21* $-$ 1

END
END ;

Trans_Load_1P receives the load of node $mm(= 2)$ and updates the estimate of the load of the sender while registering that the sender has committed to node 1 ($rec12 := TRUE$)

$estim12\_0$, $rec12\_0 \longleftarrow Trans\_Load\_1P(mm , loadm , rec12)$ $\hateq$
    PRE $mm = 2 \wedge loadm \in \mathbb{N} \wedge rec12 \in BOOL$ **THEN**
        SELECT $rec12 = FALSE$
        THEN $estim12\_0 := loadm \parallel rec12\_0 := TRUE$
        END
    END ;
$estim21\_0$, $rec21\_0 \longleftarrow Trans\_Load\_2P(mm , loadm , rec21)$ $\hateq$
    PRE $mm = 1 \wedge loadm \in \mathbb{N} \wedge rec21 \in BOOL$ **THEN**
        SELECT $rec21 = FALSE$
        THEN $estim21\_0 := loadm \parallel rec21\_0 := TRUE$
        END
    END ;

Release_Refl releases the commitment to the sender $mm(= 2)$ by assigning $rec12$ to *FALSE*

$rec12\_0 \longleftarrow Release\_Refl\_1P(mm , rec12)$ $\hateq$
    PRE $mm = 2 \wedge rec12 \in BOOL$ **THEN**
        SELECT $rec12 = TRUE$
        THEN $rec12\_0 := FALSE$
        END
    END ;
$rec21\_0 \longleftarrow Release\_Refl\_2P(mm , rec21)$ $\hateq$
    PRE $mm = 1 \wedge rec21 \in BOOL$ **THEN**
        SELECT $rec21 = TRUE$
        THEN $rec21\_0 := FALSE$
        END
    END
END

Expanding the procedure calls in the actions *Commit* and *Release_Nodes* in *Actions2P* will result in the operations *Commit* and *Release_Nodes* in *Actions2*. Hence, this step involves merely a re-writing of the machine. All the 30 proof obligations generated in this step were automatically discharged.

7.8 Refinement Step 3: Distributing the Estimates

In the machine *Actions2P* we refer to variables of node 2, *estim21* and *rec21*, in the operation *Commit_12* of node 1. Since an operation of a node should only refer to its own variables in a distributed algorithm, we need to introduce a mechanism for

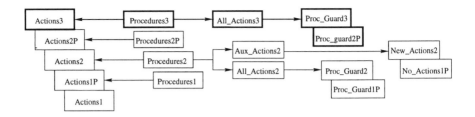

Fig. 7.13. Overview of the Derivation After the Third Refinement Step

a node to know what estimates its neighbours have about it without referencing the estimate of that neighbouring node. In the third superposition step we, therefore, add the variables *oldload12, oldload21, send12* and *send21*. The variable *oldload12* gives the value of the load of node 1 last sent to node 2, i.e. the estimate node 2 has about *load1*. The boolean variable *send12* has the value *TRUE*, if the value of *load1* has been sent to node 2 and node 1 is committed to change loads with node 2. When the commitment is released *send12* is assigned the value *FALSE*. The variables *oldload21* and *send21* are interpreted similarly. This refinement step is given in the machines *Actions3* and *Procedures3* below. Their relations to the previously developed machines are shown in the overview in Fig. 7.13. The enabledness of the procedure guards are checked via the machines *Proc_Guards2P*, *Proc_Guards3* and *All_Actions3*.

REFINEMENT   *Actions3*

REFINES

　Actions2P

SEES

　Bool_TYPE , *TaskProcessing*

INCLUDES

　Procedures3

VARIABLES

　load1 , *load2* , *task1* , *task2* , *estim12* , *estim21* , *rec12* , *rec21* ,
　oldload12 , *oldload21* , *send12* , *send21*

---

oldload12 contains the value of *load1* latest sent to node 2, i.e. the estimate node 2 has about *load1*

send12 has the value *TRUE* if the value of *load1* has been sent to node 2 and node 1 is comitted to node 2, when the nodes 1 and 2 are not committed it has the value *FALSE*

INVARIANT

　$load1 \in \mathbb{N} \wedge load2 \in \mathbb{N} \wedge task1 \in TASKS \wedge task2 \in TASKS$
　$\wedge\ estim12 \in \mathbb{N} \wedge estim21 \in \mathbb{N} \wedge rec12 \in BOOL \wedge rec21 \in BOOL$
　$\wedge\ oldload12 \in \mathbb{N} \wedge oldload21 \in \mathbb{N} \wedge send12 \in BOOL \wedge send21 \in BOOL$
　$\wedge\ (\ rec12 = TRUE \Rightarrow load2 = estim12\ )$

$\wedge$ ($rec21 = TRUE \Rightarrow load1 = estim21$)
$\wedge$ ($send12 = TRUE \Rightarrow oldload12 = load1$)
$\wedge$ ($send21 = TRUE \Rightarrow oldload21 = load2$)

When node 1 is committed to node 2, the load of node 1, *load1*, is the same as the load last sent from node 1 to node 2, *oldload12*

$\wedge$ ($send12 = TRUE \Rightarrow rec21 = TRUE$) $\wedge$ ($rec21 = TRUE \Rightarrow send12 = TRUE$)
$\wedge$ ($send21 = TRUE \Rightarrow rec12 = TRUE$) $\wedge$ ($rec12 = TRUE \Rightarrow send21 = TRUE$)

---

send12 is a mirror of *rec21* and *send21* is a mirror of *rec12*

$\wedge$ $oldload12 = estim21$ $\wedge$ $oldload21 = estim12$

---

oldload12 and *estim21* always correspond to each other, as well as *oldload21* and *estim12*

INITIALISATION

$load1$, $load2 := 0 , 0$ $\parallel$ $task1 :\in TASKS$ $\parallel$ $task2 :\in TASKS$
$\parallel$ $estim12$, $estim21 := 0 , 0$ $\parallel$ $rec12$, $rec21 := FALSE , FALSE$
$\parallel$ $oldload12$, $oldload21 := 0 , 0$ $\parallel$ $send12$, $send21 := FALSE , FALSE$

Initially $oldload12$ and $oldload21$ are 0 and $send12$ and $send21$ have the value *FALSE*, since no nodes are committed

---

OPERATIONS

New_Load_1P assigns a new load to node 1, if node 1 is not committed to another node

---

$New\_Load\_1P(ll)$ $\widehat{=}$
    PRE $ll \in \mathbb{N}$ **THEN**
        SELECT $rec12 = FALSE \wedge send12 = FALSE \wedge ll \geq 0$
        THEN $load1 := ll$
        END
    END ;
$New\_Load\_2P(ll)$ $\widehat{=}$
    PRE $ll \in \mathbb{N}$ **THEN**
        SELECT $rec21 = FALSE \wedge send21 = FALSE \wedge ll \geq 0$
        THEN $load2 := ll$
        END
    END ;

Commit_12 sends *load1* to node 2 to update the load estimates in node 2 and register this load as sent. Furthermore, it commits node 1 to node 2. *Commit_12* is enabled in case of an imbalance, a too bad estimate in node 2 or a commitment of node 2 to node 1

Commit_12 $\;\widehat{=}$
> **SELECT**
>> *Imbalance (load1 , estim12)* $\lor$ *BadlyEstimated (load1 , oldload12)*
>> $\lor$ *rec12 = TRUE* $\land$ *send12 = FALSE*
>
> **THEN**
>> *estim21 , rec21* $\longleftarrow$ *Trans_Load_2P (1 , load1 , rec21)* ;
>> *oldload12 := load1* ; *send12 := TRUE*
>
> **END** ;

Commit_21 $\;\widehat{=}$
> **SELECT**
>> *Imbalance (estim21 , load2)* $\lor$ *BadlyEstimated (load2 , oldload21)*
>> $\lor$ *rec21 = TRUE* $\land$ *send21 = FALSE*
>
> **THEN**
>> *estim12 , rec12* $\longleftarrow$ *Trans_Load_1P (2 , load2 , rec12)* ;
>> *oldload21 := load2* ; *send21 := TRUE*
>
> **END** ;

Bal_Loads_Down_21 sends a task from node 2 to node 1 and updates the loads and the estimates in nodes 1 and 2, if the nodes are committed to each other and there is an imbalance between them

---

Bal_Loads_Down_21 $\;\widehat{=}$
> **SELECT**   *estim21 < top* $\land$ *load2* $\geq$ *top* $\land$ *rec21 = TRUE* $\land$ *send21 = TRUE*
> **THEN**
>> *load1 , estim12 , oldload12* $\longleftarrow$
>> *Trans_Task_1P (2 , task2 , load1 , estim12 , rec12 , oldload12 , send12)* ;
>> *load2 := load2 − 1* ; *estim21 := estim21 + 1* ;
>> *oldload21 := oldload21 − 1*
>
> **END** ;

Bal_Loads_Up_12 $\;\widehat{=}$
> **SELECT**   *estim12* $\leq$ *top* $\land$ *load1 > top* $\land$ *rec12 = TRUE* $\land$ *send12 = TRUE*
> **THEN**
>> *load2 , estim21 , oldload21* $\longleftarrow$
>> *Trans_Task_2P (1 , task1 , load2 , estim21 , rec21 , oldload21 , send21)* ;
>> *load1 := load1 − 1* ; *estim12 := estim12 + 1* ;
>> *oldload12 := oldload12 − 1*
>
> **END** ;

Release_Nodes_12 releases the commitment synchronously between nodes 1 and 2, when there is no imbalance between these committed nodes

---

Release_Nodes_12 $\;\widehat{=}$
> **SELECT** $\neg$ *(Imbalance (load1 , estim12))* $\land$ *rec12 = TRUE* $\land$ *send12 = TRUE*
> **THEN**
>> *rec12 , send12 := FALSE , FALSE* ;
>> *rec21 , send21* $\longleftarrow$ *Release_Refl_2P (1 , rec21 , send21)*
>
> **END** ;

$Release\_Nodes\_21 \quad \hat{=}$
> **SELECT** $\quad \neg\,(\,Imbalance\,(\,estim21\,,\,load2\,)\,)\,\wedge\,rec21 = TRUE \wedge send21 = TRUE$
> **THEN**
> > $rec21\,,\,send21 := FALSE\,,\,FALSE\,\textbf{;}$
> > $rec12\,,\,send12 \longleftarrow Release\_Refl\_1P\,(\,2\,,\,rec12\,,\,send12\,)$
> **END ;**

Exit_Cond represents the exit condition

$Exit\_Cond \quad \hat{=}$
> **SELECT**
> > $\neg\,Guard\_Commit\_12 \wedge \neg\,Guard\_Commit\_21$
> > $\wedge \neg\,Guard\_Bal\_Load\_Down\_21$
> > $\wedge \neg\,Guard\_Bal\_Load\_Up\_12$
> > $\wedge \neg\,Guard\_Release\_Nodes\_12 \wedge \neg\,Guard\_Release\_Nodes\_21$
> **THEN** skip
> **END**

DEFINITIONS

$Imbalance\,(\,x\,,y\,) \quad \hat{=} \quad x < top \wedge y \ge top \vee (\,x > top \wedge y \le top\,)\,\textbf{;}$
$BadlyEstimated\,(\,x\,,y\,) \quad \hat{=} \quad x > top \wedge y < top \vee (\,x < top \wedge y > top\,) \vee$
$\quad (\,x = top \wedge y \ne top\,) \vee (\,x \ne top \wedge y = top\,)\,\textbf{;}$
$Guard\_Commit\_12 \quad \hat{=}$
$\quad Imbalance\,(\,load1\,,\,estim12\,) \vee BadlyEstimated\,(\,load1\,,\,oldload12\,)$
$\quad \vee\,rec12 = TRUE \wedge send12 = FALSE \wedge rec21 = FALSE\,\textbf{;}$
$Guard\_Commit\_21 \quad \hat{=}$
$\quad Imbalance\,(\,estim21\,,\,load2\,) \vee BadlyEstimated\,(\,load2\,,\,oldload21\,)$
$\quad \vee\,rec21 = TRUE \wedge send21 = FALSE \wedge rec12 = FALSE\,\textbf{;}$
$Guard\_Bal\_Load\_Down\_21 \quad \hat{=} \quad estim21 < top \wedge load2 \ge top \wedge rec21 = TRUE$
$\quad \wedge send21 = TRUE \wedge rec12 = TRUE \wedge send12 = TRUE\,\textbf{;}$
$Guard\_Bal\_Load\_Up\_12 \quad \hat{=} \quad estim12 \le top \wedge load1 > top \wedge rec12 = TRUE$
$\quad \wedge send12 = TRUE \wedge rec21 = TRUE \wedge send21 = TRUE\,\textbf{;}$
$Guard\_Release\_Nodes\_12 \quad \hat{=} \quad \neg\,(\,Imbalance\,(\,load1\,,\,estim12\,)\,) \wedge rec12 = TRUE$
$\quad \wedge send12 = TRUE \wedge rec21 = TRUE \wedge send21 = TRUE\,\textbf{;}$
$Guard\_Release\_Nodes\_21 \quad \hat{=} \quad \neg\,(\,Imbalance\,(\,estim21\,,\,load2\,)\,) \wedge rec21 = TRUE$
$\quad \wedge send21 = TRUE \wedge rec12 = TRUE \wedge send12 = TRUE$

END

The variables $oldload12$ and $oldload21$ are initially assigned 0 and the variables $send12$ and $send21$ are initially *FALSE*. During the execution the variables $oldload12$ and $send12$ reflect the changes in the variables $estim21$ and $rec21$, respectively. We strengthen the invariant of *Actions2P* to include this relation between the new variables ($oldload$, $send$) and the old ones ($load$, $estim$, rec) considering that $E = \{(1,2)\}$. The variable $oldload\_ij$ is always updated when the nodes i and j are committed:

$$(\forall i,j.\ i,j \in V \wedge ((i,j) \in E \vee (j,i) \in E).$$
$$send\_ij = TRUE \Rightarrow oldload\_ij = load\_i).$$

Furthermore, the variables *send* and *rec* correspond to each other in the following way

$$(\forall i,j. \ i,j \in V \wedge ((i,j) \in E \vee (j,i) \in E). \ send\_ij = rec\_ji),$$

and the variables *oldload* and *estim* as follows

$$(\forall i,j. \ i,j \in V \wedge ((i,j) \in E \vee (j,i) \in E). \ oldload\_ij = estim\_ji).$$

All the operations are updated to reflect the changes in the variables. The operations are modified only to refer to local variables, which for example means that operation *Commit_12* of node 1 only refers to variables of node 1, except for the parameters in the procedure call on *Trans_Load_2P*.

The local procedures are also changed to model the distribution of the estimation with the new variables *oldload* and *send*.

MACHINE   *Procedures3*

SEES

Bool_TYPE , *TaskProcessing*

OPERATIONS

Trans_Task_1P receives a task from node $mm (= 2)$ and updates its loads and estimates, if the nodes 1 and mm are committed

---

$load1\_0$, $estim12\_0$, $oldload12\_0 \longleftarrow$
$Trans\_Task\_1P(\ mm\ ,\ taskm\ ,\ load1\ ,\ estim12\ ,\ rec12\ ,\ oldload12\ ,\ send12\ )$ $\widehat{=}$
    PRE $mm = 2 \wedge taskm \in TASKS \wedge load1 \in \mathbb{N} \wedge estim12 \in \mathbb{N} \wedge rec12 \in BOOL$
        $\wedge\ oldload12 \in \mathbb{N} \wedge send12 \in BOOL$
    THEN
        SELECT $rec12 = TRUE \wedge send12 = TRUE$
        THEN
            $Process\_Task\_1\ (\ taskm\ )\ \|\ oldload12\_0 := oldload12 + 1$
            $\|\ load1\_0 := load1 + 1\ \|\ estim12\_0 := estim12 - 1$
        END
    END ;
$load2\_0$, $estim21\_0$, $oldload21\_0 \longleftarrow$
$Trans\_Task\_2P(\ mm\ ,\ taskm\ ,\ load2\ ,\ estim21\ ,\ rec21\ ,\ oldload21\ ,\ send21\ )$ $\widehat{=}$
    PRE $mm = 1 \wedge taskm \in TASKS \wedge load2 \in \mathbb{N} \wedge estim21 \in \mathbb{N} \wedge rec21 \in BOOL$
        $\wedge\ oldload21 \in \mathbb{N} \wedge send21 \in BOOL$
    THEN
        SELECT $rec21 = TRUE \wedge send21 = TRUE$
        THEN
            $Process\_Task\_2\ (\ taskm\ )\ \|\ oldload21\_0 := oldload21 + 1$
            $\|\ load2\_0 := load2 + 1\ \|\ estim21\_0 := estim21 - 1$
        END
    END ;

Trans_Load_1P receives a load from node $mm(=2)$ and updates its estimate of this load, if the sender mm is not committed to node 1 upon the procedure call

$estim12\_0$, $rec12\_0 \longleftarrow$ *Trans_Load_1P*(mm , $loadm$, $rec12$) $\hat{=}$
   PRE $mm = 2 \wedge loadm \in \mathbb{N} \wedge rec12 \in BOOL$ **THEN**
      SELECT $rec12 = FALSE$
      THEN $estim12\_0 := loadm$ $\|$ $rec12\_0 := TRUE$
      END
   END ;
$estim21\_0$, $rec21\_0 \longleftarrow$ *Trans_Load_2P*(mm , $loadm$, $rec21$) $\hat{=}$
   PRE $mm = 1 \wedge loadm \in \mathbb{N} \wedge rec21 \in BOOL$ **THEN**
      SELECT $rec21 = FALSE$
      THEN $estim21\_0 := loadm$ $\|$ $rec21\_0 := TRUE$
      END
   END ;

Release_Refl_1P releases the commitment between nodes 1 and $mm(=2)$

$rec12\_0$, $send12\_0 \longleftarrow$ *Release_Refl_1P*(mm , $rec12$, $send12$) $\hat{=}$
   PRE $mm = 2 \wedge rec12 \in BOOL \wedge send12 \in BOOL$ **THEN**
      SELECT $rec12 = TRUE \wedge send12 = TRUE$
      THEN $rec12\_0 := FALSE$ $\|$ $send12\_0 := FALSE$
      END
   END ;
$rec21\_0$, $send21\_0 \longleftarrow$ *Release_Refl_2P*(mm , $rec21$, $send21$) $\hat{=}$
   PRE $mm = 1 \wedge rec21 \in BOOL \wedge send21 \in BOOL$ **THEN**
      SELECT $rec21 = TRUE \wedge send21 = TRUE$
      THEN $rec21\_0 := FALSE$ $\|$ $send21\_0 := FALSE$
      END
   END
END

We can prove the Conditions (S1) - (S3) and (S5) in the superposition rule by proving the 42 proof obligations generated for the refinement *Actions3*. There are no auxiliary actions in this refinement step. Hence, the Conditions (S4) and (S7), concerning the refinement and the termination of the auxiliary actions, need not be proven here.

The guards of the global procedures are changed in this refinement step, such that we, for example, have *send12* instead of *rec21* and *oldload12* instead of *estim21* in the procedure *New_Load1P*. This change means that we would need to check the enabledness of the global procedures in Condition (S6). The change is, however, trivial since the invariant states that *(send12 ⇔ rec21)* and *(oldload12 = estim21)*. Thus, the guards of the global procedures *New_Load* in the machine *Actions2P* are equivalent to the corresponding ones in the machine *Actions3*. We have proved this condition using the B-Toolkit by creating similar machines as in the previous step. The step generated 75 proof obligations of which 63 could be discharged automatically. The rest could again be discharged with the interprover by adding the definition of the variant to the proof rules. We have omitted this part here, since it is similar to the previous step.

7.9 Decomposition of the Load Balancing Algorithm

In a distributed action system each action and procedure is local to a node referring only to variables of that node. The values of the variables of a node are only visible to other nodes by explicitly communicating them to that node via procedure calls. When embedding an action system within the B-Method a distributed algorithm consists of machines, where the operations in each machine refer to variables of one node. Several machines can belong to the same node.

Even though the load balancing algorithm, *Actions3* and *Procedures3*, that we have derived is distributed in action system sense, the operations of both nodes 1 and 2 are given in the same machine construct. Because of this we also have to declare the variables of both nodes in the machine *Actions3* and perform the changes to the state space in *Procedures3* with parameters. We can, however, decompose the system so that operations in a machine construct only refer to variables of one node and make the system explicitly distributed. The decomposition is the reverse procedure to the parallel composition of action systems, as explained in Chapter 5.

Let us now decompose the load balancing algorithm within the B-Method. If we included all procedures and actions of a node into one machine, we would have a cyclic reference between the machines of node 1 and node 2, since the actions of node 1 call the procedures of the neighbouring node 2 and vice versa. If we separate all the operations that represent local procedures of a node into one machine and all operations that represent actions and global procedures of a node into another machine, we avoid these cyclic references. We then have an action-machine and a procedure-machine for each node in the network. These machines will, however, both assign the same variables, which is not allowed within the B-Method. The solution to this is to create a third component for a node, a variable-machine. In this machine the variables are declared and given types. The variables are assigned via the operations in the variable-machine. All the assignments in the action-machine and the procedure-machine are replaced by calls to these operations. In the decomposed algorithm each node then controls itself and we have a decentralised control in the system. The overview of this decomposition is shown in Fig. 7.14.

We now reorganise the actions and the procedures in *Actions3* and *Procedures3* according to the description above. Here we have chosen to show only the machines of node 1. The machines of node 2 are similar.

MACHINE   *Node1_Actions (top)*

CONSTRAINTS

$top > 0$

The threshold *top* giving the preferable load of a process

SEES

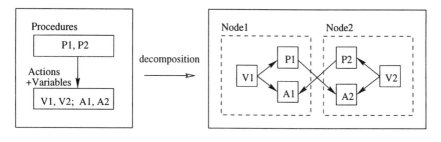

——► INCLUDES

Fig. 7.14. Decomposition of Action Systems Within B-Method

Bool_TYPE , *TaskProcessing*

INCLUDES

Node1_Var , *Node2_Proc*

The variables of node 1 and the procedures of the neighbouring node 2

OPERATIONS

The global procedures of node 1 assigning the variables of node 1 via assignment operations:

New_Load_1P(ll) $\hat{=}$
   PRE $ll \in \mathbb{N}$ **THEN**
     SELECT $rec12 = FALSE \wedge send12 = FALSE \wedge ll \geq 0$
     THEN   *load1_assign (ll)*
     END
   END ;

The actions of node 1 assigning the variables of node 1 via assignment operations:

Commit_12 $\hat{=}$
   SELECT
     Imbalance (load1 , estim12) $\vee$ *BadlyEstimated (load1 , oldload12)*
     $\vee$ *rec12 = TRUE* $\wedge$ *send12 = FALSE*
   THEN
     Trans_Load_2P (1 , load1) ||
     oldload12_assign (load1) || *send12_assign (TRUE)*
   END ;

Bal_Loads_Up_12 $\hat{=}$
   SELECT   *estim12* $\leq$ *top* $\wedge$ *load1* > *top* $\wedge$ *rec12* = *TRUE* $\wedge$ *send12* = *TRUE*
   THEN
      Trans_Task_2P (*1* , *task1*) $\|$ *load1_assign* (*load1* − *1*)
      $\|$ *estim12_assign* (*estim12* + *1*) $\|$ *oldload12_assign* (*oldload12* − *1*)
   END ;
Release_Nodes_12 $\hat{=}$
   SELECT $\neg$ (*Imbalance* (*load1* , *estim12*)) $\wedge$ *rec12* = *TRUE* $\wedge$ *send12* = *TRUE*
   THEN
      rec12_assign (*FALSE*) $\|$ *send12_assign* (*FALSE*) $\|$
      Release_Refl_2P (*1*)
   END ;

The exit condition of the action system of node 1:

Exit_Cond_1 $\hat{=}$
   SELECT
      $\neg$ *Guard_Commit_12* $\wedge$ $\neg$ *Guard_Bal_Load_Up_12*
      $\wedge$ $\neg$ *Guard_Release_Nodes_12*
   THEN   skip
   END

DEFINITIONS

Imbalance (*x* , *y*) $\hat{=}$ *x* < *top* $\wedge$ *y* $\geq$ *top* $\vee$ (*x* > *top* $\wedge$ *y* $\leq$ *top*) **;**
BadlyEstimated (*x* , *y*) $\hat{=}$ *x* > *top* $\wedge$ *y* < *top* $\vee$ (*x* < *top* $\wedge$ *y* > *top*) $\vee$
   (*x* = *top* $\wedge$ *y* $\neq$ *top*) $\vee$ (*x* $\neq$ *top* $\wedge$ *y* = *top*) **;**
Guard_Commit_12 $\hat{=}$
   Imbalance (*load1* , *estim12*) $\vee$ *BadlyEstimated* (*load1* , *oldload12*)
   $\vee$ *rec12* = *TRUE* $\wedge$ *send12* = *FALSE* $\wedge$ *rec21* = *FALSE* **;**
Guard_Bal_Load_Up_12 $\hat{=}$ *estim12* $\leq$ *top* $\wedge$ *load1* > *top* $\wedge$ *rec12* = *TRUE*
   $\wedge$ *send12* = *TRUE* $\wedge$ *rec21* = *TRUE* $\wedge$ *send21* = *TRUE* **;**
Guard_Release_Nodes_12 $\hat{=}$ $\neg$ (*Imbalance* (*load1* , *estim12*)) $\wedge$ *rec12* = *TRUE*
   $\wedge$ *send12* = *TRUE* $\wedge$ *rec21* = *TRUE* $\wedge$ *send21* = *TRUE*

END

We give the imported global variables as parameters of the action-machine, *Node1_Actions*, since this is the machine with the main operations of the node. We do not declare any variables in this machine, but we include them via the variable-machine, *Node1_Var*. The procedures of the neighbouring nodes, here *Node2_Proc*, should also be included. The global procedure *New_Load_1P* of node 1 is an operation of *Node1_Actions*, as well as the actions *Commit_12*, *Bal_Loads_Up_12* and *Release_Nodes_12* of node 1. These operations assign the variables via calls to the assignment operations in *Node1_Var*. Furthermore, the parameters only needed for changing the state space in *Actions3* and *Procedures3* are not included in the procedure calls here.

In the machine *Node1_Proc* the operations consist of the procedures of node 1: *Trans_Task_1P*, *Trans_Load_1P* and *Release_Refl_1P*. We include the variables of node 1 in this machine in the same way as in the machine *Node1_Actions*. The variables are also here assigned via assignment operations. Since the variables of node 1 are included in this machine, they need not be referenced and changed via procedure parameters as in *Procedures3*.

MACHINE   *Node1_Proc*
SEES
    Bool_TYPE , *TaskProcessing*
INCLUDES
    Node1_Var

The variables of node 1

OPERATIONS

The local procedures of node 1 assigning the variables of node 1 via assignment operations:

Trans_Task_1P(mm , taskm) $\hat{=}$
    PRE $mm = 2 \wedge taskm \in TASKS$ **THEN**
        SELECT $rec12 = TRUE \wedge send12 = TRUE$
        THEN
            Process_Task_1 (taskm) $\|$ *oldload12_assign (oldload12 + 1)*
            $\|$ *load1_assign (load1 + 1)* $\|$ *estim12_assign (estim12 − 1)*
        END
    END ;
Trans_Load_1P(mm , loadm) $\hat{=}$
    PRE $mm = 2 \wedge loadm \in \mathbb{N}$ **THEN**
        SELECT $rec12 = FALSE$
        THEN   *estim12_assign (loadm)* $\|$ *rec12_assign (TRUE)*
        END
    END ;
Release_Refl_1P(mm) $\hat{=}$
    PRE $mm = 2$ **THEN**
        SELECT $rec12 = TRUE \wedge send12 = TRUE$
        THEN   *rec12_assign (FALSE)* $\|$ *send12_assign (FALSE)*
        END
    END
END

The state space, i.e. the variables of nodes 1 and 2, is split up in the decomposition and therefore the actions and procedures of node 1 in *Node1_Actions* and *Node1_Procedures* only refer to variables of node 1, while the actions of node 2 in *Node2_Actions* and *Node2_Procedures* only refer to the variables of node 2. All the variables of node 1 are declared and initialised in the machine *Node1_Var*. Furthermore, each variable has an assignment operation and can only be assigned via this operation. The value to be assigned is given as a parameter of the operation.

MACHINE   *Node1_Var*

SEES

Bool_TYPE , *TaskProcessing*

VARIABLES

load1 , *task1* , *estim12* , *rec12* , *oldload12* , *send12*

The variables of node 1

INVARIANT

load1 $\in \mathbb{N}$ $\wedge$ *task1* $\in$ *TASKS* $\wedge$ *estim12* $\in \mathbb{N}$ $\wedge$ *rec12* $\in$ *BOOL*
$\wedge$ *oldload12* $\in \mathbb{N}$ $\wedge$ *send12* $\in$ *BOOL*

The types of the variables of node 1

INITIALISATION

load1 $:= 0$ $\|$ *task1* $:\in$ *TASKS* $\|$ *estim12* $:= 0$ $\|$ *rec12* $:=$ *FALSE*
$\|$ *oldload12* $:= 0$ $\|$ *send12* $:=$ *FALSE*

Initialisation of the variables of node 1

OPERATIONS

Assignments to the variables of node 1:

---

load1_assign(ll)	$\widehat{=}$	**PRE**	$ll \in \mathbb{N}$	**THEN**	*load1* $:= ll$	**END ;**
task1_assign(tt)	$\widehat{=}$	**PRE**	$tt \in$ *TASKS*	**THEN**	*task1* $:= tt$	**END ;**
estim12_assign(ll)	$\widehat{=}$	**PRE**	$ll \in \mathbb{N}$	**THEN**	*estim12* $:= ll$	**END ;**
oldload12_assign(ll)	$\widehat{=}$	**PRE**	$ll \in \mathbb{N}$	**THEN**	*oldload12* $:= ll$	**END ;**
rec12_assign(bb)	$\widehat{=}$	**PRE**	$bb \in$ *BOOL*	**THEN**	*rec12* $:= bb$	**END ;**
send12_assign(bb)	$\widehat{=}$	**PRE**	$bb \in$ *BOOL*	**THEN**	*send12* $:= bb$	**END**

END

The invariant contains only the type information here, because a single assignment operation does not establish the whole invariant of *Actions3*. However, since the decomposition step only involves re-arranging the variables and the operations of the system, all the operations and variables of node 1 in *Actions3* and *Procedures3* can also be found in *Node1_Actions*, *Node1_Proc* and *Node1_Var*. By creating these machines containing actions, procedures and variables for each node in the network we have developed a distributed load balancing algorithm using the B-Method.

7.10 Discussion

In this chapter we have derived a distributed load balancing algorithm from a non-distributed specification using the B-Method. The specification of the algorithm was given as an action system translated into an abstract machine specification. The algorithm was then refined in three steps within the B-Method. The refinement steps were constructed in such a way that the proof obligations generated from them corresponded to the conditions of the superposition rule within the action systems framework. In the first step of the derivation we distributed the loads by introducing procedures to the system. As the following step we added an estimation mechanism using the superposition refinement. When proving that step we needed to introduce two extra constructs within the B-Method: one implementation machine for checking the enabledness of the global procedures and another for checking the termination of the auxiliary actions. The computation in the auxiliary actions was distributed by introducing more procedures. As a final superposition step we added a new mechanism to keep track of the estimates of the neighbours. Since we did not introduce any auxiliary actions in this step, we only needed to create one extra B construct, the one for checking the enabledness of the global procedures, when proving the last superposition step using the B-Method. An overview of the derivation was given in Fig. 7.13. By decomposing the resulting algorithm so that each machine contains operations and refers to variables of only one node, we have reached a distributed load balancing algorithm within the B-Method.

Using the B-Toolkit as a mechanical aid to prove the superposition refinement of a system gives us some advantages compared to performing the refinement steps manually. It is easier to detect errors in the algorithm, as well as inadequacies in the invariant. These shortcomings are usually detected when studying the proof obligations that cannot be automatically proved. Additionally, using the autoprover in the B-Toolkit for the superposition proofs gives us more confidence in these proofs.

There are, however, also drawbacks when using the B-Method for deriving action systems. The substitutions allowed in the specifications and refinements are very restrictive. For example, a WHILE-loop cannot be introduced until the last refinement step, the machine implementation. Therefore, in order to be able to prove the superposition rule within the B-Method, we need to create extra B constructs.

In conclusion, we can say that even if the B-Method is intended for refining sequential programs, we are able to use it in the derivation of distributed programs. This is due to the fact that we can write an action system within the B-Method. However, to carry out the derivation of distributed programs within the B-Method demands some efforts with the original B-Method. The extensions discussed in the next chapter and elsewhere [18] would facilitate this process.

7.11 Exercises

Exercise 7.1 (Verification of Decomposition). Show that the decomposed system is a refinement of *Actions3* and *Procedures3* in the last refinement step.

Exercise 7.2 (Load Balancing in C). Generate C-code for the decomposed load balancing algorithm.

Exercise 7.3 (Expanding the Network). Derive the load balancing algorithm for a network with more than two nodes.

8. Distributed Electronic Mail System

Michael Butler

8.1 Introduction

In this chapter, we use an action system/AMN combination to design a distributed email system. The design starts with the abstract specification of an email service as a single machine with a simple state structure. The goal is to implement this abstract service on a store-and-forward network, where not all nodes are directly connected and messages may pass through a number of intermediate nodes before reaching their recipient. The first refinement of the abstract machine involves the introduction of data structures more closely resembling the store-and-forward architecture. Subsequent design steps involve the parallel decomposition of the system into subsystems representing the agents at each node in the network and the direct communications links in network.

Chapter 5 introduced the state-based view of action systems. In this chapter, we take an event-based view of action systems. In the event-based view, the execution of an operation is regarded as an event, but only the identity of the event is observable and the state is regarded as being internal and not observable. The event-based view corresponds to the way in which system behaviour is modelled in various process algebras such as ACP [10], CCS [55] and CSP [38]. An exact correspondence between action systems and CSP was made by Morgan [56]. Using this correspondence, techniques for event-based refinement and parallel composition of action systems have been developed in [19, 20]. In this chapter, we shall use the event-based view of action systems, applying the techniques of [19, 20] to B abstract machines.

Before going through the case study, we look more closely at the event-based view of action systems. In particular, we look at how actions can represent communication events, how such events can be hidden from the environment, and how systems can be combined in parallel such that they interact through shared actions.

8.2 Event-Based Actions Systems

Fig. 8.1 contains an action system, called *VM1*, specified as a B abstract machine. This is intended to represent a simple vending machine. The state of the machine is represented by the variable n. The machine has two actions represented by the operations *coin* and *choc*. Initially n is set to 0 so that only the *coin* action is enabled. When the *coin* action is executed, n is set to 1, and only the *choc* action is enabled. Execution of the *choc* action then results in *coin* being enabled again and so on. Thus *VM1* describes a system that alternatively engages in a *coin* action then a *choc* action forever.

```
MACHINE    VM1

VARIABLES    n

INVARIANT    n ∈ {0,1}

INITIALISATION

    n := 0

OPERATIONS

    coin ≙ SELECT n = 0 THEN n := 1 END

    choc ≙ SELECT n = 1 THEN n := 0 END

END
```

Fig. 8.1. Simple Vending Machine

An event-based view means that the environment of an abstract machine can only interact with the machine through its actions and has no direct access to a machine's state. The environment of a machine can also control the execution of actions by blocking them. This will be seen clearly in Sect. 8.4, where parallel composition of action systems is described.

For any abstract machine M, we write $\alpha(M)$ for the set of action names in M. For example,

$$\alpha(VM1) = \{ coin, choc \}.$$

We refer to $\alpha(M)$ as the *alphabet* of M. We write $M.a$ for the action named a in machine M. For example,

$$VM1.coin = \textbf{SELECT } n = 0 \textbf{ THEN } n := 1 \textbf{ END}.$$

8.2.1 Parameter Passing

The actions of an action system can be input actions, with associated input parameters, or output actions, with associated output parameters. An input action will be represented by a B AMN operation of the form

$$name(x) \ \hat{=} \ S.$$

where x represents the input parameter(s). An input action models a channel through which a machine is willing to accept an input value whenever that action is enabled. An output action will be represented by a B AMN operation of the form

$y \longleftarrow name \ \widehat{=} \ S.$

where y represents the output parameter(s). An output action models a channel through which a machine is willing to deliver an output value whenever that action is enabled.

We shall assume that no action can be both an input action and an output action. See Sect. 8.7 for a discussion of this issue.

Fig. 8.2 specifies an action system representing an ordered buffer. It is always ready to accept values of type T on the *left* channel, and to output on the *right* channel a value that has been input but not yet output. Values are output in the order in which they are input.

MACHINE   *Buffer1*

VARIABLES s

INVARIANT $s \in seq \ T$

INITIALISATION

   $s := \langle\rangle$

OPERATIONS

   $left(x) \ \widehat{=} \ $ **SELECT** $x \in T$ **THEN** $s := s ^\frown \langle x \rangle$ **END**

   $y \longleftarrow right \ \widehat{=} \ $ **SELECT** $s \neq \langle\rangle$ **THEN** $y, s := \text{head}(s), \text{tail}(s)$ **END**

END

Fig. 8.2. Ordered Buffer

8.2.2 Refinement

When refining an action system M by an action system N, both M and N must have the same alphabet, though they may have different state-spaces. Refinement is defined as follows:

Definition 8.1. *For abstract action system M and concrete action system N, where* $\alpha(M) = \alpha(N)$, *M is refined by N with abstraction invariant AI, denoted* $M \sqsubseteq_{AI} N$, *provided each of the following conditions hold:*

1. $M.init \sqsubseteq_{AI} N.init$
2. $M.a \sqsubseteq_{AI} N.a, \qquad each \ a \in \alpha(M)$
3. $AI \wedge gd(M.a) \Rightarrow gd(N.a), \qquad each \ a \in \alpha(M).$

This definition is a special case of the definition introduced in Chapter 5.

8.2.3 Example Refinement: Unordered Buffer

We specify and refine a buffer that does not guarantee to output values in the order in which they are input. An unordered buffer is described by an action system that has a *bag* of values as its state variable. A bag is a collection of elements that may have multiple occurrences of any element. We write *bag T* for the set of finite bags of type T. Bags will be enumerated between bag brackets $\prec$ and $\succ$. *Addition* of bags b, c, is written $b + c$, while *subtraction* is written $b - c$. Bag containment is written $x \in b$.

The action system *UBuffer1* of Fig. 8.3 describes an unordered buffer that communicates values of type T. The initialisation statement of *UBuffer1* sets the bag to be empty. The input action *left* accepts input values of type T, adding them to the bag a. Provided a is non-empty, the output action *right* non-deterministically chooses some element from a and outputs it.

MACHINE   *UBuffer1*

VARIABLES a

INVARIANT $a \in bag\ T$

INITIALISATION

   $a := \prec\succ$

OPERATIONS

   $left(x) \; \widehat{=}$
      SELECT
         $x \in T$
      THEN
         $a := a + \prec x \succ$
      END

   $y \longleftarrow right \; \widehat{=}$
      ANY y' **WHERE**
         $y' \in a$
      THEN
         $a, y := a - \prec y' \succ, y'$
      END

END

Fig. 8.3. Unordered Buffer

It can be shown that *UBuffer1* is refined by *Buffer1* of Fig. 8.2. As an abstraction invariant, we use

$$AI \; \widehat{=} \; a = bag(s),$$

where $bag(s)$ represents the bag of elements in sequence s. The proof obligations generated by Definition 8.1 are as follows:

- *UBuffer.init* $\sqsubseteq_{AI}$ *Buffer.init*
- *UBuffer.left* $\sqsubseteq_{AI}$ *Buffer.left*
- *UBuffer.right* $\sqsubseteq_{AI}$ *Buffer.right*
- $AI \wedge gd(UBuffer.left) \Rightarrow gd(Buffer.left)$
- $AI \wedge gd(UBuffer.right) \Rightarrow gd(Buffer.right)$

8.3 Internal Actions

In this section, action systems are extended to include internal actions. Internal actions are not visible to the environment of a machine and are thus outside the control of the environment. Any number of executions of an internal action may occur in between each execution of a visible action. Any state from which internal actions can be executed infinitely is said to be *divergent*. Internal actions do not have input or output parameters.

An example of an action system with internal actions is given in Fig. 8.4. *UBuffer2* represents an unordered buffer with an input channel *left* and an output channel *right*. However, instead of having a single bag as its state variable, *UBuffer2* has two bags, *b* and *c*. The *left* action places input values in bag *b*, while the *right* action takes output values from bag *c*. Values are moved from *b* to *c* by the internal action *mid*, which is enabled as long as *b* is non-empty. Since *b* is finite, *mid* will eventually be disabled, so it cannot cause divergence.

We write $\beta(M)$ for the set of internal actions in system *M*.

8.3.1 Refinement with Internal Actions

Intuitively it can be seen that *UBuffer2* behaves in the same way as *UBuffer1* of Fig. 8.3. We shall introduce a proof rule that allows us to verify that *UBuffer1* $\sqsubseteq$ *UBuffer2*. This rule is a special form of simulation in which the concrete system has some internal actions, and the abstract system has no internal actions.

To ensure that the internal actions do not introduce divergence, we use a well-foundedness argument. A set WF, with irreflexive partial order $<$, is *well-founded* if each non-empty subset of WF contains a minimal element under $<$. For example, the natural numbers with the usual ordering, or the cartesian product of two or more well-founded sets with lexicographic ordering, all form well-founded sets. The well-foundedness argument requires the use of a well-founded set WF and a *variant*, which is an expression in the state-variables. The variant should always be an element of WF, and it should be decreased by each internal action of the concrete system.

The simulation rule is as follows:

Definition 8.2. *Let M and N be action systems where* $\alpha(M) = \alpha(N)$ *and* $\beta(M) = \{\}$. *M is simulated by N with abstraction invariant AI, well-founded set WF, and variant E, denoted M $\sqsubseteq_{(AI,WF,E)}$ N, provided each of the following conditions hold:*

1. *$M.init \sqsubseteq_{AI} N.init$*

```
MACHINE     UBuffer2

VARIABLES    b, c

INVARIANT    b ∈ bag T  ∧  c ∈ bag T

INITIALISATION
     b, c := ≺≻, ≺≻

OPERATIONS
     left(x)  ≙
          SELECT
             x ∈ T
          THEN
             b := b + ≺x≻
          END

     y ⟵ right  ≙
          ANY y' WHERE
             y' ∈ c
          THEN
             c, y := c − ≺y'≻, y'
          END

INTERNAL OPERATIONS
     mid  ≙
          ANY z WHERE
             z ∈ b
          THEN
             b, c := b − ≺z≻, c + ≺z≻
          END

END
```

Fig. 8.4. Unordered Buffer with an Internal Action

2. $M.a \sqsubseteq_{AI} N.a$,   each $a \in \alpha(M)$
3. $skip \sqsubseteq_{AI} N.h$,   each $h \in \beta(N)$
4. $AI \Rightarrow E \in WF$
5. $AI \wedge E = e \Rightarrow [N.h](E < e)$,   each $h \in \beta(N)$
6. $AI \wedge gd(M.a) \Rightarrow gd(N.a) \vee \exists h \cdot (h \in \beta(N) \wedge gd(N.h))$,   each $a \in \alpha(M)$

Conditions 1, 2, and 3 are data-refinement conditions. Conditions 1 and 2 are the same as in Definition 8.1. Condition 3 ensures that each internal action of N causes no change to the corresponding abstract state. Conditions 4 and 5 are referred to as non-divergence conditions. Condition 4 ensures that the variant E is an element of WF, while Condition 5 ensures that the internal actions of N always decrease E when executed. Together, Conditions 4 and 5 ensure that the internal actions of N are eventually disabled and so cannot introduce divergence. Condition 6 is a progress condition and ensures that, whenever an action of M is enabled, either the corresponding action of N is enabled, or some internal action of N is enabled.

8.3.2 Example

To show that $UBuffer1 \sqsubseteq UBuffer2$, we use the abstraction invariant

$$AI \mathrel{\widehat{=}} a = b + c.$$

We use the size of bag b, written $\#b$, as a variant, with $\mathbb{N}$ as a well-founded set. Note that $UBuffer2.mid$ is a refinement of $skip$ under this abstraction invariant since the bag sum $b + c$ is unchanged by its execution. Also $UBuffer2.mid$ decreases the variant $\#b$.

8.3.3 Hiding Operator

Let M be an action system, and C be a set of operation names, with $C \subseteq \alpha(M)$. We write $M \backslash C$ for the machine M with each action named in C converted into an internal action. The input/output parameters of an internalised action should be localised using the **VAR** $x \cdot S$ **END** construct. Note that action hiding is simply a syntactic transformation of M.

Action hiding is monotonic: if M is refined by N, then $M \backslash C$ is refined by $N \backslash C$.

8.4 Parallel Composition

In this section, we describe a parallel composition operator for action systems. The parallel composition of action systems M and N is written $M \parallel N$. M and N must not have any common state variables. Instead they interact by synchronising over shared actions (i.e., actions with common names). They may also pass values on synchronisation. We look first at basic parallel composition and later look at parallel composition with value passing.

8.4.1 Basic Parallel Composition of Actions

To achieve the synchronisation effect, shared actions are "fused" using the parallel operator for actions $(S \parallel T)$. This operator satisfies the following properties:

- $x := E \parallel y := F \quad = \quad x, y := E, F$
- **SELECT** G **THEN** S **END** $\parallel$ **SELECT** H **THEN** T **END** $=$
  SELECT $G \wedge H$ **THEN** $S \parallel T$ **END**.

Since the variables changed by constituent actions are independent, the only effect of the parallel operator for actions is to ensure that the composite action is enabled exactly when both component actions are enabled.

8.4.2 Basic Parallel Composition of Action Systems

The parallel composition of action systems M and N is an action system constructed by fusing shared actions of M and N and leaving independent actions independent. The state variables of the composite system $M \parallel N$ are simply the union of the variables of M and N.

MACHINE $N1$
VARIABLES m
INVARIANT $m \in \{0,1\}$
INITIALISATION
$\quad m := 0$
OPERATIONS
$\quad a \; \widehat{=}$
$\qquad$ **SELECT**
$\qquad\quad m = 0$
$\qquad$ **THEN**
$\qquad\quad m := 1$
$\qquad$ **END**
$\quad c \; \widehat{=}$
$\qquad$ **SELECT**
$\qquad\quad m = 1$
$\qquad$ **THEN**
$\qquad\quad m := 0$
$\qquad$ **END**
END

MACHINE $N2$
VARIABLES n
INVARIANT $n \in \{0,1\}$
INITIALISATION
$\quad n := 0$
OPERATIONS
$\quad b \; \widehat{=}$
$\qquad$ **SELECT**
$\qquad\quad n = 0$
$\qquad$ **THEN**
$\qquad\quad n := 1$
$\qquad$ **END**
$\quad c \; \widehat{=}$
$\qquad$ **SELECT**
$\qquad\quad n = 1$
$\qquad$ **THEN**
$\qquad\quad n := 0$
$\qquad$ **END**
END

Fig. 8.5. Action Systems with Common Actions

As an illustration of this, consider $N1$ and $N2$ of Fig. 8.5. $N1$ alternates between an a-action and a c-action, while $N2$ alternates between a b-action and a c-action. The system $N1 \parallel N2$ is shown in Fig. 8.6. The a- and b-actions of $N1 \parallel N2$ come directly from $N1$ and $N2$ respectively, while the c-action is the fusion of the c-actions of $N1$ and $N2$. The initialisations of $N1$ and $N2$ are also fused to form the initialisation of $N1 \parallel N2$. The effect of $N1 \parallel N2$ is that, repeatedly, the a- or the b-actions can occur in either order, then both systems must synchronise on the c-action.

8.4.3 Parallel Composition with Value-Passing

We extend the parallel operator to deal with parameterised actions and value-passing. An output action from one system is composed with a similarly labelled

---

MACHINE $N1 \parallel N2$

VARIABLES m, n

INVARIANT $m, n \in \{0, 1\}$

INITIALISATION
  $m, n := 0, 0$

OPERATIONS

  $a \ \widehat{=} \ $ **SELECT** $m = 0$ **THEN** $m := 1$ **END**

  $b \ \widehat{=} \ $ **SELECT** $n = 0$ **THEN** $n := 1$ **END**

  $c \ \widehat{=} \ $ **SELECT** $m = 1 \wedge n = 1$ **THEN** $m, n := 0, 0$ **END**

END

Fig. 8.6. Parallel Composition of Action Systems

input action form another in such a way that the output value generated by the first is passed on as the input value for the second. For example, given an output action of the form

$$y \longleftarrow name \ \widehat{=} \ \textbf{SELECT } G \textbf{ THEN } u, y := U, Y \textbf{ END}$$

and an input action of the form

$$name(x) \ \widehat{=} \ \textbf{SELECT } x \in A \wedge H \textbf{ THEN } v := F(x) \textbf{ END},$$

their value-passing fusion is represented as:

$$y \longleftarrow name \ \widehat{=} \ \textbf{SELECT } H \wedge G \textbf{ THEN } u, y, v := U, Y, F(Y) \textbf{ END}.$$

Notice how $F(x)$ becomes $F(Y)$, modelling the passing of the output value from the output action to the input action. Notice also that the fused action is itself an output action.

More generally, let $M.name$ be an output action of machine M and $N.name$ be an input action of N. We shall assume[1] that $M.name$ has the form:

$$y \longleftarrow name \ \widehat{=} \ \textbf{ANY } u', y' \textbf{ WHERE } P \textbf{ THEN } u, y := u', y' \textbf{ END}$$

and that $N.name$ has the form:

$$name(x) \ \widehat{=} \ \textbf{SELECT } x \in A \wedge H \textbf{ THEN } v := F(x) \textbf{ END},$$

where H is independent of x. The value-passing fusion of these two actions is defined by:

---

[1] We only make these assumptions on actions that are to be composed in parallel with other actions.

Definition 8.3 (Value-passing Fusion).

$y \longleftarrow name$

$\widehat{=}$ **ANY** u', y' **WHERE** $P \wedge H$ **THEN** $u, y, v := u', y', F(y')$ **END**.

Furthermore, the composition of M.name an N.name is only permitted provided

$I_M \wedge P \Rightarrow y' \in A,$

where I_M is the invariant of M.

This restriction ensures that the output value generated by the output action is always acceptable by the input action.

The composition of two systems M and N is then constructed by fusing commonly named input-output pairs of actions as described by Definition 8.3. As before, independently named actions remain independent. The fusion of input-input pairs of actions is also permitted: assume $M.name$ has the form

$name(x) \widehat{=}$ **SELECT** $x \in A \wedge G$ **THEN** $u := F(x)$ **END**,

and that $N.name$ has the form:

$name(x) \widehat{=}$ **SELECT** $x \in B \wedge H$ **THEN** $v := G(x)$ **END**,

The fusion of these two actions is defined by:

Definition 8.4.

$name(x)$

$\widehat{=}$ **SELECT** $x \in (A \cap B) \wedge G \wedge H$ **THEN** $u, v := F(x), G(x)$ **END**.

Fusion of output-output pairs of actions is not permitted.

Fig. 8.7 describes the action systems *UBufferL* and *UBufferR*. The system *UBufferL* is simply an unbounded buffer with *right* renamed to *mid*, while *UBufferR* has *left* renamed to *mid*. When *UBufferL* and *UBufferR* are placed in parallel, they interact via the *mid* channel, with values being passed from *UBufferL* to *UBufferR*. This can be seen by constructing the composite action system *UBufferL* || *UBufferR* as described above (see Fig. 8.8). The only proof obligation (from Definition 8.3) associated with this composition is that the *UBufferL.mid* is guaranteed to output a value of type T, i.e.,

$b \in bag \, T \Rightarrow [UBufferL.mid](y \in T).$

If the *mid* action of *UBufferL* || *UBufferR* is hidden, then the resultant action system is the same as *UBuffer2* of Fig. 8.4. Since *UBuffer1* $\sqsubseteq$ *UBuffer2*, we have that:

UBuffer1 $\sqsubseteq$ (*UBufferL* || *UBufferR*)\{*mid*}.

```
┌─────────────────────────────────────┐  ┌─────────────────────────────────────┐
│ MACHINE    UBufferL                 │  │ MACHINE    UBufferR                 │
│                                     │  │                                     │
│ VARIABLES   b                       │  │ VARIABLES   c                       │
│                                     │  │                                     │
│ INVARIANT   b ∈ bag T               │  │ INVARIANT   c ∈ bag T               │
│                                     │  │                                     │
│ INITIALISATION                      │  │ INITIALISATION                      │
│                                     │  │                                     │
│    b := ≺≻                          │  │    c := ≺≻                          │
│                                     │  │                                     │
│ OPERATIONS                          │  │ OPERATIONS                          │
│                                     │  │                                     │
│    left(x) ≙                        │  │    y ⟵ right ≙                      │
│       SELECT                        │  │       ANY y′ WHERE                  │
│       x ∈ T                         │  │       y′ ∈ c                        │
│       THEN                          │  │       THEN                          │
│       b := b + ≺x≻                  │  │       c, y := c − ≺y′≻, y′          │
│       END                           │  │       END                           │
│                                     │  │                                     │
│    y ⟵ mid ≙                        │  │    mid(x) ≙                         │
│       ANY y′ WHERE                  │  │       SELECT                        │
│       y′ ∈ b                        │  │       x ∈ T                         │
│       THEN                          │  │       THEN                          │
│       b, y := b − ≺y′≻, y′          │  │       c := c + ≺x≻                  │
│       END                           │  │       END                           │
│                                     │  │                                     │
│ END                                 │  │ END                                 │
└─────────────────────────────────────┘  └─────────────────────────────────────┘
```

Fig. 8.7. Buffers

8.4.4 Design Technique

The derivation of the system $(UBufferL \parallel UBufferR) \setminus \{mid\}$ illustrates a design technique that may be used to decompose an action system into parallel subsystems: refine the state variables so that they may be partitioned amongst the subsystems, introducing internal actions representing interaction between subsystems, then partition the system into subsystems using the parallel operator in reverse. The refinement of the single system can always be performed in a number of steps rather than a single step.

Most importantly, the parallel composition of action systems is monotonic: if M is refined by M' and N is refined by N', then $M \parallel N$ is refined by $M' \parallel N'$. This means that when we decompose a system into parallel subsystems, the subsystems may be refined independently.

8.5 Email System

The action systems of this case study contain indexed sets of channels, each one offering similar behaviour. An indexed statement is used to specify the actions associated with such channel sets. For example, to specify an indexed set of input channels $\{ i.in \mid i \in F \}$, with associated actions, the following notation is used:

MACHINE   *UBufferL* ‖ *UBufferR*

VARIABLES b, c

INVARIANT $b \in bag\ T\ \wedge\ c \in bag\ T$

INITIALISATION

$b, c := \prec\succ, \prec\succ$

OPERATIONS

$left(x)\ \ \widehat{=}\ \ $**SELECT**
           $x \in T$
        THEN
           $b := b + \prec x \succ$
        END

$y \longleftarrow right\ \ \widehat{=}\ \ $**ANY** y' **WHERE**
           $y' \in c$
        THEN
           $c, y := c - \prec y' \succ, y'$
        END

$y \longleftarrow mid\ \ \widehat{=}\ \ $**ANY** y' **WHERE**
           $y' \in b$
        THEN
           $b, c, y := b - \prec y' \succ, c + \prec y' \succ, y'$
        END

END

Fig. 8.8. Parallel Buffers

$i.in(x)\ \ \widehat{=}\ \ S_i.$

The intention is that the i-indexed statement represents a set of input actions. S_i should constrain i to be an element of F. An indexed set of output channels is written:

$y \longleftarrow i.out\ \ \widehat{=}\ \ S_i.$

When an indexed input action such as $i.in(x)$ is internalised, it is collapsed into a single parameterless statement by transforming it to

$left\ \ \widehat{=}\ \ $**VAR** $i, x \cdot S_i$ **END**.

Similarly for an indexed output action.

8.5.1 Abstract Specification

We suppose that an email service allows a set of users to exchange messages amongst themselves. Each user resides at a node, and each user may engage in either a *send* action, or a *receive* action. Let *Node* represent the set of nodes in the system. We shall assume that *Node* is finite. Let *Mess* represent the type of messages that may be exchanged, and let *Env* be the cartesian product of *Node* and *Mess*. In the pair $(r,m) \in Env$, r is the recipient node, m is the message, and we say that (r,m) is an *envelope*.

The initial specification of the email service, *MailSys1*, is given in Fig. 8.9. Variable *mail* contains all messages sent but not yet received. Initially *mail* is empty. For each node n, there is a *send* action and a *receive* action. Action *s.send* accepts an envelope (r,m) at sending node s and adds it to the bag *mail*. If there is at least one message for recipient node r in *mail*, then action *r.receive* chooses one of these messages and outputs it.

MACHINE   *MailSys1*

SETS

    Node, *Mess*,
    Env = *Node* × *Mess*

VARIABLES   *mail*

INVARIANT   *mail* ∈ *bag Env*

INITIALISATION

    mail := ≺≻

OPERATIONS

    s.send(r,m) $\widehat{=}$
      SELECT
        $s \in Node \wedge (r,m) \in Env$
      THEN
        mail := *mail* + ≺(r,m)≻
      END

    $m \longleftarrow$ *r.receive* $\widehat{=}$
      ANY *n* **WHERE**
        $(r,n) \in mail$
      THEN
        mail := *mail* − ≺(r,n)≻ ‖ *m* := *n*
      END

END

Fig. 8.9. Electronic Mail Service

8.5.2 First Refinement of MailSys

Our goal is to implement *MailSys1* as a *store-and-forward* network, where not all nodes are directly connected, and envelopes must pass through a number of intermediate nodes before reaching their recipient. In the first refinement step, we introduce data structures more closely resembling the store-and-forward architecture, and introduce internal actions for passing envelopes between these data structures.

In *MailSys2*, *mail* is replaced by a set of stores, one per node, and a set of buffers representing direct links between nodes. The constant relation $net \in Node \leftrightarrow Node$ represents the connectivity of the network: $(a,b) \in net$ means there is a direct communications link from node a to node b.

Routing relations are used to determine which intermediate nodes an envelope may pass through. Before defining a *route*, we present some simple graph theory concepts. We say that a *graph* G is a relation on a set of nodes N (e.g., *net* is a graph on *Node*). A *path* from a to b in G is a non-empty sequence p of nodes from N, such that p_iGp_{i+1}, for each $1 \leq i < \#p$, and $p_1 = a$ and $p_{\#p} = b$. Let G^* be the reflexive transitive closure of G. Then aG^*b means there is a path from a to b in G. Note that there is always a path from a to a in G, i.e., $\langle a \rangle$. An *arc* from a to b in G is a path from a to b in which all nodes are distinct. If N is finite, then the *elongation* from a to b in G, written $e_G(a,b)$, is the length of the longest arc from a to b in G. Since the only arc from a to a is $\langle a \rangle$, we have $e_G(a,a) = 1$. We define *routes* as follows:

Definition 8.5. *Let G be a graph on nodes N. Then Routes(G), the set of routes of G, is the set of subgraphs of G such that for all $R \in Routes(G)$, and all $a,b,c \in N$, where $a \neq c$,*

$$aRb \wedge bR^*c \quad \Rightarrow \quad e_R(a,c) > e_R(b,c).$$

Here, each $R \in Routes(G)$ is a routing relation, (a,b) is a single step in R, and c is a destination node. The definition says that as we move from node a to node b on route R, the elongation to the destination node c decreases.

MailSys2 will use a fixed set of routes, each one uniquely identified by a tag from a set *Tag*. These routes are represented by the constant function

$$route \in Tag \to Routes(net).$$

In order that each distinct pair of nodes be connected by at least one route, we shall assume that the constant function *route* satisfies:

$$\bigcup i \cdot (i \in Tag \mid route(i)^*) = Node \times Node.$$

For convenience, the constants associated with routing are collected in the machine *Routing* of Fig. 8.10

On input, each envelope will be assigned one of these routes by being tagged with the route identifier. At any point on its journey the choice of the next node to which an envelope is sent will be determined by its destination and its assigned route. Since a route is a relation, the choice of next node may be non-deterministic. Elongations are used as a variant to ensure that all envelopes eventually reach their destination.

MailSys2 is then specified in Figs. 8.11 and 8.12. Corresponding to each node in the network, there is a store (bag) of tagged envelopes. These are modelled by the variable *store*. Corresponding to each direct link in the network, there is an unordered buffer of tagged envelopes. These are modelled by the variable *link*. The

MACHINE   *Routing*

SETS   *Tag*

CONSTANTS   *net, route*

PROPERTIES

$net \in Node \leftrightarrow Node \; \wedge$
$route \in Tag \rightarrow (Node \leftrightarrow Node) \; \wedge$
$ran\ route \subseteq Routes(net) \; \wedge$
$\bigcup i \cdot (i \in Tag \mid route(i)^*) = Node \times Node$

END

Fig. 8.10. Routing Information

invariant states that there is always a path from the current position of an envelope to its recipient in the assigned route.

MACHINE   *MailSys2*

REFINES   *MailSys1*

SEES   *Routing*

VARIABLES   *store, link*

INVARIANT

$store \in Node \rightarrow bag\ (Tag \times Env) \; \wedge$
$link \in net \rightarrow bag\ (Tag \times Env) \; \wedge$

$\forall (i,r,m) \cdot (\ (i,r,m) \in Tag \times Env \; \wedge \; a,b \in Node \Rightarrow$
$\quad (\ (i,r,m) \in store(a) \;\Rightarrow\; (a,r) \in route(i)^* \ ) \; \wedge$
$\quad (\ (a,b) \in net \wedge (i,r,m) \in link(a,b) \;\Rightarrow\; (b,r) \in route(i)^* \ )\ ) \; \wedge$

$mail = \Sigma a \cdot (a \in Node \mid env(store(a))) \; +$
$\qquad\quad \Sigma(a,b) \cdot ((a,b) \in net \mid env(link(a,b)))$

VARIANT

$\Sigma(a,i,r,m) \cdot (\ a \in Node \wedge (i,r,m) \in store(a) \mid e_i(a,r) * 2\ ) \; +$
$\Sigma(a,b,i,r,m) \cdot (\ (a,b) \in net \wedge (i,r,m) \in link(a,b) \mid (e_i(b,r) * 2) + 1\ )$

Fig. 8.11. Refined Email System

The abstract and the concrete variables are related by equating *mail* with the sum of envelopes in each store and each link. We write $\Sigma i \cdot b_i$ for the summation of a set of bags b_i. Let *env* be the function that removes tags from tagged envelopes, i.e. $env(i,r,m) = (r,m)$. If b is a bag of tagged envelopes, then $env(b)$ is the corresponding bag of untagged envelopes. The abstraction invariant, AI, is then the conjunction of the invariants of *MailSys1* and *MailSys2*.

The variant must be shown to be decreased by the internal operations of the refined system. We use the elongation from the current position of each envelope to its destination in its route to define the variant. Let $\Sigma j \cdot n_j$ represent the summation of a set of naturals n_j, and let $e_i(a,b)$ be the elongation from a to b on *route(i)*, i.e. $e_{route(i)}(a,b)$. The variant E is then defined as in Fig. 8.11.

INITIALISATION

    $store := \lambda a \cdot (a \in Node \mid \prec \succ) \parallel$
    $link := \lambda a,b \cdot ((a,b) \in net \mid \prec \succ)$

OPERATIONS

    $s.send(r,m) \ \widehat{=}$
        ANY *i* **WHERE**
          $s \in Node \wedge i \in Tag \wedge$
          $(r,m) \in Env \wedge (s,r) \in route(i)^*$
        THEN
          $store(s) := store(s) + \prec(i,r,m) \succ$
        END

    $m \longleftarrow r.receive \ \widehat{=}$
        ANY *i,n* **WHERE**
          $r \in Node \wedge (i,r,n) \in store(r)$
        THEN
          $store(r) := store(r) - \prec(i,r,n) \succ \parallel m := n$
        END

INTERNAL OPERATIONS

    $forward \ \widehat{=}$
        ANY *a,b,i,r,m* **WHERE**
          $(i,r,m) \in store(a) \wedge r \neq a \wedge$
          $(a,b) \in route(i) \wedge (b,r) \in route(i)^*$
        THEN
          $store(a) := store(a) - \prec(i,r,m) \succ \parallel$
          $link(a,b) := link(a,b) + \prec(i,r,m) \succ$
        END

    $relay \ \widehat{=}$
        ANY *a,b,i,r,m* **WHERE**
          $(a,b) \in net \wedge (i,r,m) \in link(a,b)$
        THEN
          $link(a,b) := link(a,b) - \prec(i,r,m) \succ \parallel$
          $store(b) := store(b) + \prec(i,r,m) \succ$
        END

END

Fig. 8.12. Operations of the Refined Email System

All stores and links are initially empty. The action *s.send* accepts an envelope (r, m), chooses a route i that (directly or indirectly) connects s to r, and adds (i, r, m) to the bag *store(s)*. If there is at least one message for recipient r in *store(r)*, then action *r.receive* chooses one of those messages and outputs it.

The internal action *forward* takes a tagged envelope that has not yet reached its recipient from some *store(a)*, chooses the next node b to forward the envelope to, and places the envelope in *link(a,b)*. The internal action *relay* simply takes an envelope from some *link(a,b)* and places it in *store(b)*.

By a sequence of *forward* and *relay* actions, a message sent at node s is eventually delivered to the store of its recipient node r. This is the case since *MailSys1* is refined by *MailSys2*, which may be checked using Definition 8.2 and the invariant and variant of Fig- 8.11.

8.5.3 Parallel Decomposition of MailSys

In this step, *MailSys2* is decomposed into two parallel systems, *Agents* and *Media*, specified in Figs. 8.13 and 8.14. *Agents* represents the behaviour of all the nodes of the network, and has a *send*, *receive*, *forward*, and *relay* channel for each network node. *Agents* only has the state variable *store*. *Media* represents the direct communications links of the network, and has a *forward* and a *relay* channel for each network node. *Media* only has the state variable *link*. *Agents* and *Media* communicate via *forward* and *relay* channels, and we have that

$$MailSys2 = (Agents1 \parallel Media1) \backslash$$
$$\{ a.forward \mid a \in Node \} \cup \{ b.relay \mid b \in Node \}.$$

8.5.4 Parallel Decomposition of Agents

In this step, *Agents1* is decomposed into a set of parallel action systems, each one representing the behaviour of an individual node of the network. Each action, *a.name*, of *Agents1* only refers to *store(a)*, so that *Agents1* may be partitioned into a set of independent parallel subsystems:

$$Agents1 = \parallel a \cdot (a \in Node \mid LocalAgent1(a)),$$

where *LocalAgent1(a)* is specified in Fig. 8.15.

For any $a \in Node$, we equate *store(a)* of *Agents1* with the variable *lstore* of *LocalAgent(a)* and action *a.send* of *Agents1* with action *send* of *LocalAgent(a)* and similarly for the other actions. Since *Node* is finite, the generalised parallel composition of statements used in the initialisation is defined by iterated use of the binary operator. The only statements that are fused in the construction of $\parallel a \cdot (a \in Node \mid LocalAgent1(a))$ are the initialisations; otherwise the decomposition simply involves the partitioning of *store* and the indexed actions.

MACHINE   *Agents1*

VARIABLES   *store*

INVARIANT $store \in Node \rightarrow bag\ (Tag \times Env)$

INITIALISATION

   $store := \lambda a \cdot (a \in Node \mid \prec\succ)$

OPERATIONS

   $s.send(r,m)\ \widehat{=}$
      ANY i **WHERE**
         $s \in Node \wedge i \in Tag \wedge$
         $(r,m) \in Env \wedge (s,r) \in route(i)^*$
      THEN
         $store(s) := store(s) + \prec(i,r,m)\succ$
      END

   $m \longleftarrow r.receive\ \widehat{=}$
      ANY i,n **WHERE**
         $r \in Node \wedge (i,r,n) \in store(r)$
      THEN
         $store(r) := store(r) - \prec(i,r,n)\succ \parallel m := n$
      END

   $b',i',r',m' \longleftarrow a.forward\ \widehat{=}$
      ANY b,i,r,m **WHERE**
         $a \in Node \wedge$
         $(i,r,m) \in store(a)\ \wedge\ r \neq a \wedge$
         $(a,b) \in route(i)\ \wedge\ (b,r) \in route(i)^*$
      THEN
         $store(a) := store(a) - \prec(i,r,m)\succ \parallel$
         $b',i',r',m' := b,i,r,m$
      END

   $b.relay(a,i,r,m)\ \widehat{=}$
      SELECT
         $a,b \in Node\ \wedge\ i \in Tag\ \wedge\ (r,m) \in Env$
      THEN
         $store(b) := store(b) + \prec(i,r,m)\succ$
      END

END

Fig. 8.13. Network Agents

```
MACHINE    Medial

VARIABLES    link

INVARIANT    link ∈ net → bag (Tag × Env)

INITIALISATION
    link := λa,b · ((a,b) ∈ net | ≺≻)

OPERATIONS
    a.forward(b,i,r,m)  ≘
        SELECT
            a,b ∈ Node ∧ i ∈ Tag ∧ (r,m) ∈ Env
        THEN
            link(a,b) := link(a,b) + ≺(i,r,m)≻
        END

    a',i',r',m' ⟵ b.relay  ≘
        ANY a,i,r,m WHERE
            (a,b) ∈ net ∧ (i,r,m) ∈ link(a,b)
        THEN
            link(a,b) := link(a,b) − ≺(i,r,m)≻ ||
            a',i',r',m' := a,i,r,m
        END

END
```

Fig. 8.14. Network Media

8.6 CSP Correspondence

In CSP [38], the behaviour of a process is viewed in terms of the events in which
it can engage in. Each process P has an alphabet of events A, and its behaviour
is modelled by a set of *failures* F and a set of *divergences* D. A failure is a pair
(t,X), where t is a trace of events and X is a set of events; $(t,X) \in F$ means that
P may engage in the trace of events t and then refuse all the events in X. A divergence is a trace of events d, and $d \in D$ means that, after engaging the trace d, P
may diverge (behave chaotically). Process (A,F,D) is refined by process (A,F',D'),
written $(A,F,D) \sqsubseteq (A,F',D')$, if

$F \supseteq F'$ and $D \supseteq D'$.

In [56], a correspondence between CSP and an event-based view of action systems is described. This involves giving a failures-divergence semantics to action
systems, with action names representing events. Let $\{\!\mid\!M\!\mid\!\}$ represent the failures-
divergence semantics of action system M. The definition of $\{\!\mid\!M\!\mid\!\}$ may be found in
[19, 56]. The observable behaviour of an action system is represented by its failures-
divergence semantics and it can be shown [19, 85] that if M is refined by N (Definitions 8.1 and 8.2), then any observable behaviour of N is an observable behaviour

MACHINE $LocalAgent1(a)$

CONSTRAINTS $a \in Node$

VARIABLES $lstore$

INVARIANT $lstore \in bag\,(Tag \times Env)$

INITIALISATION

    $lstore := \prec\succ$

OPERATIONS

    $send(r,m) \; \widehat{=}$
      ANY i **WHERE**
        $(r,m) \in Env \wedge i \in Tag \wedge (a,r) \in route(i)^*$
      THEN
        $lstore := lstore + \prec(i,r,m)\succ$
      END

    $m \longleftarrow receive \; \widehat{=}$
      ANY i,n **WHERE**
        $(i,r,n) \in lstore$
      THEN
        $lstore := lstore - \prec(i,r,n)\succ \; \| \; m := n$
      END

    $b',i',r',m' \longleftarrow forward \; \widehat{=}$
      ANY b,i,r,m **WHERE**
        $(i,r,m) \in lstore \; \wedge \; r \neq a \; \wedge$
        $(a,b) \in route(i) \; \wedge \; (b,r) \in route(i)^*$
      THEN
        $lstore := lstore - \prec(i,r,m)\succ \; \|$
        $b',i',r',m' := b,i,r,m$
      END

    $relay(a',i,r,m) \; \widehat{=}$
      SELECT
        $a' \in Node \; \wedge \; i \in Tag \; \wedge \; (r,m) \in Env$
      THEN
        $lstore := lstore + \prec(i,r,m)\succ$
      END

END

Fig. 8.15. Individual Agent

of M, i.e.,

$$\{\!|M|\!\} \sqsubseteq \{\!|N|\!\}.$$

CSP has both a hiding operator $(P\backslash C)$ for internalising events and a parallel composition operator $(P \parallel Q)$ for composing processes based on shared events. Both operators are defined in terms of failures-divergence semantics: Let $[\![P]\!]$ be the failures-divergence semantics of a CSP process P. Then $[\![P\backslash C]\!]$ is defined by $HIDE([\![P]\!], C)$ and $[\![P \parallel Q]\!]$ is defined by $PAR([\![P]\!], [\![Q]\!])$, where $HIDE$ and PAR are described in [38]. It can be shown [19] that the hiding and parallel operators for action systems correspond to the CSP operators; that is, for action systems M and N:

$$\{\!|M\backslash C|\!\} = HIDE(\{\!|M|\!\}, C)$$
$$\{\!|M \parallel N|\!\} = PAR(\{\!|M|\!\}, \{\!|N|\!\}).$$

Since $HIDE$ and PAR are monotonic w.r.t. refinement, our earlier claim that the hiding and parallel operators for action systems are monotonic is justified.

8.7 Concluding

Although operations in B AMN can have both input and output parameters, it was stated earlier that actions can either be input actions or output actions, but not both. Consider an AMN action of the form

$$y \longleftarrow name(x) \mathrel{\widehat{=}} S.$$

In the implementation of this operation, we would expect a delay between receipt of x and the delivery of y. In particular, we may want to push the computation of y into some internal actions. In order to do this using simulation (Definition 8.2), the operation should be broken into an input action, representing receipt of x, and an output action, representing delivery of y. In this way, we can introduce internal actions that are executed in between receipt of x and delivery of y, contributing towards the computation of y. It also allows us to interleave other visible actions between receipt of x and delivery of y.

Abrial has proposed an approach to the design of protocols using the B method [3]. With this approach, a protocol is specified as a single operation which is subsequently decomposed into a sequence of steps through a series of refinements. The introduction of each new step in the protocol is justified by showing that it is a data-refinement of the *skip* action. This is the same as our data-refinement condition on internal actions being introduced by a simulation step (Definition 8.2).

We have seen the close correspondence between action systems and the abstract machines of B and seen the similarity between their notions of refinement. Because of this close correspondence, we are able to apply action system techniques such as internalisation of actions and parallel composition to abstract machines. These techniques provide a powerful abstraction mechanism since they allow us to abstract away from the distributed architecture of a system and the complex interactions between its subsystems; a system, such as the email service, can be specified as a single abstract machine and only in later refinement steps do we need to introduce explicit subsystems and interactions between them. The reasoning required to use these techniques involves refinement arguments and variant arguments, which is the sort of reasoning already used in B. The techniques are also very modular since the parallel components of a distributed system can be refined and decomposed separately without making any assumptions about the rest of the system.

8.8 Exercises

Exercise 8.1 (Defining bags). Define a B machine providing bags and the bag operations for containment, addition and subtraction.

Exercise 8.2 (Message broadcast). Extend the specification of the email system to include an operation to broadcast a message to all users. Refine this extended system in such a way that the broadcast operation is implemented as efficiently as possible.

Exercise 8.3 (Distributed database). Specify a simple database in B. Using the techniques described in this chapter, refine this specification into a distributed database where the records of the database are distributed throughout several nodes. When a database request cannot be serviced locally, it should be passed on to the relevant remote node.

References

1. M. Abadi and L. Lamport, The existence of refinement mappings, Theoretical Computer Science 82(2):253–284, European Association for Theoretical Computer Science 1991.
2. J.-R. Abrial, The B-Book: Assigning Programs to Meanings, Cambridge University Press 1996.
3. J.-R. Abrial, Cryptographic Protocol Specification and Design, March 1995.
4. R.J.R Back, On the Correctness of Refinement Steps in Program Development, PhD. Thesis, Dept. of Computer Science, University of Helsinki, 1978.
5. R. J. R. Back and R. Kurki-Suonio, Decentralisation of process nets with centralised control, Proc. 2nd ACM SIGACT-SIGOPS Symposium on Principles of Distributed Computing pp 131–142, ACM Press 1983.
6. R. J. R. Back and K. Sere, Action systems with synchronous communication, E. R. Olderog ed. Programming Concepts, Methods and Calculi, IFIP Transaction A–56, North-Holland 1994.
7. R. J. R. Back and K. Sere, From action systems to modular systems, Proc. Formal Methods Europe (FME'94): Industrial Benefit of Formal Methods, Lecture Notes in Computer Science 873, pp 1–25, Springer-Verlag 1994.
8. R. J. R. Back and K. Sere, Superposition refinement of reactive systems, Formal Aspects of Computing 8(3):324–346, Springer-Verlag 1996.
9. R. J. R. Back and J. von Wright, Trace refinement of action systems, Proc. CONCUR'94, Lecture Notes in Computer Science 836, pp 367–384, Springer-Verlag 1994.
10. J. A. Bergstra and J. W. Klop, Algebra of communicating processes with abstraction, Theoret. Computer Science 37:77–121, 1985.
11. G. Berry and G. Gonthier, The esterel synchronous programming language: Design, semantics, implementation, Science of Computer Programming 19(2):87–152, Elsevier 1992.
12. B.W. Boehm, A spiral model of software development and enhancement, IEEE Computer 21:61–72, 1988.
13. Th. Boutell, cgic: an ANSI C library for CGI programming. http://www.boutell.com/cgic/.
14. F.P. Jr. Brooks, The Mythical Man-Month: Essays on Software Engineering - Anniversary Edition, Addison-Wesley, 1995.
15. M. Büchi and W. Weck, A plea for grey-box components, Proc. Foundations of Component-Based Systems '97. http://www.abo.fi/~mbuechi/.
16. M. Butler, J. Grundy, T. Långbacka, R. Ruksenas, and J. von Wright, The Refinement Calculator: Proof support for program refinement, Lindsay Groves and Steve Reeves eds. Formal Methods Pacific'97: Proceedings of FMP'97, Discrete Mathematics and Theoretical Computer Science, pp 40–61, Springer-Verlag 1997.
17. M. Butler, E. Sekerinski, and K. Sere, An action system approach to the steam boiler problem, J.-R. Abrial, E. Börger, and H. Langmaack eds. Formal Methods for Industrial Applications: Specifying and Programming the Steam Boiler Control, Lecture Notes in Computer Science 1165. Springer-Verlag 1996.

18. M. Butler and M. Waldén, Distributed system development in B, Proc. 1st Conference on the B Method, pp 155–168, 1996.

19. M. J. Butler, A CSP Approach To Action Systems, D.Phil. Thesis, Programming Research Group, Oxford University, 1992.

20. M. J. Butler, Stepwise refinement of communicating systems. Science of Computer Programming, 27(2), September 1996.

21. B. Dehbonei and F. Mejia, Formal Development of Safety-critical Software Systems in Railway Signalling, M.G. Hinchey and J.P. Bowen eds. Applications of Formal Methods, pp 227–252. Prentice Hall 1995.

22. E. W. Dijkstra, A Discipline of Programming, Prentice-Hall International, Englewood Cliffs, New Jersey, 1976.

23. E.W. Dijkstra, Discussion at ifip working group 2.3.

24. E.W. Dijkstra, Notes on structured programming, Structured Programming, 1972.

25. E.W. Dijkstra, Guarded commands, nondeterminacy and formal derivation of programs, Communications of the ACM, pages 453–457, 1975.

26. M.B. Dwyer, V. Carr, and L. Hines, Model checking graphical user interfaces using abstractions. Proc. ESEC/FSE '97, Lecture Notes in Computer Science 1301, pp 244–261. Springer-Verlag 1997.

27. F. Erasmy and E. Sekerinskin Stepwise refinement of control software - a case study using raise, In M. Naftalin, T. Denvir, and M. Bertran eds. FME'94: Industrial Benefit of Formal Methods, Lecture Notes in Computer Science 873, pages 547–566, Barcelona, Spain, 1994. Springer–Verlag.

28. Ph. Facon et al., Mapping object diagrams into B specification, A. Bryant and L. Semmens eds. Methods Integration Workshop, electronic Workshops in Computing, Springer-Verlag 1996.

29. C.J. Fidge and A.J. Wellings, An action-based formal model for concurrent, real-time systems, Formal Aspects of Computing 9(2):175–207, Springer-Verlag 1997.

30. N. Francez and I. R. Forman, Superimposition for interactive processes, Proc. CONCUR'90 Theories of Concurrency: Unification and extension, Lecture Notes in Computer Science 458, pp 230–245, Springer-Verlag 1990.

31. I. Jacobson G. Booch, J. Rumbaugh, Unified Modeling Language User Guide, Addison-Wesley 1998. http://www.rational.com/uml/.

32. J.V. Guttag, The Specification and Application to Programming of Abstract Data Types, PhD. Thesis, University of Toronto, 1975.

33. J. J. Lukkien H. P.Hofstee and J. L. A. van de Snepscheut, A distributed implementation of a task pool, J. P. Banatre and D. Le Metayer eds. Research Directions in High-Level Parallel Programming Languages, Lecture Notes in Computer Science 574, pp 338–348, Springer-Verlag 1991.

34. D. Harel, Statecharts: A visual formalism for complex systems, Science of Computer Programming 8:231–274, Elsevier 1987.

35. D. Coleman, F. Hayes, and S. Bear, Introducing objectcharts or how to use statecharts in object-oriented design, IEEE Transactions on Software Engineering 18(1), IEEE Press 1992.

36. S.D. Hester, D.L. Parnas, and D.F. Utter, Using documentation as a software design medium, Bell System Technical Journal, 60:1941–1977, 1981.

37. J. V. Hill, Microprocessor Based Protection Systems, Elsevier 1991.

38. C. A. R. Hoare, Communicating Sequential Processes, Prentice–Hall, 1985.

39. C.A.R. Hoare, Proof of correctness of data representations, Acta Informatica, 19:271–281, 1972.

40. J.P. Hoare, Application of the B-Method to CICS M.G. Hinchey and J.P. Bowen eds. Applications of Formal Methods, pp 97–123, Prentice Hall 1995.

41. IEC, Software for computers in the application of industrial safety-related systems 1992. IEC 65A 122.

42. R. Janicki, D.L. Parnas, and J. Zucker, Tabular representations in relational documents, In C. Brink and G. Schmidt, eds. Relational Methods in Computer Science, pages 184–196. Springer Verlag, 1997.

43. C.B. Jones, A rigorous approach to formal methods, IEEE Computer, pp 20–21, IEEE Press 1996.

44. S. M. Katz, A superimposition control construct for distributed systems, ACM Transactions on Programming Languages and Systems 15(2):337–356, ACM Press 1993.

45. J.B. Kruskal, On the Shortest Spanning Subtree of a Graph and the Traveling Salesman Problem, Proc. Amer. Math. Soc. 15, pp 48–50, 1956.

46. K. Lano, The B Language and Method: A guide to Practical Formal Development, Springer-Verlag 1996.

47. K. Lano, Integrating formal and structured methods in object-oriented system development, S.J. Goldsack and S.J.H. Kent eds. Formal Methods and Object Technology, Springer-Verlag 1996.

48. K. Lano and J. Dick, Development of concurrent systems in B AMN, In He Jifeng, eds. Proc. of 7th BCS-FACS Refinement Workshop, Workshops in Computing. Springer–Verlag, 1996.

49. K. Lano and H. Haughton. Specification in B: An Introduction Using the B Toolkit, Imperial College Press, London, 1996.

50. C. Lewerentz and Th. Lindner, eds. Formal Development of Reactive Systems - Case Study Production Cell, Lecture Notes in Computer Science 891, Springer–Verlag, 1995.

51. B.H. Liskov and S.N. Zilles, Programming with abstract data types, ACM SIGPLAN Notices, 9:50–59, 1974.

52. J.A. McDermid, ed. Theory and Practice of Refinement, Butterworth, 1989.

53. H. D. Mills, The new math of computer programming, Communications of the ACM, 18:43–48, 1975.

54. H. D. Mills, Stepwise refinement and verification in box-structure systems, Computer, pages 23–26, 1988.

55. R. Milner, Communication and Concurrency, Prentice–Hall, 1989.

56. C. C. Morgan, Of wp and CSP, In W. H. J. Feijen, A. J. M. van Gasteren, D. Gries, and J. Misra, eds. Beauty is our business: a birthday salute to Edsger W. Dijkstra, Springer–Verlag, 1990.

57. C. Morgan, The generalised substitution language extended to probabilistic programs, Proc. B'98: the 2nd International B Conference. Lecture Notes in Computer Science, Springer Verlag, 1998.

58. C. Morgan, A. McIver, and K. Seidel, Probabilistic predicate transformers, ACM Transactions on Programming Languages and Systems 18(3):325–353, ACM Press, 1996.

59. D. S. Neilson and I. H. Sorensen, The B-technologies: a system for computer aided programming, B-Core (UK) Ltd., Oxford, U.K. 1996. Including the B-Toolkit User's Manual, Release 3.2.

60. D.L. Parnas, On the criteria to be used in decomposing systems into modules, Communications of the ACM, pages 1053–1058, ACM Press, 1972.

61. D.L. Parnas, On a 'buzzword': Hierarchical structure, IFIP Congress '74, pages 336–339, North Holland, 1974.

62. D.L. Parnas, On the design and development of program families, IEEE Transactions on Software Engineering, 2:1–9, IEEE Press, 1976.

63. D.L. Parnas, Precise description and specification of software, In V. Stavridou, ed. Mathematics of Dependable Systems II, pages 1–14, Clarendon Press, 1997.

64. D.L. Parnas and P.C. Clements A rational design process: How and why to fake it, IEEE Transactions on Software Engineering, 12:251–257, IEEE Press, 1986.

65. D.L. Parnas, Clements, and D.M. P.C., Weiss, The modular structure of complex systems, IEEE Transactions on Software Engineering, 11:259–266, IEEE Press, 1985.

66. D.L. Parnas and J.A. Darringer, Sodas and a methodology for system design, AFIPS 1967 Fall Joint Computing Conference, pages 449–474, 1967.

67. D.L. Parnas and J. Madey, Functional documentation for computer systems engineering, Science of Computer Programming, 25:41–61, Elsevier, 1995.

68. D.L. Parnas, J. Madey, and M. Iglewski, Precise documentation of well-structured programs, IEEE Transactions on Software Engineering, 20:948–976, IEEE Press, 1994.

69. J. Rumbaugh, M. Blaha, W. Premerlani, and F. Eddy, Object-Oriented Modeling and Design, Prentice Hall 1991.

70. R. S. Pressman, Software Engineering : A Practitioner's Approach, McGraw Hill, 4th edition, 1996.

71. R.C. Prim, Shortest Connection Networks and Some Generalizations, Bell System Technical Jr. 15, pp 1389–1401, 1957.

72. P. J. G. Ramadge and W. Murray Wonham, The control of discrete event systems, Proc. of the IEEE 77(1):81–98, IEEE Press 1989.

73. M. Rönkkö, E. Sekerinski, and K. Sere, Control systems as action systems, R. Smedinga, M.P. Spathopoulos, and P. Kozák eds. WODES'96: Workshop on Discrete Event Systems, pp 362–367, IEEE Press 1996.

74. E. Sekerinski, Statecharts in B, Proc. B'98: the 2nd International B Conference, Lecture Notes in Computer Science 1393, pp 182–197, Springer-Verlag 1998.

75. K. Sere and M. Waldén, Data refinement of remote procedures, Proc. International Symposium on Theoretical Aspects of Computer Software (TACS97), Lecture Notes in Computer Science 1281, pp 267 – 294, Springer-Verlag 1997.

76. R. Shore, Object-oriented modelling in B, Proc. 1st Conference on the B method, pp 133–154, 1996.

77. I. Sommerville, Software Engineering, Addison-Wesley, 5th edition, 1995.

78. J.M. Spivey, ed. Understanding Z: A Specification Language and its Formal Semantic, Cambridge University Press, 1988.

79. Stéria Méditerranée, Atelier-B, France, 1996.

80. N. Storey, Safety-Critical Computer Systems, Addison-Wesley, 1996.

81. R. Tarjan, On the Efficiency of a Good but not Linear Set Merging Algorithm, Journal of the ACM 22, pp 215–225, ACM Press 1975.

82. M. Waldén and K. Sere, Reasoning about action systems using the B-method, Formal Methods in System Design 13(1), Kluver 1998.

83. J.W.J. Williams, Algorithm 232: Heapsort, Communications of the ACM 7:347–348, ACM Press 1964.

84. N. Wirth, Program development by stepwise refinement, Communications of the ACM, 14:221–227, ACM Press, 1971.

85. J. C. P. Woodcock and C. C. Morgan, Refinement of state-based concurrent systems, In D. Bjørner, C. A. R. Hoare, and H. Langmaack, eds. Proc. of VDM '90, Lecture Notes in Computer Science 428. Springer-Verlag, 1990.

86. J. Wordsworth, Software Engineering with B, Addison-Wesley, September 1996.

87. F.W. Zurcher and B. Randell, Iterative multi-level modelling: A methodology for computer system design, IFIP Congress 68, pages D138–D142, 1968.

Appendix

Expressions

The full syntax of expressions can be found in the B-Book of Abrial [2] and in Chapter 1 of this book. In this section we remind the reader of the syntax and semantics of some of the expressions used in the case studies of this book.

Let E and F be expressions, z a list of variables, P a predicate, S and T sets, and let m and n be natural numbers. Let additionally $r, r1, r2$ be relations from S to T and assume that $s \subseteq S$ and $t \subseteq T$.

$E \mapsto F$	Ordered pair
$n..m$	The set of non-negative integers between n and m inclusive
$\Sigma z \cdot (P\|E)$	The sum of values of the natural number expression E for z such that P holds
$S \leftrightarrow T$	Set of relations from S to T: $\mathbb{P}(S \times T)$
$s \triangleleft r$	Domain restriction: $\{x,y\|x,y \in r \wedge x \in s\}$
$r \triangleright t$	Range restriction: $\{x,y\|x,y \in r \wedge y \in t\}$
$s \triangleleft\!\!\!- r$	Domain subtraction: $\{x,y\|x,y \in r \wedge x \in S - s\}$
$r \triangleright\!\!\!- t$	Range subtraction: $\{x,y\|x,y \in r \wedge y \in T - t\}$
r^{-1}	Inverse of r: $\{y,x\|y,x \in (T \times S) \wedge x,y \in r\}$
$r[s]$	Image of set s under relation r: $\{y\|y \in T \wedge \exists x.(x \in s \wedge x,y \in r)\}$
$r1 \triangleleft\!\!\!+ r2$	Overriding of $r1$ by $r2$: $(\text{dom}(r2) \triangleleft\!\!\!- r1) \cup r2$
$r1 \triangleright\!\!\!+ r2$	Overriding of $r2$ by $r1$: $r2 \triangleleft\!\!\!+ r1$
$p \otimes q$	Direct product of p and q: $\{x,(y,z)\|x,(y,z) \in (S \times (U \times V)) \wedge x,y \in p \wedge x,z \in q\}$
r^n	The n:th iterate of r:

	$r^0 = \text{id}(S),\ r^{n+1} = r; r^n$
r^*	The reflexive transitive closure of r:
	$\bigcup n.(n \in \mathbb{N} \mid r^n)$
$S \nrightarrow T$	Set of partial functions from S to T:
	$\{r \mid r \in S \leftrightarrow T \wedge (r^{-1}; r) \subseteq \text{id}(T)\}$
$S \rightarrow T$	Set of total functions from S to T:
	$\{f \mid f \in S \nrightarrow T \wedge \text{dom}(f) = S\}$
$S \nrightarrowtail T$	Set of partial injections from S to T:
	$\{f \mid f \in S \nrightarrow T \wedge f^{-1} \in T \nrightarrow S\}$
$S \rightarrowtail T$	Set of total injections from S to T:
	$(S \nrightarrowtail T) \cap (S \rightarrow T)$
$S \nrightarrow\kern-1.2ex\rightarrow T$	Set of partial surjections from S to T:
	$\{f \mid f \in S \nrightarrow T \wedge \text{ran}(f) = T\}$
$S \twoheadrightarrow T$	Set of total surjections from S to T:
	$(S \nrightarrow\kern-1.2ex\rightarrow T) \cap (S \rightarrow T)$
$S \twoheadrightarrowtail T$	Set of bijections from S to T:
	$(S \twoheadrightarrow T) \cap (S \rightarrowtail T)$
$\lambda z \cdot (z \in S \wedge P \mid E)$	Function construction

Substitutions

In the Generalised Subsitution Language (GSL), substitutions are interpreted as statements of a sequential imperative programming language.

The application of a (generalised) substitution G to a predicate R, written $[G]\,R$, is interpreted as the weakest precondition (weakest predicate) such that statement G terminates in a state satisfying R. In Dijkstras original notation [22], this is written as $wp\ (\,G, R\,)$. If P implies $[G]\,R$, then this is equivalent to stating the under precondition P statement G establishes postcondition R, i.e.:

$$\{P\}\,G\,\{R\} \quad \text{iff} \quad P \Rightarrow [G]\,R$$

Generalised substitutions are axiomatised as follows:

$[xx := E]\,R$	$\widehat{=}$	R with free occurences of xx replaced by E	*simple*
$[\text{skip}]\,R$	$\widehat{=}$	R	*skip*
$[P \mid G]\,R$	$\widehat{=}$	$P \wedge [G]\,R$	*preconditioned*
$[P \Longrightarrow G]\,R$	$\widehat{=}$	$P \Rightarrow [G]\,R$	*guarded*
$[G\,[]\,H]\,R$	$\widehat{=}$	$[G]\,R \wedge [H]\,R$	*alternate*
$[@zz \cdot (G)]\,R$	$\widehat{=}$	$\forall\, zz \cdot ([G]\,R)$, if xx not free in R	*unbounded choice*
$[G\,;H]\,R$	$\widehat{=}$	$[G]\,[H]\,R$	*sequential*

Here xx are variables, E an expression, P, R predicates, and G, H substitutions.

Precondition and Guard

The precondition *pre (G)* of a generalised substitution *G* characterises its domain of *definedness*. When *G* is started within that domain, then *G* is guaranteed to execute in a well-defined manner and to terminate. When *G* is started outside its precondition, any arbitrary behaviour is possible, including nontermination. The precondition is defined by:

$$pre\ (\ G\ )\quad \widehat{=}\quad [G]\ true \hspace{4cm} precondition$$

Following laws can be used in determining the precondition of generalised substitutions:

$$
\begin{aligned}
pre\ (\ xx := E\ )\ &=\ true\\
pre\ (\ P\ |\ G\ )\ &=\ P \wedge pre\ (G)\\
pre\ (\ P \Longrightarrow G\ )\ &=\ P \Rightarrow pre\ (\ G\ )\\
pre\ (\ G\ []\ H\ )\ &=\ pre\ (\ G\ ) \wedge pre\ (\ H\ )\\
pre\ (\ @xx\ .\ (G)\ )\ &=\ \forall\ xx\ .\ pre\ (\ G\ )
\end{aligned}
$$

The guard *gd (G)* of a generalised substitution *G* characterises the domain of *enabledness*. Within that domain, *G* may be executed. When *G* is started outside its domain of enabledness, it will not execute at all. The guard is defined by: is defined by:

$$gd\ (\ G\ )\quad \widehat{=}\quad \neg\ [G]\ false \hspace{4cm} guard$$

Following laws can be used in determining the guard of generalised substitutions:

$$
\begin{aligned}
gd\ (\ xx := E\ )\ &=\ true\\
gd\ (\ P\ |\ G\ )\ &=\ P \Rightarrow gd\ (\ G\ )\\
gd\ (\ P \Longrightarrow G\ )\ &=\ P \wedge gd\ (\ G\ )\\
gd\ (\ G\ []\ H\ )\ &=\ gd\ (\ G\ ) \vee gd\ (\ H\ )\\
gd\ (\ @xx\ .\ (G)\ )\ &=\ \exists\ xx\ .\ gd\ (\ G\ )
\end{aligned}
$$

Equality and Refinement of Substitutions

Two substitutions *G* and *H* are considered to be equal, written *G = H*, if they always lead to the same postcondition:

$$G = H\quad \widehat{=}\quad \text{for all predicates } P\text{: } [G]\ P = [H]\ P \hspace{2cm} equality$$

Substitution *G* is refined by substitution *H*, written $G \sqsubseteq H$, if whenever *G* establishes a postcondition, so does *H*:

$$G \sqsubseteq H\quad \widehat{=}\quad \text{for all predicates } P\text{: } [G]\ P \Rightarrow [H]\ P \hspace{2cm} refinement$$

AMN Substitutions

BEGIN G **END**	$\widehat{=}$	G

PRE P **THEN** G **END**	$\widehat{=}$	$P \mid G$

IF P **THEN** G **END**	$\widehat{=}$	$P \Longrightarrow G \; [] \; \neg P \Longrightarrow \mathsf{skip}$

IF P **THEN** G **ELSE** H **END**	$\widehat{=}$	$P \Longrightarrow G \; [] \; \neg P \Longrightarrow H$

IF P **THEN** G
ELSIF Q **THEN** H
$\cdots$
ELSIF R **THEN** K
END

$\widehat{=}$

$P \Longrightarrow G \; []$
$\neg P \wedge Q \Longrightarrow H \; []$
$\cdots$
$\neg P \wedge \neg Q \wedge \cdots \wedge R \Longrightarrow K \; []$
$\neg P \wedge \neg Q \wedge \cdots \wedge \neg R \Longrightarrow \mathsf{skip}$

IF P **THEN** G
ELSIF Q **THEN** H
$\cdots$
ELSIF R **THEN** K
ELSE L
END

$\widehat{=}$

$P \Longrightarrow G \; []$
$\neg P \wedge Q \Longrightarrow H \; []$
$\cdots$
$\neg P \wedge \neg Q \wedge \cdots \wedge R \Longrightarrow K \; []$
$\neg P \wedge \neg Q \wedge \cdots \wedge \neg R \Longrightarrow L$

CHOICE G **OR** $\cdots$ **OR** H **END**	$\widehat{=}$	$G \; [] \cdots [] \; H$

SELECT P **THEN** G **END**	$\widehat{=}$	$P \Longrightarrow G$

SELECT P **THEN** G
WHEN Q **THEN** H
$\cdots$
WHEN R **THEN** K
END

$\widehat{=}$

$P \Longrightarrow G \; []$
$Q \Longrightarrow H \; []$
$\cdots$
$R \Longrightarrow K$

SELECT P **THEN** G
WHEN Q **THEN** H
$\cdots$
WHEN R **THEN** K
ELSE L
END

$\widehat{=}$

$P \Longrightarrow G \; []$
$Q \Longrightarrow H \; []$
$\cdots$
$R \Longrightarrow K \; []$
$\neg P \wedge \neg Q \wedge \cdots \wedge \neg R \Longrightarrow L$

CASE E **OF** $\widehat{=}$ $E \in \{\, l \,\} \Longrightarrow G \,[]$
 EITHER l **THEN** G $E \in \{\, p \,\} \Longrightarrow H \,[]$
 OR p **THEN** H $\cdots$
 $\cdots$ $E \in \{\, q \,\} \Longrightarrow K \,[]$
 OR q **THEN** K $E \notin \{\, l \,, p \,, \ldots , q \,\} \Longrightarrow \mathsf{skip}$
 END
END

CASE E **OF** $\widehat{=}$ $E \in \{\, l \,\} \Longrightarrow G \,[]$
 EITHER l **THEN** G $E \in \{\, p \,\} \Longrightarrow H \,[]$
 OR p **THEN** H $\cdots$
 $\cdots$ $E \in \{\, q \,\} \Longrightarrow K \,[]$
 OR q **THEN** K $E \notin \{\, l \,, p \,, \ldots , q \,\} \Longrightarrow L$
 ELSE L
 END
END

VAR x **IN** G **END** $\widehat{=}$ @ $x \,.\, G$

ANY x **WHERE** P **THEN** G **END** $\widehat{=}$ @ $x \,.\, (\, P \Longrightarrow G \,)$

LET x **BE** $x = E$ **IN** G **END** $\widehat{=}$ @ $x \,.\, (\, x = E \Longrightarrow G \,)$

$x := bool\,(\, P \,)$ $\widehat{=}$ $P \Longrightarrow x := TRUE \,[]$
          $\neg\, P \Longrightarrow x := FALSE$

$x :\in E$ $\widehat{=}$ @ $x' \,.\, (\, x' \in E \Longrightarrow x := x' \,)$

$x : P$ $\widehat{=}$ @ $x' \,.\, (\, [x := x']\, P \Longrightarrow x := x' \,)$

$f\,(\, x \,) := E$ $\widehat{=}$ $f := f \lhd \{\, x \mapsto E \,\}$

Machines and Proof Obligations for Consistency

The syntactic structure of an abstract machine specification is as follows:

MACHINE   *Machine_name(f)*

CONSTRAINTS
  F
CONSTANTS
  c
PROPERTIES
  C
VARIABLES

x

INVARIANT
  I
INITIALISATION
  H
OPERATIONS
  $Operation\_name \mathrel{\hat{=}} \textbf{PRE} \quad P\ \textbf{THEN} \quad G\ \textbf{END}\ ;$
  $\vdots$

END

A machine can include other machines via an **INCLUDES**-clause. The included machines become part of the including machine. An included machine can be renamed by prefixing its name with some identifier followed by a dot in the **INCLUDES**-clause. Renaming may be used to include multiple copies of a single machine. A machine can get access to other machines via the **USES**-clause. The variables, sets, and constants of the used machine can be refered to in the invariants and AMN substitutions of the using machine provided the variables are not modified. When a machine **SEES** another machine the variables, sets, and constants of the machine become known to the seeing machine. They can only appear in AMN substitutions provided they are not modified. The **EXTENDS**-clause includes machines. All the operations of the included machines become operations of the including machine. Used, seen, and extended machines can be renamed.

The B-Method supports the checking of the internal consitency of an abstract machine. The internal consitency of the machine above is proved via the following five proof obligations:

(C1) $(\exists\ f.\ F)$

(C2) $F \Rightarrow (\exists\ c.\ C)$

(C3) $(F \wedge C) \Rightarrow (\exists\ x.\ I)$

(C4) $(F \wedge C) \Rightarrow [H]I$

(C5) $(F \wedge C \wedge I \wedge P) \Rightarrow [G]I$

Machine Refinement and Associated Proof Obligations

The syntactic structure of an abstract machine refinement is as follows:

REFINEMENT   *Refinement_name*

REFINES
  Machine_name
VARIABLES
  x'
INVARIANT

R
INITIALISATION
  H'
OPERATIONS
  Operation_name $\hat{=}$ **PRE**   *P'* **THEN**   *G'* **END ;**
  $\vdots$

END

The name of the machine beeing refined is given in the **REFINES**-clause. The parameters, sets, constants, and properties are inherited from the refined machine. The variables of the refined machine can appear in the invariant of the refining machine, but they cannot be referensed in the AMN substituitions of the refining machine. A refinement can see a list of machines using the **SEES**-clause.

The correctness of a refinement step w.r.t. the machines *Machine_name(f)* and *Refinement_name* above is proved by verifying the following four proof obligations:

(B1) $(\exists(x,x').\ I \wedge R)$

(B2) $[H']\neg([H]\neg R)$

(B3) $(\forall(x,x').\ (I \wedge R \wedge P) \Rightarrow P')$

(B4) $(\forall(x,x').\ (I \wedge R \wedge P) \Rightarrow [G']\neg([G]\neg R)).$

Machine Implementation

The syntactic structure of an abstract machine implementation is the same as that of an abstract machine refinement except that the **REFINEMENT**-clause is replaced by an **IMPLEMENTATION**-clause. The **OPERATIONS**-clause gives implementations to all the operations specified in the machine denoted in the **REFINES**-clause. When an implementation **IMPORTS** a list of machines, the variables and constants of these machines can be used in the invariant of the importing machine. They cannot, however, appear in the operations. The operations of the imported machines can be used by the importing machine. An implementation machine can see other machine via the **SEES**-clause.

The proof obligations for an implementation are basically the same as those for refinement. However, in an implementation we can use more programming like construct not allowed in the other machines. The loop construct is one of them. The proof obligations for a loop

Loop=T; **WHILE** *P* **DO** *G* **INVARIANT** *R* **VARIANT** *E* **END**
for some predicate *R* are as follows:

(T1) $[T]R$

(T2) $R \Rightarrow E \in NAT$

(T3) $(\forall l.(R \wedge P) \Rightarrow [G]R)$

(T4) $(\forall l.(R \wedge P) \Rightarrow [n := E]([G](E < n)))$

$(T5)$ $(\forall l.(R \wedge \neg P) \Rightarrow Q)$.